DATE DUE

MAY 1 3 2011		
JUL 0 1 2011		
AUG 1 1 2011		
JAN 0 3 2012		
JAN 3 1 2014		
DEC 0 5 2014		
MAY 2 0 2015		

Why School Antibullying Programs Don't Work

Why School Antibullying Programs Don't Work

Stuart W. Twemlow
and
Frank C. Sacco

JASON ARONSON
Lanham • Boulder • New York • Toronto • Plymouth, UK

About the front cover: Positive vibrations is in a verse from a Bob Marley song; "Rastaman vibration positive, you can't live that negative way." The song rallies people to be positive and strong and to speak honestly and stand up for their rights, while taking care of themselves. Although Jamaican in origin, it has universal application to be a gentle warrior in one's personal life for the good of self and others. The biracial character is surrounded by and holds a bead bracelet. Making bead bracelets was one way a Jamacian school harnessed the power of positive vibrations through their altruistic natural leaders.

Published in the United States of America
by Jason Aronson
An imprint of Rowman & Littlefield Publishers, Inc.

A wholly owned subsidiary of
The Rowman & Littlefield Publishing Group, Inc.
4501 Forbes Boulevard, Suite 200, Lanham, Maryland 20706
www.rowmanlittlefield.com

Estover Road
Plymouth PL6 7PY
United Kingdom

British Library Cataloguing in Publication Information Available

Library of Congress Cataloging-in-Publication Data

Twemlow, Stuart W.
   Why school antibullying programs don't work / Stuart W. Twemlow and Frank C. Sacco.
      p. cm.
   Includes index.
   ISBN-13: 978-0-7657-0475-7 (cloth : alk. paper)
   ISBN-10: 0-7657-0475-7 (cloth : alk. paper)
   eISBN-13: 978-0-7657-0612-6
   eISBN-10: 0-7657-0612-1
   1. Bullying in schools—United States—Prevention. 2. Bullying in schools—United States—Psychological aspects. 3. School violence—United States—Prevention. 4. School environment—United States. I. Sacco, Frank C., 1949– II. Title.
   LB3013.32.T88 2008
   371.7'82—dc22   2008011241

Printed in the United States of America

♾ ™ The paper used in this publication meets the minimum requirements of American National Standard for Information Sciences—Permanence of Paper for Printed Library Materials, ANSI/NISO Z39.48-1992.

To EDUCATORS all over the planet,
who are the backbones of civil societies

Contents

Acknowledgments

Several thousand students and their families and dozens of school teachers and other staff of USD 501, Topeka, Kansas, together with several doctoral and master's students in the Clinical Child Psychology Program at the University of Kansas, particularly Anne Jacobs, Edward Dill, Michael Wright, Bridget Biggs, Jennifer Mize, and Tim Nelson, deserve much of the credit for the enormously complex randomized trial that formed the backbone of our research. Many of the project ideas came from staff of the schools and thus reflect personal experience and investment, not some disembodied research hypotheses. Renshi Stephen Twemlow and students of the School of Martial and Meditative Arts created the format and enthusiasm for the Gentle Warrior and much of the Bruno group work. Pat McElliot, Marty Gies, Debora Hess, and Ruth Mott did much of the implementation work. Jim Fultz, Larry Wolgast, and the staff of the development office and Child and Family Center of the Menninger Clinic, Topeka, Kansas, created the material support and statistical help to make the project work. Karl Menninger and his legacy inspired us, and Joshua J. Wagner, a Topeka student who was a victim of lethal bullying, motivated us to do this work.

Co-principal investigators for the study included professors Twemlow, Vernberg, and Fonagy, all of whom contributed chapters to this book.

Sharon Stredde and Walt Duy of Aurora, Illinois, put many research ideas into practical operation, and over years these clinical trials greatly improved the framework for the work.

Principal Somerville, Vice Principal Manning, and Ms. Henry, the reading teacher, have helped greatly in the Sheffield all-age school in Negril, Jamaica. Jennifer Malcolm, David Konovitch, and Audley Samuels created the atmosphere and did the work there. John Brandon kindly contributed housing for the Jamaican research team.

Chris Hill blended our ideas into the culture of New Zealand and Australia, aided by Eve Steel and Doug Kirsner. We are very grateful to them for their time, energy, and creativity.

Nicholas Twemlow offered expert and sensitive support for our literary efforts, Erica Bernheim created a manuscript from our ideas, and Art Pomponio, Ph.D, gently supported and guided us through the publication process. We thank them deeply.

*   *   *

Some of the material used in this book has been previously published in the following:

Twemlow, S. W., Fonagy, P., and Sacco, F. C. (2001). An Innovative Psychodynamically Influenced Intervention to Reduce School Violence. *Journal of the American Academy of Child and Adolescent Psychiatry* 40 (3): 377–379.

Twemlow, S. W., Fonagy, P, and Sacco, F. (2002). Feeling Safe In School. *Smith College Studies in Social Work* 72 (2):303–326

Twemlow, S. W., Fonagy, P., and Sacco, F. (2004). The Bystander Role of Teachers and Students in the Social Architecture of Bullying and Violence in Schools and Communities. *Annals New York Academy of Sciences* 1036, 215–232.

Twemlow, S., Fonagy, P., and Sacco, F. (2005). A Developmental Approach to Mentalizing Communities: I. The Peaceful Schools Experiment. *Bulletin of the Menninger Clinic* 69 (4):281–303.

Twemlow, S. W. (2004). Preventing School Violence. *Psychiatric Times*, April 21 (4).

Sections 1 and 2 of the teacher questionnaire were adapted from items in the Positive Learning Climate Scale of the Staff Assessment Questionnaire, School Self-Assessment Instrument. (1986). University of Washington, Seattle. Contact Jerry Bamburg P.O. Box 353600, Center for Effective Schools, University of Washington, Seattle, WA 98195-3600

There are many unnamed others who helped these intricate processes, and to all we wish thanks and hope the altruistic effort and natural leadership each showed was a source of personal satisfaction.

The high school version of the K–12 questionnaire has a few questions derived from vaguely remembered sources: Questions 1–10 of part 5 from the Center for Disease Control; part 7, 10, and 11 are from studies of Mitch Prinstein, a student of Eric Vernberg. We have acknowledged what we can remember and hope nobody else is offended. It was certainly not deliberate.

Introduction

An ex-FBI director told the following joke, as a way of focusing the attention of a large and varying group of individuals gathered together under FBI sponsorship to study the problem of the "school shooters," a problem that had created immense urban and suburban panic and fear that we were on the edge of some violent national epidemic.

The joke was about Sherlock Holmes and Dr. Watson. Dr. Watson was always trying to measure to Sherlock Holmes's brilliance and originality. One day the two of them went camping, and in the early hours of the morning, Holmes woke up Watson and said, "Watson, what do you make of all those stars in the sky?" Watson, then seizing his chance to be clever, said: "Astrologically it seems as if the moon is really in Venus; theologically it means God is in heaven; chronologically it means it's 3:00 A.M. What do you make of it Holmes?" Holmes said, "My sense, Watson, is that somebody stole the tent!"

What is the tent and why the chuckle? The burgeoning number of school antiviolence and antibullying programs that have developed in the past ten years in the United States, and the many others that have undergone much more detailed research over several decades in Britain and Europe, have generally not worked very well. It is hard to measure significant academic performance; it's hard to measure whether or not there is less bullying (children are generally unreliable reporters); effect sizes for interventions range under one—in fact an effect size of one would be truly brilliant; school statistics for things like truancy, suspension, and so forth, are unreliable—all these events make interventions look quite ineffective.

The question really posed by Sherlock Holmes and facing us is that clearly it is *not* about a competition for who can create the best program; the real issue is that we are not doing the things that allow any of these very well-intentioned and original programs to work.

1

A psychotic patient, who washed dishes in a local hospital, gave a gem of wisdom one day. He pointed out, "Doctor, some things are too big for you to see." We believe it is *just* those sorts of issues that are taken for granted and not thought about or rarely thought about that determines whether a rather sensible simple and doable antiviolence program works. We will address only these issues in this book, not the individual programs.

Why did you pick up this book? If you are a teacher or school administrator, concerned parent, or someone who is about to have children in the public school system or has children there and is not happy the way things have been going, you are our audience. What made you pick up the book may have to do with the title. You have probably heard discussions over the years about cheap and simple programs that are usually curriculum add-ons—devised often by teachers—but don't work, partly because they are too simple for a problem with this complexity. Ten sessions of social and emotional education will not change a poisoned school environment. We have been criticized for failing to include detailed research documentation in this book. This was deliberate. We want the reader to have the straight scoop. Research literature is easy to find on the Internet. Ours is freely available at www.backoffbully.com.

There is another group of programs that have been used as part of an experimental protocol with exhausting demands on children and teachers to test out an intervention. Tiring as this is, if the protocol is well devised it often shows results, although this type of intervention generally shows relatively low effect sizes for an enormous amount of time and money invested by people who expect to have an intervention later that will help them. Many such experimental programs are not useful because the program is not feasible and realistic. So now we have the problem that an experimental program that may not approach reality closely enough to be useful later, so what is the point?

A third type of school would be one that has had problems, maybe even a shooting or two, or some other serious school violence, and has tried to find a program that will address its individual school needs. There are literally hundreds of programs that vary enormously in approaches, from those focused on identifying bullies and victims as disturbed individuals who need psychiatric care and counseling, to the ones that are "out of the box." An example is the Positive Deviance Program that evolved from observations at World Health Organization sites in which certain people who should be starving to death were not, because they learned to make use of local wild plants to keep themselves healthy. Applied to schools, the positive deviant selected and studied the children who were doing well in the bullying school environment whereas other children were not.

How you choose for your school is a problem, because what in your school needs the intervention? Even if you are an off-site expert, how could you pick a program for a particular school that you know only by name? Who should pick programs for individual schools and how should that be done? These are all questions that we discuss in this book. We have concluded that it is really not *what you do*, but *how you do it* that matters: the program needs to be simple and the process crisp and continuous. In other words if you notice the large "invisible" background issues that may be critically important to success of a specific intervention, then virtually any intervention will have a chance of working. Well maybe not any—but many. If this is why you picked up the book, then we can only strongly encourage you to read on.

Chapter One

Myths, Fallacies, and Truths About School Violence Prevention

All parents want their children to attend safe schools, and all educators and administrators want to provide safe schools for children to attend. This book contains the collective and extensive experience of two professionals who have examined the problem of school violence from a number of different angles, trying to find a way of creating solutions for parents, educators, and children. For instance, as researchers, we studied ways of changing a school's climate using a random, controlled study costing nearly a million dollars, involving nine schools and thousands of children. We learned that *what* you did to change a school was secondary to *how* you did it, and that the most powerful tool in changing a school is the "buy in" of teachers.

As program developers we were instrumental in attracting a Safe Schools Grant for bully prevention to a particular city, but we were ironically bullied out of the grant by a school system desperate to allocate those resources to other projects. They used our research to get the money and then spent those funds on other school expenses. Tragically, not long after receiving this Safe Schools Grant, a teacher was murdered by a student, the first in the city's history. In a school infamous for its aggressive students, the metal detector bought with the grant money had been stored "safely" in the basement.

We also worked in exclusive schools in the suburban United States, private boarding schools in Australia and New Zealand, and schools on the island of Jamaica, which has the third-highest murder rate in the world. Schools in the inner city have become war zones, while suburban schools ooze toxic social aggression. Our work has targeted both individuals referred to us from schools for mental health services and also entire communities concerned about the quality and safety of their children's education. As consultants to the FBI's National Center for the Analysis of Violent Crime's Critical

Incident Response Group, we looked for reasons why suburban white youth were embarking upon seemingly senseless lethal rampages.

This book draws on a large number of diverse experiences to create a conceptual framework for understanding, planning, and sustaining a process capable of creating and maintaining safe-school learning environments. Most schools begin this process after a public embarrassment or tragedy. We are generally called in when a school or community is already in trouble and wants the outside doctors to cure the disease. This has been especially true as the emphasis in education has shifted toward the creation of a corporate mindset in public education, holding teachers and administrators personally and directly responsible for the achievements of their students. Schools around the world are under immense pressure to create more competitive academic results, yet there seems to be a crucial oversight in this process: children are not bags of information trained to spit out good grades on command. They are little humans in the process of growing up, and the role of the school is to provide the community's stage on which its children begin their social-emotional journeys toward adulthood.

Our experiences with a variety of schools have been as diverse as the schools themselves. While touring a very prestigious boarding school renowned for educating royalty and steeped in centuries of tradition, we met one of the counselors in charge of these children. Although he appeared very reserved and proud of the school, he was quick to request and accept our assistance in improving the quality of the learning environment. In other words, he did not hide behind the status of the school; he sought out knowledge and served as a willing sponge for ideas and information.

Conversely, we consulted at a West Coast elementary school in an urban area. The proud principal let us know immediately that there was no violence in *her* school and told us it was very unlikely we would be able to offer her anything useful in bully prevention. We politely nodded, then asked to visit the school's lunchroom. She gladly agreed and we were not in the lunchroom longer than one minute before two fights broke out. What this taught us was that the higher you go in the school system, the less is known by those in charge about what a school is really like. We also learned that the amount of resources or status a school enjoys does not guarantee it to be a safe and creative place; it is the people who run the school who set the tone, good or bad.

Our mission over the past three decades has been to find the common denominators in this complex range of experiences. What factors make a group feel peaceful? What makes a community, a school, or a workplace violent, unpleasant, and noncreative? As our experiments progressed, our initial plan was to create the ultimate antiviolence program, package it, sell it to schools, and retire early as rich men. This quickly proved to be the wrong idea. As we will discuss in greater detail later, schools do not like programs. Instead of marketing one program to many schools, we decided to shift our focus toward studying the implementation process of violence-prevention programs in a variety of academic environments.

Our basic idea is that changing schools is everybody's responsibility, not just the schools'. Regardless of the manner in which we entered a troubled situation, the critical elements of understanding the bullying or violence problem and tracing its roots within larger groups was fundamentally the same. It was consistently true in schools, and we believe that this approach will work in a variety of other large group formats, such as companies, city departments—in fact, in any dysfunctional social system

This book takes the unusual, and often misunderstood, theoretical approach we have called "community psychoanalysis," or the use of psychodynamic principles in the understanding of tendencies and instances of social deviance in large groups. Specifically, we have developed a theoretical approach to understanding the power dynamics that occur within larger social contexts. The role of the unconscious is stressed, and group climate is the focus of change. In order for change to be sustainable, we posit that a process needs to be implemented and followed consistently over time. The *process* is the key element to change, rather than the content of any one program.

Often, climates are impacted by certain unconscious yet blatant behaviors or attitudes. We call these "undiscussables," and they are the proverbial giant elephants lurking in the corners of many rooms and conversations. Everybody knows they are there, but no one can point to them definitively, describe them, or even acknowledge their contributions to a problem. These undiscussables often represent the catalysts for trouble within schools. For example, the fact that teachers bully their students is often one of the many undiscussables we have encountered in a number of schools. Parents bully schools, and then school committee members sit idly by while schools tolerate sustained bullying, and the cycle perpetuates itself to the detriment of everyone involved.

We must remember that schools represent a community's investment in its future through the safe education of its youth. The community in question may be a local government charged with operating and overseeing a public school district, or it may be the collective parent community of a boarding school. No matter what form a community takes, the bottom line is that the school is entrusted with that community's young people, and it contains a structured leadership system designed to protect and nurture students. We have worked with the Jamaican schools, for example, alongside highly dedicated teachers working under draconian conditions ranging from overcrowding, no equipment, or student transportation, to abject poverty.

The issues impacting safety in these schools, however, are the same as those present in the best suburban American schools or the most prestigious private schools. The same cast of characters always appears, beginning with the leaders of the community, and then moving from the government sectors into the business arenas, such as the social control agencies, health and welfare organizations, and then eventually into the school administration itself, namely teachers, parents, students, and support personnel. This is the social context within which schools exist. We encourage anyone involved in changing schools to begin by understanding the factors necessary to create a peaceful school.

The first step in changing schools always involves one person or a small group of people, who first experience the need for change. Sometimes this group appears reactively following a public crisis. For example, if a school system is embarrassed in the media, a group will form or the school superintendent will designate a panel of sorts to deal with the situation. The group process that follows is what will determine the success of any efforts to make a school environment more peaceful.

Through our efforts in trying to help schools change, we have encountered certain universal fallacies, or mistaken beliefs, that create barriers to creating and sustaining change. These false assumptions resurface regardless of the country or the status of the school, and they create unsuccessful, frustrating, and potentially dangerous processes that hinder serious attempts to address school violence, whether physical or psychological. The following fallacies we have collected over time represent how social systems consistently avoid reflecting on their own collective selves and assuming responsibility for a problem.

FALLACY ONE: THIS SCHOOL IS TOO GOOD OR TOO BAD

Many schools have a vision about their own situation, which is often mistaken for safety or danger. If a school is impoverished and in a violent neighborhood, people may assume that the school is unsafe. Conversely, a school that is neat and clean, with students in uniforms not engaging in physical fights, has no guarantee that students and teachers are free from nonphysical types of social aggression. Good schools that strive for perfection and indulge students and teachers with resources can still be very unhealthy and unhappy environments for students. Struggling schools, on the other hand, often lose hope; communities frequently abandon their schools when they are considered beyond repair, unconsciously allowing them to become breeding grounds for future violence.

Columbine High School, for instance, was an example of a great school, and everyone in Jefferson County, Colorado, thought so. As we now know, this fantasy ended tragically because of two unhappy boys in a climate that tolerated the humiliation of students by other students. Having spent time with many of the teachers and principals who have had shootings in their schools, we definitely believe there is a potential school shooter in every suburban school. When social aggression is allowed to continue unchecked, the social climate becomes infected by humiliation. When an injustice collector (someone who blames problems on others and resentfully feels like the victim of social injustice), begins to break away from adult and peer connections, the likelihood of such an individual becoming an avenging victim increases dramatically. The Columbine High School shooters were known to have been targets of social aggression from their peers. Their lethal acts became their final way of communicating their despair with a system that considered itself "too good" to be harboring this degree of unhappiness.

On the other end of the spectrum, in an evolving nation such as Jamaica, it would be easy to understand why people might give up hope and succumb to the paralyzing impacts of poverty. Surely, schools in Jamaica would think that things were "too bad." During our research, however, we were continually struck by the pure intensity of Jamaican teachers and how this affects the school environment. They teach in open, overcrowded classrooms with no doors and children pressed together trying to learn. Jamaican students value education even though it is beyond their reach. When a child stops learning, he or she usually turns to crime and violence in order to survive. These schools struggle every day, yet are not dissuaded by the despair or the lack of resources. They do not believe that their schools are too bad to be saved.

You can observe this same phenomenon throughout urban public schools in the United States as well. Proud teachers control their classrooms and expect learning and self-control from their students. The school environment may be rough, but the teacher does not cave in to the idea that the school is too bad for its students to thrive. It is simply where the kids are, and that is where a good teacher wants to be, making a difference.

The fashionable term for schools that are viewed as bad has become "underperforming." Some schools have great academic numbers, but various groups of students are miserable every day they spend in these schools. The "No Child Left Behind" approach is only the latest example of blaming the victims for their situations. Judging schools and placing them under pressure to perform academically plays into this community fantasy of schools that are too good or too bad. When schools receive high scores on their tests, they can easily convince themselves they are too good to worry about climate. This mistaken idea allows for many barriers to successful climate programming. Schools tend either to coast on their academic numbers or to despair over chronic underachievement or even to fake academic results, by coaching their students, such as occurred recently in Houston, Texas.

FALLACY TWO: SCHOOL VIOLENCE IS SOMEBODY ELSE'S PROBLEM

This fallacy is very common in a staggering number of schools. In a private school, parents may be paying big money for their children's education. Their expectation may also be that they are paying for the right not to have to parent while the children are at school. Public-school parents, however, are often busy working or struggling in poverty, and they also believe that the school should handle its own problems. Parents see their responsibility ending when their children go out the front door. If the school calls the parents about their child's misbehavior, the modern response appears to begin and end with a finger-pointing process. The days of administrators, educators, and parents being automatically on the same page about their children's school behavior are all but gone. Regardless of whether a school is private or public, parents are letting their children's schools do much of the parenting and guiltily criticizing school personnel who are not suited to do this, nor adequately trained.

The mayor of a city may think he or she is done with the job of educating children when the community's education budget has been completed and approved. A business in a town may not feel that the problems of the local junior high school are theirs as well, certainly not as members of the private sector. The community's fantasy is that the school can handle its own issues independently from its ongoing connection to the community. Teachers and police are quick to receive the blame when something goes wrong. After all, it was "their" job to protect our schools and to teach the children and we (the community members) pay their salaries.

Our experience has shown us time and again that successfully resolving school problems must be a community priority. When a school stands alone in the community, it becomes isolated and loses its ability to be enriched by its environment. Instead, this sort of school devours its own energy internally until something tragic occurs and causes the school to implode. We must remember that the school represents a critical social context that actively promotes the development of a community's future. Public schools are funded by local, state, and federal taxes, property taxes often providing a high percentage of funding. Thus affluent families have access to more-affluent schools. When a family has a child in school, they tend to pay more attention to the allocation of funds, but still may not become heavily involved with ensuring their children's safety and well-being.

Unfortunately, parents are transferring more responsibilities to the school for a variety of understandable reasons. Urban schools in the United States are populated by an increasing number of children from dysfunctional homes with absent or abusive fathers, overwhelmed and traumatized mothers, and increasing numbers of children living in foster homes. Many of these children suffer from environmentally induced behaviors that are both self-destructive and disruptive. By contrast, in American suburbs, parents are working harder than ever before. There are more two-parent working families who send their children to school, leaving them to fend for themselves or to spend their time in after-school programs until their exhausted parents finish work and come to collect them.

The net result of these different pressures is that parents are more likely to point their fingers at the school, demanding service and dealing out blame after their child underperforms or gets into trouble. The idea that the education of children is purely a school job stems from different sources, but it quickly becomes a convenient way to avoid accepting collective responsibility for the creation of peaceful schools. For instance, some members of the community have already raised children who have graduated and moved away. When the school asks for a budget increase, these older citizens may feel less connected to their community's schools, and again, the school is considered an isolated institution continually in need. Then, when the school fails, the community resorts to blame, further isolating the school.

FALLACY THREE: ZERO TOLERANCE REDUCES DESTRUCTIVE DECISIONS

It can be comforting to fantasize that simply forbidding something can be sufficient to solve a problem like bullying at school. It is, of course, common sense to reason that tolerating bullying should not be tolerated, but this is a gross oversimplification of the work that needs to be done in order to eliminate bullying. The spirit of zero tolerance is punitive and results in expulsions, conflict, denial, and favoritism. At the other end of the continuum is the implementation of dismissive social contexts. In this scenario, the school turns a blind eye to bullying and dismisses the value of reporting bullying or of taking steps to intervene.

This form of avoidant bystanding is stimulated by many factors. For example, in the No Child Left Behind program, staff members can lose their jobs in low performance schools. Some feel that problems come in cycles and we just have to wait them out, while teachers often believe that positive thinking eliminates negativity. There are elements of truth in all of these attitudes, but in school environments distorted by nonmentalization and power struggles, more has to be done to provide the backdrop for a sound antibullying program to succeed in any way.

Both extremes of this continuum can produce very unhealthy and dangerous circumstances in a school. Zero tolerance is arguably the most extreme approach to take, however, because it leaves the school and community little room in which to be creative and to sustain policies that prevent bullying and reward prosocial behavior at all levels of the school and in the community. When there is inadequate wiggle room, extreme actions become necessary in order to maintain the necessary sense of equilibrium in a social system.

Zero tolerance also leads to prejudice in how situations in a school are handled. When a collective mindset engages in nonreflective, overly simple reactions to very complicated problems, the thinking becomes stereotypical and narrow-minded. The fact remains that students are children who are still growing up and making mistakes across a wide range of parent constellations existing within the community. Mandating punishment for bullying drives it underground and avoids dealing with the more complex reasons why coercive energy exists in the system. Zero tolerance harshness may be applied inappropriately and can result in very destructive effects on children and their families.

The practical disadvantage of the zero tolerance approach to bullying is that it closes out potentially valuable field intelligence gathered by the other students. If the peer group at any age thinks that telling an authority figure about bullying might result in harsh punishment, they will be less likely to report that someone is being humiliated, has made a threat, or has a drug problem. This becomes a critical issue especially for middle- and high-school students. When the FBI and Secret Service studied school shooters, both agreed that most shooters gave plenty of advance warning, especially to their friends. Teen suicide has a very similar pattern. These tragedies occur when desperate young people act in extreme ways to relieve the unending burdens and intense emotional pain they experience, while we all deny the seriousness of the messages they give.

The Secret Service has developed a nonpunitive alternative approach to dealing with people who make threats against public figures. Like bullying, making threats is not always an immediately punishable crime, but it is a problem that cannot and should not be ignored. When the Secret Service identifies someone who has made a threat, they case-manage that individual or group using teams of specially trained agents and psychiatrists to monitor the behavior of the individual or group making the threat. The Secret Service solution is a no-nonsense response that is not simply punitive. The person making the threat is monitored, not incarcerated. There certainly is no part of the Secret Service that takes safety lightly, and they use this approach because it is effective, flexible, and sustains contact over long periods of time in various stages.

We should have zero tolerance for denial of the impact and origins of bullying. This will send a vital message to students, teachers, parents, and the community: we have zero tolerance for nonaction. Responding to bullying takes a team headed in the same direction with the best interests of the child, teacher, parent, and community in mind. Anything less will fall flat. The best programs to prevent bullying begin early and continue throughout the educational cycle. In chapters 3 and 4, we will describe our theory of understanding bullying, victimization, and the vital important role bystanding behavior plays.

FALLACY FOUR: SIZE OF THE SCHOOL MATTERS

Every school has unique climate zones. There is little argument that smaller schools and classes are better learning and teaching environments, all other things being equal. Simply being small or exclusive, however, does not guarantee a peaceful school. Columbine was large, while Pearl, Mississippi, was small, and both had shootings. The size of a school in and of itself defines only a small part of the formula for understanding what is needed to create a more positive school climate. The small schools movement, exemplified best in Chicago, is a beginning to a much more complicated, larger effort needed outlined in this book.

We worked in one Chicago high school, New Trier, which breaks all the rules about size. It has four thousand students who are very high achieving for a public high school. GPA for the senior class is 3.6. This is not the secret to their success. They have managed to create a peaceful and functioning school. This school invests twenty-five minutes each day to discuss with students problems and successes experienced at the school. The school is large but it created a way for students and faculty to make one-on-one connections. New Trier metaphorically shrunk the school by increasing student and teacher time focused on relationships rather than just academics.

New Trier invested tremendous amounts of time to organize meetings to bring together groups interested in improving the learning environment. They were not afraid to discuss the undiscussables. They talked about problems of excellence and the potential to lose track of alienated kids left out of the academic achievement frenzy. Here we have an example of a very large school that creates closeness by focusing on human connection and facilitating communication. It was not the size of this school that mattered. In this case, New Trier developed ways to make the school a safe and connected place but with a hidden "problem of excellence," that is, children were devastated by parental insistence on achieving high enough grades to gain entrance to Ivy League schools.

FALLACY FIVE: TODAY'S KIDS ARE NO DIFFERENT THAN WHEN WE WERE YOUNG

Most parents and teachers are often amazed at how different new generations seem from "when *we* were young." Nowhere is this generation gap more obvious than in schools. Every generation reflects changing cultures, and history is full of examples of this inevitable process. Just as the 1960s represented a rebellion against traditional values, in the twenty-first century, a new generation has had to cope with a completely new set of challenges unknown to their own parents.

The arrival of the digital era has created a culture that is connected by more devices than at any other time in history. The Internet has created a connected world; digital phones provide new ways to stay in touch; e-mails can be received on phones that are also mini computers. Phones can take pictures and send them in turn to computers and to other phones. Technology shapes how children live from an increasingly younger and younger age. Maintaining a sense of self in the face of such easily dispersed images and information is a challenge this generation faces.

With regard to bullying and violence, we must consider technology as a factor with two sides. On the positive side, being tremendously connected offers unlimited opportunities for the sharing of positive feelings, information, images, and resources. It offers the curious researcher a world of information accessible from the comfort of a home computer. Families can stay connected "in real time" with distant relatives. Pictures and e-mails can keep people together and involved in each other's life. Children who are trapped in poverty can reach out to the world and create hope for themselves. Shy people can meet other shy or trapped people and create virtual realities that help them cope with their lives in more positive ways. Communication is facilitated with virtually every task once done on paper now being completed online. In our own research, we have used the Internet to connect American and Jamaican schools, and we hope to expand this concept to include a worldwide network of students, parents, and teachers interacting about ways to improve school climates.

The negatives, however, involve the misuse of the Internet's connection power to exploit others sexually, financially, and emotionally. It is not surprising that child predators thrive online. This virtual world allows for the faster evolution of deviant interests. Reality television has exposed some of these predators through staged sting operations that lure predators to a house where they are filmed as they are confronted and then arrested. Access to information can also lead to exposure to hate and deviance online. Many of the recent American school shooters used the Internet to explore resources and to develop plans for murder as an act of revenge for being bullied. An alienated child who sits at home and types "hate" into a search engine will be connected to an unimaginable number of active and technologically savvy hate mongers. These virtual connections espousing hate often masquerade as understanding male figures offering to help "set things right." The Internet has also broken down the barriers between the social world of the school and the home. Social aggression that begins at school is carried through the Internet to the home through techniques such as instant messaging. Groups and cliques form online and can be used to create mean-spirited dialogues, which, in turn, are continued when the participants are back in school.

FALLACY SIX: ELIMINATING THE BULLY SOLVES THE PROBLEM

It is impossible to dispute the periodic need to identify disturbed children and refer them for treatment. Certainly, when a child hurts someone, carries a weapon to school, or in other ways seriously threatens himself—or herself—or the school at large, a school suspension is warranted. This, however, does not solve the problem if the social context continues to allow bullying to occur.

We have observed this phenomenon at work in the war on drugs as well. As soon as one street corner dealer is arrested, another takes his place. Nothing in the neighborhood changes, so nothing will prevent another drug dealer from claiming the momentarily vacant spot. Bullies act the same way in schools. Schools that target and suspend bullies are missing the point. When a bully is suspended, plenty of "bully bystanders" are simply waiting to be activated as soon as a bullying role opens. Eliminating one person playing a role does not solve the problem of how a bully gains power using mean tactics.

If finding and suspending bullies from their schools worked, then school violence would be a very easy problem to solve. The problem would instead become a matter of who is bullying "too much," since everybody bullies a little at one time or another. While the finer points about just how much is too much for one student compared to another are debated, the social role of bully still is allowed to achieve a measure of social status for the individual who inhabits it. In other words, the goal of bullying is to gain social status.

Consider that thirty years ago the Marlboro Man was considered cool because smoking itself was cool. It was just as cool to have a pack of Lucky Strikes rolled up in your tee shirt. Smoking became a sign of social inclusion and dominance. Today, because smoking has lost so much of its appeal as a way to be included, the role of smoker, too, has been substantially diminished. If bullying were like smoking, then, discovering and removing the smokers, even the casual smokers, would be easy. A zero tolerance policy would eliminate all smokers from the environment. In fact, after decades of legal battles, smoking is no longer permitted indoors and smokers are not allowed to spew their smoke on those who choose not to smoke. The process of smoking was not tolerated in the social context and smokers no longer captured the social status formerly associated with the glamorous Marlboro Man riding off into the sunset. Children are learning earlier now about the dangers of smoking and see that fewer places allow it to occur within their walls. This process shares several striking similarities with bullying, being a victim or a bystander. The status gained by being mean, for instance, needs to be addressed, and the bystanders have to pull their support away from the bully. And, finally, those in leadership roles must delve into the peer culture and find ways to shift the status of bullying.

FALLACY SEVEN: MORE MONEY
LEADS TO MORE PEACEFUL SCHOOLS

There are undeniably many elements of education that require money to operate more effectively. Science is taught better when students have access to expensive laboratories with new equipment and cutting-edge technology. Computers are needed in order to teach successful computer science courses. Peaceful learning environments, on the other hand, do not cost a lot of money, and creating one does not require as much funding as a new roof, a set of computers, or renovating a gymnasium. Having a peaceful learning environment requires some time and the changing of attitudes. It does not cost more to have a peaceful school than it does to have a troubled one. Having an abundance of resources is no guarantee that there will be a peaceful school.

Some of the schools we visited and worked with had very little funding at all. One school in Jamaica had so few resources that students shared desks, pencils, and had no reliable transportation to and from school. This school jumped at the chance to work on a project to redirect some of the nonpeaceful energy. Using a craft project, the school created a reason for older kids to be nicer to teachers and the younger students. Being included in the craft class was a sign of social status. The price of admission was helpful bystanding. This project was begun with very few donated dollars, but ultimately it proved extremely successful at ridding the school of nonpeaceful energy.

Some social systems are corrupt by nature. Our work in Jamaica taught us very early on that if you bring resources in through the top, they get sucked dry before they hit the bottom. This is also true in many American cities where the FBI is continually investigating and prosecuting corrupt officials. Evolving nations provide many examples of how desperately poor nations' funds are skimmed by corrupt leaders. Unfortunately, corruption often eats up the resources that are designed to help the human infrastructure and the larger social context. When the poor get angry or do not improve their quality of life, the victims get blamed for their situations, and prejudice helps weave yarns about various elements. Some cities pay upward of ten thousand dollars to educate a child in war zone schools that are desperate and run down. It costs more money to run corrupt systems, and the corrupt system ensures that circumstances will not change.

The reality of corruption often creates a sense of despair in schools. Municipal workers also share this feeling of being underappreciated and mistreated; everybody gives up. Some individuals, however, disconnect from the reality of corruption and unfairness. They define their classrooms or their municipal duties as a reflection of their own characters. We have seen many examples of dedicated, underappreciated teachers inspiring their students in school systems known for failure. We watched Jamaican teachers growing hoarse while teaching packed rooms of children, combating open classrooms, oppressive heat, low pay, and uncertain futures. They stood tall and took pride in teaching math or helping their students learn to read and write. These classrooms were pure and immune from corruption. The "raw teacher" response is a personality trait that wants to teach, wants to see children grow and learn, and needs to be respected by the community for these noble efforts. Money is not the necessary ingredient that guarantees peaceful schools. In fact, it may spoil schools.

When visiting private boarding schools in Australia, we learned that, again, it was not the fancy quarters or prestigious history that made the school what it was; it was the staff. The elite nature of the school, in fact, adds a burden to these teachers. They are working under close scrutiny and always are walking a delicate line. Teachers often serve as houseparents to children, many of whom are from split families. We thought we would see spoiled and entitled teachers not open to our ideas of bully-victim-bystander, but to our surprise, the most elite school we visited had the most focused and open-minded counselors and teachers. It was not the money or prestige; it was the kids who motivated the staff. These teachers were the most hungry for new ways to improve their learning environments.

FALLACY EIGHT: LACK OF
PHYSICAL VIOLENCE MEANS A SCHOOL IS SAFE

The violent rampages of Columbine exploded the myth that violent schools can only be found in blighted urban areas. To the surprise of many, these shootings bore no resemblance to the stereotypical image of inner-city scenarios in which young minorities are shooting each other in gang-related wars and retaliations. The Columbine school shooters, however, were young white men from the suburbs. They were not openly aggressive, were not constantly in trouble, and were not considered obvious violent threats. In fact, Columbine was the jewel of Colorado. It was a large and apparently successful school with many trophies on display as a testament to the students' athletic and academic achievements. The shootings in 1999 opened the door to a new phenomenon active in suburban schools: social aggression. Both the FBI and the Secret Service have studied these school-shooting cases intensively, and both agree that bullying or social aggression in middle and high school was a key causal ingredient in the evolution of the modern school shooting.

The invisible force at work in seemingly safe schools like Columbine can be considered a silent killer. It has notably few outward symptoms that can easily slip below the radar and remain there until unexplained explosions of violence, high rates of addiction, suicide, and sudden academic failures become visible. The school in question may not have many open fights. There may be no weapons at all inside the building because the weapon of choice in social aggression is the spoken word and its subsequent echoes over the Internet. There is no way to detect how social aggression will impact a student population. Some students may be particularly at risk for victimization or for assuming the victimizer's role. Bystanders are everywhere, and it is up to schools to look deeper into the larger group climate in order to recognize the signs of this type of violence. Simply patrolling to ensure that there are no guns or knives in a school is clearly not sufficient.

Furthermore, bullying shifts from predominantly physical intimidation in middle school to a more social form of bullying in high school, based primarily on social inclusion and exclusion. The violence in poor city schools is based on pressures placed by economic deprivation, addiction, fatherlessness, crime, and limited resources and opportunities. Urban violence tends to reflect this competition and results in the physical imposition of social dominance. Street gangs control the flow of drugs, and schools often become battlegrounds.

We must remember, however, that this is not the whole picture. Schools can also become psychological battlefields with no overt aggression being displayed. An urban school can hire a police officer and use conventional law enforcement to intervene in overt violence, while a suburban school with social aggression cannot take this direct approach. The incidents of social aggression are not in and of themselves punishable events. Excluding someone or playing a mean trick may be cruel, but not illegal. This quandary is comparable to the Secret Service's approach to people who make threats rather than committing acts of violence. There are markedly few penalties for simply speaking and not acting. As a result, more creative and prevention-oriented approaches need to be taken to respond to social aggression. For the Secret Service, the key to protecting public officials is case management of people who make threats. In schools, a critical element in protecting the school climate is developing an awareness of how social aggression is being acted out in the school and to reducing it before tragedy strikes through, we propose, case management.

FALLACY NINE: BULLYING IS JUST A KID THING

For many people the word "bullying" evokes a normal part of childhood, a familiar childhood scene on a playground. It is very common for adults to minimize or dismiss bullying as a "kid thing," and even to mock those parents who complain about nonphysical bullying. The victim is often perceived as thin-skinned with overinvolved parents. It is not common for people to think of adults as bullies, but by definition, bullying entails the frequent use of humiliating communications learned from adults. Kids today may use the Internet to entrap their victims in an almost inescapable social web of shame and humiliation. This sequence of activity is virtually untraceable unless a parent can obtain printed versions of these interactions, video phone images, and can disprove the "my friend used my computer defense." Again, while none of this activity is in and of itself punishable or physically aggressive, its impact can be far more lethal than a punch, a shove, or a kick.

FALLACY TEN: FOCUSING ON
PROBLEM KIDS WILL IMPROVE THE CLIMATE

There is no doubt that some students in a school will require special services in order to deal with medical issues and psychiatric disorders such as attention deficit hyperactivity disorder, posttraumatic stress disorder, bipolar illness, and disruptive and oppositional disorders. They become easy prey or targets in a school that allows coercive roles to thrive unchecked. It is not the psychiatric disorder that causes the school dynamic, but the school climate that fans the flames and allows children with emotional conditions to be bullied or targeted for social aggression. Simply noticing, referring, and treating these students will not solve the problem of a socially aggressive school climate. These problem children often come from homes that are emotionally toxic, lack basic nurturance, and they may already suffer from seriously dysfunctional family dynamics.

When there are fewer visible "problem kids," then, the school climate may be the place where problems develop because of the opportunities allowed within a school. Many suburban and private schools fantasize that they have successfully screened out potential problem kids. Parents are recruited and attracted by the fantasy that their children's school will not have problem kids. This illusion leads to the denial of a problem with social aggression and to a subsequent lack of commitment to creating and maintaining peaceful schools. Social aggression feeds off of achievement-driven adults. The competition to succeed academically or athletically may be unwittingly condoning socially aggressive behavior on the part of the more successful students and their parents. Teachers and coaches are easily pulled into the competition game. The survival of the fittest mentality leads to a lack of focus on the marginalized students who then become the problem kids. These problems follow them home and are further inflamed by the pressures of human development, especially beginning in middle school. Often high academic schools position learning disability training in the basement away from the achievers!

The main fallacy in the "problem child" fantasy is that expelling such children will result in a problem-free or peaceful school. Our experience has taught us that removing and expelling problem students, although sometimes necessary, does not solve the problem in the school climate. The social roles of bully-victim-bystander will remain unchanged by the removal of any one player in the power struggle, as there are always more players waiting in the wings. Essentially, the face may change but the destructive structure and impact of each role remains the same. The problem lies with the system, and not the person—child or adult—who fills the social role of victim, victimizer, and bystander. Focusing on the problem child distracts from the need to examine the school climate. Creating peaceful schools demands a separate process that does not have to require enormous amounts of time or money. At the end of this chapter, we will outline the critical elements involved in designing a peaceful school, elaborated in more detail in the later chapters.

FALLACY ELEVEN: QUICK FIXES, COOKBOOKS, AND PROGRAMS CAN SOLVE THE PROBLEM

When tragedy strikes a school, the first response is often to point to a program already being used. In addition, schools tend to react to a crisis by choosing a "cookbook" and beginning to train teachers using one specific antibullying or antiviolence program. There are, quite literally, hundreds of programs created to assist in dealing with bullies. Typically, the programs are selected by the top administrators and enforced as a mandate on the already burdened and overly pressured teachers. The initial reactions may include a subgroup of teachers who hate the new idea, some who may try it out, and others who go for it wholeheartedly and become trainers. We have seen numerous programs introduced and we have watched them fail because teachers do not buy into the program.

As you might imagine, we learned this lesson the hard way. Years ago, thinking we had discovered the cure for bullying, we created materials and "cookbook manuals," completed and published our research, created a Web site, submitted proposals to this committee and that federal group, and allowed outsiders to review the program. Finally, we received a grant to have a school use all our materials to develop programs, sat back, and waited for our millions to roll in. This is when we learned that the very idea of introducing a program from the outside is doomed to fail. A program will immediately be viewed as a suspicious foreign agent and the antibodies in the school will undermine the program, whatever it may be. The people introducing the program will be attacked and the program seen as worthless. This failure is not because of financial concerns or due to an evidenced-based controversy. It is a fact of nature in social groups, and one that must be considered before attempting to implement and create ways of dealing with bullies and violence in our schools.

FALLACY TWELVE: ONE PROGRAM FITS ALL

The resource section of this book will list a variety of Web sites and books you may consult to see summaries of the hundreds of programs now available, and some of the Web sites that assess them for you. The question then becomes: how do you choose a program for *your* particular school? In our opinion, long before you consult a book or a Web site, the ten chapters in this book address matters you can and must address before you tackle the problem of bully proofing your school.

There is no one program that will fit every school, as each institution represents an individual case; even schools within the same school district may have very different needs, depending on location and bussing; the social, economic, and education levels of the community it draws children from; and the quality of the leadership, style, and focus of the leadership. In many ways, race, religion, ethnicity, gender bias, socioeconomic level, and the quality of the physical environment all affect a school's needs and determine the kind of program needed to address specific issues. For example, a program addressing improving communication skills in already well-situated children from happy homes and reasonable social economic environments will work there, but if implemented in Harlem is highly unlikely to have any focus or, for that matter, meaning for the students.

Over the course of our work, we have noted an interesting dynamic present in the schools in poorer parts of town with gang activity and frightened teachers. While the children get along with each other very well and consistently support each other, they fight the teachers. Compare this situation to the affluent middle-class schools, where the socioeconomic level is much higher and where children have their basic needs provided and feel protected. These children tend to "suck up" to the teachers and fight with each other instead. The dynamic between the environment and the students alone will vastly affect the success of whichever program you choose. A program that focuses, for example, on improving the richness and depth of communication between children won't have as much impact immediately in an impoverished school as it would in a more affluent school.

We eventually stopped marketing ourselves to schools and began giving away our ideas and materials free of charge. We discovered that the process of changing schools is a very personal one that requires certain critical elements: the content of this book. Our mission is to outline the backbone of a process in a way that any school from around the world can understand and use to improve unique and particular school environments.

FALLACY THIRTEEN: VIOLENCE IS AN INFECTION THAT MUST BE ELIMINATED

When bullying children and children who are victims of bullying are treated as if they have an infectious disease, specific medical care will be sought out, as it often is, and many schools have mental health programs situated within the schools. Although the disease metaphor for violence is grossly oversimplified—if not incorrect—if the "disease approach" to bullying and violence is used, once you eliminate the disease from an infectious situation, certain preventive measures must be put into place so that the individual doesn't recontract that infection. For instance, if you have pneumonia caused by pneumococcus, there are certain things that you need to do maintain your body's health and integrity after you have recovered from the initial infection. Schools are not dissimilar; eliminating the disease alone without following up with an effective program—one with a prevention action component—

ensures that the problem will return. The aforementioned prevention component should be put into place for roughly five years. Research data gathered in most countries to assist with school violence prevention are gradually highlighting a shift in interests. The data indicate a shift away from pathological roles for bullying victims and management of them, aiding instead those individuals who need various medical interventions or counseling, and moving toward a focus on school climate itself.

Another issue that has become more noticeable recently is that the length of time a particular approach needs to be maintained in order to show lasting effects is significantly longer than many people might expect. In one of our studies in the Midwest, we monitored the program in question for about three years, but, ideally, we would have extended that time to five years.

CRITICAL STEPS FOR CREATING A MODEL SCHOOL VIOLENCE PREVENTION APPROACH

This book seeks to break down the process of creating a peaceful and creative learning environment. Here is a quick overview of the book's critical elements.

"Buy In"

Arguably the most critical step of all, a buy in is not a commonly used term outside of the United States. It refers to two main issues: first, it demonstrates the degree to which all the staff and students involved with schools prioritize the need to make an antibullying program successful. An institution with a high level of buy in has a group of concerned and engaged individuals who consider the program essential and necessary to follow. The factors that render the buy in as high rather than low are variable, but a high buy in is rarely mandated. Most of the time, this level of concern is a result of a crisis.

We observed this tendency during our first experience with a small elementary school. This particular school had the highest out-of-school suspension rate and the poorest academic performance in the school district when a second grade girl was sexually assaulted by several second grade boys. As a result, we observed a group of concerned individuals who were extremely eager to buy in or support an antiviolence program in their school. This school is now a model for others, not only quiet, orderly, and altruistic, but with higher academic performance levels for African American students. Is there another way to enhance buy in before waiting to react to a tragic or critical incident? We believe there is, and part of that process entails ensuring the program will work for individual situations, regardless of the opinions of the expert consultants.

The second main issue included in the idea of a buy in is that a program also requires institutional support and must be compatible with the institution's mission and culture. Creating a framework designed by teachers and students working together to change their particular school will lead to noticeably higher levels of buy in, and a relatively smooth development and implementation process, as we observed during the pilot phase of our research and work. In the aforementioned school where the project was devised, for instance, the teachers actually did the project. They compiled their ideas and worked together creatively to set up the criteria to measure change, and, with assistance, they devised and selected the use of instruments to measure change. They administered the instruments and teachers even volunteered to score them. Although this process initially developed because we simply didn't have a lot of funding for a research evaluation, we inadvertently created a very smooth data collection process, method of evaluation, and a program that fit seamlessly into that particular school, causing virtually no problems.

Why did the program in this case seem so easy, compared to the endless problems created by experimental programs devised in universities by disconnected academics? Because the school designed it and instituted it, their buy-in level of acceptance and dedication to it was high.

Feeling Safe

This basic step is critical to any organizational system. A program's internal functioning depends on whether or not the individuals in it feel safe. What does it mean to "feel safe?" Obviously, physical safety is a crucial part of feeling safe, and that's the area we unfortunately are compelled to focus on most in schools, with the use of metal detectors, security guards, and other visible methods. In New York City, all schools in the Bronx have school security guards who have been elevated to the level of police officer and are responsible for matters of discipline. Little, if any, disciplining is done by teachers. Schools like these resemble war zones or prisons, places where each day begins with metal detector screenings before first period. Can these schools also function as learning environments? Generally not. It takes a huge amount of work to make sure an environment is safe enough so that individuals can thrive and relax enough to absorb new knowledge.

Understanding Power Issues, Power Struggles, and Power Dynamics

When choosing a program, every school needs to consider whether or not the power differential between the various roles and positions of authority within the school are reasonably balanced. Failing to understand and acknowledge this issue will undermine the chances a program has for success. It should be noted that Columbine High School had an antibullying program prior to the shootings in 1999, but it was completely ineffective due largely to the unresolved power differential between the athletically inclined "white cap" students and the intellectuals or "trench coat mafia." Many types of power issues exist in everyday life and people continue to experience power struggles long after they have left the school environment.

In some cases, an individual allows himself—or herself—to be dominated. For example, if you are reading this, you have made a choice, as a reader, to be dominated by us, the producers of the knowledge you require in order to improve your understanding of a problem. And although you are being dominated, you don't experience conflict. If, however, you were forced to read this book and you were not interested in schools at all, the domination would feel like a coercive pressure, and the power issue would then mutate into a power struggle between an expert with an opinion to share (us), and an audience unwilling to take it in (you).

The impact of power struggles between groups, rather than between individuals, is most prominently felt in school environments. Most people can remember feeling bullied, bullying other children, or playing the role of a pathological bystander, either enjoying the bullying without punishment or feeling too scared to move and react. Please note, the incredibly important issue of pathological bystanding will be explained and dealt with more thoroughly in a later chapter.

In a nutshell, the circle of power in power dynamics has everything to do with the cocreated nature of the following interchangeable roles: victim, victimizer, and bystander (see figure 1.1). These are not medical diagnoses, mainly

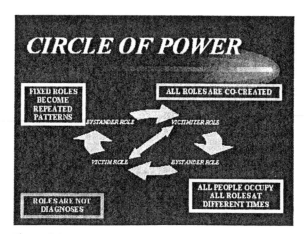

Figure 1.1.

because we are all capable of playing all three; these roles are part of our normal everyday "psychopathology." They are cocreated; one cannot exist without the other, and the roles are generally fluid in most people. If they become fixed, however, the victim may turn into an avenging victim, who then focuses total attention on revenge, as we learned from studying the tragic events. We must remember that patterns, when fixed, tend to repeat themselves.

Pathological Bystanding

If, for example, you have taken the time to find an antiviolence program that stresses character development and positive values that recognize the existence of others for your particular school, you want the whole school to participate. The "whole school" includes not just students but teachers, volunteers, parents who fill in as teachers, the administrative staff, the superintendent, the school board, and even the surrounding community.

Earlier in this chapter we outlined a variety of forms of bystanding, which we will discuss in further detail in chapter 4. Because these forms of bystanding are unconsciously adopted by various individuals, we consider them pathological. At times the dynamic between bullies, victims, and bystanders can resemble a play in which the bully and victim are the actors on stage and the bystanders are the rapt audience. If there is no audience, however, there is no incentive to act out or to perform.

In many situations, the "abdicating" bystander group gathers together after the fact and wonders what can be done about school violence. They tend to place blame on those in work roles, such as poorly functioning teachers and security guards. Both teachers and security guards may then feel overly pressured to solve problems they cannot solve without the participation of the community as a whole. The community has become the group we have called "abdicating bystanders." Even though you may be instituting a program that has little, if anything, to do directly with power issues, it may prove well worth your time to look carefully at the extent to which bystanders avoid taking part in the essential role of changing the structure of your school's climate. Teaching the importance of honesty, for example, as an element of character structure will not work well in an environment with high rates of pathological bystanding.

In one sense, we can summarize this situation in the following rather dense and critical statement: the bully in a community or school is the agent of a group of abdicating bystanders, the community members themselves, who project their dynamics and problems onto the bully. The bully then, as an agent of the abdicating bystanders, inflicts their conflicts as well as his or her own onto the agents' victim. From this perspective, the agent and the agents' victim are symptoms of a pathological and dysfunctional social system. The change element certainly would involve managing the actions of the abdicating bystanders. The actualization of this dynamic partially opens up a path to creating a school social system more receptive to school antibullying programs.

Natural Leadership, Mentalization, Altruism, and School Change

As you begin implementing the program you have chosen for your school, specific types of people will play major roles in making that program succeed. We have noted that natural leaders become very important in this role. A natural leader may not organize the group using Robert's Rules of Order, but functions more like a group facilitator. In our work with elementary schools we call these natural leaders "helpful bystanders." They are bystanders in the positive sense, as opposed to abdicating bystanders, and they display a number of qualities that would likely render them excellent individuals to engage with or involve in the elements of the program that you have chosen for your school.

In a later chapter, we will explain more about natural leaders, and we will explain in greater detail the difference between a natural leader and a charismatic leader. The critical element that distinguishes the natural leader from the charismatic leader is that natural leaders—who often do not think of themselves as leaders—are nonetheless persons motivated to act for the good of the group as a whole. They may not volunteer like charismatic leaders tend to, but they feel the need to "show" people and to lead by example. Natural leaders tend to promote creativity, to reach benevolently out for help, and always to provide for their successors a natural flow of their nonself-centered leadership style. In other words, this style models altruism to others and encourages them to become natural leaders as well. Any school that wants a program to succeed might want to make the natural leader or helpful bystander their key person in planning, selected, and instituting the program.

Hidden Problems: The Undiscussables

However well your program focuses on the needs of your school, if it does not address some of the more hidden or difficult elements of the problem, there is no way it can be successful. For example, in some areas where busing is used, community schools have become a thing of the past. Children are often not brought up in the school districts surrounding the school; they instead come to school from a great distance. We often encounter factors like this one that will fragment a school, and yet they do not appear in the average day-to-day discussion of what program will work best in schools.

We contributed one of the first papers dealing directly with the problem of teachers who bully students; we have also become very aware of students who bully their teachers, especially in high school, as well as parents who bully teachers, and administrators who bully teachers. Are these variations of traditional bullying situations easy to address? No, they are certainly not. Teachers' unions in the United States have functioned more like labor unions than professional associations and are understandably defensive about how their teachers work. We were able to carry out our research only because we had a record of years of altruistic action aimed at helping schools, and the teacher's unions in each situation were subsequently positive about our efforts and supported our work.

Bullying administrators, corruption, labor disputes, and sore spots created by teacher whistle blowers, and the prejudice and stigma over the issue of whether or not schools encourage orientation of new students to the group rather than forcing them into subgroups are among the problems faced by teachers' unions. And this is just the tip of the iceberg. The "problem of excellence," the role of high grade point averages, and students' desires for acceptance into Ivy League Schools are also part of the story. In high school, students *do* bully teachers. In one school we reviewed, teachers were so scared of students that every teacher in the break room was asleep from stress and exhaustion.

Evaluation, Communication Between Disciplines, and Accountability

Measuring and evaluating the impact of an antiviolence intervention seems like common sense. People don't like to do it, however, because it smacks of research, although often the necessary instruments are quite painless, and the procedures themselves are brief. This step is very helpful as a way to evaluate an entire school district or group of schools in an anonymous way using a variety of instruments. For example, a school principal who knows quite well that his or her school needs an antibullying approach could convince a mayor with other agendas to promote and financially support the purchase of such a program, provided the necessary data are available and compelling.

Bringing together people, including students and administrators, who take account of and monitor all of these steps is essential. We recommend that data be collected for school districts as a whole, rather than focusing on individual classes. Grade-by-grade analyses with anonymous questionnaires provide the most useful data. Schools are not hospitals and should not use the same kinds of general questionnaires to gauge the climate of their institution. For instance, if you ask a question about how well the students are performing you will generally get most answers indicating that students are performing well; in a very well-behaved school we consulted with, 85 percent of the children felt the school was excellent. While this is nice to read, common sense suggests that it only takes one or two unhappy individuals to kill people, regardless of what statistics suggest.

Schools already collect statistics pertaining to many areas, such as daily attendance, expulsions, and out-of-school and in-school suspensions. These statistics are heavily influenced by politics and, with rare exceptions, are not reported if the school doesn't want the knowledge to become public. We worked in a school district where the most violent school reported no out-of-school suspensions. This school was like a lockdown war zone with serious threats for nonperformance, not unlike maximum-security prisons and equally expensive. Privatization of performance had produced massive staff financial incentives for high academic and discipline performance. Certain criminal behaviors are extremely serious and must be reported for legal reasons, but the vast majority of events that causes a school to become dysfunctional would not appear on mandatory reports at all. Truancy and attendance are, of course, state laws in many places, but whether or not a child who is truant is actually prosecuted depends largely on the workload of a district attorney in a given area. School truancy is hard to prove, because it involves the parents, and the penalties are relatively minor. Many district attorneys simply won't prosecute truancy and school truancy statistics are artificially low, as a result. In other words, the statistics collected by a school system don't always indicate what is going on in the school itself, or in this case, how the problem of truancy can be a factor in creating a hostile school environment.

Chapter 10 reviews resources in the literature on the Internet and in the community. The key point is how to assess validity and reliability of programs and how to ask the right questions.

The People We Work With

Creating change in a social system is all about people; it's not really dependent upon specialized programs or unusual levels of expertise. People on the same page move in the same direction and will, if allowed, create a peaceful school-learning environment.

How you train people involves several basic steps:

1. Identify a leader, preferably a natural leader, and gathering the stakeholders together.
2. Establish a process that defines similarities, acknowledges differences, and creates a safe outlet for negative emotions.

3. Discuss undiscussables and stimulate and humanize each other.
4. Set boundaries, agree on a common language, define the problem, and establish a long-term time table and resist quick fixes.
5. Take action to identify and select the natural leaders.
6. Create collaborative work groups, give feedback, monitor, and establish interdisciplinary communication.
7. Train future trainers in the particulars of small group dynamics.

The goal is to facilitate action within the group by following these rules and laws in order to establish a highly mentalizing climate of critical self-reflection.

Chapter Two

Buy In:
Nothing Happens Without It

We have spent a lot of time over the past fourteen years conducting careful research to verify ideas some people might classify as simple common sense. Essentially, no violence prevention program can or will work in any school without the presence of the factor we refer to as the "buy in" on the part of that school's leaders, key teachers, students, and the students' concerned parents. Successful implementation of any antibullying program demands that you understand the barriers and techniques for creating the buy in within your school. A school's climate can be changed, but it takes more than a program to effect that change. Think of it this way: you can have all the fancy snow shovels in the world, but without people to shovel it, the snow stays right where it is. In the field of violence prevention, even the best programs can fail when people do not address buy in, the key component in getting started and creating positive changes.

We consider ourselves among the groundbreaking experts in exploring ways of understanding and reducing school violence. Before our research could even begin, however, we had to accept that bullying was not an easy phenomenon to be understood. Too often, people dismiss bullying as part of normal children's development, although we all victimize, act as a victim *and* bystander in ever-changing roles. It is when the roles are fixed that the problems begin.

When we brought a martial arts and psychological perspective to the behaviors we observed, we learned that bullying involves a variety of rotating social roles, including those of the bully, the victim, and the bystanders. We noted how the role of the bystander was the most understudied element of behaviors in school and at home. Oversights such as these may compel researchers to pursue the wrong goals and to overlook the solutions others may dismiss as common sense.

This leads us back to the term we began explaining at the opening of this chapter. What is buy in? Why is it so important? Buy in can be defined as "joining" a group of teachers and earning their investment of time and talent in a process designed to improve overall school climate. Change cannot be solely directed from the top. This process of responding to the administration is called compliance. Buy in goes more to the core of why a teacher teaches, rather than selling real estate or opening a restaurant. When teachers buy into a process, what they are doing is agreeing to participate and invest in a guided process that will ultimately enrich their own environments and careers.

We must also remember that teachers can become overworked and over-stressed, sagging under the pressures of ungrateful communities, unreasonable parents, and troublesome kids. Teachers feel chained to expectations and may resent outside demands on their time and skills beyond academic matters. In fact, when a teacher is tired or stressed, the most irritating event must include being talked to about positive behavior plans and new approaches. No one wants to give teachers more tasks to balance. Some successful initiatives, however, have been taken by schools to discover ways to ensure teachers' buy in. The struggle to convince teachers is comparable to convincing them, for instance, to embrace new technology. In other words, despite the huge number of important advantages for teachers to embrace technology, often these initiatives are met with resistance. To motivate teachers to learn new teaching approaches calls for more than choosing a training manual, showing off the basics, and expecting the rest to fall magically into place. Even the best program and manual will gather dust on busy teachers' desks if they have not decided to buy in.

One incentive, therefore, for teachers to buy in, is to emphasize an important connection our research has shown: in a controlled study of elementary schools, schools with a bullying prevention program demonstrated a significant improvement in their students' scores on standardized achievement tests. There is a definite link between a peaceful school and improved learning. It is not a waste of time for a teacher to invest or buy into a procedure that improves the quality of the school climate. Students can learn freely, and teachers can be more creative and unburdened to do what they do best: teach. Simply *knowing*, however, that there is a potential benefit does not always get the job done when it comes to bullying and violence prevention in our schools.

It might seem impossible to imagine that a group of diverse teachers would truly and wholeheartedly buy into anything as a whole. In fact we have found that 75 percent of teachers and 100 percent of administrators, including principals, must buy in for a program to be successful in schools. The basic formula behind preparing your school for an antiviolence program, in our opinion, consists of a universal set of principles based on human behavior.

HOW NOT TO EARN BUY IN

Jamaicans have a wonderful idiomatic expression that defines people who seem to be all talk and no action: "a bag full of mouth." Buy in involves more than just fantasizing about change, complaining about the people in power, or listing the endless difficulties presented by the children and their families. Buy in requires action in a specific direction. Buy in can be seen as the polar opposite of empty talk. Teachers are very sensitive when they feel they are being judged and told what to do in their classrooms. A teacher's sense of territorial pride is something that can bring a classroom alive with learning, but if improperly or aggressively challenged, even by those with the best of intentions, teachers will tune out, rebel, or fake compliance. There will be, of course, no buy in, and any program implemented will have no chance of succeeding in the long term.

One sure way to kill the possibility of a buy in is to promise too much and not deliver. This can be the result of misunderstanding or underestimating the challenges and obstacles facing teachers on a daily basis. A group of teachers can become dysfunctional as a result of feeling pressured or offered solutions that will never work, given the reality of daily life in most schools. We learned this lesson very quickly in dealing with Jamaican schools and have since applied it to our findings in other countries as well. If you want to get the teachers on your side, it is vital to produce what you promise. It is better to promise and deliver small things over time. This builds buy in and opens the door to change.

Another sure way to kill buy in is to present your ideas from a mistaken perspective, such as by using a "know-it-all" or "old pro teacher" speech. We have seen this approach often in teacher professional training or in presentations by outside consultants. Your school's climate is a highly protected entity functioning as a social group with visible and invisible social norms that direct its inhabitants' behaviors. Invisible rules can be difficult to know or recognize until they are broken, and schools can be the same way. The school climate is both generated and changed by addressing the social norms, as well as the power dynamics existing within this climate. Before this is possible, a change agent needs to build buy in.

A good example of how teachers think about outside "shrink-type" consultants involves one of our experiences at an inner-city elementary school having considerable behavior problems. The school's consultant was hired through a federal grant and spent ten hours per week at the school. The consultant presented a teacher training program in which the main technique shared showed teachers how to increase their levels of self-control, and how not to be pulled into the students' bad behavior. Everybody seemed very interested at first; some teachers may have been daydreaming after a long day of teaching, while others were polite, listened, and asked the typical questions. The next day, the consultant was asked to fill in for thirty minutes while a kindergarten teacher took a quick lunch break. The consultant quickly agreed and pranced confidently into the room, while the teacher left. It took about five minutes before sheer chaos broke out. The students immediately sensed the adult's discomfort and saw an opening for acting out. They all took turns creating dramas around the food, and all the clever strategies presented the previous day were useless, even if the consultant had been able to remember them.

After what seemed like forever (but was less than half an hour), the teacher returned. The consultant spent the rest of the day hiding in the counselor's office. The teachers and counselors were laughing and good-naturedly mocking the consultant for the remainder of the day. The consultant learned firsthand the burden and intensity of teaching young children in a public school, one classroom at a time. Interestingly, this experience led to the buy in of that particular school. It was not the techniques from the training presentation that stimulated the buy in, but rather the consultant's willingness to listen to and try out the teachers' experiences. Of course, the consultant's humble pie experience also contributed to the overall inclusion of the consultant, but listening is truly the most important catalyst for the buy-in process.

Judging teachers is another sure way to kill buy in. We learned this lesson early during our research in Jamaican schools. Bear in mind that the average Jamaican teacher earns less than $100 per week. The average class contains over fifty students, often with three sharing a single desk. Teachers have extremely limited resources and are faced with staggering educational problems. Kids stabbing each other and fighting endlessly for every bit of resource or adult attention are daily occurrences. The teachers can seem quite harsh and disinterested at times when they are asked to supervise multiple classrooms at a time, and yet the more time we spent in Jamaican schools, the more we began to understand the power, dignity, and courage of these teachers.

Although we were warned that these teachers would be hard to engage, and that none of them would take the time even just to listen to our ideas, they *did* meet with us. We began by presenting them with some much-needed school supplies before beginning our presentation. This donation was teacher-focused and relatively minor, but it did open the door a bit and showed them that we understood and cared about their needs. We engaged the teachers by listening to them in small groups. Our focus was to find ways we could help the older students become helpful bystanders instead of bullies. At the teachers' suggestions, we instituted a craft program that involved the older students in a highly valued extracurricular program. The combination of a student program that targeted these difficult older students and our listening to teachers opened the door to buy in and toward a solution that benefited everyone. It would have been tempting to judge these teachers, or to try to convince them to think differently, but doing so would have eliminated the possibility of their buy in.

Earlier, in another Jamaican school, we learned the hard way how barging into a school with preconceived notions kills buy in. We began our intervention by offering to support the school's newly formed computer-lab room through funding their high speed Internet connection. Next, we proposed a teacher-based essay project and suggested some other activities that *we* thought would be the most appropriate. We met with teachers and presented our ideas, but we failed to stop and listen to what they had to tell us. We tried to transpose what had worked well in the United States onto Jamaican schools, not taking into account key differences between the two systems. We spent a year preparing the project site, working with the Peace Corps to develop a program design and funding a high speed online connection. We just put up the money and tossed ideas related to antibullying out through the Internet. The end result, as you might have guessed, was a dismal failure. The principal was offended and enraged when we shared our data with her. She railed that the instrument was wrong and that the results did not make sense. The school personnel used the Internet connection for their own personal goals, ignoring all the elements of the climate program we suggested. Our goal of linking up teachers and schools never got off the ground because we completely failed at securing buy in.

Every time we stumbled early in our research, we learned extremely valuable lessons about what works, and just as important, what does *not* work. In another instance, while working with an urban American school district, we used our research data to secure a grant. As soon as the grant was awarded, the bully prevention component began enlisting elementary schools. We developed literature, workbooks, signs, posters, and a wide array of program materials to be used in each school. We had a large manual and a generous budget for teacher training. Our goal was to involve ten schools per year; instead, we got two in three years. Eventually, our portion of the grant was entirely phased out. Think of it this way: the bullying prevention program was itself bullied out of the school system. Our materials were attacked or ignored, and the administration used our share of the grant for other school expenses. Buy in requires support from the top and from leaders who hold schools accountable for creating plans that improve school climates. Without this support from the top, buy in is very hard to attain. If your school does not buy in, it cannot support a successful antibullying program.

Support from the top, however, does not guarantee buy in. In fact, an outside helper or consultant may be viewed as a hired gun doing the boss's dirty work. Schools can become closed systems that do not tolerate outside intervention. The system is closed for a good reason; it needs to protect the children and to foster learning. If teachers smell a possible "rat," they may play along, be polite and wait for the outsider to wither away from lack of internal support. The benefits of any program you attempt to implement will be lost in the process of trying to earn buy in. Simply being appointed and financed by the top does not translate to automatic acceptance at the teacher level. Nothing works without the active cultivation over time of this teacher-level support.

EARNING BUY IN

The first step in this process requires that the outside consultants acknowledge the need to earn buy in within a school. Teachers view their internal worlds from a very different perspective than a school district's administration. Entering this system is a delicate process that can easily be ended if you take the wrong approach. There is little doubt that teachers will use and value helpful strategies, however, if they feel that they have been adequately involved in the process from the beginning. The first step in this process of earning buy in is to learn and show respect for the inner circle of the teacher's world. Compare this approach to that of martial artists bowing and shedding their shoes when entering a dojo or fighting area. The area itself and the people in it are shown respect every time anyone enters the space. While these might seem like small gestures, or simple pageantry, failing to make them will affect the environment and everything that happens within it.

The first sign of respect is shown by simply listening. The best program ideas often come from the teachers themselves. When the teachers help build the process of change, then they will remain invested in its success and in keeping it going. This might seem like common sense, yet many well-intentioned individuals often overlook this idea entirely. We learned this at our very first experimental school. The school was underperforming and had a high record of disciplinary actions, expulsions, and suspensions. The outside agents were a psychoanalyst and martial artists from the School of Martial and Meditative Arts.

This particular elementary school had a very active group of teachers who brainstormed with the principal to find a way of teaching about and reducing instances of bullying, victimization, and bystanding behavior. We brought our research and theoretical ideas and the "hook," or the high interest activity. In this case, the hook was adapted defensive traditional martial arts to be added to all students' physical education classes. The altruism of the outside experts and their role as facilitators of the ideas of the staff, in this project, added to the power and sustainability of the program effort. It is easy to succumb to the idea that the outsider is the expert and that the teachers need to be taught what to do. We learned quickly that the teachers understandably need to feel in control and shape the way in which change principles are enacted on a day-to-day basis.

THE FOUR ELEMENTS OF A BUY-IN PROCESS

Schools may differ in different parts of the world. We have certainly experienced a broad spectrum in various countries. There are communities and countries where the governments seem to spoil their schools by throwing money at problems. Other countries struggle simply to provide a roof and a teacher. But, no matter their differences, all schools must have teachers. We believe there is a universal quality to this buy-in process that reflects human group dynamics. It is no surprise to sociologists or to social psychologists that people in groups develop their own unique psychologies. While most groups fear outsiders, its members almost never share the exact same motivations, for example, life conditions, or employment status and need for recognition. As a result, approaching a group of teachers in a school requires awareness and understanding of how group processes work. Changing schools demands the building of support among those closest to the children, and this often means the teachers.

Building trust is, as you might imagine, a tricky business, but one which must be mastered before even the most enlightened and sensitive antibullying program can effect change. The main players in the change process include first an inside agent, then an outside altruistic expert, and the third is the school's leader. Parents can be either helpful or deadly to the buy-in process. It only takes a few parents with motivation, tenacity, and a sense of boundaries to help your school change its climate. They represent extra hands, minds, and hearts that can share the load with your already overburdened teachers. This combination of change agents is the core group, whose primary job is to attract those willing to try new things for the sake of the school climate. Once a core group of early believers is recruited, then the buy-in process is ready to proceed.

Element One: Understanding the Pressures on Teachers

Teaching in the digital era can feel like being trapped in a strange new world. Students are now connected literally all day and all night. Whatever a student does at school follows them home through text messages, digital phones, instant messaging, chat rooms, blogs, and video phones. Whether the student is living in a fancy residential school or attends a public suburban junior high, the digital connection must be factored in to his or her experience. Kids can be mean and the more they want to stay that way, the harder it is to teach them otherwise, and as a result the entire school becomes more troubled. We have seen teachers compelled to act as referees, police officers, parents, state agencies, judges, and juries, dragged into the endless conflicts spurred by the digital obsessions of modern students. The students in turn tend to become violent, depressed, self-destructive, drug addicted, unmotivated to perform academically, and likely to develop dangerous mental impairments.

Many communities have no idea how children have changed and how the rules of teaching are impacted by modern forces. School may be the only time in a child's day when an adult can successfully compete with phones, iPods, and the Internet. Teachers may have to work harder to control their classrooms because of having to compete with digital devices for the minds of our children. The problem becomes how to keep the teacher strong, supported, valued, and full of enough tricks to survive and thrive. Teachers already know how to teach the academic material; the hard part is to maintain control of a classroom when the students are acting out in distracting, nonfunctional behavior patterns. We need teachers to be able to turn their classrooms into safe havens separated from the social problems children may be experiencing outside. Teachers need to be able to capture the minds of our children and hold them open while they introduce new ideas and facts.

Because of this vital role they play, and their ubiquitous presence at schools in every location imaginable, teachers need to be included and involved in any efforts you make to change your school. Many schools have been labeled "underperforming" and may in fact be inadequate physical settings with disproportionate numbers of "problem" students. Even in these schools, however, there are teachers who manage to create safe and positive learning environments. How is it that some teachers treat their classes like temples of learning, while others seem completely indifferent? The key ingredient to creating positive classrooms is a teacher who is in charge because she or he earned the buy in from students. The good teacher builds relationships with the students over the course of the school year, respecting differences and seeking the positive in all students. This is what gets and keeps the students' attention.

In other words, teachers have a choice. They can retreat to their classrooms and restrict their efforts to their own particular group of students. The alternative is to buy in to a larger climate change in the schools. Schools need to prioritize practices that target school climate as a whole.

This demands that teachers believe in the selected approach to improving school climate. Simply teaching a technique is not enough. Teaching is like wrestling, in that you have to constantly try new moves to break away from old obstacles or barriers.

School climate programs need teachers to buy into a process that strives to improve the quality of learning environments. Eliminating power struggles, bullying (involving students, teachers, the administration, and parents) or mean and coercive behavior takes effort, discussion of the undiscussables, and the time and goodwill of the community and its educational leaders. Helping teachers create more creative and safe learning environments is in everybody's best interest. Outside experts may have the skills teachers need, but they have to be willing to earn the teachers' confidence. The community and educational leadership must commit time and available resources to allow this process to happen. Peaceful classes thrive in positive educational climates.

Element Two: Create a Simple Process

Changing your school's climate does not begin with a program, but rather, with a process. Many schools begin to address their climates only *after* a tragic event has occurred. Yet, if you think about it, the time immediately after a school has been traumatized is perhaps the worst time to create a reflective process for change. It is more common for a school or any social system to react by seeking out a quick fix at this time. Blue Ribbon Panels are a good example of this reflexive impulse to quickly fix whatever it was that caused a particular problem or a tragedy. These panels gather to reflect on how such a tragedy could befall their school. Experts give their opinions; educators state the reality of day-to-day life in school. The media gets involved, sometimes for better and sometimes for worse. Reports are often generated, a few programs may start, and funding is quick to follow. Then, the aftermath of the tragedy lessens and less pressure and attention are focused on the issue of school climate. Soon the school returns to normal and the underlying climate problems remain to fester and potentially reignite.

The goal of the climate-change process is to set up a dialogue and to foster mentalization, or self-reflection. This may begin as simply as weekly discussions among a principal, a guidance counselor, and a local expert. The goal of this core group is to attract the input of others in practical and useful ways. The core group needs to stay in continuous contact, but not everybody has to be similarly involved at that level.

For example, in a Topeka, Kansas, elementary school project, the local Parent Teacher Organization had two very active members. They offered to help the team by making hand-embroidered "peace flags" to hang outside each classroom door. The teachers loved that idea and found that the students rallied around the peace flags. When a class was disrupted, the disruptive student(s) had to take down the class's flag. As you might imagine, kids hated to do that. This example shows how a few parents jumped into the core group's planning process and set an integral part of this school's climate-change strategy into motion. This approach worked not because of the flags, but because the teachers bought into the parents' idea and supported it wholeheartedly. This probably would not be as effective if we just had stuck flags on classroom doors in any school we entered. It was the process of the involvement of the parents with the teachers that gave those flags special meaning. This is what climate change is all about.

The simple process can easily become entwined with other parts of the change process. Somebody has to chair and help the group stay focused, or the process can become too abstract and lose sight of its mission. Here are the four guidelines we found most helpful:

1. Assign a group chair who creates agendas and takes notes.
2. Limit meeting times to forty-five minutes or less.
3. Try a climate campaign quickly to kick off.
4. Meet weekly and include the school's principal in all communications.

The most effective groups are very efficient and remember to plan events targeting the climate issues. Fitting in, or matters of social inclusion and exclusion, are fairly universal human interpersonal processes. The specific nature of how they are acted out varies from school to school and from country to country, but in general, young people need action to keep them interested. We have found that physical education classes are excellent places to practice physical skills of assertiveness that lead to reduced fears of being harmed by a bully. Posters and contests are a great way to increase awareness and build relationships with the community and are good supplements to physical education classes.

Element Three: Take Action

Getting teachers involved takes some effort. If you're expecting a buy in, you have to be ready to do some selling! Taking action that impacts a teacher's world is one way to start revving the buy-in engine. For instance, we have witnessed some very successful climate campaigns that began with small community donations for a poster contest. A local bank donated a savings bond, the nearby amusement park donated free passes, and a local sporting goods store offered fifty-dollar gift certificates. Remember that including a teacher-oriented prize also will attract attention and get the teachers interested. Involving judges and award presenters from local elected officials always elevates an event, as can adding other celebrities in a school's area. Bill Cosby "adopted" some deserving Springfield public school students and paid for them to attend college when he was convinced to speak at an event in Springfield, Massachusetts. He was recruited because he lived nearby, received his doctorate from University of Massachusetts, and became involved with Springfield as the closest city to his family home in Shelburne, Massachusetts.

Once empowered, change agents can start their mission with the proverbial bang, a type of visible kickoff. These ceremonial-style events create interest and draw attention, presenting your team to your school's teachers, students, and their parents as an action-oriented practical group, one committed to listening and responding to what is said about improving the learning environment. Speakers can present very simple ideas to large groups about ways of building and creating peaceful schools. Teachers are still working when they attend assemblies and this is an excellent time to show them some of the potential fruits of their input and to motivate their buy in.

Element Four: Leadership Notices Buy In

Your principal is the official leader of your school. Often, as leaders, they are not capable of participating in everything they support. Principals want to be noticed and they want the best for their schools. It takes no extra resources to notice good deeds, however, and not just to focus on academic successes or missteps. The best way we have learned to teach students this lesson is to start from the top and model the behavior down the line or chain of command. When leaders accept the challenges of understanding and changing school climates, teachers will be more motivated (being noticed is very rewarding) to buy into a project. Again, the higher up a leader is the more power she or he will have to generate.

For example, we worked in an East Coast public school with a truly visionary superintendent. He took a school system that was sinking and began to create change by recruiting minority principals. The school had a 19 percent Caucasian student body and 90 percent Caucasian teachers. He held every principal responsible to implement a program to fight bullying. A healthy sense of competition ensued as each principal became motivated to please the superintendent. This is smart leadership, and it needs to be as contagious as the factors that can work against it all too often.

GETTING IT DONE: IMPLEMENTATION

Teachers have become bogged down by the constant need to deal with disruptive behaviors in their classrooms that negatively impact a school's overall climate. Disruptive behavior is an attack on any teacher's ability to teach, and when disruptions overflow into recess, hallways, cafeterias, and school buses, the entire school experience can become a series of destructive power struggles among students and also between students and teachers. School administrators and parents alike will be sucked into those struggles. The net result is a noncreative learning environment burdensome to everybody. Savvy and aware school administration members and principals can anticipate these problems before they become manifest in increased disciplinary referrals and decreased academic achievement. A parochial K–8 school we studied in Springfield, Massachusetts, adopted a program to deal with the unhappiness of younger children who felt excluded by the older children. The parent-teacher organization in that school was active in bringing this problem to the principal's attention before it was reflected in any of the typical parameters of disruption. It was at this very early stage that we recommended the incorporation of an antibullying program for that particular school, and for older children to welcome the younger students, a problem easily solved by the Student Council.

An errant approach to this implementation would be for a school to mandate this program without full cooperation, especially of the school's teachers and the students' parents. School administrators often walk a tightrope when making a decision to institute programs like this. If the situation is serious, involving frequent acts of extreme violence and weaponry, students may be so frightened that they are unable to institute any comprehensive programs due to the mind-numbing, demoralizing effect of fear. On the other hand, an urgent need created by violence in the school may instead be a strong motivator to make such programs successful.

As experienced clinicians, we are acutely aware that it is the people running the program that make this or any program work and doing that involves complicated decisions. The components themselves of *any* program are useless without the enthusiasm and inspiration of the administration, principals, and teachers. For example, a school board member whose child has been bullied may force a school into adopting a program that it does not want. We recommend, when evaluating a school for the program, such factors be carefully evaluated instead of being mandated unilaterally by the school administration or school board.

GETTING STARTED

Now that you know the key factors for implementing a program successfully, how do you get started? We recommend an initial evaluation of the needs of your particular school district, including assessment of other schools in the district or region. Chapter 9 outlines a relatively objective way to do all this with simple anonymous questionnaires, including a violence audit, which we have found consistently insightful and useful in preparing schools for antiviolence programs. By studying a sampling of children in grades three through twelve using questionnaires such as these, we learned to evaluate feelings of safety and ways in which aggression, victimization, and responses to aggression and victimization occur within schools. This material is summarized and included in the sample recommendation to the school administration. Chapter 10 lists other useful resources.

ADDRESSING THE DEVELOPMENTAL NEEDS OF THE CHILD

Very young children often find school a frightening place, since it is their first separation from home. School also represents their first real exposure to a large number of peers in a regimented classroom style. Even within typical elementary schools, spanning kindergarten through fifth grade, children experience a variety of normal developmental phases. The key to preventing bullying is to include specific activities and messages as organic parts of the educational process the students are already involved in, appropriate to their developmental needs.

Consider that from kindergarten through third grade children have not yet fully developed their verbal skills. At these ages, children tend to relate to their teachers as parental surrogates. Teachers who work with very young and elementary age children often comment that they feel more like mothers or fathers than they do teachers. Much of what children do at that age is designed to get attention with a desire to please or irritate the teacher rather than to achieve or master any academic skills. Young children learn by doing, as they are constantly active and yearning to be in motion. Attempts to hold their attention and keep them in their seats are often fruitless. Programs that include physical activities, such as an emphasis on martial arts, can function as excellent teaching devices that address the readiness of children at a specific developmental stage.

Later, in fourth and fifth grades, children tend to form peer groups that evolve natural leaders. Their verbal and symbolizing skills are also developing, and children begin to become more competitive. Their goals are often focused on mastering their own skills by competitively challenging others as part of the resolution of normal strivings and assertiveness. Competitive sports are excellent metaphors to use to teach children at this age about bullying. In making use of peer leadership through healthy competition, older children are taught to help younger children learn and integrate. For example, by being assistant instructors in the Gentle Warrior program or being part of the Honor Patrol in the Bruno Adult Mentor program, children can learn to be leaders and how to help others find their places.

Among middle- and high-school-aged children, competitive sports are also invaluable metaphors to inspire and motivate a child. In later years of high school, power struggles begin to change a child's character. The schoolyard physical bully has a decreased social status in the later years of high school as children become more abstract, intellectual, and verbal in their thinking. Often, students at these stages of development have mastered the verbal means to solve conflicts. In these schools, purely intellectual metaphors can be selected. Forensics and debate are often popular activities in high schools and represent other ways in which a whole school can bully in areas other than athletics. Table 2.1 summarizes basic developmental metaphors from kindergarten through early adulthood.

In summary, we have seen the following factors affect buy in in the direction in which the school system moves, rather than forcing a series of changes. People that run schools are generally good hearted, experienced, and highly dedicated to the care and the education of children. It is not that anything needs to change necessarily; they just need to be redirected, which is a matter of how their priorities are assessed.

The first is the complicated problem of whether the teachers are there to teach or to take care of children both as parental figures and as "therapists." It is a problem that is immensely variable, depending on the social context. As one inner-city teacher told me wearily, "Dr. Twemlow, you are preaching to the choir here." In this particular high school teacher's classroom, there was a boy with a black eye from his mother's boyfriend, another girl who had been sexually abused by her mother's boyfriend, and another girl who had just started her period and thought she was bleeding to death because she had no education in this area at all. As the teacher said, "Do you think I taught mathematics?" It is much easier in a more peaceful, more settled, and safe school

Table 2.1. Normal Developmental Stages of a Student's Relationship to Teachers

K–3: Teacher as good enough parent/protector
• Child does most good and bad things to please or annoy the teacher

Grades 4–7: Peer groups and leaders emerge
• Giving up the "good enough" teacher
• Competitiveness evolves naturally as peer leaders emerge
• Much preoccupation with peer groups and projects

Grades 8–12: Development of abstraction and verbal skills
• Separation from the good enough teacher
• Identity formation and premature identity foreclosure under peer pressure
• Capacity to be alone is emerging and growing

Early Adulthood (up till age 25)
• A psychosocial moratorium (Erik Erikson)
• Young person often tries on many hats in career, relationships, jobs

Questions
• If many children don't think about the responsibilities of being grown and independent, then maybe they may only learn when it is fun (K–12). Teachers remembered are the ones that acknowledge the psychological needs of children.
• Parents have as much difficulty letting their children go as children have in letting their parents go.

to do what teachers feel they have been hired to do: teach. Our sense really is that teachers enjoy the caring and social-emotional aspects of learning as much as the intellectual content, yet they just need the impetus to include it as part of being a valid teacher, not just an intellectual scribe!

We have seen this model of a teacher appear where there has been some major catastrophe, such as in the very first school we visited, following an attempted rape of a second grade girl by a group of second grade boys. When a school is motivated mainly by a catastrophe, it is not an ideal buy-in situation. Such schools are so desperate to get something done that they generally fail to think through what they actually need to do within their school structure, and instead they search desperately for a quick solution to settle the crisis. Politics are often motivated by complaints from both community and parents, and although schools will quickly buy in to programs, they won't necessarily implement them in a measured and steady way, such as for five years of consistent work, by teachers, students, volunteers, and consultants.

Buy in can be achieved as a safety measure in schools that are not experiencing a crisis. Where data are collected on schools, issues surface that often provide evidence for the need for a proactive approach to school bullying and victimization. It is not always easy to get schools to use questionnaires that ask very specific questions. Some schools are more comfortable with the school equivalent of patient satisfaction surveys. "How do you like your school?" This provides data generally that confirm the wishes of the school to find nothing particularly problematic. But violence assessment from behaviorally and psychologically oriented questionnaires can be extremely helpful, especially if conducted in schools throughout the school district, since it provides a comparison of schools for further work.

Another approach to the challenge of attaining buy in is to ask the school for a small amount of what is possible. Schools are often able to provide free time even though they cannot free up money, for instance. Ask for an hour or two a week and create a school climate group consisting of teachers, parents, students, volunteers, and consultants willing to talk through what needs to be done, the priorities, and the unique problems of your school. Many principals will often allow a small amount to be done, which then can grow as your core group continues to be active and makes its presence known as a proactive and peace-focused force.

Another possibility is to create an atmosphere in which the school administrators are made to look good, by utilizing projects that involve the community but also highlight the strengths of the school. For example, creating partnerships between businesses and schools and awarding community-focused prizes to students who excel in positive activities will present the school to the media as innovative and progressive. This approach will tend to set up a more positive view of dealing with the more negative and difficult issues since budget personnel typically think this way. Recasting negative issues, such as bullying and power dynamics, into a more positive light makes it easier for school administrators to accept the possibility of addressing these issues.

One issue for students, teachers, and volunteer staff to tackle is to start recording instances of bullying. Then they can send numerous e-mails or petitions to the principal highlighting these records of specific instances of bullying noted by both staff and students. This should not be performed in a judgmental way, but in a consistently matter-of-fact and everyday tone that lets the principal know how the school is doing from the inside out.

Don't overlook school staff members who might not occupy academic roles. Many bullying behaviors can also be handled through the actions of coaches, for example, who themselves may well bully students as part of an ill-conceived attempt to get the best possible performance out of children. Working directly with coaches may, in some cases, seem less threatening to schools than asking teachers directly. The main challenge to focus on is guiding the movement of the school in a painless but inevitable fashion toward a process that later may expand into a much more comprehensive antibullying approach.

CHAPTER 3: KEY QUESTIONS

Step 1. Identify: Who are the key figures whose buy in is crucial? What sorts of incentives can help ensure the buy-in factor at your school?

Step 2. Evaluate: Describe the current relationships between teachers, students, administrators, and parents in your school. What would you like to see change?

Step 3. Act: Getting started . . . find your core group members. Remember: "Don't assume it is present"; "It might change over time"; "What is the need?" and "How intense is it?," can't be mandated by the higher-ups.

SUMMARY AND REVIEW

- Buy in is the commitment by teachers to give a program a chance to work, learn about the program, not resist and mock the ideas of the program, and ultimately work together to make the program work in their school.
- Bullying is a complex problem that needs everybody to be involved in order to keep up with the shifting nature of bullying. It needs the teachers input every step of the way.
- Buy in is not compliance to authority. Buy in is earned by a team that is seen to be working to help improve the school. A superintendent cannot mandate buy in.
- Buy in must respect the overburdened teacher and not place unwanted tasks on them. Volunteering is the next step after buy in; you don't have to volunteer to buy into a program.
- We have demonstrated the connection between peaceful schools and improved achievement. Teachers need to be shown how the program can lead to better student achievement. A safe school can achieve more.
- Quick list of DON'TS in creating buy in.

  —Just talk and direct.
  —Make promises you can't keep.
  —Be a know-it-all.

—Judge and criticize.

—Try to ask too much, take small steps.

- To improve buy in, direct resources to the teachers to motivate and reward participation. These can be symbolic such as trips, donated meals, or specialized supplies.
- Four Elements to Building BUY IN:

    —Start slow and respect the ongoing culture.
    —Create a simple process and team.
    —Take action, do some small project (see project list).
    —Create public leadership support (involvement gets you noticed).

- Address the developmental needs of the children.

    —K–3 (primary targets for primary prevention)
    —Grades 4–9 (Middle School—two very difficult transitions from elementary to middle and from middle to high school)
    —High School
    —College

PROJECT SUGGESTIONS

Ideas for Quick Starts with Low Resources

- Poster Contests: Use violence prevention or health information to send to parents in K–10 and then create a local competition with some small prizes (movie tickets, teen meals, sports equipment, etc.). Winner is recognized, receives the prize, and winning poster adopted as a peace flag.
- Teacher Classroom Decoration: Offer prizes for the most creative room that promotes program messages. Involve the library and support staff.
- Essay Contests: Sponsored by local newspapers, attract local sponsors to judge and award the best teacher/student/parent essay on the topic. This helps form bridges to the community.
- Student Awareness Events: Can be sponsored, using the themes of anti-bullying, positive vibrations, social acceptance, and a social disregard for mean social behavior.
- Sports Adoption of Socially Vulnerable Children: This is a great way to have socially strong athletes adopt a student who is having trouble socially or is predicted by counselors to be at high risk for victimization during a transition to junior or senior high school. The athletes can use bead bracelets to make a friend, coaches will value it, and everybody benefits.

- Using Creativity and Altruism Projects (Adopt A School-Country): We use beads made in a Jamaican school, purchased by U.S. community sponsors, and used in U.S. schools as signs of friendship between the athlete and his new friend. U.S. schools can work internationally to expose students to the massive cultural differences that exist in schools around the world. This can be done in the United States between privileged schools and underperforming schools.

Chapter Three

Understanding Power Dynamics, Power Struggles, and Power Issues

Throughout the many projects we have worked on over the past fifteen years, it has become clear that bullying, or the use of coercive power, is one of the most basic issues contributing to the evolution and expression of aggression. This is not only true in schools, but also throughout countries, government organizations, and other groups present in larger social contexts outside of the educational sector. While bullying may take many different forms over time, the fundamental dynamic of creating humiliation remains consistent in all forms of bullying. Bullying is the behavior that pervades school climates in many forms and by all age groups, creating the exact opposite of a desirable and peaceful school. Eliminating bullying is the key element in all attempts to build and maintain peaceful school environments, and it can prove helpful in creating peaceful adult environments as well.

In approaching any social context experiencing coercive behavior problems, we have learned the importance of acknowledging the underlying power dynamics already in place. Schools are the classic example of social climates that can become, even with the best of initial intentions, unconsciously coercive environments. Peaceful environments are, by definition, intolerant of coercive activities. School leaders are often distracted by conflicting societal demands, and increasing responsibilities tend to replace the structure, boundaries, and attention families have stopped providing for their own children.

This conflict is clearly illustrated in the current No Child Left Behind Act of 2001. This education-reform legislation (based on a corporate incentive model) aims for increased accountability without a full understanding of the problems and extra burdens this model creates for schools. This corporate pressure leads to the devaluation of the time invested in reflecting on positive climates, creating instead a fertile ground for the unconscious development of coercive dynamics that invade a school's culture. These coercive processes are part of the underlying or preexisting power dynamics potentially within any social context and must be addressed before *any* antibullying program can be successful. Focusing on the underlying power dynamics is a crucial first step in preparing your school to begin any antibullying program, as it shifts the emphasis from the pathologizing and punishing model of action to the prevention and positive alternative models.

Schools are generally the first places in which society at large begins to notice bullying behavior; school is the first place bullying truly displays itself. Since bullying involves the misuse of a power differential to create public humiliation, the power differential being used can range from an individual's size, style of dress, money, social adroitness, appearance, ethnic characteristics, to any number of other valued social qualities. Remember, schools are the first major social experience for many children. There are, of course, differences in the ways bullying behaviors are manifested. For example, younger children tend to use size to physically intimidate. Boys tend to express outward aggression, while girls generally express their bullying more indirectly, using social aggression and self-directed or self-defeating expressions of victimization, such as eating disorders, promiscuity, self-injury, and suicide. Bullying does tend to become a more social rather than physical activity as children age, beginning in earnest after the shift to high school.

Bullying is a process that does not happen in a vacuum, independent of other circumstances in an environment, yet our conviction is that bullying is largely misunderstood. There is too little focus placed on the audience of bystanders and the social context within which the bullying occurs. To understand bullying, it is critical to view the social context of not only the bully and the victim, but also the dynamics and power struggles enacted by different kinds of bystanders. We believe they exist in a trialectic, or an inextricably linked fashion in which one group is cocreated by the others. It is important to remember that these are not necessarily fixed or permanent roles. The social roles of bully, victim, and bystander comprise the fundamental architecture for many scenarios that occur within a given social context, with schools representing the most dramatic examples of how bullying plays out at various levels.

One main feature of bullying is that typically if the behavior exists and continues unrecognized, damage to various individuals occurs. Table 3.1 summarizes the process, illustrating the trialectic relationship among the victim, victimizer, and bystanders.

The key element in all bullying behavior is the generation of humiliation. In these cocreated roles, the process that develops creates a sense of social

Table 3.1.   Redefining Bullying

Dyadic

- Bully and victim are primary focus
- Individual roles as bully or victim seen as fixed
- Bystander audience is passive observer
- Purely external definition
- Bully and victim are behavioral roles
- Focus on behavioral change
- Intervention targets individuals

Triadic

- Social context bully and victim is primary focus
- Cocreated B-V-B roles in flux
- Bystander initiates the stress
- Have complex internal meanings
- B-V-B are social roles
- Focus on mentalizing
- Interventions aimed at climate

Dyadic Definition of Bullying:

- The repeated harmful exposure of a person to interactions that produce social reward for the bully, are hard to defend against, and involve an imbalance of power with the bully stronger and the victim weaker.

Triadic Definition of Bullying:

- The repeated harmful exposure of an individual or group perceived as weaker than the bully, to negative interactions inflicted by one or more dominant persons and caused mainly by the active or passive role of the bystander linked with the bully and victim in complex ever-changing dynamic roles and social rewards. NOTE: the helpful bystander can play a major role in reversing this process.

dominance for the bully. Bullying can be seen as the basic virus of coercion within a climate. Positive factors, such as active learning and open-mindedness, cannot exist within coercive situations. When social dominance is achieved through coercion, the school climate becomes dominated by a nonpeaceful feeling, compounded by the sense that a faceless individual is controlling the social behaviors in the school. The opposite of bullying is being a friend; the opposite of a coercive environment is a peaceful and creative one. At times, this form of "attack" can be lethally damaging as we have seen in school shootings. Figure 3.1 outlines the sequence and destructive progression of emotions felt by someone who is shifting from giving up to feeling given up upon by others.

GIVING-UP/GIVEN-UP-ON
SYNDROME

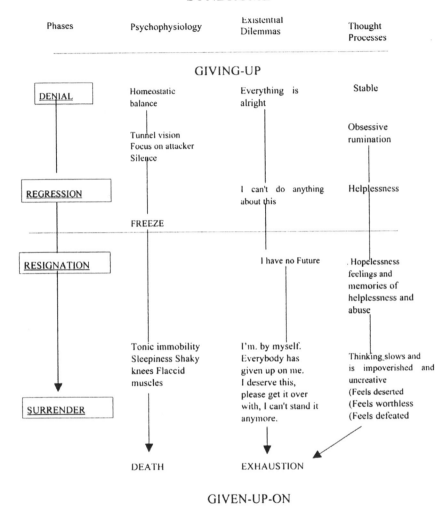

Figure 3.1.

As you can see, it is possible that individuals may begin in a state of denial, not acknowledging the problems around them that will negatively impact the possibility of any antiviolence program completing its mission. From denial, individuals may move into regression, manifested by detrimental feelings of powerlessness in their own environments. Resignation and surrender typically follow, leaving individuals both physically and emotionally compromised.

It should be noted that the twentieth and twenty-first centuries have created new sets of dynamics responsible for shaping bullying in our schools. The traditional view of school violence typically elicits a mental image of an impoverished, urban public school in which gangs and graffiti are simply part of the social context. However, as our society becomes more connected through digital technology, computers, blogging, and unprecedented access to various media outlets, the shift in bullying within our schools has also evolved to more advanced forms of social aggression. Suburban American schools are rife with instances of social aggression in which students are exposed to high levels of exclusion and social humiliation at the hands of their unmonitored peers. These students are living in a virtual world unknown by or disconnected from sustained adult attention. It is within this context that social aggression steps forward as a primary engine for the development of unhealthy learning climates.

This shift from physical to social aggression is particularly true in private schools and is not a phenomenon that can be eliminated through the use of strict rules. While it may be an alluring fantasy for parents to believe while writing a check for their child's private school, tradition and exclusivity do not necessarily add up to a peaceful learning environment. Problems with subtle, but destructive aggression are more prominent in private than public schools in the United States. A horizontal dynamic exists between children in public schools. Children are often close to each other and bullying and other aggressive actions are in the service of survival. Such bullying has a perverted rationale that we can all understand even if we can't accept or welcome it. Private schools have a vertical dynamic, where children suck up to the teachers and don't necessarily like each other. Cruelty and a full range of dirty tricks without severe or lethal violence thrive in affluent private schools and are also the harbinger of the lethally violent actions of the 1990s. Social aggression is in part normal, especially in first and second grade, but without containment, monitoring, and alternative mindsets, young people can be pulled into destructive patterns due to the dynamics of underlying social aggression played out in their schools.

When a school defines success academically or athletically, there is a risk that power dynamics will dominate the climate and create fixed roles that lead to nonpeaceful environments. We must remember that most students who come to school are neither academic nor athletic superstars, and this is perfectly natural. The bulk of a school's population is composed of hard-working children trying to reach their maximum potentials. These individuals tend to make up the bystanding audience we consider the target *and* the source of social aggression. The bystanders act as the audience that determines what roles the leaders in your school play. If the socially dominant peers within the school are not challenged and are allowed to be coercive, then bullying will result.

WHAT IS BULLYING?

Bullying is more than "simply" fighting. Bullying is an interpersonal process that creates humiliation for a victim in front of a bystanding audience. Table 4.1 in chapter 4 illustrates this phenomenon. In order to be considered bullying, the humiliation needs to be sustained, not just an isolated occurrence. Bullying tends to be an almost compulsively repeated psychological process that begins between individuals and then may evolve into a peer-group phenomenon. Cliques grow quickly, forming social war zones within the school environment. Bullying is not the periodic stupidity of young people hurting one another's feelings; it is a sustained process of a peer or adult consciously using humiliating strategies in public toward a targeted individual. Bullying clearly needs to be coercive. Bullying is not just one misplaced comment or broken allegiance to a friend; it is by definition a mean-spirited and sadistic sequence and series of activities targeting an individual. Bullying involves clear intention to humiliate a victim as a stepping-stone toward overall social dominance. In tens of thousands of children we have studied in a number of countries, the pattern is that as children move from earlier grades to later grades, they shift from physical intimidating—pushing, shoving, and threatening to harm—to more socially based bullying, such as exclusion, name calling, humiliating photos, Internet bullying, and other forms of nonphysical coercion.

Humiliation is the foundation of bullying. The cocreated connection between the bully and the victim becomes a scene that is enacted in front of a passively bystanding audience, since bullying cannot happen without both a victim and an audience. This audience includes the adults within your school environment, as well as the leadership elements in your community. Regardless of how the bullying takes shape, humiliation or shaming are the essential and necessary ingredients for it to be defined as bullying.

Dr. James Gilligan has eloquently described the role of shame in the evolution of violence, using firsthand experience with what may represent an endpoint for bullies or victims who act out violently. Drawing on decades of working as a prison psychiatrist in Massachusetts state prisons, Gilligan describes the powerful role that shame plays in the causal factors in the evolution of violence. Gilligan's writings, such as *Violence: Our Deadly Epidemic and Its Causes*, provide numerous examples of how young people may be incarcerated for long periods of time over seemingly petty crimes. When interviewed, many of these young prisoners explained that they were not fighting over material goods, but to gain the respect of others, or to create better images for themselves. Being shamed eventually led to the commission of a murderous act, and this can go both ways. A victim can be shamed into a compressed mental state and then suddenly turn into a victimizer who lashes out at the source of the shame.

School shooters in the United States provide a prime example of this phenomenon. These school shootings have been investigated and studied by both the FBI and Secret Service, both groups ultimately agreeing on the huge role bullying played in the evolution of the despair and the mindset of the avenging shooters. Shame is a causal factor in many of the destructive decisions made by adolescent students. The personal shame experienced by a student may be minimized by overworked parents and by teachers and school administrators under misguided pressure to produce artificial achievement numbers. These busy adults are busy doing society's work as they understand it, but there is little incentive for these individuals to change their patterns and for most educational systems around the world to invest enough time and energy into creating peaceful climates to create lasting changes. No one will deny wanting peaceful climates, but precious few are interested in stepping up to the plate to take the steps necessary to create those environments. Some of the programs that will help a school are very expensive, such as Promoting Alternative Thinking Strategies (PATHs), and failing to take the necessary steps in order to ensure it will work will not only waste your school's money and resources, but also can discourage people from believing change is even possible. You must take into account a number of important considerations before attempting to implement any program you choose.

One of the preexisting conditions you must therefore consider is the perennial victim within this power dynamic. The victim role is characterized by submission. It is the victim's public outcry that activates both the attention of the bystanding audience and the sadistic wishes of the bully. These observable victim-victimizer interactions are played out in the school corridors, at bus stops and playgrounds, on athletic fields and in gymnasiums, and continue after hours at students' homes, thanks to the Internet and cell phones. The roles of bully, victim, and bystander are, however, surprisingly fluid. Most people at some point in their lives assume one or all three of the roles, often over the course of any given day. Certain victim roles can become fixed to an extent, and life for that targeted victim becomes burdened and publicly humiliating. Bullies tend to seek out easy targets to ensure their public displays of humiliation achieve the desired submission from the victim. People picked out as problems will be the ones who make the loudest noise and these tend always to be the bullies and their victims.

Victims seem to attract the bully, by role suction, just as the bully hunts the victim. The result of this dynamic is, again, a public show of shame. The most forgotten element in this equation is the audience of bystanders, upon whom we will elaborate in chapter 5. Essentially, however, this audience fuels the process of bullying. There would be little reinforcement for the bully and victim without the presence and involvement of the bystanders. This group of audience members is engaging with a coercive process from a number of different positions within the larger group. This may seem like simple common sense, but it is a fact all too often ignored by experts and laypersons alike. For instance, some bystanders identify with the victim, while others may instead live vicariously through the bully, all but forgetting how their own engagement can be fueling a destructive and harmful process.

The bystanding audience is the third cocreated role in the bully-victim-bystander equation. Again, many different people glide through various permutations of these social roles in the course of an average day. Bystanders represent both an active collective presence and a principle causal factor in the evolution of violence and coercive school environments; they are not just backdrops for the drama.

Victims of the drama of bullying are typically easily targeted by the school for help. They tend to withdraw and act in self-defeating ways. The school will notice the withdrawn and miserable states of mind that the child displays. Counselors can diagnose a victim's condition and begin to try to help him or her deal with the residual effects of the bullying process. However, it is often very difficult for school administrators to know what happens to these students when they are not at school. They may be bullied at home by parents or older siblings, or they may be experiencing problems that play a role in their victimization at school as well. These children can become targets very early in their school lives. Some children have dysfunctional parents who neglect them and send them to school unprepared and dressed for ridicule.

While studying a large group of Jamaican school children, all of whom wear uniforms, we were surprised to learn that the children still honed in on the differences in each other's appearance. The uniforms may have been the same color, but their conditions varied greatly as did the footwear, belt, accessories, or lack thereof. Children will always find differences and pick on them. Caring parents take the time to make sure their children look their best, and students show the result of that parental investment. Many of the very poor children from rural Jamaica had uniforms that looked military pressed and creased. The children's teeth sparkled and they had clearly benefited from what Jamaicans call "good broughtupsy," or concerned caretaking, from their families, whether extended or immediate. Distracted parents may heap material goods on their student, forgetting to invest the time and involvement needed to create positive values. Victims often are the spoiled and entitled, as well as the unkempt and neglected. Schools are becoming parental substitutes and the behaviors of both parents and teachers mold the way children manage power in their social relationships.

THE BYSTANDER AT THE ROOT OF VIOLENCE

Violence is a tricky nonphysical organism. Just when you think you understand how people become violent or why they act in certain ways, the patterns shift. History is filled with examples of how wars were fought for the widest array of reasons. Today's children may be exposed to very different forces—especially in this modern digital era—that shape how they act, but certain elements of violence seem to remain painfully the same, and this is what makes it human.

The search for a cure of any problem begins with understanding its most basic form. Before you can use a program like the Incredible Years Series, you must understand the relationship between violence and its genesis in the social behaviors of children. There are many forces that shape our children's predisposition to violence. These forces can be understood as part of a social context that begins to shape how our children experience life. Children in this "digital era" face the unique challenge of surviving and rising above the onslaught of information (both wanted and unwanted) thrust onto them by the Internet, television, instant communication methods, and untraceable video recordings. Parents of this new "digital generation" are often clueless when it comes to what is happening in their children's lives. Most parents grew up in stricter homes and are baffled at how differently our own children react to us than how we reacted to our parents. We must remember, though, that the demands of kids living in a digital era are unique, yet strangely the same as those of generations past. The human element of being a kid requires that caregivers be alert, loving, and protective.

There are many ways, unfortunately, in which children can experience the lack of love and connection they need in order to grow up into resilient, freethinking beings, free from major life baggage and emotional problems. We will argue throughout this book that a child's connection to positive adult models is the key to all levels of violence prevention for our children. Communities need to be connected; individuals must avoid becoming abdicating bystanders who contribute to the evolution of violence. Standing by and watching can no longer be accepted as a passive process, but must be recognized as a stronger causal link in the evolution of violence.

Two examples from vastly different worlds help illustrate two of the main ways violence is enacted in high schools. The first is the tragic case of Corey Ramos, a seventeen-year-old Puerto Rican young man who stabbed Reverend Brown to death in front of two bystanding teachers and twelve students in Springfield, Massachusetts. The second is the case of a young Alaskan boy whose self-inflicted severe incapacity was the result of unrelenting bullying that was not dealt with by the school. Both these incidents involved a frozen social context that became an ingredient in the evolution of violence.

In the first case, a young inner-city high school student engaged in a five-minute interaction that ruined his own life and ended another person's. The student and teacher become physically violent in an interaction that was in great part ignited by their frozen social context. The Reverend followed Corey down the hall, and they entered a classroom of a dozen students with two teachers present. They squared off. The Reverend was pulled down to the level of the defiant student. Both the Reverend and Corey became the "center stage" or the core power struggle directly influencing the evolution of the lethal incident. In Corey's mind, they were struggling to win honor. The Reverend's mission was to maintain control and social order. In the end, neither goal was accomplished; a courageous school counselor died and a student was incarcerated. The cost to the school, the observers, the parents, the relatives, and friends of all involved is impossible to quantify.

The question persists: why did the Reverend have to die? Our view is that the larger school system can be a causal ingredient, exposing both the teachers and students to unnecessary risks. The role of the social context in the evolution of this violence is the main theme of this book. We hope to explore ways of understanding the evolution of violence as a process involving the interaction of the internal and the external, as well as the individual and the surrounding community.

In the other case we alluded to, the victim of ongoing bullying wanted to show his community how badly being bullied had hurt him: In Alaska, a middle school student hung himself, and although he survived his suicide attempt, he is now severely mentally and physically impaired. Where was the school while this was happening? Where were his friends? How could a child become so desperate and miserable without any adult noticing and intervening? Again, in this case, the social context became a causal ingredient in the escalation of violence. The school dismissed the importance of bullying, and the parents would be the last to know, unless informed by their son's friends or by his school. It is up to schools to penetrate this often-undiscussable underground "peer conspiracy" of silence. Without information from the peer network, it is impossible to predict and stop violence within a school. Multi Systemic Therapy, designed to help with at-risk students and substance abuse problems in high schools, for instance, cannot be successfully implemented unless you first identify adults students will trust and confide in.

Whether a victimized student is an East Coast inner-city kid or comes from a rural Alaskan middle school, the social context of their learning environments irrevocably changed their lives by allowing violent interactions to percolate within abdicating educational environments. The school personnel acted as avoidant bystanders with little incentive or training to do otherwise. John Devine approached this problem in his social anthropological work in New York City schools. His conclusion is that schools have distanced the teacher from the student by procedures and policies that stress mechanical safety over the teacher's relationship with students. Teachers are forced into roles by institutional policies that promote fear of the student and encourage abdicating "hands-off" approaches because of the fear of lawsuits.

We hope to help broaden the perspectives you use in understanding violence, particularly how it impacts our children at school. We feel that all humans experience power struggles. How they are enacted varies over time and across culture, yet we believe that teaching children ways of resolving and dealing peacefully with power struggles now will benefit everyone involved in the process.

We believe that the central causal agent for the escalation of bullying and violence at schools is the bystanding audience. Consequently, when you're deciding which antibullying program is the best for your school, you're likely to get the most bang for your buck by targeting bystanders. Our research supports this notion. In a controlled study, our team documented the success of an intervention that targeted the school's climate rather than targeting the bully or the victim. The entire school became proactively involved in preventing coercive behavior; the social status of the bully was decreased, and yet this approach did not address the problems of the bully or the victim in any specific way. The net result was an increase in scholastic achievement, decrease in disciplinary problems, and some indications of increased racial tolerance (despite our not including any specific references to race or culture).

HOW BULLYING UNFOLDS

In younger children, bullying generally takes a very physical or concrete form of expression. Much like Jean Piaget's concept of the stages of development of cognitive thinking, the way bullying is enacted evolves over time. Children are by nature developmental, concrete, and magical beings. They begin to be able to create abstractions in their minds and to think critically as they approach ten years of age. This pattern can be seen, unfortunately, in bullying, as well as in the natural development of children. We studied over ten thousand young students in an eastern urban public school and found that bullying generally manifested physically up to sixth grade. After that, it takes a developmental turn away from the physical and becomes, in our opinion, more deadly, in the form of social aggression.

Little children bully by intimidation. They threaten to steal things or to beat a child up. They tease a child based on appearance. This appears to be a rather universal way in which children bully each other all around the world. In several countries we studied, appearance was always rated as a top way to demean or bully another. This method of targeting children at school can be seen at a very early age. By first grade, children can become aware of physical differences and how some children stand out. The different appearance could be based on racial characteristics or such other elements of physical appearance such as weight, teeth, and disfiguring scars. The victim role becomes incubated in these early social years. The child who stands out becomes a consistent victim of prey and eventually becomes stalked by the more aggressive bullies. Similarly, children who gain social dominance through bullying become empowered to continue bullying and disrupting peaceful school activities. This stalking and humiliating of children can only happen if adults allow it, model it, or deny it. It is natural to expect that children will only do what is allowed; as adults, we make certain choices that create the social context for this bullying process to exist.

Children are very impressionable and vulnerable to the social behavior of adults who model aggression. If teachers are verbally abusive or target individual students publicly, this will set a tone and an example for more dominant children to model this behavior. If teachers are afraid of their own students, and are forced by the administration, the student body, or angry parents to become noninvolved bystanders, the learning environment will become less peaceful and creative.

As children begin to transition away from the parent-child model with their teachers, their peer group and notions of social inclusion become the most important issues for them. Students move from having one teacher (and maybe an aide present) for all of their classes to moving between different teachers and classrooms. In other words, the social group becomes less localized and involves a much wider geography and sphere of social influence. In boarding schools, children move into a peer-dominated routine under strict adult supervision. Many of the children from elite schools also have very emotionally difficult family relationships. School becomes the most predictable social environment. In this situation, the stakes are even higher. The higher the standards are, the higher the stakes. Regardless of the stakes, however, the bottom line is this process is about children.

Preoccupation with peer acceptance is a known element in developmental psychology. When this stage is reached and children attend school, they look for a social perch to rest on while trying to learn. Social subgroups form. This makes the school more pivotal in the role of managing social aggression. Just as school athletes, students should be considered representatives of the school and held accountable for their behavior off the field, and in and out of the school's limits. For instance, behavior at school that becomes broadcast through the Internet should be considered school behavior; interventions to stop it need to involve parents. Again, the earlier, the better and the more prevention and education is invested, the less punitive and reactive responses need to be in order to maintain a peaceful school.

School counselors, who know what is happening, can, however, function as the symbolic ears of the school. If something is happening in your school and the counselor has the respect of the students, the specific power struggles and methods of bullying will be known and dealt with. What the counselor's role becomes, in this model, is a change agent of the underlying power dynamics. This climate focus looks for larger root causes and defines them in useful power dynamics formats. The counselor may identify that certain hateful activities emanate from one class with a teacher who is passive (bystander) and a principal who is close to retirement (bully bystander) and a group of athletes (bullies). These individuals should be the target of your intervention and whichever program you use must be one that can help resolve these issues.

THE DENIAL OF VIOLENCE IN SCHOOLS

No school wants to think it is being continually exposed to the threat of violent attack. But denying that bullying and violence can infiltrate any school environment exposes the school to unforeseen high levels of risk percolating within a school environment. Becoming aware of violence and bullying in your own school may be painful initially, but it is a necessary first step in preparing your school to become a more peaceful learning environment. It is impossible to read, watch television, or listen to the radio without feeling that the world is becoming increasingly more violent. International, national, and local news reports create an inescapable barrage of real-life violence every day.

It is, therefore, easy to understand the allure of denial. Awareness is frightening, while preparation is tough and demands discipline and commitment. Safety begins and ends with a school's awareness and alertness to danger. Denying violence is a natural and common method of human behavior in modern society. The demand for daily survival awareness has decreased as society and human beings have evolved into a more industrialized culture that allows modern humans the time to think obsessively about themselves, forgetting the basic instincts that have kept us alive for eons. Denying violence and bullying in a violent world is an unnatural act that is leaving schools vulnerable to preventable tragedies.

Denying violence is also a quick way to reduce the constant anxiety and fear of living in a violent world. Schools, especially private schools, can believe that they exist as oases from violence. Putting violence on the back-burner allows schools to live without the uncomfortable and constricting effects of fear and anxiety. By collectively allowing people to close their eyes to danger, we encourage schools to perceive themselves as magically clean and clear learning environments without the inconvenient discomfort of fear. A school can guarantee itself invincibility by simply closing its eyes and not thinking about coercive processes. The more tightly our eyes are closed, the more illusions can be constructed to make us feel safe.

Why is this denial such an attractive option? Most people don't have the necessary tools and resources to prepare their schools correctly against violence and bullying. In the face of being ill equipped, the simplest solution to mounting fear and anxiety is quick and easy denial. Shutting out reality is uplifting, even if it is ultimately a delusional escape. Illusions of survival can be easily spun from this free (very alluring to cash-strapped schools) web of denial. Feeling in danger is averted by denying or closing the school's eyes to violence and how it may affect education.

This book will continue to outline some critical elements we found to be useful in starting and maintaining peaceful schools in many different cultures. What we want to emphasize is that the process of building a peaceful school has become more important than the program itself. Even the best program cannot work in a school with a negative social context existing unchecked. Understanding these critical elements is the foundation for building good climate responses to bullying and reducing violence. Please read on!

CHAPTER 3 : KEY QUESTIONS

Step 1. Identify: List the preexisting conditions involving power issues and struggles that your school must overcome before implementing an antibullying program.

Step 2. Evaluate: Name instances in which you have represented a bully, a victim, and a bystander. How did each role make you feel?

Step 3. Act: Talk to your school's counselors. They are the symbolic ears of the school. What can they tell you about the state of your school's power dynamics? What are the issues they feel must be prioritized, then decide what to do, and how to do it.

SUMMARY AND REVIEW

This chapter deals with the underlying theory of what makes a social environment coercive. It introduces a way to understand power dynamics and the role this social drama has in the creation of a peaceful learning environment and as a backdrop for a selected program.

- Bullying is the result of shame in a public setting.
- Bullying is a group power dynamic.
- Bullies will only do what bystanders allow.
- Bullying is a coercive action that spreads through a school, like rust on metal.
- Changing a school climate demands that the underlying power dynamics be understood, whatever program is used.
- Bullying is a social process with three main roles:

  1. Bully or victimizer,
  2. Victim or target, and
  3. Bystanding audience.

- Denial of bullying leads to a group sense of powerlessness, leading to resignation and eventually to physical and emotional disturbances.
- Bullying can take many forms and exists all over the world.
- Bullying is different based on the type of school. In a European private school, the main type of bullying is based on social inclusion/exclusion while in inner cities of the United States or in evolving nations bullying is more survival oriented and based on intimidation.
- Within evolved nations there is a greater increase in social or interpersonal aggression fueled by the hyperconnectivity of the Internet and digital phones.
- Adults play a huge role in shaping how children manage social power. When adults in elementary schools allow bullying to occur, then children's mean-spirited social aggression becomes reinforced. This is further complicated by the role of the parent who may come into conflict or agree with the school and might be the cause of the oft-reported decrease in empathy for victims of bullying as the student grows up.
- Bullying is NOT NORMAL, it involves:

  1. Intention to shame and cause discomfort,
  2. Sustained humiliation,
  3. Predatory stalking of victims,
  4. Lack of empathy, and
  5. Sadomasochism.

- Bystanders are a causal link in the evolution of coercion in a social environment. School systems can become abdicating bystanders and spark violence by their dismissiveness.
- The bully-victim-bystander relationship involves cocreated roles. You can't have a bully without a victim, and the bully will not be reinforced without the audience of bystanders. People change roles through the day. Kids may be victims of domestic violence and then bully other kids at school. There are, of course, many variations in the cocreation of all of these power roles.
- Within schools, it is essential to keep the door open for peer communication about bullying and victimization. Social cliques evolve as hiding places within the war zone that can develop in socially aggressive schools. Peer communication to adults is a key pressure valve and primary prevention tool.
- The Internet and cell phones have collapsed the boundaries between home and school. This greatly amplifies the role of the bystander in these cyber bullying activities.
- Bullying is developmental: K–3 is physical/intimidation. Grades 4–6: Social aggression is manifested in the development of peer leaders. Grades 7–10: Beginning of social awareness and the creation of cliques, continuing to grades 11–12 with the worst years being the TRANSITION years and the bullying hidden behind sophisticated metaphors that are subtle and not physical.

School is the community's stage for modeling acceptable ways to show peer dominance and acceptance. Peaceful and creative school environments promote friendship!

Chapter Four

Bystanding: The Forgotten Causal Factor in Violence

It's hard to believe now, but the seriously disturbed Columbine High was once called "the jewel of Colorado," and considered a school with high academic performance and high rates of its graduates enrolled in Ivy League schools. They also had an antibullying program in place before the slaughter, which, as history has shown, proved completely ineffective most likely because of its failure to deal with and resolve the power issues between the "White Caps" and the "Trench Coat Mafia."

By looking at high school settings, we can see how bullying evolves and how it manifests itself in children over time. While the bullying power differential is repetitive and dependent on coercive and humiliating actions, in boys it is more directly manifested than it is in groups of girls. Interestingly, in a cross-cultural study of differences between men and women, the sole difference in terms of psychological characteristics was that in group situations, males tend to use aggression more directly and females, indirectly.

Bullying tends to manifest itself according to the physical and psychological skills of the child. This is still true in many American schools, but is becoming less so as young girls are adapting to a different set of expectations. More now than for previous generations, women have become visible presences in the business world and workplace. According to a recent *USA Today* article,[1] more than 60 percent of women over the age of twenty were either working or looking for jobs. It stands to reason that these changes also affect the way children behave in academic environments as they prepare themselves for the eventual pressures of life after school.

After puberty, bullying becomes a primarily social behavior, visible through the forms of aggression that manifest themselves during high school.

A great deal of this "new" bullying behavior occurs below the radar in most cases, and includes:

- Spreading rumors
- Scapegoating and blaming
- Exclusion games and shifting of loyalties
- Nasty pranks
- Teasing and public humiliation
- Feuds and backbiting
- Cyberbullying, including increasingly mean bullying using the Internet, instant messaging, and cell phones

While middle school has a reputation for the most bullying problems, we believe that bullying is much more prevalent in high schools, but in more subtle ways. It is the biggest, strongest kid who can beat up everyone who dominates when children are younger; it can be a little runt who later dominates in high school, thanks to cleverness and an innate capacity to read people accurately. This ability to read other people is, by the way, not a healthy form of mentalizing, but a pseudo mentalizing. While the child can read mental states accurately, he or she does not feel them. Experiencing the emotion is what makes the reaction of the mentalizer more human and connected to other people. It's not difficult to imagine how a small quiet psychopath in middle school can easily become a bully by high school.

BULLIES WILL ONLY DO WHAT BYSTANDERS ALLOW

What does this statement mean? It may sound quite extreme, and we say it only after decades of experience working with schools. The idea itself—that the bully-victim dialectic is controlled by the bully-victim-bystander trialectic— generated from our years of experience working in schools across the United States, Jamaica, Australia, and New Zealand.

The statement is relevant, no matter which program you deem most appropriate for your own school. For instance, if you choose to implement a program such as Character Matters, you might emphasize honesty as a trait to model for a given month. All the children will try to enact and write essays about honesty and will prime the whole school atmosphere to be thinking about honesty and its implications.

What could possibly go wrong? Imagine this activity taking place in a school with a strong bully victim-bystander dialectic thriving beneath the radar. What could happen if one of the children learns how important honesty is and subsequently reports a dishonest action seen in a basketball game to another student? If the other child is a bully, he or she recognizes the first child as a threat and later terrorizes him until he eventually drops out of school. What if this plays out in a more seriously disturbed school, perhaps one with a major gang problem? A gang leader capable of reading the weaknesses of those around him can make use of the most well-intentioned character education activities to perpetuate pathologically oriented groups. The idea of honesty can be easily twisted by a gang leader into a way of exploiting the need for peer acceptance and recruiting and holding members.

The hypothesis of this chapter is that the social context (from the Latin *contextus*, meaning "a joining together") situates the pathological bystander in an avoidable active role created, in the case of school violence, by the interactions between victims and their victimizers. In other words, the bystander is by no means passive in terms of the etiology of bullying and violence. If the power differentials are not too great, it may be possible for some schools to handle these issues simply by discussing them openly. With more disturbed schools, it may be also necessary to have an additional approach to dealing with the power differential; this depends, of course, on the conditions of your particular school, rather than the specific program you choose to implement.

In situations with cases of institutional and individual bystanding, the bystanders themselves can be viewed as an audience watching and responding to a play. If there is no audience, there can be no play. In front of a small or hostile audience, the actors don't do well; the real key to an audience is how it motivates the actors. In the case of bullying, the "actors" are agents of the social system, the bully being the primary agent of the system that victimizes a smaller child who is the agent's victim. From this perspective, bullies and victims will only do what the bystanders allow and the bully, essentially, is the agent of what we call "abdicating bystanders."

> At every quarterly examination a gold medal was given to the best writer. When the first medal was offered, it produced rather a general contention than an emulation and diffused a spirit of envy, jealousy, and discord through the whole school; boys who were bosom friends before became fierce contentious rivals, and when the prize was adjudged became implacable enemies. Those who were advanced decried the weaker performances; each wished his opponent's abilities less than his own, and they used all their little arts to misrepresent and abuse each other's performances.
>
> —Robert Corman, *Political Inquiries* (1792)

The epigraph above documents school bullying and bystanding in a way that is particularly relevant to this chapter. Corman's description underscores the potential for destructive interaction following the apparently innocuous effort made by the school to promote excellence by offering a medal. The school's efforts do not imply any deliberate or malicious intent on the part of teachers and other members of the community to promote bullying, yet sometimes these bystanders' actions have backfired. The main point is that the bystanders—teachers and school administrators—should have been aware from the beginning of the potentially negative social impact of creating healthy competition based on interpersonal relationships.

Basically, the bystander role is an active one with a variety of manifestations listed in the Table 4.1, a list that is by no means exhaustive. It's one in which an individual repeatedly and indirectly participates in the victimization process as a member of the social system, rather than as a bully or a victim. Bystanding either facilitates or ameliorates victimization, and the bystander is propelled into the role by his or her interaction with the victim or the victimizer. The roles of bully, victim, and bystander can also be seen as a part of a dissociating process. The victim is dissociated by the bully from the school community as being "not us." On behalf of the bystanding community, the community bystander could be described as the abdicating one.

Successful interventions in the school setting, therefore, must focus on the transformation of the bystanders into a committed community and active witnesses. Whether you are using PATHS or Multi Systemic Therapy, you must identify the helpful bystanders and make use of them as part of reducing violence and bullying problems in your school, since, if you do this, the chances of the program working will be increased.

From this perspective, the bully—as the dissociated agent of the system—and the agents' victim are both members of the abdicating bystander group themselves. The abdicating bystander who projects blame onto the bully and the victim who is allowing the process to continue without acknowledging his or her own role in it have become part of the larger problem, even if unconsciously. A peaceful school environment begins by interrupting the dissociating process and seeing it as a largely unconscious effort to deal with the anxiety felt by all in response to a dysfunctional social system. The desire then begins to transform group power into a passionate statement and consistent respectful communication.

Character education is a very critical part of many antiviolence programs, but character education alone will fail if not included as part of an overall process that deals with, or at least assesses, the degree to which pathological bystanders exist in your school. Bystanding as a symptom is not merely a problem to solve, but a dysfunctional solution or adaptation that keeps a larger more painful or more meaningful problem lurking unseen within the system.

Table 4.1. A Variety of Bystander Roles

Type	Mentalization	Subjective State	Role In The System
Bully (aggressive) bystander	Collapse of mentalisation	Excitement, often sadomasochistic	Establishes a way to set up victimization within the school community
Puppet-master variant of bully bystander	Authentic empathy and reflectiveness collapses; capable of logical planning and non-feeling empathy	Arrogant grandiose sense of powerfulness	Committed to violent outcomes, achieved by conscious manipulation
Victim (passive) bystander	Collapse of mentalisation	Fearful, apathetic, helpless	Passively and fearfully drawn into the victimization process
Avoidant bystander	Mentalization preserved by denial	Defensive euphoria; and individual action	Facilitates victimization by denial of personal responsibility
Abdicating bystander	Mentalization preserved by projection and projective identification	Outraged at the "poor" performance of others; an agency or group action	Abdicates responsibility by scapegoating
Sham bystander	Mentalization preserved	Uses conscious largely verbal manipulation; deliberate and calm	Neither victim nor victimizer role is authentic, but is adopted for personal political reasons
Helpful (altruistic) bystander	Mentalization enhanced	Compassionate, sometimes outraged at harm to others; not a "do-gooder"	Mature and effective use of individual and group psychology to promote self-awareness and develop skills to resist victimization

When abdicating bystanders engage their pathologies, the environment for the struggling new character education program is also influenced by the unconscious collusion of the parental influence on the school structure. For example, "goal focus" is a largely positive byword, especially if linked with those seeking a dominate/win mentality. In other words, the best role you can play is a nonconflictual one. The solution is to reduce the power of the pathological bystander, while at the same time increasing the power of the altruistic helpful bystander, also called a "natural leader." The natural leader role will be dealt with much more in detail in chapter 6.

Another idea common in a bullying, abdicating bystander group is that obstacles to success needed to be attacked so that they can be removed. The fact of the matter is that many obstacles don't need to be attacked. In fact, if you attack an obstacle that has a function in another phase of a lifecycle of an event then you may damage the ecosystem as a whole. Children then perform in the affluent schools for adult approval, and in less affluent schools for personal approval. Performing for others and self-development is a problem, but parents who are aware of the role of the abdicating bystander will modulate their child's performance and be sure their child is developing in a healthy way, rather than performing solely for adult approval.

In one case we studied, a man took a second mortgage on his house so he could follow his son's progress at Little League games. As a result of his father's overcommitment, his son eventually learned to hate playing ball so much that he ended up in therapy, unable to tell his father, who, like many middle-aged people, had been acting out his own midlife sports goals using his child as a mediator. Consider the famous quote from the eminent football coach, Vince Lombardi, "Winning is the not the best thing, it's the only thing." On the surface, it sounds like this sentiment would foster togetherness and cohesion between people with the common goal of winning. But if the goals of that competition exclude certain children, or damage them because of the pressure of the pathological bystander role, the system becomes inherently dysfunctional, unstable, and attempts at teaming are simply noninclusive. All of these roles are filled by an intensively competitive population if the school in question has achieved notoriety and fame for its performance in academics, sports, or other extracurricular activities, such as forensics and debate.

SELECTED LITERATURE REVIEW OF THE ROLE OF THE BYSTANDER IN SCHOOL CONFLICTS

The recent spate of school shootings has placed bystanders squarely in the public eye, thanks to numerous articles highlighting the inaction or aborted actions of teachers, parents, or students, who were aware of threats, but did not act because of denial (avoidant bystanding) or fears that they would be targeted for tattling on their peers (the conspiracy of silence). In some troubled California schools, for instance, bystanders who did not report a shooter's previous threats were considered in need of protection from the families of the victims. On a more positive note, some high schools now encourage bystanders to help prevent or stop violence by providing confidential or anonymous online and phone reporting.

Until recently, however, bystander behavior has largely been overlooked in the literature on victimization, although the role of the bystander is an important determinant of chronic victimization. Bystanders in the school environment are those who witness bullying and other acts of violence but are not themselves acting in the role of bully or victim. Bystander behaviors may perpetuate bully-victim patterns, such as when passively allowing bullying to occur, or encouraging bullying by encouraging the exclusion of others. Teachers who openly discourage the use of aggression have students who are less likely to show the usual developmental increases in aggressive behavior over time. Teachers who do not intervene in bullying often have students who will not help victims. The effectiveness of programs aimed at promoting helpful bystanding is clearly dependent on teacher modeling, as our own research has shown.

One study of the ability of teachers and counselors to differentiate between bullying and other forms of conflict noted that both groups displayed a rather poor understanding of bullying. Teachers, for instance, often rated all physical conflict as bullying, underestimating the seriousness of verbal, social, and emotional conflicts and abuse. One researcher studied whether or not teachers could identify bullies and victims, finding that they were more likely to do so accurately in elementary rather than in middle school. A study of Greek children reported that teachers and students felt that teachers rarely talked about bullying, and children tended to speak more to their parents about such problems. Studies have indicated that if children cannot handle problems on their own, they may be perceived as wimps, and therefore targets for bullying. Interventions must address the overall social climate of a school, particularly the complicated peer-group interactions, in order to effectively deal with this problem.

These factors are influenced by teacher training and the awareness of children's psychological needs and subjective states. In a Finnish study of several hundred children, various bystander roles were categorized into several groups: defenders of the victim, bystanders from an outside perspective, assistant to the bully, reinforcer of the bully, and outsider. Boys were found to be more closely associated with the role of bully, reinforcer, and assistant, while girls identified more often with the roles of defender and outsider. In other studies, passive bystanders were found to reinforce the bully by providing a consenting audience, which sent the implicit message that aggression is acceptable.

Bystanders have been found to be less likely to help when they observe others doing nothing (the norm of nonintervention). When adults intervene in response to bullying, lower levels of aggressive bystanding were found in elementary schools.

THE "MURDEROUS" ABDICATING BYSTANDING

On December 5, 2001, Reverend Brown, an African American family life counselor and minister was stabbed to death by a seventeen-year-old student in front of two teachers and eight students, the first recorded case of a teacher murdered by a student in Massachusetts. The student is now serving a life sentence for second-degree murder, with the possibility of parole after fifteen years. The murder took place in an alternative school designed for adolescents with behavior disorders. The murderer was a young man who had been shuttled between living with his mother, his grandfather, and with his friends, transient situations resulting from ongoing conflicts with his mother. Reports indicate that he felt overburdened and devalued by his family, specifically by his duty to care for his two younger siblings. He was also resentful and angry at what he experienced as a devaluation of his social status by his mother.

Life events seemed to create a pattern of fear-based responses against perceived shame and humiliation in this boy, a response called "injustice collection" in recent school homicide literature. Reports also indicate that the boy worked with counseling services in order to try to repair his relationship with his mother. He also participated in individual psychotherapy, as well as case management efforts by state agencies, probation personnel, and private-sector therapists to motivate a process to reconnect him to a more positive relationship with his mother. In fact, the murdered teacher was trying to find a place for him to stay because of these conflicts. The lethal interaction began after the boy entered the classroom. Just prior, in the hallway, the victim had asked the boy to remove his hood. The boy remarked to two other students that he was sick of "the same old thing every day."

One of the students who witnessed it described the lethal incident:

> We were going to sit down at our desks when I heard the student and the teacher arguing by the teacher's desk, which is near the hallway door. I heard the teacher

ask the student again if he would "just take the hood off." The student told the teacher that he wanted to be left alone. The teacher moved as if he was about to touch the student and the student told him not to. The teacher said something like, "what is that going to solve or do?" The student then said again, "Don't touch me." The teacher then said something that I couldn't hear. I then heard the student say, "you ain't going to leave me alone about it." The student then took off his coat that had the hood underneath. When the student took his coat off, it looked like he wanted to fight the teacher. The teacher looked like he was squaring off, too. The student shrugged his shoulders a few times and brought his hands up in front. The teacher then made a fake left at the student. He came close but didn't hit him. At this time, they both started going at it. They were both throwing punches.

The teacher was fatally stabbed in the abdomen using blows that looked to the observers like punches and, initially, the teacher seemed unaware that he had been seriously injured. He left the classroom and various people asked him if he was okay, to which he replied that he was, until finally the school nurse noted he was "covered in blood from his shirt to his shoes." After he passed out, attempts at resuscitation failed, and he was dead on arrival at a local hospital. In this tragic example, the murdered teacher had been put in a complicated, undefined role, a role the students did not fully understand. They called him a "security guard or counselor."

The boy in this tragic confrontation had a history of repeated and prolonged absenteeism, was disconnected from any positive environment in the school, and had expressed feelings of being picked on and regularly provoked by his teachers and peers. His past history of psychiatric disorder was relatively insignificant, although there was a single experience of trauma due to kidnapping when he was about seven, which resulted in the development of night terrors. His father was functionally absent, a street criminal visible to him in that role from time to time. His mother was a hard-working but overburdened social service worker. He experienced her as an exhausted victim of the system and engaged in regular fights with his stepfather. He was often unkempt and had poor hygiene, which was the reason he gave for wearing his hood, concerned about how others would see him. He noted to his therapist on one occasion that he "had to fight in order not to be seen as weak by other kids." He spoke regularly of the victim, whom he felt was accusing him of things he did not do.

In a discussion between Frank Sacco and a former classmate of Reverend Brown, who had discussed some of his feelings with him on the night before the murder, we learned further information about Reverend Brown's background and experiences with classroom dynamics and bullying. The former classmate remembered Reverend Brown as the only male in a class about theories of counseling. He was considered a popular member of the class because he was naturally good with children. The teacher, however, was distant and had a rather unforgiving classroom demeanor. She became critical of Reverend Brown because he didn't seem to appreciate her interpretations of the theories that she was describing. She told him, "You are not getting this and if you don't start learning, you are not going to make a good counselor." This went on throughout the class because he was unable to grasp the theory she was teaching.

As a teacher, this particular woman was not brutally cruel to students and was considered intelligent. The classmate didn't remember the teacher being abusive to others in the class, but after class, everyone in the room would gather around Reverend Brown as a way of supporting him. She said, "I thought maybe you could see it in his face that he felt like crap. You know, because he had been put down in front of the class, and I think he was thinking that what if it was true, that he wasn't good at his job, or what he hoped to be his job as a counselor." The teacher had indicated to him that he might not pass the class. The day following his murder, the same teacher debriefed Reverend Brown's classmates in a cold but supportive way. Not much was discussed and the class went on to study statistics.

The school administration, school board, and people in the community collectively assigned a very confusing role to Reverend Brown, and in doing so they collectively functioned as an abdicating bystander in this situation. He happened to be of imposing stature and had been recruited to monitor behavior problems as well as to counsel and teach students. It is often assumed that a big strong individual with the authority of a teacher may know how to handle these complicated and contradictory roles, but he was not trained for the dangers of such a situation, especially in how to activate a helpful bystanding role for himself.

When it comes down to it, the abdicating bystander can take over the agent so that they act in meaningful ways. What if Reverend Brown had thought to himself, "I am no good at this, perhaps in the end I have to confront this boy using street language in the way that he knows, bring him out, maybe that would be better than the counseling theory?" We cannot know what went through his mind, but we do know that the encounter ended with his untimely death. Someday perhaps the victim, who is now serving a fifteen-year sentence for murder, will give his side of the story, but in the meantime, what can we learn from this tragic event? Rare as it is, injury to teachers is gradually increasing each year, and that's only taking into account the teachers who do report problems. There are probably five or six times more frequent violent problems occurring that teachers may be too embarrassed to mention, such as that a smaller child "hurt" them, in a position where they are supposed to be in charge.

Can parents become so aggravated over sports that they commit murder? Can the murderous abdicating bystanding also appear in this setting? It does happen periodically. One such case occurred in Cambridge, Massachusetts, in 2000. A large and imposing man, the son of an ice hockey player, beat the father of another man to death on July 5, after they argued about rough play in a hockey practice. The aggressor was a suburban Boston father with a job and a reasonable education who embodied all of the features of the typical abdicating bystander's attitude to winning. The jury found the man guilty of voluntary manslaughter, sentencing him to eight to twelve years in prison.

Newspaper reports suggest that "during recent years, the experts say, there is more involvement by fathers and mothers in their children's sports. Greater pressure to see their offspring win athletic scholarships or big monies for professional contracts and a tendency to over identify with the children, who the parents hope they will become the sports star that they themselves never were."[2]

There is a general agreement that parents often behave badly at their children's sports games. I have seen the same things occur in schools intensely committed to forensics and debate: the same heat, the same lack of light, and the same bullying of children into roles that perhaps their parents wanted at one time to fulfill. As a karate teacher, more than once Stuart Twemlow had to reprimand fathers who berated their children, often a tiny child of no more than six or eight years old for crying after being hit in a fight. It is as if the fathers, some of whom apologized later, forgot their roles and allowed themselves to be carried away at the expense of their children.

Stimulating a group to remain free of the troubles created by power differentials may be a lot easier than it was thought to be. At a karate tournament, for example, in which three hundred people attended from five different states, Twemlow led a meditation with the whole group, including the audience, every thirty minutes. We focused on the importance of thinking about the bushido code of conduct, considering other people before acting, and remembering those who have given their lives in the service of others, trying to appeal both to the sacrificial aspect of altruism and the common golden rule aspect of altruism present in most people, even "bad" people. That tournament finished two hours ahead of time; there was not a single conflict about a match or a demonstration, and there were no fights or disagreements, not even in the children's division. Once again, managing the background of bystanders keeps the focus on the antibullying program. Large social systems are easily distracted and the reminders must be at least daily, incorporated into the language of the school as a whole.

CHAPTER 4 : KEY QUESTIONS

Step 1. Identify: Who are the key students in your school that you emulate or look up to? Do these figures consider themselves active participants in school life or are they "simply" bystanders?

Step 2. Evaluate: What strategies do these individuals currently have in place to deal with bullying and violence issues? How have they been trained to deal with potentially explosive situations in their classrooms and outside of them?

Step 3. Act: Remember to involve and to include teachers and administrators in your program. Bullying behaviors are not just problems for bullies and their victims; bystanders play a crucial role as well.

SUMMARY AND REVIEW

- The key to understanding bullying lies in the role of the audience of by-standers who reinforce the bully.
- Bullies will only do what bystanders allow.
- As children develop into puberty, the role of peer acceptance peaks and makes the impact of social aggression more acute and dramatic. This increases the impact of bystanding on the lethality of any bullying that may occur in a school. This places higher socioeconomic status or resourced schools at more risk earlier in a child's development. The earlier a child has a cell phone, the quicker these factors come into play as an issue of self-worth for the child.
- The main elements in interpersonal aggression as a form of bullying are social inclusion and exclusion not intimidation, as seen in younger grades and poorer countries and schools.
- The Internet is the ideal engine to amplify the role of the bystander in the continuation of the process of bullying. Remember, again, that the Internet brings the school and home into the same cyber arena.
- The bully's behavior can be seen as what the group unconsciously projects into the bully who acts it out for the group. The bystander keeps the process going. The abdicating bystander (school) determines the lengths to which this destructive bystanding will be permitted. Bystanding is both an individual process (a parent who listens to mean talk about other girls and says nothing) and a group one (as when a school system fails to adequately ensure the safety of its teachers and students).

- Many schools do not abdicate and bystand intentionally. Most large-group abdication is unintentional and can be sustained for well-intentioned reasons that unwittingly contribute to destructive ends.
- The roles of the victim and the bully (main protagonists) are fueled by the tastes and tolerances of the bystanders. There would be no reason to bully if the audience failed to value the show.
- Bystanders are the key to change in a school. The bully will follow the changing taste of the audience. The ideal is to motivate the bystander to stand up for positive values and character strengths.
- Within the bystanders there will be natural leaders who can be used to direct the tastes of the bystanding audience. These natural helpers defend against the misuse of the positive program messages and model the prosocial behaviors espoused in the program.
- Bystanders legitimize aggression by valuing its expression within a social environment.
- Studies of school shootings in the United States reinforce that peers (bystanders) are key to the prevention of lethal violence. Children know what's going on and need to feel that they can safely speak to adults about it. Prevention of violence in a school needs intelligence gathered from students about their peers.
- When a school has no plan to face bullying, the adults are confused, roles in the school become confusing, and dangerous situations can begin and grow into lethal tragedies.

NOTES

1. www.usatoday.com/money/economy/employment/2006-09-02-women-work_x.htm

2. *New York Times*, July 11, 2000, p. A14, "A Fatality, Parental Violence in Youth Sports," Fox Butterfield.

Chapter Five

Feeling Safe at School

Feeling safe is necessary for the human mind to operate properly. When the mind freezes from the lack of feeling safe or being afraid, everybody's actions become reactive (fight/flight), nonreflective, narrow, and stereotypical. The point of a changed social system is that it is reflective or uses what Peter Fonagy has described as mentalization (reflective thinking). In order to mentalize, a school has to feel safe. This feeling safe is the fundamental foundation for all programs. A school would be silly to try a simple antiviolence program while gangs rule the hallway, and incredibly, that has been tried! In one inner-city school where serious gansta gangs ruled, the principal decided to give the elected classroom leaders control over discipline and curriculum content. Gang leaders were, of course, elected and ruled with threat and money, and the school was pseudo-quiet for a brief period before, as you might expect, chaos descended. There is a huge debate about how to create this feeling of safety. Some say, especially after 9/11, increase physical security, get more metal detectors. Others, like John Devine working as a social anthropologist in New York City's most disadvantaged schools, believe that this approach marginalizes student's relationship with teachers. Security is subcontracted to police, and teachers are forced into a hands-off bystander role.

This chapter attempts to explore what is needed for children and teachers to feel safe. We have come to understand that children face a wide array of experiences and behaviors from peers and adults that are experienced as real threats to feeling safe. The traditional view of violence as being only physical is quickly changing with the appearance of highly sophisticated digital photo and Internet connectivity. Now, school and home are one cyber place. Children may become trapped by Internet bullying that starts at home and haunts them at school. Many children experience bullying waiting for their bus or on the bus. Bullying may be very different in different cultures. What does

81

remain the same worldwide is that children and teachers need to feel safe at school. We believe that the strongest ingredient to a child's capacity to feel safe is the relationship they have with the adults in the school.

What schools should be and what they actually are, or have become, as a result of molding social cultural features, is an interesting lesson itself. Historically, schools have functioned as safe havens that promote the self-improvement and growth of young people, as Bertrand Russell, the famous English philosopher, described his views on teaching, in a well-known essay, "The Functions of a Teacher." He says,

> The civilized man, what he cannot admire, will aim at understanding rather than at reprobating. He will seek to discover and remove the impersonal causes of evil than to hate the man that is who is in his grip. All this should be in the mind and the heart of the teacher, and if it is in his mind and heart he will convey it in his teaching to the young who are in his care.

These pedagogical ideals were also applied to higher education, as in Thomas Jefferson's vision of an "academical village," once considered the ideal model for the creation of an academic utopia. This ideal layout is actually exemplified at the University of Virginia, where the main campus is designed around a centered lawn and the faculty, students, classrooms, and library are arranged together in a circle of buildings connected to each other. Jefferson's ideas also included faculty and students living together and learning from each other in personal and academic ways, with intensity and devotion to learning, brought about by a personal as well as an academic relationship. But students should not have to wait until attending college to feel safe and academically challenged, yet free to grow and learn. If our schools were to become those safe havens again, is some version of Russell's and Jefferson's visions necessary? We believe so. Are such ideas easy to design and implement on a nationwide basis? No, they certainly are not! We realize that proposing and implementing such radical changes to our current educational structures and philosophies will take many years, even if viewed as essential and prioritized by lawmakers and school administrators alike.

What, then, does this mean to a school about to adopt an antiviolence program today? There are a number of programs adapting behavioral models that would ease the process, such as the Center for Social and Emotional Education. Such approaches allow teachers to become models for their students as an organic part of their teaching process. Teachers do model a great deal already, not only in what they teach *about*, but *how* they teach it, and how they embody that model in handling day-to-day problems in their own lives.

A safe and well-disciplined classroom is one in which teachers manage their classrooms by treating disciplinary problems as potential opportunities for learning. For instance, teachers may reward good behavior more intensely than they punish bad behavior. They may also try to find out whether individuals or groups have learned their own roles in each new disciplinary experience, but again, this is only possible in a safe classroom where the teacher is able to manage his or her students and communicate with them in a healthy and productive way. If this happens children learn from a calm, safe teacher who embodies discipline in her personal habits, and they will internalize the example. An unsafe teacher punishes erratically and children despise the example and act out whenever the teacher leaves the room.

FEELING SAFE IS AN INTERNAL DECISION

It is interesting to note the etymological roots of the word "safe," meaning "whole." The Latin *salvus* also implies healthiness. In other words, a whole and healthy person feels safe both internally and externally. These added dimensions of experiencing safety are often overlooked or even forgotten. That feeling of safety derives from feeling whole and then spreads to encompass both the individual and the community. Secure human relationships create a feeling of safety.

Of course, *feeling* safe and *being* safe are not synonymous, and while this may seem like an obvious statement, it's important to remember that psychopathological conditions (such as mania and other grandiose psychotic states) may cause an individual to deny potential danger completely. Dependant and avoidant character pathology can create a spurious feeling of safety for different reasons. Recognizing and dealing with this sort of pathology allows for more creative and resilient efforts to make the environment safe, as we mentioned. Feeling safe also requires an awareness of danger and how to respond to it, including self-defense and negotiation skills, especially in our contemporary climate that includes strong political support for the continued controversial availability of handguns.

Unfortunately, pathologically cohesive communities, like street gangs, offer little forgiveness, little freedom of choice, and no permeability to or from the outside, and create increasingly more dangerous communities in which young people may find the attachment figures they have been looking for since childhood. It is not only gangs that form these structures; many dictatorships are similarly organized. A colleague from Paraguay pointed out that between 1955 and 1989 under a national dictatorship, the climate was quite peaceful, yet there was a striking lack of individual and personal freedom. In the countries of the former Soviet bloc, personal safety was hardly an issue through the 1960s and 1970s, although the government regulated its citizens' personal liberties to varying degrees of control. With the shift toward democracy and freedom came also a massive increase in violent crime, particularly Mafia and gang-related criminal activity. The dilemma for us today is to achieve safety without relying on overwhelming bureaucratic and potentially tyrannical control.

WHAT QUALIFIES AS A SAFE COMMUNITY OR SCHOOL?

In the mid-1960s, a group of clinical psychologists gathered in Swampscott, Massachusetts, to discuss a new direction of psychology, one that we now call "community psychology." The initial tenets of community psychology emphasized the importance of a long-term vision for a mutual social-support network to prevent, as well as treat, mental illness. Community psychology also stressed the central importance of learning from each other and the respecting of individuals' differences, regardless of race, intellect, gender, age, religion, socioeconomics, education, or sexual orientation. Community psychology takes for granted that collective decision making leads to an enhanced sense of empowerment on the part of the individual who, by acting in concert with the group, enhances his or her own power as well as that of the entire group.

We must remember that schools function as a form of community, not unlike neighborhoods, and each needs a team devoted to protecting it from violence and fear. Consider the following definition of a general community, and remember that it is also quite applicable to schools: "a dynamic whole that emerges when a group of people participates in common practices; depend upon one another; make decisions together; identify themselves as larger than the sum of their individual relationships; and commit themselves for the long-term to their own, one another's, and the group's well-being."

Numerous studies have proven the importance of recognizing how disconnected children feel in their schools. One study of nearly four thousand children ranging from seventh to twelfth grade, demonstrated that early signs of disconnection and alienation from the school environment (creating a child who feels unsafe) are often indicated by a child's withdrawal from the peer group. A child may also adopt specific habits that distinguish the child from his or her peers, such as cigarette smoking and alcohol consumption.

Time and time again, studies have proven that as children become more and more excluded from their peer groups or withdraw from these groups, the resulting environment becomes a tinder box for violence. A school filled with disconnected students is likely to experience vicious power struggles as children are either targeted by the group or become bullying—even homicidal—tyrants who aggressively try to force their way back into the group, or they withdraw and become depressed and even suicidal victims.

A successful approach to school violence must ensure connectedness among children, provide a conceptual framework and language for the problems, and must also pay close attention to the dynamics of groups and to the roles of healthy adults and peer mentors. Without these factors, you cannot create an environment that empowers the individual within the group, and children will continue to break off into violent and pathological subgroups. Furthermore, without these factors, any antiviolence program you choose to implement is guaranteed to fail. The experiences that should ordinarily unite people and make them proud of their community become garbled and forgotten. In violent communities, both inside and outside of schools, pathological subgroups often have as their central concern the need for individuals to feel safe through coercive power using violence and money. The minicommunity of schools is no exception to this process.

A sixteen-year-old Latino boy, who served as a peer mentor in our Peaceful Schools program, wrote a graphic yet ambivalent account detailing the attractions of gang life:

It all started during the summer of 1994. It was a hot day in about mid-June. The only thing on our minds was our initiation later on that night. It was me, C. C., Dirt, Monster, and Mone. These were the names given to us by the bigger homies. Then night came around and it was time for us to join the set. So after getting drunk at our first ESC [East Side Click] get-together, the big homies, Keno, C Side, and Houston, called attention to us.

All of a sudden we was catching blows left and right; the only thing to do was fight back, but eventually I was knocked to the ground and beaten. After a few minutes it stopped, then we was given some love and started to celebrate again. Next was to show if we was down for the hood. So we loaded up into three cars and was headed for Slur Hood (Slur is a disrespectful term for Surenios 13, who is the ESC's mortal enemies).

When we got there, we spotted three of them standing outside a Kwik Shop. Our job was to beat down the enemy until they could no longer move. Only then could we return to the cars. So we did, and got respect from the older homies for what we did. This was the whole initiation night. This was the first work I did for the set; it wasn't the last.

With my two years being with the set, I did enough dirt and earned enough respect to surpass the first three ranks and now I'm a Baby Gangsta [B. G.], only two ranks away from being an O. G. With earning the B. G. rank, I'm allowed to do things I couldn't do before; for instance, I can ball the big homies' cars, teach and tell the younger homies what to do and not to do, and sell drugs. But to break it down, there is nothing wrong with representing East Side Click, one

of the many Crip sets. You get paid, known, and respected—the three things
gangbangers want.

But behind all of the glamour, like me, you get shot at; you shoot at. I've been
jumped four times and put in the hospital for stitches once, had my house shot
at, been locked up, have partners locked up, and worst of all, I lost two homies;
D-Monster and Houston, both killed in Houston, Texas, for what we believe in.
For some, this is all we got, so we're gonna represent to the fullest no matter the
pain or cost: only to live up to every gangbanger's dream of having riches, respect and to live in a world where everyone looks up to you and have worries of
watching your back 24/7. But until then, I'm gonna keep Cripping and stick to
my motto, "can't stop, won't stop; East Side Click ride, till my casket drops."

Unfortunately, this student eventually succumbed to the pressure of life within
a gang, but not without a struggle. He continued to help us "undercover!"

In the stabbing deaths of eight children in an elementary school in Osaka,
Japan, on June 8, 2001, as security at the school tightened, one mother said,
"We don't want to make schools prisons—the community as well as school
staff should be watching the children." This summarizes the dilemma in a
nutshell: schools cannot really be safe in unsafe communities where grown-
ups are insecure and do not know what to do.

WHAT MAKES CHILDREN FEEL SAFE AT SCHOOL?

This topic is elusive indeed, but there are slivers of information hinting at
factors worth examining more closely before you choose the best program for
your particular school's situation. We must remember that feelings of attachment are related to an individual's experience of belonging and feeling safe.
The models for this feeling, of course, are the adults in the school environment, beginning especially in elementary schools. As children get older and
become more verbally gifted and capable of abstract thought, natural leaders
emerge to model strong and dominant positions for other children. Recent
studies of relational aggression in African American and European American children in grades seven through twelve showed that for both genders
this form of aggression involving ostracizing, name calling, and more subtle
forms of interpersonal aggression caused children to feel more unsafe, and for
boys to carry a weapon to school.

People cannot and do not, however, feel safe when they witness violence
on a regular basis. Feeling safe is clearly related to the effectiveness of
public safety in keeping overt violence levels in a community low. When in
elementary and middle school, children feel safer when they can see and feel
their protectors and when these protectors can effectively combat the nega-

tive influences leading to bullying. We do know that some forms of media may impact the way children feel about their overall safely. While exposure of children to television has been extensively studied, other media like video games, the Internet, and rock music have been less extensively researched. Clearly unsafe feelings can be generated by repeated violence exposure on television, an effect much greater in preschoolers, and are potentially aggravated when family members or classmates mirror these unsafe feelings.

Drug and alcohol abuse are also important factors in determining how safe individuals feel in any given environment. Feeling safe is related to how much drug and alcohol abuse exists. The more drugs and alcohol problems exist in a community, the greater the risk of violence becomes. In other words, we can infer that feeling safe is directly related to the absence of drugs and alcohol.

Physical surroundings play an important role in determining a child's feeling of safety, or lack thereof. "Safe havens" where children can go to feel safe and protected often include parks and their recreation programs, community programs, Boy and Girl Scouts, and community centers and provide means of assisting community members' feelings of safety. Studies have also shown that even children who live in dangerous areas felt safer when they could rely on the routine of going to school and living with their families. Simply having a routine and a productive place or safe haven is a key element of feeling safe. Factors such as truancy and out-of-home placement are, then, the big enemies against this vitally important sense of safety. Training in personal safety can also help children feel more confident in their abilities to protect themselves.

Feelings of safety are also related to the social climate. When students engage in altruistic behaviors such as cooperating, helping, or consoling, academic achievement improves as a direct result. Having friends and being helpful as part of a larger group can contribute to children's senses of safety and success. Children need to feel valued and respected in order to attain their own sense of a positive collective and individual identity.

In general terms, it may be said that the following factors are the most likely to affect a young person's feeling of safety and sense of well-being in a school setting:

- Quality of the caregiver and child relationship
- Exposure to family and community violence
- Presence of protective adults
- The rules of the social system
- The presence of drugs and alcohol
- Media reports concerning the safety of a community

- Media violence
- The presence of a safe haven or retreat
- Training in personal safety techniques
- Good relationships with peers and friends
- Engaging in altruistic behaviors
- A sense of belonging to a community

THE SCHOOL AS A SECURELY ATTACHED FAMILY

We have noted some very interesting parallels between pathologically un-safe school environments and the practice of poor quality parenting. In an ideal situation, the child's signals are understood and responded to by the caregiver; the signals gradually acquire meaning and, through internaliza-tion, become part of a process of self-regulation. The securely attached child explores a strange environment, such as a new school, readily in the presence of the attachment figure, becomes anxious in the absence of that figure, and actively seeks contact with the caregiver upon the reunion that follows a brief separation.

The burgeoning field of attachment research has described a variety of pat-terns of attachments that create pathological outcomes later in life. The school has a responsibility to modulate the affect of its students and to create the expectation of control by its staff, which is a central factor in children feeling safe. Schools, as systems, may be characterized in terms of the manner in which they deal with fear. The attachment system has, as its primary function, the regulation of fear in the presence of conditions that biologically provoke it. In the interest of being secure, a well-balanced school system accurately recognizes the emotional state of those within its walls and creates the well-founded expectation that distress will reliably be met by comforting.

Confidence in this belief leads to a system that may be characterized as secure, one in which the systemic strategies for regulating affect would enable the school and any or all of its subsystems to restore a healthy emo-tional balance. The characteristics of this system will only be revealed when dysregulation has occurred—when the school has been challenged by some external or internal event (such as lack of discipline or community violence). A secure school will regularly adopt a tolerant open strategy and a wide range of communications patterns that permits individual expression and responds meaningfully to it. Warning signs are neither exaggerated nor minimized; language used is respectful and participatory. Communications are clearly ac-knowledged, and individual contributions are expanded by other participants rather than ignored, denied, or dramatized. Evaluative comments are taken seriously and there is a sense of coherence in communication patterns that implies an overall commitment to collaboration.

Such systems contrast notably with their insecure counterparts. An insecure school may carry the appearance of well-regulated organizations, but its appearance collapses under the pressure of a dysregulating event. Behind the apparently harmonious picture presented to a visitor are significant imbalances in communication, where there is limited self-expression for the members of the group, with the aim of avoiding tensions.

A dismissive attachment pattern can develop in a school environment where there is little interest in children, and where parents and teachers are preoccupied with their own problems and overwhelmed by feelings of insecurity, an unresponsive administration, conditions of employment, and low salaries.

As schools fail to provide a sense of safety in both children and adults, there can be no sense of belonging on the part of those who participate in these systems. This is why failing to deal with preexisting problems in your school dooms any program you select. In disconnected and dysfunctional schools, truancy and absenteeism rates on the part of both students and staff tend to be unnaturally high. The emotional nature of relationships is avoided in communications between students and their teachers and between the teachers themselves. There may be a denial of anxiety and a devaluing of the importance of human relationships as well as a false bravado, denial of all problems, and an idealization of the school environment. Members of the group will not, generally, seek each other out in times of stress. Children in avoidant or dismissive schools learn to deny the importance of interpersonal relationships and live without them; they feel alienated and isolated from others in their schools.

The school thus divides or splinters students into small subsystems within the school, which exist without reference to or concern for each other. Children who feel unknown are therefore able to perform coercive acts where a feeling of belonging might *otherwise* have served as a powerful inhibitory function. As part of the feeling safe project for a school, threat assessment has achieved priority in the United States, especially in the last decade or so, following an "epidemic" of homicides by adolescent boys from relatively stable homes. The Secret Service has a comprehensive threat assessment protocol available that provides an excellent model for such a threat-assessment approach, and which can be reduced in size by each school. We feel all schools should have this or a similar program in place. A protocol is available at the following Web site: www.secretservice.gov; click Final Report National Initiative for Safe Schools.

In other dysfunctional schools, a pattern of anxious resistance takes over. In psychosocial terms, these patterns resemble those characterized by infants who are not comforted by their parents following separation. These individuals tend to be anxious in dealing with problems, readily panic in the face of challenges, and are most likely to call in consultants to assist with the difficulties they face. However, these individuals are among the least likely subjects to be able to successfully implement any recommendations that such consultants might make. There are no clear lines of communication in these schools. There is likely also to be an absence of any clear hierarchical structure; if such structure exists at all, the participants mostly undermine it, even inadvertently. People in these schools often experience confusion about relationship issues, and domains of discipline tend to overlap unhealthily with other domains, affecting relationships and general safety. Such schools become toxic environments in which high levels of affect are often evident, and teachers frequently show anger toward students and each other. As in a securely attached family, a securely attached school is self-regulating and safe. The ideas are summarized in table 5.1.

How can these factors be overcome? Many contemporary theories rank the optimal involvement of parents as extremely important. Involving parents in a healthy way is a complicated proposition in both inner-city schools and in the more affluent schools where there is often too much parental involvement. Involved parents are often more interested in their own children getting a fair deal in the school than they are in creating positive changes as a community. Thus, parental over- or underinvolvement can be very much a double-edged sword. Lack of parental involvement should, however, not discourage you. It is very possible to influence staff members even without parental participation, to become sensitive to students as independent sentient beings with a minds, unique thoughts, and feelings. With this support, the process of mentalizing will occur more normally as the child's capacity to recognize himself or herself in others, to perceive others as separate, and to feel comfortable in expressing these thoughts increases.

In this chapter we have outlined a number of large scale relationship patterns among teachers, students, volunteers, and the community that determine in part why children feel safe or unsafe. Essentially, feeling unsafe prevents the mind from being able to think and learn (mentalize). A secure school using the model of family attachment is one that regulates with an in-control staff using nonpunitive discipline. Before implementing a program of any kind into your school, you must ensure these conditions exist. Secure schools promote respectful, open communication and ensure that individual input is sorted out and listened to. Any dysregulation, whether social or individual, is met by a balanced response, and the competence of

Table 5.1.   Attachment View of Safety in Schools

A Secure School

- Down regulates fear
- Staff in control
- Nonpunitive discipline
- Respectful open communication
- Individual input is sought and listened to
- Dysregulation leads to a balanced even response

An Insecure School (Pattern One: Anxious Avoidant)

- Limited self-expression to avoid tension
- Dismissive-avoiding (denying)
- Communication with self-absorption
- Low sense of belonging
- High child truancy and staff absences
- Denial of the importance of interpersonal relationships
- Failure of mentalization
- Fragmentation into cliques and subgroups for adults and students
- Children act with less inhibition (e.g., violence)

An Insecure School (Pattern Two: Anxious Resistant)

- Fear is unregulated
- Excessive requests for help and consultants (panic) whose recommendations are not implemented
- Unclear line of authority
- Confusion of task
- Angry teachers
- Failure of mentalization

the adults in the system to cope creates a safe and secure working environments for children.

CHAPTER 5: KEY QUESTIONS

Step 1. Identify: What does it really mean to feel safe? What makes you feel safe?

Step 2. Evaluate: What key factors are necessary to ensure that people feel safe in communities, in schools?

Step 3. Act: Which are the factors causing adults and children to feel unsafe within *your* community? What are the barriers to feeling safe? How can these factors be resolved?

SUMMARY AND REVIEW

- Teachers are the main way to create a sense of safety at school.
- Classroom discipline that strives to reward and increase understanding of a child's behavior, rather than punishing it, fosters a sense of safety.
- Secure human relationships form the foundation for feeling and being safe in a school.
- Feeling safe and being safe are not identical. There are many false senses of safety, especially in suburban U.S. schools.
- Safety can become ensnared in bureaucracy that devalues human connections.
- Schools are communities within a community. When a community does not feel safe or prioritize public safety, schools follow.
- Disconnected peer groups in schools become powder kegs that can explode onto an unsuspecting school.
- Safety is increased when connected students and educators communicate openly within a school.
- Feeling safe is an internal decision made without thinking of it consciously.
- Social or interpersonal aggression can erode a school's sense of safety without much outward sign.
- Feeling safe for younger children depends on their seeing adults protecting them; older kids are able to feel safe with more abstract ideas.
- The level of drug and alcohol abuse impacts a sense of safety. The more drugs, the less safe students feel.
- Schools need to create physical safety zones; communities need to help with after-school safety zones such as Boys & Girls Clubs.
- Predictable routines make children feel safe; broken routines frustrate children and lead to fear.
- Teaching personal safety increases children's awareness of safety.
- Safety can be amplified in schools by enhancing altruism and making friends.
- Attachment patterns in individuals can be seen in schools: secure, anxious avoidant (dismissive), and anxious resistant for example.

Chapter Six

The Natural Leader: Mentalization and Altruism

Coauthored by Peter Fonagy, Ph.D., F.B.A*

In this chapter, we will discuss and provide specific details and personal qualities you should look for and be aware of when assembling the type of leadership team we will describe in the following chapters. Both the adults and children you choose for this team will be your primary helpers throughout the process of assessing your school, and they will be absolutely critical to overall school change, whichever program you choose to implement.

First of all, what *are* these personality traits or qualities? For the sake of clarity, we have divided them into three central elements: the potential for natural leadership, the ability to mentalize, and the quality of altruism. We have noticed these qualities present in a number of children, teachers, and other individuals who proved themselves capable of taking action without becoming overwhelmed by the prospect of danger to themselves in a variety of situations. In our research, helpful bystanders and observers consistently alerted us to the importance of these three qualities, which we will describe in greater detail for you here.

NATURAL LEADERS AND NATURAL LEADERSHIP

The descriptive term "natural leader" oversimplifies the important role this person plays in any attempt to create positive changes in a given environment. We have encountered a number of individuals who have grown into leaders over the course of their personal lives, and who continue to be natural leaders without having to undergo specialized training. For instance, children who have had intensive altruistic religious training are not necessarily natural

---

*Freud Memorial Professor of Psychoanalysis, University College London; Director, Anna Freud Center, London, England.

leaders; it is not a quality that can be taught easily, although there are ways to avoid inhibiting the qualities of natural leadership. Individuals who have been taught, punished, cajoled, or ordered to place others before themselves are not necessarily going to become natural leaders.

We first encountered this "natural leader" type of personality among older police officers working in a highly corrupted third world country. These adults had spent a decade or more serving in the police force, and although they were known for acts of bravery, they continued to be underpaid and poorly treated. And yet they remained dedicated to their group as a whole, which enabled them to transcend their shared rage against the system for underpaying, undervaluing, and undertraining them. In these police officers, we found the qualities of the natural leader, which are summarized below. Natural leaders tend to be:

- Self-motivated and motivators of others, without coercion or sadism;
- Aware of and capable of taking responsibility for community problems;
- Willing to take physical risks for peace and are not easily frightened;
- More altruistic than egotistic;
- Relationship-oriented and humanistic;
- Alert, strong, and positive;
- Personally well organized;
- Self-rewarding, with little need for praise;
- Able to see potential in all people, not sadistic;
- Advocates for and protectors of the vulnerable and the disempowered;
- Passionate about and committed to their work; and
- Tenacious and patient.

It does not require much imagination on the part of a creative and concerned teacher, administrator, or parent to translate these traits into various developmental stages of childhood, and to try and find out what sort of a child might tend to emulate these natural leadership qualities. Consider the comparisons between these two possible outcomes in table 6.1.

The key issue here is not so much whether one is healthy or unhealthy, but how a natural leader functions. Not everyone will fit automatically into one of the two possibilities above. Furthermore, natural leaders may not always see themselves as leaders; sometimes when it is suggested, they are quite surprised by that designation. They are not put off by it necessarily, but they aren't looking for it. They might say something like, "I have been this way all my life." Natural leaders work for the good of the group rather than for their own good, and they are often willing to contribute to the group and all its members as a whole, rather than the actions of one or other persons in it.

The term itself was inspired by the name of a renowned and well-established program, Natural Helpers, first created in 1979. This program identifies chil-

Table 6.1. Comparison of Natural and Self-Centered Leaders

Natural Leader	Narcissistic (self-centered) Leader
Noncutting sense of humor that connects and empathizes with peers to encourage their autonomy and participation	Cutting, sarcastic, cold, aloof humor that puts down or victimizes peers
Healthy ability to empathize with peers in a way that helps self and others	Empathy that largely promotes the self above others and eventually at their expense or harm
Creativity applied to leadership that promotes creativity in group projects and in individual group members	Creativity that promotes destructive subgroups that cause isolation or alienation from the larger group
Natural leader's personal needs are met by benevolent reaching-out to challenge the peer group to connect with their community via helpful projects and activities	Narcissistic leader's personal needs or psychopathology is deepened by efforts to dominate the peer group
This leader reaches out to foster and mentor positive leaders in younger grade level children modeling future leaders	This leader bullies or puts-down younger aspiring leaders so as to maintain his or her superiority

dren who wish to help their friends and provides them with the specific formal training needed to develop into effective helpers. The training process part of this program fosters positive school connections and supports the identification of at-risk children with psychiatric problems, making sure they are given the appropriate help.

Natural leaders have high levels of mentalizing and are able to apply their leadership skills creatively within the group. Perhaps most important, their natural narcissistic needs (all human beings have some!) are met and satisfied by reaching out and through community group action, not by personal praise, accolades, and awards. Such leaders also commonly create a set of successors, while a narcissistic leader rarely does, often moving on and leaving a role empty without a second thought, or electing somebody unsatisfactory to continue on. A natural leader will have a succession of people waiting to take on the work. So natural leaders are not the same as do-gooders; they are not people who have been specially trained to be altruistic.

What roles do natural leaders play in improving the quality of our schools? They rarely occupy traditional leadership roles, but they tend to excel at listening and mentalizing, no matter what their official role in the school may be. In a study of small communities sponsored by the Kansas University School of Social Welfare, the natural helpers in a number of communities were primarily middle-aged housewives who listened, rarely advised, and had no official psychotherapy training. In schools, natural leaders intuitively realize the power of the large group. They don't go toe-to-toe with the bully, but use large groups of peers to engage in discussion instead.

Although there are no strictly evidence-based methods that can identify natural leaders, we have found many ways of encouraging them to emerge, especially if the teaching staff looks for these personal qualities in students and others around them. We currently choose natural leaders by peer and teacher opinion. People do know who they are, and you must encourage them to come forward and to reach out.

Functionally, a natural leader enhances mentalization for the group, is compassionate, uses individual and group psychology intuitively, promotes self-awareness, and resists victimization. In other words, this individual embodies the sorts of qualities one wants to promote in a nonviolent school. Encouraging such leaders, however, does require taking some action. Here are two actual cases, chosen from recent newspaper reports; the first is an eighty-three-year-old grandmother who had worked since 1957 as an elementary-school crossing guard. Students and teachers called her the heart and soul of the school in a massive celebration of her service. One grown man wrote a letter remembering her when, as a boy, she would help him find his dog and thus avoid punishment from his parents. Somewhat overwhelmed she concluded with "I never knew I'd be so popular." The other—a younger—school custodian kept the school sparkling and was feted by the schoolteachers and children. He was so popular a special schedule was needed for children to help him serve lunch. A teacher indicated that "the children would do anything to work with him." He worked on whatever needed to be done; from innovative ways to get wild animals out of the school, to helping resolve student disputes. He was so respected it was easy, a teacher mentioned. Both these natural helpers had a tenacious commitment to the task, were listeners and liberal helpers in whatever was needed to make the complex social system work. Both seemed very surprised that their work had been so widely noticed and applauded.

MENTALIZATION

If you are using an empathy training program, perhaps one involving character education or focusing on the capacity to think, symbolize, and reflect, as the PATHS program does, you may already know that a nonmentalizing mind will subvert that program. What is a nonmentalizing mind? We define it as someone who continually:

- Stereotypes or tends to classify people as an example of a group, rather than as individuals;

- Denies, avoids, and forgets issues that may be major or even life threatening;
- Tends to continue trying the same old noncreative solutions. A nonmentalizing mind cannot create solutions that are out of the box. Very often, such a person, when able to mentalize again, will kick themselves for not thinking of certain solutions previously.
- Oversimplifies issues: a nonmentalizing person may adopt simple solutions, like carrying or using pepper spray indiscriminately with undue faith in its effectiveness; and
- Misjudges affect and aggression. A victimizer who is not mentalizing may often be quite perplexed by the degree that other people consider him or her as aggressive, when he or she "was aware of no such problem and had no coercive intentions";
- Becomes caught in the middle of a fear dynamic when mentalizing. His or her levels of aggression are often misjudged and either overestimated or underestimated.

So what then does one try to achieve with mentalizing and why is it important in school antibullying programs? Can you teach these qualities in a classroom? We believe that you can, quite effectively in fact, but *not* without a solid framework dedicated to supporting and encouraging mentalization in many other formal and informal aspects of school functioning.

Mentalization ultimately requires the acknowledgement of an individual as a thinking sentient creature and not as a robotic model. It addresses whole people, not just functionaries, and addresses the process of each individual relationship, as well as the effects of it. The "opposition," whether it consists of a group or individual, is thusly humanized. Mentalizing requires us to:

- Modulate our affect, which at times can become very intense and can lead to the collapse of mentalizing;
- Reflect on what we do, allowing for action only after thought;
- Understand ourselves and others. When empathy is extended to the self as well as to others, an intuitive ability to say where a person is coming from, either implicitly with an intuitive knowledge, or explicitly by teasing it out in the process of conscious communication; and
- Behave in an assertive and healthy way. This requires the capacity to establish and maintain boundaries as well.

A mentalizing individual can also be considered "mind-minded," meaning that he or she has other people's emotional and psychological well-being in mind, can negotiate rather than fight, understands himself or herself and others, and is not fearful.

Of course, mentalizing is not an all-or-none capacity. There is no doubt that some people are more likely to show it more of the time than others and some people appear chronically lacking in "mind-mindedness." However, even the least reflective person is able to engage in interpersonal interaction to a level that confirms their capacity to mentalize. In essence, mentalization is a capacity that varies (a) in terms of the highest level a person can reach and (b) the likelihood that they reach a relatively high level given contextual challenges such as anxiety, anger, intense attachment, or other types of emotional turmoil.

How to select mentalizing natural leaders is a very interesting issue. Many schools create problem situations or tasks for natural leaders to determine who will emerge to demonstrate the most helpfulness. What we have done with groups of children indicates a wide range of children that will volunteer and wish to be in charge, to those children who help out because it makes them feel good to be of assistance to others. The motive in the end may be egoistic *and* altruistic, but the selection process must weigh on the side of altruism.

ALTRUISM

Although this is not the best forum for a detailed consideration of the extensive research literature available on the idea of altruism, we do want to stress that there is convincing evidence that altruism exists as a fundamental impulse in human beings and several other species. It is not merely a derivative emotion and can, therefore, potentially be harnessed in the service of ameliorating violence and violent environments. Such pragmatic forms of altruism focus on benefiting the community as an actual entity, not as an abstract theory or an unreachable ideal. The quality of commitment to the community as a whole often serves as an inspiring model for others, often catalyzing unexpected and dramatic changes in the system as a whole.

Some researchers have collected anecdotes and derived a theory to explain altruism, such as the tipping phenomenon, in which a sudden change occurs with little stimulus, but simply when the time is just "right." In our experience in a violent secondary school in Jamaica, a remarkable systemwide restoration of order began as an "epidemic" of helpful bystanding seemingly created by a playful chant, the brainchild of a police officer in the altruistic bystander role. In an effort to get boys to be tidier in their physical appearance, a mandate to "tuck your shirt in" was employed, which rapidly inspired songs and jokes that then became a minicraze, uniting the student body. In the space of a few days, there was hardly an untidy child in the school and, notably fewer instances of violence, too!

Advocates of egoism central to the academic elements of the altruism suggest that some of us, at least to some degree, are capable of qualitatively different forms of motivation, with the ultimate goal of benefiting someone else. Very careful clinical and sociopsychological arguments have been made for and against these points of view. Some of these theories or arguments depend on how you define altruism and egoism. From our perspective, all schools have natural leaders at all levels who are more likely to be helpful to others without direct personal benefit than others. And there are quite a number in any school: we have no specific figures, but it would exceed 5 percent of any school in our experience. It is these altruistically motivated individuals who are most likely to become the natural helpers.

Altruism from this perspective is a motivational state, with the ultimate goal of increasing another's welfare. Is there such a thing as altruism with no egoism? We will leave that debate to philosophers; the important issue here is that correcting violence is desirable. So what do altruistic helping bystanders in our ideal schools do? They encourage the positive without denying the negative; they support each other's projects. Interestingly enough, altruism is often seen in very "bad" people. One example we encountered was a young man who belonged to a gang. The altruism-egoism issue was very much central to both his altruistic work and to the group he was a member of. On one occasion, when he was unsure about whether to go with a gang or come to help needy children in a nearby elementary school, he was late for a ride to carry him to an elementary school and ran after it and jumped in it at the last minute. The lure of gang life eventually claimed him, but he did maintain an undercover helping role with the small children.

Altruism tends to build positive group thinking naturally, and it creates opportunities for altruistic actions and service projects, for example, community cleanup, like raking leaves for elderly people; delivering homework to children who are away from school for prolonged periods of time and helping keep them in touch with their classroom and classmates; and community programs such as Care for a Friend, in which certificates are exchanged between children who identify aspects of other children they wish to reward. These are the sorts of altruism-fostering projects that a natural leader would inspire and take part in. Others you should consider include:

- Dealing with the orientation of new staff and students, especially those arriving during the school year;
- Caring and showing concern for those physically and psychiatrically disturbed, and dealing with prejudice; and
- A noncoercive classroom-management plan that determines all students are responsible for discipline problems, and mandates that all students must participate in solving them.

Natural helpers may be young or old, students, staff, and volunteers. The goal is to utilize them as a natural resource to assist in school settings.

If your school has a collaborative atmosphere of naturally interacting peers, it should be easy to set up a peer-helping arrangement. This will help you to select natural leaders and to promote whatever the talents of the program being introduced happen to be. Some programs specifically address conflict resolution, others are climate focused, like the Olweus program, but any program can and will benefit from the presence of natural leaders who provide a helping environment to spread the word and to create positive changes for your school.

CHAPTER 6: KEY QUESTIONS

Step 1. Identify: Find people in your community who are natural leaders, who are altruistic and able to mentalize.

Step 2. Evaluate: How can the special skills of these individuals best be utilized?

Step 3. Act: Begin planning your first interactive event! How can you bring students, parents, administrators, and other members of your community together to accomplish a common goal?

SUMMARY AND REVIEW

This chapter defines the qualities needed to create and sustain change in school climates. In addition, the process of mentalizing is described as an individual and group way of thinking that is reflective, self-regulated, and aware of self and other. Altruism is the key motivational necessity for key players in any school climate-change plan. The key issues involve:

- Natural leaders are necessary to change school climates.
- Natural leaders must be discovered, nominated, and developed as change agents within the school. Natural leaders can be children or adults.
- Mentalizing is the individual and group process of reflective, clear thinking and includes:

    1. Modulating affect (self-control);
    2. Self-awareness, "mind mindedness";

3. Understanding inner and outer cues during social interaction; and
4. Assertive self-existing within clear boundaries.

- When either an individual or a group stops mentalizing, a series of repetitive and stereotypical responses follow. Climate will become increasingly more coercive.
- Altruism is a motivational state that can be self-rewarding. The use of altruism in climate change is critical.
- Altruism is a drive to help others, a community mindedness that causes people to get involved. Altruism in natural leaders tends to exist behind the scenes without the need for self-aggrandizement.
- Altruism builds group thinking and can be modeled by others.

Chapter Seven

Creating a Game Plan

The two most important steps in establishing a productive school violence reduction program is identifying the proper change agents and then creating a game plan that reflects the realities of the school. This game plan is your blueprint for change. It consists of properly selected and motivated "change agents" from both within and outside your school.

This plan is more than a simple proclamation by a principal against bullying or a course in social skills and character education. Every school's plan will consist of different tactics and will involve different people, taking into account both variable resources and fluctuating levels of support. A plan can succeed only when motivated and responsive change agents work together for the common good. This is an organic process that takes time and can span from one academic year to another. The plan becomes similar to an observing ego in the social system, offering another way to observe what happens inside and outside the school walls and to find answers to the evolving problems that impacts school climate.

A good game plan is critical in order to begin programs that will grow slowly in your school and will remain part of the larger school climate. The opposite of a game plan is a knee-jerk reaction. This type of response frequently follows a crisis that has already happened at a school. A diverse group of individuals might gather and identify the need for someone in a school leadership position to do something about the problem. This is clearly not a game plan, but, rather, an instinctive response to a crisis. When news of the Columbine and Virginia Tech tragedies saturated the media, for instance, there was an immediate rush to figure out, *after* the fact, how such terrible events could unfold in such good schools. The ideal game plan should involve people asking these questions, but *before* an outbreak of violence and the tragic loss of innocent lives.

A game plan is a specific set of steps that needs to be followed in order for schools to recruit the right people and to make the decisions necessary to create a peaceful school. Every school is a unique environment in need of a different and personalized game plan. All coaches know that every game involves a different opponent and demands a flexible and unique strategy. This is similar to the approach needed to create winning strategies for building peaceful schools. If a team relies on only one strategy, they will easily be defeated over the course of a season; all their moves will become recognizable and familiar, and the game plan will not prove flexible and responsive enough to achieve victory.

The first step, of course, is to establish a team. The composition of this team is critical to the success of the overall game plan. Keeping the sports metaphor in mind, remember that recruitment is a key part of building a strong and competitive athletic team. It is difficult to win games with players who are not adequately motivated, skilled, and coached. The team leader, or coach, needs to be in charge of the team. He or she must use foresight, charisma, skill, and knowledge of the opponent to guide the players to victory.

In the field of school violence prevention, this team needs to be selected by leaders and given the opportunity and resources necessary to function. The team players need to identify the time and resources they need in order to begin strategizing and building game plans to target bullying in their school. The team members are extremely critical to the success of any program. The best intentions and plans to implement change will fall woefully short if they are not accompanied by enthusiastic and skilled team players working together toward a common goal.

Let's start with the first player you should select: the team leader. The team leader's main function is to implement the plan of action agreed to by the team. To use a sports metaphor again, the "coach" in this case can be the school superintendent or board member who grants the captain the power and resources necessary to achieve the team's overall objectives. The team leader is a change agent who participates in the everyday activities of your school in a way that enables and complements the plan designed in the implementation strategy. He or she is the identified point person within the school. Nothing positive can be created and sustained within your school without this person's focus and commitment to improving your school's climate.

The single most important decision you will make at this point is choosing the right leader. The senior leadership within the school district should be involved in the selection and ongoing support of the change agents within the school. Principals need to understand the value of this leadership position. Team leaders should be visible and recognized by the school board and community leaders; it is essential that this not be an invisible or devalued task, tossed to any willing volunteer. Your leader, or change agent, needs to be empowered by the superintendent to:

- Gather a team of interested teachers, parents, students, and community leaders to meet regularly to design and evaluate climate improvement strategies.
- Set regular time aside for meetings and for program implementation.
- Have access to school resources to create strategies using these available resources in the school system.

Your team leader needs to be part of the internal structure of your school. It is understandably difficult for outside change agents to become active within a school for any sustained period of time. The team leader needs to be familiar with all parts of the school climate and should have personal and professional relationships with those who will be recruited to participate in any subsequent action strategies.

The team leader is not sufficient, however, to create an effective change strategy. This internal leader or change agent often is best used in collaboration with an outside change agent. In many of the school programs we designed, there have been outside change agents who became active and provided regular assistance to schools. These external change agents work collaboratively with their internal counterparts to strengthen the overall quality of the process, as well as to apply fresh perspectives and insights to climate issues that may elude those who have been spending all of their time within that climate. A good team is well represented by individuals coming together from both the inside and outside of the school.

The outside change agent is often someone in the mental health profession. We have worked with a number of schools where outside mental health professionals collaborated with schools to create an ongoing change process. These outside change agents can also be volunteers capable of working within the school to foster a strong sense of connection to the outside community, and to build bridges, rather than walls, between the schools and the community.

Our first experiences in helping schools change began, in fact, with a volunteer effort by Dr. Twemlow to respond to the needs of a school in Topeka, Kansas. The initial phases of the consultation were done on a voluntary basis; this proved to be a key element in the success of the program. Initially it took approximately three hours a week of Dr. Twemlow's time, but as the team strengthened and more community members became involved, this was quickly reduced. Within a short period of time, the team then recruited a local karate instructor and began to develop programs to reduce bullying, victimizing, being a victim, and being a bystander. Both Dr. Twemlow and the karate instructor's time and efforts were eventually rewarded with increases in their respective businesses. There was an increase in psychiatric referrals to the outside consultant as well as an increase in the karate school's enrollment, illustrating how involvement in the school change process can lead to mutual gains for both the school and the outside change agents.

There is often a conflict inherent in hiring outside consultants to visit schools and to offer them advice on how to operate peacefully on a day-to-day basis. While these outside consultants may often have excellent ideas, teachers and administrators rarely buy in, as we discussed in chapter 2. Superintendents or school boards may entertain the fantasy that expensive outside experts will magically resolve issues in their schools and will immediately implement a process they believe will lead to reduced levels of violence. This fantasy does not always come true for a number of reasons. For instance, the very process of being evaluated and told what to do by an outside expert often undermines or defeats the purpose of creating a team to problem solve from within the school.

A good outside change agent needs to have certain skills that can be useful in establishing a game plan. To begin with, your outside consultant needs to have prior experience working as part of a group and knowledge of group process. In fact, the role of the outside change agent could be likened to that of a group facilitator, not as an inspirational expert delivering the answers. The group consultant will respond to your inquiries or list experience and training on his/her professional curriculum vitae. The partnership between the internal change agent and the external change agent forms the nucleus of the change process within the school. These two leaders must work from both sides of the school to establish realistic goals, timelines, and other group processes. There are many useful consultants available to schools we will list in the resource guide. Informally, volunteers can be helpful but are not paid, with potential need for support and praise without being financially obligated. Many volunteers are very reliable, but some are not. Get them involved early on to test their commitment, so that you are more prepared later.

GATHERING STAKEHOLDERS

Once a leadership team is in place, a team of stakeholders must be recruited to participate in this ongoing change process. Changing a school is not a sprint; it is more like a marathon, where strategy and endurance can be more important than speed. Change does not happen overnight, and antiviolence programs may experience years of trial and error, recruitment, changes of team composition, shifts in leadership, and other challenges before succeeding.

The process of building a successful antiviolence climate is very similar to building a successful sports team. The end result may be a championship team, but certainly this does not happen overnight. Successful athletic programs develop time lines and benchmarks to evaluate their progress toward specified goals. There are three keys to this process: patience, acceptance of the time it will take to build a team, and smart recruitment of key players.

The sports metaphor you may have noticed recurring here is not accidental. It is critical that a successful antiviolence program implementation strategy be valued at the same level as a school's athletic success. We have noticed that many schools consider their basketball or football teams more important than extracurricular activities that foster antiviolence within the school. These antiviolence teams have no cheerleaders and might not attract large crowds, but they are critical resources for the entire student body and for members of the community. Athletic programs generate a sense of pride in the school while antiviolence programs build a sense of safety from within the school. Both are important to the community and follow very similar rules for creating successful programs. Antiviolence programs depend, of course, on buy in.

TEAM PLAYERS

Successful antiviolence programs require that a dedicated and focused group of people remain committed to a process over a sustained period of time. This model does not call for a blue ribbon panel approach in which individuals gather after a tragic event to theorize about what could have been done to prevent this crisis. This process is a low-key and behind-the-scenes process in which the key team players convince community members to look honestly at the climate of the school. They will work together to discover root causes and to determine what can be done to decrease coerciveness and improve the school's climate and then select a program.

The team needs to have at least several teachers invested in the process. Teachers are clearly the frontline players in the school. As the adult role models in a school environment, teachers reflect the values of the community. Teachers are also familiar with conditions in the school on a daily basis and can bring a sense of reality and immediacy to any discussion about what is happening within the school's walls. It would be difficult to have a successful team without including dedicated teachers.

Students are, of course, also a very important part of any violence prevention team. It is critical to get the student perspective on what is happening on a day-to-day basis. Both teachers and students are aware of their respective sides of the issues and can be brought together under skilled leadership to heighten both the awareness of problems and the realistic approaches that can be tried. Students are often quite motivated and want to be involved in what is happening in their schools. You will frequently find these students participating in activities such as student council and other leadership activities.

Parents are another great resource to consider when you are assembling your team players. In recent years, we have noted a decline in parents' involvement with their children's school activities. Attendance at parent-teacher meetings has been sparse, and many after-school parent activities (such as workshops on bullying or child development seminars) do not generate much interest. Parents seem busier than ever before and report having less time available for activities planned by their children's schools. While these factors present a challenge, remember that one or two motivated parents can be sufficient to offer the parental perspective, as opposed to a large number of parents.

Your team can also be greatly enhanced by participation from local community leaders. Often large companies will allow their employees or senior management staff to work as mentors in local schools. Having someone from the business or the political world involved in this team brings a tremendous amount of energy and potential resources into play. Once again, involvement of these outside community resources needs to be voluntary and should rely on altruism. One such commonly available program is Business Partnerships with Schools, which, as the name suggests, helps local businesses reach out to schools.

For example, in a school violence prevention program we observed in Jamaica, the Jamaican Tourist Board became involved, along with local business leaders, in working toward reducing violence in a troubled secondary school. The Jamaican Tourist Board helpfully offered ideas, as well as in-kind resources such as airline fares, hotel accommodations, and meals for visiting experts used in the antiviolence effort. This generosity allowed for the recruitment of the team of law enforcement and psychology specialists needed to develop training programs for both police and school teachers. This was not a purely economic contribution; these leaders met weekly with schools and communicated regularly with outside consultants in order to design training strategies to assist in reducing school violence. It was the work of the outside community resources that allowed for the creation of a three-year plan to reduce the violence in this school, as well as in the larger tourist community.

Similarly, in Springfield, Massachusetts, a large insurance company (Mass Mutual Insurance) offered senior executives the opportunity to help a group of students develop an antibullying and mentoring program. The corporate executives reached out to the community and became involved with the school and students. Each school in Springfield was eventually adopted by a business in the community. The end result was a very successful after-school program supervised by the Boys & Girls Clubs that greatly enhanced the school environment.

Once you have assembled your team, it is important to establish a realistic group process. Team members need to commit to a long-term reflective process designed to identify and respond to the problems impacting the school's sense of safety. The leader needs to create a low-key, altruistic, and realistic identity for the team. Your team is not intended to be a high visibility group striving for recognition and accolades, quite the opposite, in fact. The key element to a successful team is longevity. Many committees and commissions are formed and exist for a school year or part of a school year, then die a rather unceremonious death. Frequently, these change-focused teams can morph into other types of groups unrelated to the original goals of establishing safe and creative learning environments. The goals and boundaries of the group need to be kept simple and achievable, yet focused exclusively on improving the quality of the school-learning environment. The team's identity is one that should be routinely discussed and kept in check through a group process led by insiders and outsiders.

ESTABLISHING A PROCESS

The key element in establishing a successful process for a team gathered to change the school climate is that it be realistic and meet regularly. The group needs to be action-orientated and willing to try out various strategies. The process should also be action-oriented and goal-directed, rather than simply an open and reflective series of steps in which problems are discussed with no concrete plans for following through.

This process must also refrain from generating ideas that cannot be studied by the group over time (to measure their impact on the overall school climate) or implemented at all. The first order of business for this group should be to establish its goals and the rules of operation that will enable it to function effectively. Meeting times must be set, attended, and become routine. Agendas need to be created and the team leader must keep the other members on task. The process for these groups is comparable to the Total Quality Management approach to meetings in the business world. The key is not to allow these meetings to be mere rap sessions where gripes are aired but nothing significant is accomplished, but to create a process that gets things done while allowing ample time for airing the gripes and doubts. The ideal leader is one who can keep the group mentalizing, which entails allowing fear to be expressed and managed.

Establishing a meeting process can be as simple as setting aside one hour per week immediately after school, or designating a free period during the day (for instance, either just before school or during homeroom) to gather the team together in a regular fashion. This may sound easy, but it is arguably the primary reason why many of these teams do not succeed! The initial phases of team development may be embraced enthusiastically by everyone, but eventually motivation declines and discouragement ensues as the group becomes reduced in size and focus. It is critical to stay realistic and to encourage team members who are able and sufficiently motivated to sustain their commitment to the process. This may require that the goals be adjusted to meet the realities of the people involved in the teams.

Be sure your prospective team members are willing and able to adhere to the following basic set of requirements:

- To meet regularly for a specified amount of time with the team leader;
- To follow mutually agreed upon rules of order (not necessarily Roberts Rules of Order) that will allow leaders to manage communication. Group process needs to create a way to follow the agenda and allow free expression of doubts and thorough working through of ideas, before a decision is made;
- To set priorities for the group;
- To identify targeted problems;
- To establish realistic timelines for the initiation of trial projects;
- To understand and remember all projects aim to create increased compassion, empathy, and to improve students' skills at making friends and having peaceful interpersonal relationships; and
- To create a system for measuring and evaluating the results of trial projects.

Boundaries must be established and respected in order to allow a non-blaming way of communicating about experiences and activities that affect the climate in the school. It is critical for this group to avoid finger pointing and not to personalize potentially volatile issues discussed within the group. The group needs to develop an identity as a safe place to discuss problems, ideas, and solutions. There must be clear boundaries between members of the group, with specific roles assumed for the purposes of discussion and future implementation of projects.

Interactive projects are an easy way to establish a process and to get started, as they can be inexpensive, capable of involving the whole community, and create every politician's dream: good publicity. In a suburban community we observed, a team decided to hold a poster competition for the four elementary schools. The team began by creating a handout describing the roles of bullies, victims, and bystanders. Teachers sent the handout home, offering it in the spirit of the solar system projects many parents help their children complete.

This assignment, however, called for parents and children to develop a poster or slogan advocating against any of the negative behaviors outlined in the handout. A local bank donated a fifty dollar savings bond, and a local sporting goods company donated another fifty dollars in sports equipment. The judges were chosen from the school committee, local churches, and the mayor's office. All four of the schools' principals supported the idea and passed it down to the teachers. Every teacher shared the assignment and passed out and collected the entries. The team collected the posters and arranged for anonymous judging. One team member contacted the media who arranged for coverage in the local paper complete with the winner and celebrity group photo and story in the newspaper. The winning poster was announced at a televised school committee meeting, and the poster itself was made into a flag that was prominently displayed in all four elementary schools for the next year. This is just one of many examples of how a team began with a simple idea and enhanced it by adding their available local resources. The whole intervention cost less than one hundred dollars, and everyone involved came out a winner. The awareness of the roles played by bullies, victims, and bystanders was raised by the teachers and parents from the four elementary schools through an existing educational process and tradition. This low-cost project succeeded because the surrounding community, not just school personnel and students, was involved. Total commitment of the surrounding community will ensure total success for virtually any school project.

Your group needs to start by defining the similarities among its members as well as respecting their differences. It is easy for groups to become competitive and personalize their opinions and positions, and it is the leader's responsibility to keep the group focused on the overall good of the school climate. Ultimately, it is less important that one member's ideas be chosen over another than it is that the group understands the value of trying out a variety of projects. While differences need to be acknowledged and respected, a well-led group will avoid getting stuck in this self-preoccupation stage and will instead redirect the group's energies to planning and implementing strategies.

An example of this self-preoccupation could involve the different perspectives brought by police or probation officers versus those of community activists or parents. The law enforcement perspective may stress punishment for those who engage in coercive activities within the school. It is important that this perspective be respected, even if a parent or a community activist perceives it as a destructive force. A successful group will tolerate its differences and work to identify ways to compromise in developing its responses.

This is where the outside change agent needs to use his or her skills as a group facilitator to help keep the group focused and moving, rather than trapped by power struggles. The group must be able to model this cooperative spirit in its day-to-day operations, not only to succeed in its mission, but also to set an example of compassion and empathy for the rest of the school. We used this process in a citywide antihomicide intervention in Jamaica. We called it "engineered conflict." The warring groups were gathered and the fights developed under a tight structure to allow the participants to realize that they were more the same than different in their goals.

In other words, the group needs to develop the ability to tolerate and contain the potential negativity of its members. Imagine, for example, that your team contains both a parent whose child had been arrested and a police officer. However wronged by the police parents may feel, they need to remember that the police officer in the group is not their enemy. It is essential that everyone in this working group go beyond their own personal experiences and focus instead on the larger group goal of establishing a peaceful school climate. Positive alternatives include beginning with an open discussion of difficult problems and accepting the notion that some problems are beyond the reach of the team.

One team we encountered was able to overcome potentially difficult team dynamics and resolved a teacher-bully situation. This urban team began by discussing the topic of bully teachers and what can be done to reduce the problem. The teachers on the team were initially very quiet, and the school resource officer focused instead on the troubled nature of the students. Once the team had accepted that there were no *official* ways to address one particular teacher, a discussion ensued about how to address the problem of this teacher *informally*. The team leader then approached the school's principal and inquired about stress management training seminars for all the school's teachers, emphasizing how teachers could help one another cope with stress. The team's next step was to contact an outside expert to present ideas for helping a colleague who might be unaware of a bullying pattern of behavior. The presentation was codesigned and reviewed by the team to target specific behaviors identified as problematic within their schools, and specifically with this bully teacher. The presentation itself focused on the role of bystanding teacher; the main idea involved the description of the impact of remaining a bystander when a colleague bullies or is bullied by a student. The key to this group's success was in going beyond personal preoccupations and creating a nonblaming and nonpunitive orientation to facing their problem.

It is this spirit of safety and acceptance within the group that will allow its members to discuss the undiscussables. It is these "no-touch topics" that often reside at the base of many of the systemic problems that generate coercive school climates. Your group needs to feel safe discussing difficult and controversial subjects that are all too often left undiscussed. These topics can range from labor disputes to teacher bullying, as in the previous example, but they all contribute to the construction of a school's climate.

Your group also needs to stay focused on everyday experiences. It is easy for groups to wander off topic and into larger issues that may be related to the more general problems experienced in schools, yet not specifically tied to the everyday problems being experienced within their own specific school. While it is important to understand the implications of certain laws, such as No Child Left Behind, it is not specifically relevant to responding to a bullying elementary school teacher. Staying focused on solving real everyday problems is critical to maintaining the group's motivation to stay together and maintain a working relationship toward mutually agreed-upon goals.

The group also needs to establish a timetable that is realistic. Most schools work based on a school calendar year, therefore many programs and processes begin at the start of the school year in August or September and end in May or June. You must establish timelines that are realistic, and different timetables may be necessary for projects that depend on the existence of the group or upon school being in session. The group needs to, like their athletic counterparts, continue its operations from year to year or season to season. Just as it is important for athletic coaches to build skills in certain areas and recruit for certain positions, this group needs to share that attitude in their approaches during the school year as well as from one school year to the next. A focused group is more likely to experience success and will be more likely to stay together to form a permanent ongoing presence at the school.

Remember, one of the key tasks of the group leader is to ensure that members of this group are humanized. Many groups attempt to function with individuals remaining in their respective roles and forgetting that they are also just simply people. Police officers behave like police officers, and parents only think of their own children. The act of humanizing group members will create an atmosphere more conducive to problem solving and cooperative action. Group members should be encouraged to step outside their roles and to become people who think outside of themselves. This can be done by beginning to discuss and attempting to solve less conflicted issues before tackling the more complex problems. In other words, the group should begin with a project that is not controversial, is fairly easy to coordinate, and has a good chance of succeeding. For example, most people would agree that a school's climate could be improved with some antibullying messages incorporated into classroom and school decorations in the common areas of the school.

The group process needs to reflect what the British psychoanalyst Wilfred Bion called a "work group model." In this style of group operation, the members stay focused on specific tasks and are not derailed from their objectives by the intrusion of their personal feelings. With this sort of dynamic in place, team members are free to create hypotheses that can be tested in simple ways, and then the action steps designed to follow up any successful strategies.

Perhaps you have already experimented with forming groups to deal with bullying within your own school. If so, you may have already realized that simply discussing the problem and identifying a program will not result in an immediate victory. Remember that you must begin with a testable hypothesis in order to evaluate in real time whether or not a group's efforts are proving effective. It is this group that tailors the responses to the specific problems identified thanks to the hypotheses underlying the problem statements.

Consider, for example, a student member of your group who shares the knowledge that ninth graders in your high school are often targeted and victimized by upperclassmen. To some bystanders, this problem may be seen as a natural and traditional hazing ritual or as a good-natured way of welcoming new students. A parent, however, may disagree strongly with this perspective, leading her to discuss the negative impact hazing had on her child during ninth grade, which led to her permanent alienation from school and subsequent substance-abuse problems. Another team member, such as a coach, might then hypothesize that this process might be reduced by recruiting the school's higher social status athletes and involving them in a buddy program designed to assist new ninth grade students identified as at-risk targets for victimization. This is an example of a hypothesis-driven project that is simple, realistic, and based on the everyday experiences of the group.

Ultimately, such an effort could lead to the implementation of a program that recruits varsity lineman to adopt specially identified students likely to be victimized during their first semester at school. This program has been used in a variety of high schools for physically disabled and developmentally delayed students. This is a simple program requiring no outside funding, simply the motivated involvement of the coaches and team members. There is nothing a superintendent likes more than a successful program that does not cost money. Here we see a simple idea based on a coach's hypothesis; the program succeeded because it could be evaluated using identifiable benchmarks that could be adjusted in real time to suit the unique needs of a particular school.

The success of this program was easily evaluated by simple observation and feedback from the involved athletes, school counselors, and the teachers of high-risk children. Parents of both the mentors and potential-victim targets can also be brought together to offer feedback and support to their children's efforts at school. Realistically, it may happen that some of the athletes are more motivated than others, and competition or sadism may be exhibited by the mentor buddies. This unfortunate behavior could be identified by teachers or parents, and then corrected by the coaches. What is critical in this process remains the focus on feedback and the adjustment of the hypothesis to meet the stated goals of improving the quality of life for these high-risk students during their transition to high school.

After engaging and involving one group of prominent students, an anti-violence team might also establish groups of natural leaders among other students and school members. The creation of a friendly competition, such as an antibully poster competition between schools, as we mentioned earlier, is one such example. Recently, a middle school we observed began one of these poster competitions. The winning poster was of a tee-shirt that said, "It's not what's on the label, but what's under the label that counts."

In a Midwestern elementary school, two parents participated in a similar type of creative project. They quilted flags that were used outside of class-rooms to indicate whether or not the classroom was having a peaceful day. This idea was generated by parents and teachers and implemented organically from within the school. Beginning as a simple idea, it eventually grew into a schoolwide project that resulted in a significant reduction in bullying. We have noticed that typically, it is the small "do-able" ideas that actually have the most impact.

CHAPTER 7: KEY QUESTIONS

Step 1. Identify: What are the first problems your school's team will address?

Step 2. Evaluate: Can your team's members successfully adhere to the rules and requirements of working together? Are they aware of what these condi-tions are?

Step 3. Act: Think creatively! Are there nontraditional or outside-the-box ways of tackling some of your school's problems?

SUMMARY AND REVIEW

Team selection is key and the following are some principles to guide in the creation of this team:

• A team will need an inside change agent who becomes the school's point person using his or her daily activities at the school to help develop information from students as well as stay in close contact with the teachers and administration.

- The team also needs an outside change agent with altruistic motives to help and the skills necessary to garner community resources as well as help with group processing and psychological issues as they may appear.
- Teams should span between school years (like basketball or cheerleading) and not become stale and reactive to specific incidents.
- The team should strive to stay small, simple, and organic. Simple plans that produce buy in will strengthen the team's image of itself as well as how it is seen by the rest of the school and community.
- Inside team leader must have:

  1. Access to school every day;
  2. Full support of the superintendent and principal; and
  3. Ability to schedule regular meetings with school staff and community members.

- Outside team leader should:

  1. Volunteer;
  2. Have group-processing skills; and
  3. Be well connected to community resources.

- Once leaders are chosen, then stakeholders are recruited for the group or to be included in projects from a wide spectrum including law enforcement, outside mental health experts, parents, students, teachers, and local public officials.
- A climate change group needs to create an identity for itself and adopt simple rules:

  1. Low key, positive, nonblaming tone with attention to group process (with help of outside consultant);
  2. Task focused, not just talking about problems;
  3. Establish the GROUP GOAL: PEACEFUL LEARNING CLIMATES;
  4. Define similarities and difference between group members and respect different opinions;
  5. Share tasks that might not be your expertise but will give you a chance to empathize with others on the team;
  6. Try different projects, keeping them small and easy to evaluate;
  7. Contain negativity, resignation, and giving up;
  8. Focus on everyday activities; and
  9. Create timelines and adhere to realistic goals.

- The group needs to be humanized and members shed their professional roles and work together to identify problems and create realistic solutions, in an area where nobody has the right answer.

Chapter Eight

Discussing the Undiscussables

When implementing school antiviolence programs, it is often difficult to develop a strategy capable of encompassing all of the ingredients necessary for a cohesive school climate. Everyone knows about the problems, yet no one wants to be the one in charge of tackling them. An undiscussable is, by definition, a topic that ignites a tremendous amount of anxiety in a group, and will either be avoided or will allow fragmentation to halt all forward progress the group has made. Your undiscussables may be rooted in a wide spectrum of school policies and quite possibly extends into many levels of your school's hierarchy. The role of the undiscussables and how to discuss them is vital in selecting and using a program that will actually work for your particular school and situation.

Consider, for instance, this situation: everybody might know that a school's politically connected principal is burned out, but no one wants to bring the issue up. The principal is disinterested in change or progress, but plays along in order to keep from creating more problems. Or imagine implementing a program meant to eliminate the schoolyard bully but fails to address the question of whether or not teachers may also be bullying students. In both examples, the problem is that the overall school climate will remain distorted by an underlying abuse of power that will create unhealthy school climates. There isn't a program in existence that can succeed in this kind of an environment, and trying to implement one without addressing the undiscussables is a waste of time, resources, and effort.

We have conducted extensive studies on teachers bullying students and have found this to be an understandably delicate issue. People are reluctant to characterize teachers across the board as engaging in this type of behavior. Too often, we cling to an unrealistic illusion that teachers are somehow superhuman, immune to the coercive behaviors we condemn in children. Teaching is a noble profession to be sure, albeit one accompanied by a number of elements that *increase* the pressures while they *decrease* the healthy resistances to acting coercively. Teaching is one of the few occupations in which employees can be trapped in a contained environment with their charges on a daily basis. Many teachers suffer headaches and lower back pain from the stress of classroom teaching. As correctional officers and psychiatric ward nurses would understand, being in charge of troubled individuals is both an inescapable burden and an omnipresent responsibility. There is an ever-present psychological impact within the classroom that carries over and exists in a teacher's daily life.

Teachers bullying students is but one of a wide range of undiscussables that exist in every school or organization. Many corporations experience similar types of pressures in which certain topics in the workplace are considered off-limits, and discussing them can lead to ostracism and hostile or negative action. We will begin our discussion of undiscussable topics with an analysis of teachers bullying students, and then we will examine other potentially relevant undiscussables that negatively affect contemporary school climates and reduce the likelihood of positive change.

TEACHER BULLYING

Based on our research, we define teacher bullying as a teacher using his or her power to punish, manipulate, or disparage a student beyond the point most would consider a reasonable disciplinary procedure. In one study we conducted, 116 elementary school teachers responded to an anonymous questionnaire about their perceptions of teachers who bully students in their broad school experience. Surprisingly, the results indicated that over 40 percent of teachers openly reported bullying students themselves. As a group "bullying teachers," compared to other nonbullying teachers, had bullied more students, experienced more bullying when they were students, and had worked with and observed more bullying teachers over the past three years. In a larger study of 214 teachers in elementary, middle, and high schools, a similar profile to the bullying teacher occurred in teachers working in schools with the highest suspension rates. These results strongly suggest that suspensions and disciplinary problems are connected to the problem of teacher bullying, as well as to teachers' perceptions of their own and other teachers circumstances.

We were struck by the courage and honesty of the teachers who openly admitted to being bullies or victims of student bullying themselves. While some of the teachers resented being asked the question, a greater majority recognized that bullying students was a hazard of teaching and that they had themselves taken on the role of bully, victim, or bystander in both student-to-student bullying as well as teacher-to-student bullying. There was also a clear indication that it was not just teachers bullying students, but also teachers being bullied by students. This study further served to confirm our hypothesis that bullying teachers represent a minority in the overall profession. Teachers readily admitted to observing and experiencing being a bully and a victim of students, as well as by their parents and administrators.

Clearly, it is more than "just" the students who most stand to benefit from a successful school intervention program. We identified two types of bullying teachers present in most situations. The first type includes the more sadistic teachers who use their positions of power to bully, shame, and humiliate their students. The second type of teacher fits into a more defined bully-victim-teacher role, characterized by a pattern of provoking victimization by students and then reacting in an inappropriate and coercive fashion. Many of these bully-victim-teachers appear burned out and are unable to generate the energy necessary to stay ahead of the power dynamics within their classroom or the larger school environment. The questionnaire was, as we later learned, experienced by some of the participating teachers as a wake-up call, highlighting some of their key concerns, and showing them that they were not alone in their frustrations and responses.

The problem of sexual exploitation of children by adults in positions of authority has also been a very hot topic over the past decade. A special 2006 issue of the renowned *Virginia Child Protection Newsletter* contained an overview of the problem of sexual abuse by educators. This type of teacher bullying is a crime, unlike the bullying that results from a teacher being needlessly coercive with a student during class, while supervising lunch, or monitoring schoolyard activities. Judging the full scope of the problem of sexual abuse by teachers is quite difficult. A study by the American Association of University Women reported that two-thirds of both male and female respondents reported having been the target of unwanted sexual comments, jokes, gestures, or looks. Additionally, about half the students reported having been touched, pinched, or grabbed at some point by their teachers. Student-to-student sexual harassment was the most common, accounting for nearly 80 percent of the incidents, while teachers, custodians, and coaches accounted for about 20 percent of the incidents. One respondent noted that verbal harassment occurs mostly in the classroom, while physical contact, sexual, or clearly defined sexual harassment is obviously more likely to occur outside of the classroom.

Teacher bullying in the classroom is, we believe, a far more difficult issue to deal with than sexual exploitation. When a teacher exploits students sexually, it is considered a crime, clearly a legal and criminal matter. But there are more subtle ways in which teachers abuse their students, and these incidents are more difficult to prosecute. Instances of both teacher bullying and teacher exploitation of students are grossly underreported because of the nature of the shameful activities. This undiscussable has had and continues to have a tremendous impact on the overall climate of a school. In one case, an eight-year-old complained that his teacher, an experienced and widely respected woman, would call him by a girl's name to make the class laugh at him, but only when there were no other adults in the room. Although people did not believe him at first, he clinched the matter one day with a tape recording he had made in the classroom!

Several prominent authors have outlined a response pattern that could be used for both teacher bullying as well as teacher sexual exploitation. Their suggestions include:

- Implementing a code of conduct that details the exact boundaries for teachers in responding to students both verbally and physically;
- Establishing grievance procedures for harassment victims that can be distributed, understood, and adhered to by teachers, parents, administrators, and students;
- Protecting against false complaints and allegations. These recommendations include severe punishments for false allegations against a teacher by a student or parent;
- Impartially adhering to policies that involve a due-process procedure for all parties identified as bullies, victims, or bystanders; and
- Training teachers to assist them in avoiding false allegations of any type of bullying.

ADMINISTRATOR BULLYING

Teachers work within a hierarchical system, led by administrators following policies set by elected or appointed school board members. It is not uncommon for schools to be forced into accepting arbitrary and politicized decisions as a matter of policy. Principals may be forced to protect a bullying teacher because that teacher is politically connected or may be involved with organized labor groups. In some cases, administrators will bully those who stand up for other teachers and may treat them unfairly. These issues are frequently the topic of informal conversations among teachers while sitting in lunchrooms. Many teachers report having heated interchanges among themselves about the unfairness of how the administration mistreats teachers. In one instance a school superintendent was known to regularly cuss out principals who did not obey his infantilizing demands. In another quite a number of school principals learn not to place vulnerable children with bully teachers but do not want to confront the issue for fear of the possible response.

In too many cases, administrators assume a punishment surveillance model when responding to teachers. This results in a climate within the school in which the external disciplinary presence of the administrator is the primary way of relating to teachers on a day-to-day basis. This in turn creates a climate in which teachers are left on their own to control situations that occur in their classrooms or while supervising students in everyday school activities.

The general pattern of administrative bullying can take several forms. One common form of administrative bullying involves an administrator taking an abdicating bystander role. In this instance, administrators do very little to acknowledge the existence of certain problems, and they fail to protect teachers from unreasonable and aggressive parents and irrelevant or contradictory policies handed down from school boards. This type of bullying administrator is primarily concerned with maintaining the illusion of a healthy school and will ignore issues impacting teachers' abilities to control and maintain a positive school environment. Often, this type of bullying will lead teachers to form their own unhealthy and often-coercive subgroups. Some teachers are able to function independently of the larger support of their colleagues and peers. They simply survive by controlling their own classrooms and existing in a vacuum, but the result is a fragmented social climate rendered fertile for the growth of coercive activities by both students and teachers. When teachers are alienated from administrators, feel that they are devalued, and ignored by the administration, they will far too often take matters into their own hands.

Another type of bullying administrator is a more sadistic individual who uses his or her power to make decisions that impact the quality of life for both teachers and students. This type of administrator is likely to target specific teachers, engaging in a pattern of creating humiliating tasks, disciplinary actions, and transferring of responsibilities as a way of maintaining power and superiority. These sadistic administrators are very self-absorbed and care only for their own welfare, leaving teachers essentially to fend for themselves. This type of administrator will always appear to be strict and concerned with maintaining discipline in a rather controlled environment, but his or her dictatorial stance will alienate the teachers. This dilemma represents the quintessential undiscussable.

A school with this type of administrator will have a hard time implementing any type of antiviolence program unless they are able first to deal with the problem. Sadistic principals may indicate that they are interested in having antiviolence programs but will minimize the potential value by eliminating those resources necessary to complete the tasks of climate interventions, slowly undermining or devaluing the activity. This type of school might try a number of different programs with promising outcomes, only to find that they are paying lip service to administrators who are simply creating an image in turn for their own superiors. These schools will tend to rely more on expulsion and suspension as a way of dealing with student misbehavior. Authoritarian teachers who talk a good game will be supported and favored by this type of bully administrator.

Bullying administrators are more concerned with numbers and orderliness within their schools than with the human beings who both teach and learn in that school. Eliminating students who do not achieve through suspension for behavioral reasons is one way to maintain higher academic scores, but how does it help the problem of student behavior? In a controlled study we conducted, an antibullying program was initiated and embraced by the teachers and the principal, as well as students. The net result of this program was a significant increase in academic performance, especially on the part of bystander children who said they hated school initially. In other words, when a school works together to eliminate coercive activities at all levels, children learn better because teachers are freer to focus on teaching.

The problems of administrators who bully are not easily addressed by anyone in the school hierarchy. Again, the most prevalent way of coping with this type of problem is informal modes of communication, such as gossiping between demoralized teachers who feel unable to perform because of the seemingly hopeless structural captivity they experience working under a bullying administrator.

BULLYING COACHES

It is not uncommon for high schools to define themselves by the successes or failures of their extracurricular programs. In schools with successful athletic programs, there is the increased risk of harboring a bullying coach who pressures students inappropriately to succeed. Other schools may pride themselves on their success in nonathletic events, such as debate or forensics, but the same bullying can exist in these arenas as well. Whatever the competitive extracurricular activity is, there is generally a coach of some sort who selects students to participate as representatives of their school. As part of this process, the coach is trusted to choose a team, train that team, and guide its members through the season. Whether it is a forensics competition or a debate, a gymnastics or wrestling meet, a football game, a cheerleading competition, or a spelling bee, the process of an adult being charged with selecting a group of children for competitive activities remains the same.

Remember, in most high schools, coaches are also teachers. During the extracurricular activities, coaches are placed in the position of having to prepare their teams for "battle," or competition, getting their team into an excited and competitive mindset. We have observed a number of coaches being needlessly coercive in their selection and training approaches. Even seemingly well-intentioned coaches often forget that the main point of extracurricular activities is to develop students as overall human beings rather than as robotic athletes or performers, charged with defending the honor of the school and the prowess of their coach. In other words, it becomes more about the coach than the success of a team or its individual members. Coaches often forget that they are role models, and they may engage in bullying behavior as a way to motivate their team. Bullying coaches often use exclusion and failure to motivate students in games or practices. If students complain to their parents or to the extracurricular director, they frequently are told to return to the team and simply "work it out." If questioned or held accountable by concerned parents or administrators, coaches can fire back by withholding playing time or participation opportunities for students who might have spoken out.

Also, coaches have a tendency to personalize their criticism of students participating in their activities. The coach is supposed to be in charge. If a parent questions a coach's approach or decision during practice or a game, the athletic director or school administrator frequently supports the coach, maintaining the status quo under the guise of creating "tough" students, able to participate in the competitive world they will encounter outside of school.

Recent television shows such as MTV's *Two a Day*, or NBC's critically acclaimed *Friday Night Lights*, illustrate the differences between coaches functioning in different communities. In *Two a Day*, we are presented with a coach who is a clear example of a bully. He is, however, protected by the academic institution because of its single-minded determination to win football games at any cost. The point of the football team in this program is ostensibly to prepare the students to become scholarship students at various highly competitive colleges. The coach is depicted as a highly aggressive and competitive individual with a team of assistant coaches who follow his every lead. The focus is not on the impact of any of the adult behavior on the students, but instead emphasizes the effects in the school that follow a student's failure to perform, putting even more pressure on the young athletes. By contrast, the coach depicted in *Friday Night Lights* is more concerned with the overall lives of the team members. This authority figure is a nonbullying coach who exists within a community that also insists on a winning football team. The program demonstrates how a nonbullying coach can hold his ground and continue to place the welfare of his students ahead of the "needs" of the community to succeed as a condition of his employment.

There is no lack of media coverage of instances in which coaches have lost control or engaged in highly questionable tactics to motivate their teams. When a school overvalues its extracurricular participation, as we see happening more and more often, the role of the coach becomes idealized, and the ability to question the wisdom of a coercive coach becomes increasingly difficult. Competition is used as a way of justifying coercive behavior by an adult toward a student. When a winning coach bullies a student through excessive personal criticism in public or by excluding them from participation, the behavior is excused as a part of coaching, rather than being recognized as bullying. The bullying coach is clearly an undiscussable that may be on many teachers' minds. Teachers may clearly see the negative impact of a bullying coach on their students' achievement or participation in class, but they will be unable to address the issue because of the undiscussable nature of the problem and the idealized role of the coach in certain schools.

Bullying coaches may also act as abdicating bystanders if their athletes or scholars are engaged in bullying activities. For example, if a senior quarterback sexually abuses a freshman, the impact of this transgression may become minimized and misdirected. We have observed instances in which the victim is even blamed for seducing a popular athlete and making problems later. The coach in this scenario may well become an abdicating bystander if the school allows him or her to position the importance of extracurricular activities over the individual experience of the student within that school environment.

SCHOOLS WHO SUPPORT BULLIES

Children may be exposed to bullying by nonteaching adults in the schools. Students often have few options to communicate about this to anyone. Often, teachers and administrators downplay the impact of this type of adult bullying of children because they lack the awareness of the impact this has on children. There is no question that schools require a wide range of adults to be employed and present in order to sustain the school building itself, to fulfill students' nutritional needs, and to ensure their extracurricular programs and activities. We have encountered numerous instances, for example, of secretaries and librarians acting in bullying ways toward the student body. Custodians, who have a large role to play in the maintenance of a school's physical appearance, frequently have contact with students during the conduct of their business. Maintenance workers are often protected because of their labor contracts and are not trained to the level of teachers and administrators in skills necessary to interact with students in a safe and positive manner.

In a small private school we recently studied and consulted with, a custodian was found to have evaded the typical background check and had engaged in a repeated pattern of sexual exploitation of children over a long period of time. This protected private school setting became the ideal circumstances for a corrupt and deeply troubled adult. Because the school enjoyed a very high status in the community, the idea that some ancillary school staff member could have engaged in a systematic bullying process was not considered until it could no longer be ignored. When the events finally became known, they were minimized until the eruption of a criminal molestation case left the school no option but to reevaluate itself and then to deal with its undiscussable problems.

The support personnel within your own school can be both a source of tremendous inspiration and encouragement to the children, as well as a potential source of bullying. The role that all adults who have contact with children play must be discussed by team leaders seriously seeking to change their school's climate. The possible impact of grouchy janitors, critical librarians, or mean-spirited lunch workers needs to be consistently addressed. There is clearly a need to include these adults in any discussion involving overall school climate.

PREJUDICE

The question of prejudice and stigma is extremely difficult to discuss as a matter of policy. Nobody wants to admit they are prejudiced or playing a racial or ethnic card. This is, again, an ideal undiscussable within a school. We have witnessed extremes in responding to the issue, such as people of color targeted within a social context that tolerates prejudice with no recourse. In an elementary school intervention we led in Topeka, Kansas, we found that it was possible to reduce prejudice and stigmatization of people of color as a by-product of addressing bullying. Why? When bullying is seen as a social role shared by children and adults, it is easier to identify the coercive behavior as bullying, rather than dismissing it as some type of racial prejudice or bias. Prejudice itself can be seen as a form of bullying in which victims are targeted because of some perceived characteristics, such as race, culture, social-economic status, fashion, choice of interest, way of speaking, or physical attractiveness. The pressure to be perceived as fair rather than biased is quite high in most schools, and this pressure may lead to denial of bullying activity.

The issue of prejudice is not easy to explore. Change agents should not be viewed as part of an inquisition team looking for ways to identify and punish all prejudiced individuals. This type of zero tolerance is what renders the issue undiscussable in the first place. In our experience, prejudice is universal. Some forms of prejudice are malignant (destructively aggresive), while others exist benignly (like strongly held preferences). We have found that when people are open and nonjudgmental about prejudice—both in themselves and in others— then an open and free exploration and mentalizing dialogue becomes possible. Choosing a program that stresses the importance of tolerance and keeping an open mind is vital to the success of your intervention.

PARENT BULLYING

Parents can be horrendous bullies. While we have mentioned the detached state of some parents, many others become overly involved in their children's schools, making unreasonable demands and criticizing all aspects of the way the schools are run. Another type of parent bullying involves parents who abdicate their responsibility, then react aggressively to any questioning of their feelings about the school. When an abdicating bullying parent is contacted by the school about issues related to their children, they often will respond by bullying concerned teachers and administrators with threats and angry accusations and assertions that they are protecting the rights of their children.

A safe and creative school climate requires that parents take responsibility for their own levels of coercion and cooperation—or lack thereof—with the school. We have noticed an increasing divide or disconnect between the signals that children receive from their parents and from their schools. When the child is permitted to cause friction between the school and the parent, the parent is likely to engage in bullying behavior as a form of pseudoprotection or to demonstrate involvement with their children. This is increasingly true with parents burdened by the excessive demands of employment necessary to support a family. The inconsistency of these signals from both parent and school creates the opportunity for a child to engage in increasing amounts of coercive behavior at school. When children believe that their bullying can be neutralized by the bullying of their parents, then the child will feel emboldened to bully more at school.

A bullying parent will only have power when school administrators allow him or her to continue. If an administrator abdicates responsibility, then the bullying parent is unleashed on the teacher who may become sandwiched between an abdicating bully principal and a sadistic bully parent. The result, once again, is that this situation becomes an undiscussable.

THE "PROBLEM" OF EXCELLENCE

Not all coercive school environments are violent. Many very high-achieving and socially elite schools have extremely coercive school environments without instances of physical violence on a regular basis. In the quest for excellence, there may, however, be an unwitting commitment to a coercive style of encouraging competition among both teachers and students that builds an unhealthy school climate for all involved. All schools try to bring out the best in their students and want to set high academic standards. But when this process is taken to an extreme, both teachers and students are dehumanized. This is an ideal environment for the evolution of bullying and the creation of an unhealthy school climate.

In our experience, private schools and affluent public schools suffer from a higher level of social aggression than many of their public counterparts. There is a higher tolerance in these schools for children and teachers to behave in an elitist and mean-spirited fashion during their struggle to increase social status and academic reputation. These schools often seem clean, neat, and orderly with well-dressed articulate students and teachers. When you pierce the first layer, however, it becomes clear that many of the children are quite unhappy and the teachers feel constantly devalued and pressured. The pursuit of excellence can become a form of coercion that is presented as achievement and determination on the part of the administration. It is not uncommon for communities to set their schools on pedestals and overvalue their abilities to score in the highest levels measured by the state or the governing body. This illusion of quality schools based solely on academic scores is not unlike the way a community attracts new home buyers. We are not suggesting that schools abandon their goals and aspirations for academic excellence, but when it comes at the expense of human beings, we believe it is necessary to approach these goals differently.

The pursuit of excellence is clearly an undiscussable. Parents who pressure a school to focus solely or unhealthily on academic excellence allow coercion to grow within the school climate. Discussions that challenge the single-minded obsession with achievement are quickly seen as a wish to reduce the quality of academics at the school and all too often the focus shifts away from the real problem: bullying and coercive behaviors.

In the pursuit for excellence, children are sometimes viewed more as machines than as complex humans. Their community and parents become obsessed with pushing them steadily into higher levels of achievement, often forgetting that they are still developing human beings and not simply bags of information waiting to perform on cue. Teachers and parents can both underestimate the impact that the pressure to excel academically places on children. Again, this preoccupation with competition may lead to very unhealthy school climates. Children can become at risk for higher rates of dropping out, substance abuse, and even suicide. An example in a small private school was when a parent unabashedly indicated that his son's B grade led him, the father, to let the boy know that he had shamed the family. In another instance, in a family session following a suicide attempt by a bright but very stressed high school senior, she was angrily confronted by her father and mother regarding her failure to follow house rules. In tears she pleaded that she had gotten 93 percent in a test. Her father said, "And it would have been 98 percent if you done what you were told."

WHY DISCUSS THE UNDISCUSSABLES?

If your school decides to focus on empathy development or another type of character enhancement, but instead obsesses over problems with achievement or a bullying teacher, then any program is you invest in is, unfortunately, guaranteed to fail. Your ability to implement programs that improve the quality of your school requires that all subjects be fair game for discussion. Failure to discuss the undiscussables will absolutely inhibit any program targeted to enhance or to improve your school's climate. There is a strict relationship between what a program *can* do and what it is *allowed* to do, based on the overall openness of the system to reflect on how it manages power and to recognize its own role in the current situation.

School climate is a very difficult factor to address and change since it is an invisible entity. The undiscussables are typically embodied by the power misalignments that exist in the larger social system of the school. Any group charged with improving school climate must be free to explore and to discuss any issue that impacts the school climate, even if it is sensitive or difficult to talk about. A group of teachers and outside volunteers may not feel empowered to reflect on certain issues that affect the school without the support from the top to be able to openly talk about the undiscussables. Sometimes the undiscussable is unchangeable and that must be tolerated and creative alternatives developed. The group should be searching for ways to make these problems addressable in practical ways that stress positive approaches rather than blaming, attacking, and finger pointing. The challenge for your school is to not become trapped in one issue. You must be able to explore undiscussables and try some alternatives designed to shift the current culture away from ignoring an undiscussable.

CHAPTER 8: KEY QUESTIONS

Step 1. Identify: Which of the undiscussables you read about in this chapter apply to your school?

Step 2. Evaluate: Describe the history of activities and interactions between coaches and students in your school. How do these correlate with wins and losses?

Step 3. Act: Plan a meeting with your team in which you will all present thoughts on three undiscussable issues in your school. Accept what you can't change and identify ways to address what you can.

SUMMARY AND REVIEW

This chapter raises some touchy questions. It is difficult to point the finger at a teacher. The overwhelming majority of teachers are not bullies but outstanding role models. When there is an adult who bullies, it is often undiscussable. The best approaches for dealing with adults who bully are informal and come from peers rather than as discipline from above. We review our research into teacher bullying and identify certain patterns of adult bullying that may emerge and ways to deal with them:

- An undiscussable is an issue that is not officially talked about, but which has great impact on the learning climate. The issue, usually about adult bullying, creates group anxiety and often leads to avoidance.
- When adults bully, the abuse of power becomes the social role model for students and has a great impact on the school climate.
- Teachers are prime targets for being victims of bullying by bully administrators, parents, or coaches.
- Teaching has become an even more pressured job. More of what families cannot give to their children becomes the job of the teacher. Teachers are being unfairly evaluated and their jobs threatened if achievement does not go up in standardized testing. This shifts teachers against kids.
- Our research shows a correlation between bullying teachers and the use of student suspensions. We identified two major types of bully teacher:

  1. The sadistic type who openly humiliates children in front of their peers.
  2. The bully–victim type who provokes a negative reaction then attacks using his or her victimization to bully.

- Schools need to be aware of the sexually exploitive teacher who commits a crime against a student. This teacher psychopathology with a student is slow to evolve and often difficult to prevent.

- We suggest the team create a way to discuss the undiscussables in a positive way that strives to help rather than punish bullying adults. Reaching out informally by teacher peers is a very powerful tool.
- Administrators bully actively by attacking teachers, special treatment, and unfair labor practices or passively by doing nothing to address the problem of bullying in the school.
- Bully managers tend to use a punishment-surveillance model that disconnects them from their teachers leaving them feeling abandoned.
- There are two types of bully administrator:

  1. The sadistic type who transfers teachers, assigns unpleasant tasks unfairly, or uses his or her power to humiliate teachers, students, and parents.
  2. The abdicating bystander type who just lets bullying happen at school and does nothing but allow bullies to thrive at all levels.

- Good administrators can be seen running around their schools helping out, not locked in an office chained to paperwork. They value the human connection, which can be seen in the overall climate of the school.
- Bully coaches can impact the athletes, their families, and the whole school by placing competition above healthy child development.
- Bully coaches are full of themselves and see the team as a reflection of their needs. This is a very poor role model for adults to show children at school.
- Bully coaches use the power of inclusion-exclusion (cutting) of players to assert their own authority without regard to the impact of the decision of the athlete and often personalize criticism in front of teammates.
- Bully coaches justify coercion by improperly connecting it to winning.
- Many bullying coaches will knowingly allow bullying on the team as well as bullying off the court or field in school by athletes. This is abdicating bystanding and reinforces athlete bullying.
- Discussing prejudice can become difficult. Prejudice can be looked at in power dynamic terms without pinpointing individuals as prejudiced. Most prejudice is not malignant, but it may become so if left undiscussed.
- Parents can be bullies to teachers, administrators, or coaches. There are two types of parent bully:

  1. The absent parent
  2. The ever present, over involved parent.

- There is a growing trend in suburban U.S. education and some private residential schools in striving for academic achievement at the cost of the child's mental health. We refer to this as a Problem with Excellence. There is high parent pressure; children compete fiercely for social, athletic, and academic honors. Social aggression builds up fast and can spin off into lethal outbursts of violence, but it also contributes to eating disorders, substance abuse, depression, and teen suicide.

- Why discuss the undiscussable? There are three good reasons:

  1. Not talking about it will ruin any program tried to improve school climate.
  2. Undiscussables are often power misalignments.
  3. It allows for informal solutions person-to-person, teacher-to-teacher.

Chapter Nine

Evaluating What We Do

Coauthored by Eric Vernberg, Ph.D.*

What can you do as a way of evaluating what you want to have happen in your school with limited funding and without getting involved in a complex and expensive research protocol? Unfortunately, there is no single method that is ideal. We advocate developing a plan based on local preferences and resources, including at least two of the methods and sources of information suggested here.

School records that should reflect bully victim problems seem intuitively appealing. However, over a period from 1992 to 2007, we found that school records like out-of-school and in-school suspension, truancy, and school attendance are typically of questionable value because of differences from school to school in the recording and reporting of infractions. For example, one of the schools in our Peaceful Schools Project recorded fewer than three disciplinary infractions for the entire school year, whereas another school reported 380, although other sources of information (child self-reports, teacher reports) suggested that similar levels of bullying occurred in the two schools. If school records are to be a source of information, you must be very careful to ensure consistency and accuracy in the way these records are generated. Changes in key personnel, such as administrators or office staff, may affect how records are generated, as may changes in district policies. Simply put, school records are only useful when there is good quality control and consistency across schools and from one year to the next.

In addition to attempting to use school records, we have collected data from a variety of sources in our research, including teacher reports of bullying and victimization, children's self-reports, peer nominations, and observations

*Professor and Associate Director, Clinical Child Psychology Program, University of Kansas, Lawrence

133

of children in the classroom and on the playground. We have also surveyed teachers on their perceptions of the school learning environment and their opinions about the usefulness of bully-victim-bystander programs. Of these measures, peer nominations are likely the least familiar to most readers. For peer nominations, children circled the names of classmates who they saw as being the target or perpetrator of various forms of bullying (e.g., hits, kicks, or punches others; other kids tell rumors about them behind their backs). These "nominations" are pooled across all children in the class, so only children who are identified by several peers as frequent aggressors or victims are considered to have significant involvement as bullies or victims (or both). For teacher reports, the child's primary classroom teacher circled the names of children in her class who were frequently involved in bullying, using the same items as the peer nomination measure.

The advantage of children's self-reports is that they can be gathered quickly for a large number of students and typically do not cause much controversy. Self-reports also allow children to report on events that may not be observed by teachers or classmates and to give information on issues that may be targets of an intervention, such as their attitudes and beliefs about bullying and the reactions of school personnel to bullying. The biggest limitations of self-report concern their accuracy. We know that some children deny being aggressive or being victimized even though their peers or teachers indicate otherwise, and others report being victimized frequently when peers or teachers do not see them that way. However, we also found that children's self-reports of bullying and victimization correlated significantly with teacher reports and peer nominations and were relatively consistent over six-month intervals (indicating adequate test-retest reliability). Thus, children's self-reports are not perfect, but they do tell us something about what is going on at school in terms of their personal experiences with bullying, their personal reactions to and attitudes toward bullying, and their perceptions of adults' responses to bullying. As with other measures, it is important to tell children how their responses will be used. If the purpose is to judge whether an intervention is having an effect, rather than to identify individual children who are having problems with bullying, it is important to collect self-report information in a way that assures the children that their responses will be confidential (only authorized personnel will know the respondent's identity) or anonymous (no one will know the respondent's identity).

The advantage of teacher nominations and surveys of teachers' views toward the school learning climate is ease of administration. The teacher's nominations of bullying and victimization in the classroom can be gathered quickly, typically in less than twenty minutes per class. Surveys on teachers' opinions are similarly brief and require little time to complete. These surveys can give useful information on whether the teachers (and other school staff) see a need for prevention-intervention programs of this sort, whether they find the program to be useful, and whether they are implementing their part of the program. On the limitation side, teachers may not see children in contexts where bullying often occurs (e.g., at recess, when being coached, moving between classes, before and after school) or may not see a very large sample of children's social behavior in schools that are larger and change classes for each subject. We have also found variability between teachers in the proportion of children in their classroom who they identify as bullies or victims. Over a three-year period, some teachers seldom identified any students in their classroom as being aggressive or victimized. Other teachers identified many children, exceeding the number identified by peer nominations or self-reports. Thus, some teachers appear to regularly underreport bully-victim problems whereas others may overreport. With regard to teachers' views of the school learning climate and the usefulness of bully-victim-bystander programs, teachers will understandably be reluctant to give honest answers if their responses are individually identifiable. We recommend that teachers' responses to these surveys be anonymous.

The advantage of peer nominations is that this procedure utilizes information from many respondents, whereas self-reports and teacher reports use only a single respondent. Many researchers consider peer nominations to be the most scientifically rigorous of the methods described in this chapter. However, several issues may make peer nomination procedures difficult to administer and interpret without expert consultation, and the whole idea of obtaining peer nominations is off-putting to many people. A frequent concern is that asking children to make these judgments about peers may cause children who are nominated as bullies or victims to be teased more. Research on this issue suggests this does not happen if the purpose of the nominations is explained well and the results are kept confidential. Parents, teachers, or the children themselves may object to the idea of peer nominations, usually on the grounds that this singles out children. Again, this requires discussion and consensus on what the purpose of peer nominations would be (i.e., to get a good idea of whether bully-victim problems are becoming less frequent following intervention rather than to identify individual children). Finally, peer nominations reflect a child's reputation among their peers. Reputations can be difficult to change, even after a child's behavior changes. In some states peer nomination techniques are illegal. It is worth checking with your local authorities.

Observations of children's behavior in various areas of the school could be useful if the resources are available to do this in a systematic manner. For example, we found that children in schools that implemented our research program, Creating a Peaceful School Learning Environment (CAPSLE) were more engaged in classroom learning activities compared to children in comparison schools. This type of systematic observation is very useful for research studies, but also very labor intensive. In our project, a trained observer coded various indicators of instructional engagement (e.g., on task, not disruptive) for each child on three separate days. We also observed children on the playground at recess. However, we found it difficult to get good inter-rater agreement about whether or not bullying was occurring because many interactions between children were ambiguous and observers could seldom get close enough to hear verbal exchanges without also influencing the children's behavior.

Some age limits also apply. Self-reports and peer nominations are the most useful in children at third grade and above. Under third-grade reading skills make it difficult to obtain reliable information on bullying in a classroom context.

Whatever measures are used, it is extremely helpful if students are tracked over time. We suggest that measures should be gathered at the same time each year, because there typically are differences in responses simply due to the time of year. One strategy that yields useful information is to give measures sometime in the fall, and then again in April or May. This allows school staff to look at children's experiences over the course of the school year. If measures can be given only once a year, we would recommend a springtime administration. We also recommend that the same measures be gathered for all students and teachers in the school system. This allows tracking analyses by schools and grade level over time.

It is extremely useful to compare results for schools that implement the program with other schools in the district that are not using this program. This allows the district to understand whether changes on the measures are related to the intervention itself rather than naturally occurring changes over time. For example, children tend to report less empathy toward targets of bullying, more approval of the use of aggression, and less victimization of themselves as they move into the higher elementary grades and into junior high school. Such findings tend to work against an intervention effect and may exaggerate other effects (e.g., decreased victimization of self), and thus proof of the outcomes needs to be well controlled. Our research suggests that the teachers who buy into the programs also tend to report seeing it as more helpful.

Now what of these varying research findings can be applied in the average nonresearch setting in schools? We think there is enough evidence to suggest that anonymous student and teacher questionnaires are both reliable and valid to assess how much bullying and victimization occurs in schools, without necessarily addressing teacher and peer nominations, school records, or behavioral observation of children in these school settings. Such evaluations, however, need to be done on an at least once yearly basis toward the end of a school year, and before children are involved in final examinations.

What among these various student self-report questionnaire approaches are most useful? There are a variety of questionnaires not dissimilar to patient satisfaction surveys often used by hospitals to assess whether a patient has been well treated by staff in the hospital. Such questionnaires are often quite elaborate asking children for the varying views of their satisfaction with the school environment. We recommend against such surveys because, as the Columbine situation indicated, it only takes one or two children to bring a school down. So if even 99 percent of your children report outstanding satisfaction for the environment, the 1 percent that do not can cause an enormous amount of trouble. We have concluded that is much better to ask directly for the behavioral observations of bullying including three prime issues. First, you have to directly ask about:

• Humiliating coerciveness,
• Social isolation, and
• Legitimization of aggression by authorities.

Such questionnaires should ask, what happened to you? What you did about it? What happens when a student gets bullied or picked on? For example, how did the adults respond? How do helpful bystanders respond? How do bully-victim-bystanders respond? Such questionnaires also need to look at the role aggression plays in how children feel they can solve their interpersonal problems. How do they manage risk behaviors, like weapons, fights, alcohol, cigarettes, drugs, unprotected sex, and suicide? How do they handle harassment and intolerance, particularly in relation to race, religion, sexual orientation, wealth, and clothing? A set of questions should be asked about how they relate to each other, what friends are like, do they get into trouble, substance abuse, fights, and extracurricular activities. That is, measures of the degree to which the environment is relationship or mentalizing oriented, with an emphasis on empathy and reflectiveness rather than reactive power based interactions.

Schools that are unsure about themselves tend to choose satisfaction survey instruments. Schools in less denial will choose direct questioning. For example, it is quite common for elementary age children to have attempted or seriously contemplated suicide, maybe 5 or 10 percent of them. This is often shocking to parents and staff. Children will admit to such behavior anonymously but will not speak about it directly to adults. Asking direct questions, although full of difficulties in terms of how the child interprets the questions, will provide data that should first be discussed with the principal before making it available to parents, teachers, and students.

Our experiences suggested that such a questionnaire could be administered in one school period, once a year, supervised by teachers who may have to read out the questions and troubleshoot problems. There is also a need for a questionnaire about teacher satisfaction with the environment; such a questionnaire would cover issues like how positive the learning environment appears to teachers, including the physical plant; whether the teacher feels safe and supported; enthusiasm about teaching; attention to problems by administrative staff; incidents and discipline. Such a questionnaire should assess how teachers see the antibullying program that is currently being administered. The questionnaire would only take ten or fifteen minutes. Results can be made available to schools with inexpensive and useful power point presentations well within the possible budget of even a quite poor school.

There are many questionnaires including instruments by luminaries in the field like Dan Olweus from Norway, Peter Smith in the United Kingdom, and Ken Rigby in Australia and New Zealand, that your science advisors should review. Our questionnaires are appended, but we suggest that you contact us before using them to gain access to our very large database, comparing student responses in the United States and countries beyond. We also include a brief survey to find out where bullying happens. Such data will be valued by all personnel, but especially school security.

GENERAL CLIMATE CHECKLIST

Listed below is a set of general questions that we have used in an initial assessment of a school. They are helpful for consultants as well as for self-reflection. These are questions that the team could apportion to members and ask as they are forming into a cohesive whole.

Pre-School Elementary

1. What makes girls/boys popular at your school?

2. What is your reaction to seeing a fight? Do you like it or are you so frightened that you can't do anything?

3. Do you see certain other children frequently picked on or left out? What happens to them? What can a student do about it? Have you ever done something about it?

4. What individuals or groups bully kids?

5. Who is the scariest kid at your school and why?

6. How does your school tell you how to handle bullies?

7. If a child looks strange or is very quiet, do other students at your school reach out to him or her or is the student teased, excluded, or ignored?

8. Do you ever not want to go to school because you know you are going to be picked on?

Middle/High School

1. Do teachers appear intimidated at your school?

2. Are there teachers or counselors you can speak to about these problems?

3. What is security like at your school?

4. Have you ever reported a student being bullied? What happened?

5. What does your school tell you about how to handle bullying or what to do if you hear someone threatening to kill or hurt somebody?

6. Which groups or cliques can you clearly identify in your school? Is one group dominant?

7. Are there racial/ethnic groups that control the school?

8. Are there gangs in your school?

9. Do young people plan fights during the day and talk about who will win and when and where they will fight?

TEACHER QUESTIONNAIRE*

Please mark the categories that describe your role in the school:

Staff position ❑ Certified teacher ❑ Noncertified support staff ❑ other ❑ Grade: primary ❑ secondary ❑

Instructions: This questionnaire contains four sections with questions about general school environment, your safety at school, discipline techniques, and influences on student behavior. For each section, please circle the number that most closely resembles how you feel about each item.

---

*Parts 3, 4, and 5 were devised by Eric Vernberg, Bridget Biggs, Stuart Twemlow, and Peter Fonagy and are reproduced by permission of the authors.

Part 1—Positive Learning Environment

1 = Strongly agree, 2 = Agree, 3 = Undecided,
4 = Disagree, 5 = Strongly disagree

1. People in my school are willing to listen
   to the ideas and feelings of others,
   even when they disagree.   1   2   3   4   5

2. Students cut a lot of classes.   1   2   3   4   5

3. Vandalism is a problem in my school.   1   2   3   4   5

4. Teachers know and treat students as individuals.   1   2   3   4   5

5. I would transfer to another school if I could.   1   2   3   4   5

6. Drug and alcohol abuse are problems in school.   1   2   3   4   5

7. My principal is an effective disciplinarian.   1   2   3   4   5

8. Discipline is fair and related to violations of
   agreed-upon rules.   1   2   3   4   5

9. Stealing is a problem at this school.   1   2   3   4   5

10. A positive feeling permeates this school.   1   2   3   4   5

11. I am satisfied with the variety of
    extracurricular activities at this school.   1   2   3   4   5

12. Teachers and staff members take a real interest
    in their students' future.   1   2   3   4   5

13. I enjoy working at this school.   1   2   3   4   5

14. Student behavior is generally positive
    at my school.   1   2   3   4   5

15. Students can count on staff members to listen
    to their side of the story and be fair.   1   2   3   4   5

16. Students in my school abide by school rules.   1   2   3   4   5

17. My school building is neat, bright, clean,
    and comfortable.   1   2   3   4   5

18. Staff and students do not view security
    as an issue in my school.   1   2   3   4   5

19. This school makes students enthusiastic
    about learning.   1   2   3   4   5

20. I feel there are procedures open to me to go
to a higher authority if a decision has been
made that seems unfair.   1   2   3   4   5

21. The physical condition of my school is
generally pleasant and well-kept.   1   2   3   4   5

22. Problems in this school are recognized
and worked on.   1   2   3   4   5

Part 2—Teacher Safety at School

1 = Never, 2 = Once or twice, 3 = Three to five,
4 = Six to ten, 5 = More than ten times

1. A student threatened to hurt me.   1   2   3   4   5

2. A student threatened me with a weapon.   1   2   3   4   5

3. A student cursed at me or called me
a derogatory name.   1   2   3   4   5

4. Students spread rumors about me.   1   2   3   4   5

5. A student touched me in an inappropriate way.   1   2   3   4   5

6. I confiscated a weapon from a student.   1   2   3   4   5

7. A student pushed or shoved me.   1   2   3   4   5

8. A student kicked, punched, slapped, or bit me.   1   2   3   4   5

9. A student sexually assaulted me.   1   2   3   4   5

10. A student tried to intimidate me.   1   2   3   4   5

11. A group of students tried to intimidate me.   1   2   3   4   5

12. I feel safe on the school grounds.   1   2   3   4   5

Part 3—Classroom Discipline

1 = Not effective at all, 2 = A little effective, 3 = Somewhat effective,
4 = Quite Effective, 5 = Most effective

1. Using group comments (e.g., stating that there
is talking instead of pointing out who is talking
and asking them to stop)   1   2   3   4   5

2. Pointing out disruptive behavior of specific
   students in front of the class   1   2   3   4   5

3. Recognizing "good" behavior of the class
   in general (e.g., saying that you like how
   hard students are working at their desks)   1   2   3   4   5

4. Recognizing "good" behavior of specific
   individuals   1   2   3   4   5

5. Pointing out how behaviors affect others' well-
   being or their ability to learn (e.g., stating that
   talking keeps others from hearing the teacher)   1   2   3   4   5

6. Removing privileges (e.g., recess) for children
   who misbehave   1   2   3   4   5

7. Asking students to help establish their own
   classroom rules or goals and having them
   evaluate how they are doing on those rules
   or goals   1   2   3   4   5

Part 4—Influences on Student Behavior

1 = Not influential, 2 = A little influential, 3 = Somewhat influential,
4 = Quite influential, 5 = Most influential

1. In your opinion, how influential are teachers for
   how students behave in the classroom?   1   2   3   4   5

2. In your opinion, how influential are teachers for
   how well students get along with each other?   1   2   3   4   5

3. In your opinion, how influential are
   children's peer relationships to their
   academic performance?   1   2   3   4   5

Part 5—Use and Perceptions of Antibullying Program

Please answer part 5 *only* if you are a classroom teacher

1. How helpful do you find the program was in managing classroom behavior?

Not at all helpful	*A little helpful*	Somewhat helpful	*Generally helpful*	Greatly helpful

2. How helpful do you find the program in promoting positive relationships among students?

Not at all helpful	*A little helpful*	Somewhat helpful	*Generally helpful*	Greatly helpful

3. Not including reflection time, how often do you use program terminology or concepts to address disruptive behavior?

Rarely/ Never	*Few times/ month*	Few times/ week	*Almost daily*	1–2 times/ day	*3+ times/ day*

4. Not including reflection time, how often do you use program terminology or concepts to recognize positive, prosocial behavior?

Rarely/ Never	*Few times/ month*	Few times/ week	*Almost daily*	1–2 times/ day	*3+ times/ day*

7. In your opinion, how is the program and academics related?

   a. The program interferes with teaching.
   b. The program helps students' relationships but does not help with academics.
   c. Once the program gets rolling, it can help academics.
   d. The program has given me more instructional time so students are learning more.

Violence Audit

SECTION 1 (51 questions)*

Part 1—What Happened to You?

Circle the number to show how other students bullied or picked on you. Tell about things that happened during the past 3 months.

1 = Never, 2 = Once or twice, 3 = A few times, 4 = About once a week, 5 = A few times a week

1. A student teased me in a mean way.	1	2	3	4	5
2. A student said he or she was going to hurt me or beat me up.	1	2	3	4	5
3. A student ignored me on purpose to hurt my feelings.	1	2	3	4	5

---

*This questionnaire was devised by Eric Vernberg, Stuart Twemlow, Peter Fonagy, and Anne Jacobs and is reproduced by permission of the authors.

4. A student told lies about me so other students
   would not like me.   1   2   3   4   5

5. A student hit, kicked, or pushed me in a
   mean way.   1   2   3   4   5

6. A student grabbed, held, or touched me in a way
   I didn't like.   1   2   3   4   5

7. Some students left me out of things just to be
   mean to me.   1   2   3   4   5

8. A student chased me like he or she was really
   trying to hurt me.   1   2   3   4   5

9. Some students "ganged up" against me and were
   mean to me.   1   2   3   4   5

Part 2—What You Did

Circle the number to show how often you bullied or picked on another student
at school. Tell about things that happened during the past 3 months.

1 = Never, 2 = Once or twice, 3 = A few times, 4 = About once a week,
5 = A few times a week

1. I teased or made fun of a student in a mean way.   1   2   3   4   5

2. I threatened to hurt or beat up another student.   1   2   3   4   5

3. I ignored another student just to hurt his or
   her feelings.   1   2   3   4   5

4. I told lies about another student so other
   students would not like him or her.   1   2   3   4   5

5. I hit, kicked, or pushed another student in a
   mean way.   1   2   3   4   5

6. I grabbed, held, or touched another student
   in a way he or she didn't like.   1   2   3   4   5

7. I helped leave a student out of things just
   to be mean to him or her.   1   2   3   4   5

8. I chased a student to try to hurt him or her.   1   2   3   4   5

9. Some students and I "ganged up" and were
   mean to another student.   1   2   3   4   5

Part 3—What Happens When a Student Gets Bullied or Picked On?

Circle the number to show what you think happens when a student gets bullied or picked on at school. Tell about how things have happened during the past 3 months.

1 = Almost never, 2 = Sometimes, 3 = Most times, 4 = Always

Adult Responses

1. Teachers here help students solve their problems by talking things out.	1	2	3	4	5
2. Teachers understand what is going on with the students.	1	2	3	4	5
3. Teachers are usually in a good mood when they talk with students.	1	2	3	4	5
4. Teachers listen to the student's side of the story.	1	2	3	4	5
5. The school rules are fair.	1	2	3	4	5

Helping Bystander

1. I feel upset when I see a student left out of things on purpose.	1	2	3	4	5
2. I feel bad when I see a student get bullied or picked on.	1	2	3	4	5
3. I try to stop it when I see a student get bullied or picked on.	1	2	3	4	5
4. It bothers me a lot to see a student get bullied or picked on.	1	2	3	4	5
5. I tell a teacher when I see a student get bullied or picked on.	1	2	3	4	5

Aggressive Bystander

1. I join in or cheer when I see a student get bullied or picked on.	1	2	3	4	5

2. I think it is exciting to watch a student get
    picked on or beat up.   1   2   3   4   5

3. I usually take the bully's side when I see a
    student get bullied.   1   2   3   4   5

4. I join in on fights or bullying after they
    have started.   1   2   3   4   5

5. It is fun to jump in a fight and help pick
    on a student.   1   2   3   4   5

Victim Bystander

1. I feel too scared to help when I see a student
    get bullied or picked on.   1   2   3   4   5

2. I join in on bullying because I am afraid of
    what the bully might do to me.   1   2   3   4   5

3. I felt guilty after being pressured to join
    in bullying.   1   2   3   4   5

4. I worry that bullies will pick on me if I try
    to help victims of bullying.   1   2   3   4   5

5. It is too hard to stand up to bullies.   1   2   3   4   5

Part 4—What I Think

Circle the number to show how much you agree with each statement.

1 = I don't agree at all, 2 = I agree a little, 3 = I agree a lot,
4 = I completely agree

1. It's okay for students to fight each other.   1   2   3   4   5

2. It's important for students to show they are
    ready to fight anyone who picks on them.   1   2   3   4   5

3. When two students are fighting each other,
    other students should stop them.   1   2   3   4   5

4. Sometimes a student deserves to get pushed
    around by other students.   1   2   3   4   5

5. Bullies get what they want from other students.   1   2   3   4   5

6. Students get respect when they boss other
   students around.   1   2   3   4   5

7. When two students are fighting each other,
   it's okay to cheer for them.   1   2   3   4   5

8. It can make a student feel big and tough
   to be a bully.   1   2   3   4   5

9. Sometimes it's okay to be a bully.   1   2   3   4   5

10. Students can make other students do what
    they want by yelling at them.   1   2   3   4   5

11. Students who get picked on or pushed
    around usually did something to deserve it.   1   2   3   4   5

12. When a student is getting picked on,
    other students should try to stop it.   1   2   3   4   5

13. When two students are fighting,
    it's all right to stand there and watch.   1   2   3   4   5

SECTION 2 (62 questions)

Part 5—Risky Behaviors

Circle the number to how often you did something that might hurt you. Tell
about things that happened during the past 3 months.

1 = Never, 2 = Once or twice, 3 = A few times, 4 = About once a week,
5 = A few times a week

1. I carried a gun, knife or other weapon to school.   1   2   3   4   5

2. I got in a physical fight.   1   2   3   4   5

3. I smoked cigarettes.   1   2   3   4   5

4. I had 5 or more drinks of alcohol in a row,
   that is, within a couple of hours.   1   2   3   4   5

5. I used marijuana.   1   2   3   4   5

6. I used another type of illegal drug, such as coke,
   LSD, PCP, ecstasy, mushrooms, speed, ice,
   heroin, or pills without a doctor's prescription.   1   2   3   4   5

7. I had sex without using a condom.   1   2   3   4   5

8. I thought about hurting myself.   1   2   3   4   5

9. I made a plan to hurt myself.   1   2   3   4   5

10. I tried to hurt myself.   1   2   3   4   5

Part 6—Harassment and Intolerance

Circle the number to show how often students treated each other at school.
Tell about things that happened during the past 3 months.

1 = Almost never, 2 = Sometimes, 3 = Most times, 4 = Always

1. Students bullied other kids because they were
   of a different race.   1   2   3   4   5

2. Students bullied other kids because they looked
   or dressed different.   1   2   3   4   5

3. Students bullied other kids because they thought
   they were gay.   1   2   3   4   5

4. Students bullied other kids because they didn't
   have a lot of money.   1   2   3   4   5

5. Students bullied other kids because they
   belonged to a different religion.   1   2   3   4   5

Part 7—What My Friends Are Like

Think of the four people you know the best and spend the most time with.
Circle the number to show how many of these people fit the descriptions.

1 = None, 2 = One, 3 = Two, 4 = Three, 5 = Four or more

1. Number of your closest friends who go to
   this school.   1   2   3   4   5

2. Number of friends who are liked by teachers.   1   2   3   4   5

3. Number of friends who have been involved
   in school clubs/teams.   1   2   3   4   5

4. Number of friends who could have gotten into trouble with the police for some of the things they've done.   1   2   3   4   5

5. Number of friends who are liked by most other students.   1   2   3   4   5

6. Number of friends who get in trouble with the teachers or principal.   1   2   3   4   5

7. Number of friends who carried a gun, knife, or other weapon to school.   1   2   3   4   5

8. Number of friends who got in a physical fight.   1   2   3   4   5

9. Number of friends who smoked cigarettes.   1   2   3   4   5

10. Number of friends who had 5 or more drinks of alcohol in a row, that is, within a couple of hours.   1   2   3   4   5

11. Number of friends who used marijuana.   1   2   3   4   5

12. Number of friends who used another type of illegal drug, such as coke, LSD, PCP, ecstasy, mushrooms, speed, ice, heroin, or pills without a doctor's prescription.   1   2   3   4   5

13. Number of friends who tried to hurt themselves.   1   2   3   4   5

Part 8—How I Felt

Circle the number to show how often you felt like the statement during the past 3 months.

1 = Never, 2 = Once or twice, 3 = A few times, 4 = About once a week, 5 = A few times a week

1. I felt sad.   1   2   3   4   5

2. I felt lonely.   1   2   3   4   5

3. I felt hopeful about the future.   1   2   3   4   5

4. I had crying spells.   1   2   3   4   5

5. I did not feel like eating.   1   2   3   4   5

6. I enjoyed life.   1   2   3   4   5

7. I wanted my feelings to matter more
   to the people around me.   1   2   3   4   5

Part 9—What My School Is Like

Circle the number to show how much your school is like each statement.

1 = I don't agree at all, 2 = I agree a little, 3 = I agree a lot,
4 = I completely agree

1. I like my school.   1   2   3   4   5

2. It is easy to be myself at school.   1   2   3   4   5

3. My teachers treat me with respect.   1   2   3   4   5

4. I feel in tune with the people around me
   at school.   1   2   3   4   5

5. I feel the teachers know me well at school.   1   2   3   4   5

6. No one really knows me well at school.   1   2   3   4   5

7. I feel like I belong or fit in at school.   1   2   3   4   5

8. Students in my school are very competitive
   in grades.   1   2   3   4   5

9. Students in my school are very competitive
   in sports or other after-school activities.   1   2   3   4   5

10. I feel a lot of pressure to make good grades.   1   2   3   4   5

11. I often feel I am lost among all the other
    students.   1   2   3   4   5

12. I feel a lot of pressure to do well at sports
    or other after-school activities.   1   2   3   4   5

13. I feel that my teacher understands me.   1   2   3   4   5

14. If you are not the best at something, you do
    not matter much at school.   1   2   3   4   5

15. I wish I could go to another school.   1   2   3   4   5

Part 10—Parental Support of School

Circle the number that best describes how your parents fit with each statement.

1 = I don't agree at all, 2 = I agree a little, 3 = I agree a lot,
4 = I completely agree

1. My parents care about what happens at school.   1   2   3   4   5

2. My parents go to school meetings or other
   school activities.   1   2   3   4   5

3. My parents support me in my school activities.   1   2   3   4   5

4. My parents know a lot about what I do
   at school.   1   2   3   4   5

5. My parents ask me about my school day.   1   2   3   4   5

Part 11—What Dating Is Like

Circle the number to show how much you agree with each statement.

1 = I don't agree at all, 2 = I agree a little, 3 = I agree a lot,
4 = I completely agree

1. Some girls ask for trouble by the way they
   dress or act.   1   2   3   4   5

2. Girls like guys who are tough or macho.   1   2   3   4   5

3. Girls are pressured into doing things they
   do not want to do.   1   2   3   4   5

4. Guys are pressured into doing things they
   do not want to do.   1   2   3   4   5

5. Guys do not like girls who speak their mind.   1   2   3   4   5

6. It is easy to set limits on what you will or
   won't do on dates.   1   2   3   4   5

7. If someone takes you out on a date, they will
   usually expect something sexual in return.   1   2   3   4   5

Where Things Happen*

1. **Gender: Circle one: Boy   Girl**

2. **Grade: Circle one: 7th   8th   9th**

Directions. Please show how often you have seen a student bullied or picked on by another student in each of the following places. Circle the words that show how often you saw these types of actions happen in each place **since this school year began.**

1. **I saw a student get bullied in the restroom while classes were meeting.**
   never   once or twice   a few times   about once   a few times
                                               a week   a week

2. **I saw a student get bullied in the restroom between classes.**
   never   once or twice   a few times   about once   a few times
                                               a week   a week

3. **I saw a student get bullied in the halls between classes.**
   never   once or twice   a few times   about once   a few times
                                               a week   a week

4. **I saw a student get bullied in the halls while classes were meeting.**
   never   once or twice   a few times   about once   a few times
                                               a week   a week

5. **I saw a student get bullied in the halls before school.**
   never   once or twice   a few times   about once   a few times
                                               a week   a week

6. **I saw a student get bullied in the halls after school.**
   never   once or twice   a few times   about once   a few times
                                               a week   a week

7. **I saw a student get bullied on the school bus (leave blank if you do not ride a bus).**
   never   once or twice   a few times   about once   a few times
                                               a week   a week

---

*Reproduced with permission of Eric Vernberg.

8. **I saw a student get bullied on the school grounds before school.**

    never   once or twice   a few times   about once   a few times
    a week   a week

9. **I saw a student get bullied on the school grounds after school.**

    never   once or twice   a few times   about once   a few times
    a week   a week

10. **I saw a student get bullied in the classroom during class.**

    never   once or twice   a few times   about once   a few times
    a week   a week

11. **I saw a student get bullied on the way to school in the morning.**

    never   once or twice   a few times   about once   a few times
    a week   a week

12. **I saw a student get bullied on the way home from school.**

    never   once or twice   a few times   about once   a few times
    a week   a week

13. **I saw a student get bullied while changing for gym class (P.E.).**

    never   once or twice   a few times   about once   a few times
    a week   a week

14. **Please write down any other places where you saw a student get bullied:**

CHAPTER 9: KEY QUESTIONS

Step 1. Identify: What kind of questionnaire would be most helpful for your school?

Step 2. Evaluate: What do the results of the questionnaires suggest to you? Based on those results, what do you think the top priorities are for your school?

Step 3. Act: Suggest a schedule for administering questionnaires in your school. Remember, it should happen once a year, near the end of the school term, but not during finals week or at some time when students will be distracted with other events.

Chapter Ten

Community and Institutional Resources

Including community and informational resources as a chapter necessary to ensure a peaceful school climate makes it obvious that we consider this section a critical step. First of all, what is a resource? A resource is something you could use to provide the knowledge about what is necessary to make your school antibullying program work. Without such knowledge, it not only might be difficult to get the program to work but also what you do would not take advantage of modern research findings. Digging into the vast resources available in both the literature on the Internet and also looking around your community and asking the right people the right questions could easily be a task for beginning team building. In chapter 7 details were given on how to build a team and how to lead it. As the team is forming, checking resources might be a good way to get team members fired up over the issues and begin the process of learning to work collaboratively and to share information noncompetitively. It also might help define their roles based in systematic information rather than a haphazard way. The formal process for improving one's knowledge is available primarily through the individual work of people who are willing to take the trouble to collect resources and summarize them for other team members, on a task for which they feel passion.

An important step in making use of the resources is evaluating validity, reliability, and practicality. It is quite helpful for such a person to have a system to evaluate the resource in place even before starting the work. The following steps could be taken in evaluating any resource either informational, obtained from the Internet, read in a book or scientific paper, or in the media:

1. What is the source of the information? Does it come from an opinion that is weak in scientific merit, or does it come from an experimental trial of an experimental hypothesis. The relative statistical strength of scientific work could be roughly appraised as follows, listed from most valid to least valid.

a. Randomized controlled blinded trial
b. Randomized controlled nonblinded trial
c. Uncontrolled group pre-post outcome study
d. Single case study, time series design
e. Retrospective statistical study of cases grouped according to experimentally derived hypotheses
f. Systematic case study with a preliminary concept of what is being studied in mind
g. Anecdotal case study

Items a and b suggest strong studies; c, d, e could be recommended with moderate confidence; and f and g have value in individual circumstances, or when no other studies are available. Many search engines now have scientific papers available online. Calling a university library is a useful first step.

Once you have reached the level of deciding on a program for the school will be a good place to use the outside consultant who will presumably have knowledge of statistics and design to make sure that what you select has been subject to adequate scientific validation and is reliable.

2. Spotting the quick fix program. During your assessment be aware that programs suggesting six or ten sessions added to the curriculum, however well designed and however much they seem like common sense, are unlikely to be effective, a point I think we've made rather clearly in this book. Besides, curriculum add-ons are not liked by teachers and would have to be very valid and reliable.

3. Dealing with the bullies and victims versus climate. One way of assessing a resource is whether or not a school climate is being used as the primary intervention, that is, the intervention is focused on what the school needs as a whole. This should be compared to programs that emphasized dealing with bullying and victimization and the victim's response to such targeting as a function of abnormal or medically disturbed people (a treatment-based program). It should be quite clear that there are children who have medical problems that will make them predisposed to be either bullies (antisocial traits including Conduct Disorder and Oppositional Defiant Disorder), or victims, including predisposition to depression, preexisting sexual and physical trauma, and a variety of other environmental factors, suggests that sometimes these children do need medical services. However, they are rarely helped by selecting them out as bullies and victims because by that time whatever trauma they carry into the school from their prior existence is magnified and made much more difficult by the social process of bullying and victimization that you are trying to stop. There is a recent publication by the Centers for Disease Control showing that climate programs are preferable to those that intervene with individual children.[1] This article is worth reading although it is published as a special report rather than a scientifically peer reviewed article.

WHAT ARE THE TYPES OF RESOURCES AVAILABLE?

Obviously Web sites and a variety of other Internet resources are important, as are books and papers with varying degrees of reliability and validity. Generally speaking, books published by well-known booksellers have been subjected to relatively informal peer review. Scientific papers have been subjected to more stringent peer review but vary in their circulation and a degree to which the scientific world sees them as high-quality scientific journals. Conferring with a university consultant can determine how journals are ranked (impact factor), if this much detail is needed.

Informational Resources

Web Sites

www.backoffbully.com

This is a Web site created by the authors of this book that contains a lot of information about what they do and available scientific papers written on various trials of approaches to school climate problems that are available under the publications button. The randomized control trial manual and the school psychiatric consultation manual is also available under the peaceful schools button.

http://brnet.unl.edu

The Bullying Research Network is a virtual clearinghouse designed to bring together nationally and internationally known researchers in the area of bullying prevention and intervention research; to conduct interdisciplinary research related to bullying and aggression; and to establish an international research network for advances in evidence-based prevention and intervention initiatives in bullying prevention and intervention efforts. We highly recommend it.

www.targetbully.com

This Web site includes an evidence-based approach to the ecology of the disturbed climate. May helpful options are made available. We know the people including Professor Susan Swearer and highly recommend them.

www.csee.net

The Center for Social and Emotional Education is large and, although originating to assist programs in New York State, has now an international reputation with multiple interactions often involving teachers who are asking for information. The Web site also includes up-to-date scientific information and makes available questionnaires to assess school climate coordinated by Jon Cohen Ph.D, a highly recommended colleague.

http://www.colorado.edu/cspv/blueprints/matrix/overview.html

Blueprints provide a listing of promising programs with a link to a page that explains each program in greater detail. Blueprints Web site is considered as the gold standard for scientifically approved programs but by no means contains all the available and useful programs that have less scientific experimental information available. Table 10.1 lists some of the selected blueprint programs compared to ours.

Programs that may be useful for administrators, parents, and concerned lay people:

- Sites that deal specifically with cyber bullying strategies and resources including http://wiredsafety.org and http://www.csriu.org/about/bio.html.
- Cyber bullying is an area needing special assessment, but it is in the early stages of providing valuable and reliable measurement strategies.[2] Our group is also developing a cyber bullying questionnaire that is posted on www.backoffbully.com.
- The FBI and Secret Service have taken a great deal of interest stimulated by the adolescent homicides. The FBI published a manual, *The School Shooter: A Threat Assessment Perspective*, to which the authors of this book contributed, that is available to review at http://www.fbi.gov/publications/school/school2.pdf.

The Secret Service has done a great deal of work using an individual case management approach to threat assessment rather than profiling. They have produced a useful although complicated threat assessment program for schools and are available to teach that program, for little or no cost except expenses. The Secret Service Web site is www.secretservice.gov. Click Final Report National Safe Schools Initiative.

We have included below a list that summarizes a threat assessment approach combining the FBI and Secret Service to give a decision tree that might be helpful if your school considers the need for a threat assessment program as part of their school antibullying and antiviolence initiative (see table 10.2 here).

Books and Manuals

These resource suggestions are very broadly based. Some of the books, like Gilligan, give a conceptual background; others, like Horne, are manuals; and some, like Espelage and Swearer, give readable research findings.

Cohen, J. (2001). *Caring Classrooms/Intelligent Schools*. New York: Columbia Teachers Press.

Table 10.1. Six Programs with Promising Outcomes

Name	Target Group	Concept	Method	Design	Outcomes	References
PATHS*	Elementary: regular, special needs, and deaf	Promote social and emotional competence	Classroom curriculum	Field trials	Improved self-control, empathy, frustration, tolerance, conduct, problems, and psychiatric symptoms	Greenberg, Kusche & Mihalic (1998)
Incredible Years Series*	Preschool to 3rd grade	Addresses risk factors for conduct disorders	Classroom curriculum: teacher, child, and parent training	Several randomized trials	Decreased parental depression, conduct problems with parents, peer aggression in classroom, conduct problems at home and school	Webster-Stratton, Mihalic, Fagan, Arnold, Taylor, and Tingly (2001)
Project Toward No Drug Abuse*	14–19 year olds	Drug education, stress control, negative and positive thought pattern control, weapons carrying	Interactive 12-session curriculum	Controlled field trials	22–26% reduction in drug and cigarette use, 25% reduction in weapons carrying	Sussman, Dent & Stacy (2002)

(continues)

Table 10.1. (*continued*)

Name	Target Group	Concept	Method	Design	Outcomes	References
Bullying Prevention Program*	Elementary to junior high	School-wide classroom and individual discussion. No tolerance approach to bullying	Systemic intervention	Widespread uncontrolled field trials	Students report decreased victimization, antisocial behaviors, and increased classroom order	Olweus, Limber & Mihalic (1999)
Multi Systemic Therapy*	12–17 year olds	At risk and chronic, violent, and substance abusing offenders	Home-based delivery of family therapy, parent training, and CBT	Multiple controlled trials, cost, effectiveness, comparisons	Decrease of 25–75% in rearrest and symptomatic behavior. Increase in family functioning, cost saving	Henggler, Mihalic, Rone, Thomas & Timmons-Mitchell (1998)
Peaceful Schools Project	K–5	Positive climate, classroom management, physical and social skills training to manage bully-victim-bystander relationship, parent component	Systemic social systems approach	Randomized controlled trial	Increased: helpfulness, academic performance. Decreased: victimization, disciplinary problems	Twemlow, Fonagy, Sacco, Gies, Evans, Ewbanks (2001)** Twemlow, Sacco & Twemlow (1999)**

*Blueprint Model Program
**Available at www.backoffbully.com.

Table 10.2.   Threat and Risk Decision Making

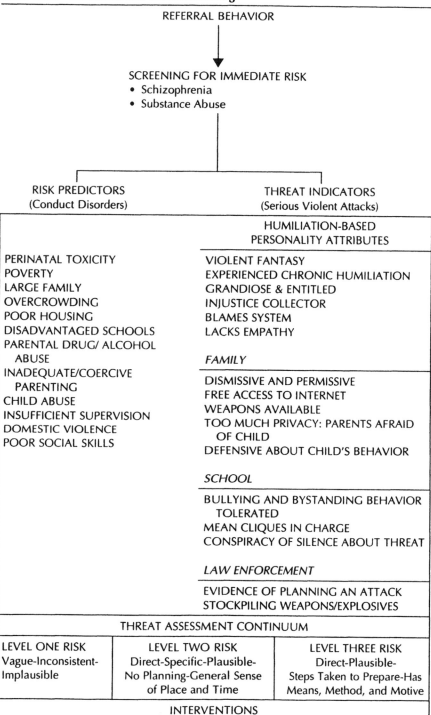

REFERRAL BEHAVIOR

SCREENING FOR IMMEDIATE RISK
- Schizophrenia
- Substance Abuse

RISK PREDICTORS (Conduct Disorders)	THREAT INDICATORS (Serious Violent Attacks)	
	HUMILIATION-BASED PERSONALITY ATTRIBUTES	
PERINATAL TOXICITY POVERTY LARGE FAMILY OVERCROWDING POOR HOUSING DISADVANTAGED SCHOOLS PARENTAL DRUG/ ALCOHOL ABUSE INADEQUATE/COERCIVE PARENTING CHILD ABUSE INSUFFICIENT SUPERVISION DOMESTIC VIOLENCE POOR SOCIAL SKILLS	VIOLENT FANTASY EXPERIENCED CHRONIC HUMILIATION GRANDIOSE & ENTITLED INJUSTICE COLLECTOR BLAMES SYSTEM LACKS EMPATHY *FAMILY*	
	DISMISSIVE AND PERMISSIVE FREE ACCESS TO INTERNET WEAPONS AVAILABLE TOO MUCH PRIVACY: PARENTS AFRAID OF CHILD DEFENSIVE ABOUT CHILD'S BEHAVIOR *SCHOOL*	
	BULLYING AND BYSTANDING BEHAVIOR TOLERATED MEAN CLIQUES IN CHARGE CONSPIRACY OF SILENCE ABOUT THREAT *LAW ENFORCEMENT*	
	EVIDENCE OF PLANNING AN ATTACK STOCKPILING WEAPONS/EXPLOSIVES	
THREAT ASSESSMENT CONTINUUM		
LEVEL ONE RISK Vague-Inconsistent-Implausible	LEVEL TWO RISK Direct-Specific-Plausible-No Planning-General Sense of Place and Time	LEVEL THREE RISK Direct-Plausible-Steps Taken to Prepare-Has Means, Method, and Motive
INTERVENTIONS		

Devine, J. (1996). *Maximum Security: The Culture of Violence in Inner-City Schools.* Chicago: University of Chicago Press.

Espelage, D., and Swearer, S. (2004). *Bullying in American Schools: A Social-Ecological Perspective on Prevention and Intervention.* New York: Lawrence Erlbaum Associates.

Garbarino, J. (1999). *Lost Boys.* New York: Free Press.

Gilligan, J. (1996). *Violence: Reflections on a National Epidemic.* New York: Vintage Books.

Gilligan, J. (2001). *Preventing Violence.* New York: Thames and Hudson.

Horne, A., Bartolomucci, C., and Newman-Carlson, D. (2003). *Bully Busters: A Teachers Manual, Grades K–5.* Champaign, IL: Research Press.

Newman, D., Horne, A., and Bartolomucci, C. (2000). *Bully Busters: A Teachers Manual, Grades 6–8.* Champaign, IL: Research Press.

Olweus, D. (1993). *Bullying at School: What We Know and What We Can Do About It.* Oxford, UK: Blackwell.

Orpinas, P., and Horne, A. (2006). *Bullying Prevention: Creating a Positive School Climate and Developing Social Competence.* Washington, DC: American Psychological Association.

Community Resources

It is known that more involvement of the community will assure the greater success of any school climate program. One could paraphrase the well-known proverb into "It takes a whole village to raise a school." Individuals in the school will have a great deal of trouble if they work against the resistant surrounding environment. A great deal of resistance in the environment, besides reflecting the role of abdicating bystanders, are also a group of people who simply don't know the school needs help, and thus an active team reaching out to them may produce a result that is quite surprisingly helpful.

Successful school programs need to connect to the community and draw from it resources needed to sustain the team as well as its projects, and to familiarize community groups and individuals with the school as an involved community member. The community has many of the ingredients to make a good program run from year to year, but it also needs help from the schools. In one Midwestern school, community cleanup projects, helping the elderly with home maintenance and raking leaves, and so on was regular and appreciated.

The three main types of resources are time, money, and materials. These can be established formally as in a letter of agreement or informally through donations. The resources can be obtained through direct application such as in grants or subsidies or through more informal channels such as personal reaching out.

Community resources can liven up the projects that the team designs. Previously we described a poster competition in which a local bank donated fifty dollars. The bank presented the check at the school committee meeting and received a nice photograph in the local newspaper. Everybody won. The project had buy in from the teachers, who sent home the projects for the parents and students. The outside prizes offered local business a chance to show their community investment and receive some free advertising.

TIME

Projects will require the donation of time from a wide range of community members. Again, these vary from formal to informal, structured to "as needed," long or short term. One example of the long-term, formal contribution of time is the business partnership with schools model. In one city, a large insurance company formally arranged for senior management to donate work time to mentoring at the school. These mentors were directed by the counseling department and used personal mentors for high-risk youth about to drop out of junior high school. This program was a resounding success. The business mentors were challenged by the extreme circumstances facing the students they were mentoring. This investment of altruism was good for the student and the mentor. The company demonstrated its commitment to the community. Everybody won.

Schools need a formal arrangement with public safety departments, even if situated in nonviolent parts of town. Often, schools call the police only when trouble happens. The climate teams need at least one public safety volunteer. This volunteer could be appointed to take several hours from his or her work day to sit with the climate team and plan prevention efforts. Most courts, probation departments, and police and fire departments would gladly dispatch a prevention officer for work in a school. Public safety and school partnerships are very attractive program models for small grants.

The community is also rich in resources from its retired population. Many highly skilled retirees from a broad range of professions are willing to donate small amounts of time as a public service and a diversion from straight retirement. In one program in the Midwest, a formal program was developed to recruit retired grandparents to supervise playground activities. This may be especially true with high-risk, inner-city juveniles who would modulate their aggression in the presence of a respected grandparent figure. Here again, simplicity is the key. The outside change agent in the team must be aware of the need to screen volunteers closely and work with the school human resources division to screen for past criminal activity or child abuse–related concerns.

We came to understand this mentoring phenomenon when we began working in a Jamaican secondary school. A police officer was assigned to this school and sought our consultation. We suggested a mentoring program and a life skills class. The police officer took on a mythical presence at the school. The kids referred to him as Bruno, or a fierce junkyard dog present for protection. We expanded this Bruno idea in our programs to apply to any volunteer. "Bruno" became another word for "mentor" and "volunteer" within the school and he often grows to be quite fiercely committed to the school. The presence of this Bruno becomes part of the climate and can have a very profound impact on the overall feeling of safety.

Some schools may have a high need for such a Bruno presence. Populations with low paternal involvement are ideal for this approach. This effect may be different in populations with higher social economic status and two-parent families. These schools may have the material resources but struggle with social aggression. The kids have a lot and sometimes get into trouble due to a lack of purpose. In this situation, programs that connect these schools to less-privileged schools can create a sense of meaning. In a current experiment with a school in Jamaica, the Jamaican school partnered with a Seattle school. The U.S. school donated computers and visited the school in Jamaica. Parents, students, and teachers enjoyed Jamaica and also visited the school, creating personal bonds between the U.S. children and Jamaican students, although the computers are idle through lack of Internet connection. Both benefited! Future trips are planned and the Jamaican students keep in touch with the U.S. students.

Celebrity always helps keep a project going in a school. Some communities are lucky and have direct access to really famous people. Springfield, Massachusetts, was adopted by Bill Cosby who donated his time to get involved in supporting local violence prevention efforts within minority communities. Climate teams can brainstorm and make a list of celebrities who could be asked to host or appear in support of a certain initiate. Having a sports or media personality present an award always brings in parents, media, and community support. It is imperative to keep the requests focused and reasonable. Celebrity endorsement can make a program stand out and increases the overall value of the program in the community's eyes. This creates a positive circle of altruism.

Local vocational talent is also available to assist in climate projects. Construction companies could donate expertise to build sandboxes or a gate. Media outlets could help students develop a television ad about making friends and not bullying. Newspapers and city-owned TV could run advice and tip columns and programs focusing on school issues. Editors could be recruited to work with existing school newspapers to include issues relating to safety and positive school climate. Local artisans could be recruited to create murals that foster positive climate. Each community has a reserve of unused talent that could be used by climate teams to improve school climate. Recruiting volunteer adults into these less defined roles is anxiety provoking initially. Sleight of hand is a wonderful talent to entertain and distract children from conflict.

Coaches are often teachers. College coaches could be recruited to assist in developing character-building programs for high school athletes. Coaches and teachers are now being pressured to deliver achievement only. This myopic focus on pure competition and winning at all costs can lead to a problem with excellence mentioned in an earlier chapter. Athletes could use their social status to help build positive school climates rather than be part of the problem of bullying and social aggression. Building this into the routines of athletic programs will institutionalize the task, so that it becomes just the way the school is.

Climate teams are urged to do a community inventory of potential resources that could fit into a project that is being planned. The power of these climate campaigns lies in their simplicity. The point is to increase mentalizing around issues of coercive power dynamics. The best programs do small projects three to four times a year, year after year. Whether the project is a publicized debate about bullying between students with grand prizes or a grandfather mentor in a disadvantaged school, the goal is the same: reducing needless aggression.

MONEY AND MATERIALS

Good projects need a little money to attract interest. Many local businesses get hit hard for youth causes, Little League, church, and school activities. This demands that the team be careful in asking for money directly as the sole ingredient to making the project run. Most schools are nonprofit and can offer tax-deductible options for local businesses to sponsor or give to an event. Selling advertisements in a program bulletin can offer a local business some advertising with large numbers of parents. These are the traditional informal means of accessing money for projects.

Once a climate team is established and evaluates its effectiveness, then, it can begin to seek more formal arrangements with community foundations. In Chicago, a community foundation funded a year of a Peaceful School program by funding a position and training for the entire suburban community. Most communities have small foundations that give out grants for projects with demonstrated success and some hope of sustaining themselves after the grant. Schools often have grant writers on their staff that could be used in this process.

Good teams work together to scratch up resources. This seems to create a more organic and direct impact than a larger grant might. Large grants can easily corrupt a system starved for resources. Outside money can be used to reinforce the projects developed by the climate team. These sums are typically quite small and may actually be more beneficial in building attachment to the community. A small contribution made in the right spirit with winners all around completes a positive cycle between the school and the community. Personal contact is made and the money is spent specifically on climate projects. This clearly does not imply that grants are not important to larger school goals. Schools need grants to stay competitive. Climate campaigns do not fall into this category; you can't simply buy a good school climate. It is the result of good people focusing, planning, and acting to make a school environment better.

Good projects need materials. Teachers should be able to pull from some outside source the materials needed for a good climate project. Gift certificates make excellent prizes for competitions. Six Flags amusement park donated free passes to a local poster campaign. This really ramped up the competition and family involvement within this disadvantaged school. Students, teachers, and parents received free passes, Six Flags received free publicity and political support, and the school benefited by improving its climate. The school was alive with posters about not bullying, being a bystander, or a victim.

SAMPLE YEAR EVENT PLAN

October 1:   Campaign Kick Off, Mayor, State Representative, District Attorney Announce the Poster Competition, Prizes

November 1:   Posters judged

Thanksgiving: Awards ceremony with prizes

December 1:   Teacher classroom decoration for peace and no bullying (prizes)

December 20:   Media-covered event for the best classroom: award grand prize

January 5:   Newspaper-sponsored essay competition with prizes of monogrammed classroom banners

February: Vacation grand prize winner announced

April: Play sponsored by local theater company about not bullying

Commencement: Awards for positive climate contribution (scholarship)

NOTES

1. *The Effectiveness of Universal School-Based Programs for the Prevention of Violent and Aggressive Behavior*, CDC Report, August 10, 2007/56(RR07); 1–12.

2. Raskauskas, J. and A. D. Stoltz. (2007). Involvement in traditional and electronic bullying among adolescents. *Developmental Psychology*, 43, (3), 564–75.

About the Authors

Stuart W. Twemlow, M.D., is a psychoanalyst and psychiatrist who has worked in communites for forty years researching the causes of violence and ways to promote peace in consultation with schools, cities, corporations, the FBI, and governments in third-world countries.

He is director of the Peaceful Schools and Communities Research program at the Baylor College of Medicine and professor of psychiatry in the Menninger Department of Psychiatry, Baylor College of Medicine, Houston, Texas. He is a founding editor of the *International Journal of Applied Psychoanalytic Studies* and has written over two hundred articles, books, and book chapters.

He is active in sponsoring educational programs and establishing community psychoanalysis within the International and American Psychoanalytic Associations. Many of his ideas are derived from a lifelong study and practice of the martial and meditative arts. He is a seventh-degree black belt and master teacher (Renshi) in Kenpo Karate and Kobudo (weapons), a student of Zen, and an exhibited black ink brush painter.

Frank C. Sacco, Ph.D., is the president of Community Services Institute in Springfield and Boston, Massachusetts. Since 1985, he has pioneered the use of home-based mental health to multiple problem families in the high-risk urban areas of Springfield and Boston. He is an international speaker on school violence and victimization and has addressed audiences in Jamaica, Paraguay, Australia, and New Zealand on the topics of violence.

He is an adjunct professor at Western New England College in Springfield, Massachusetts. He has been qualified as an expert in child and family mental health in juvenile and federal courts in Massachusetts and has been a consultant to the FBI.

He is also a martial artists with a black belt in Han-Pul Karate. He has co-authored thirty papers and book chapters on school violence prevention and threat assessment as well as several educational videos including the original song *Back Off Bully* with Dr. Twemlow and his son Stephen.

Breinigsville, PA USA
12 May 2010
237856BV00002B/6/P

DEADLY CHOICE

Recent Titles by Christine Green from Severn House

Kate Kinsella Mysteries

DEADLY BOND
DEADLY ECHO

FATAL CUT
FIRE ANGELS
VAIN HOPE

DEADLY CHOICE

Christine Green

This first world edition published in Great Britain 2004 by
SEVERN HOUSE PUBLISHERS LTD of
9–15 High Street, Sutton, Surrey SM1 1DF.
This first world edition published in the USA 2004 by
SEVERN HOUSE PUBLISHERS INC of
595 Madison Avenue, New York, N.Y. 10022.

British Library Cataloguing in Publication Data

Green, Christine
  Deadly choice
  1. Kinsella, Kate (Fictitious character) - Fiction
  2. Women private investigators - Great Britain - Fiction
  3. Detective and mystery stories
  I. Title
  823.9'14 [F]

  ISBN 0-7278-6052-6

Typeset by Palimpsest Book Production Ltd.,
Polmont, Stirlingshire, Scotland.
Printed and bound in Great Britain by
MPG Books Ltd., Bodmin, Cornwall.

One

A t six a.m. I was staring out on to Longborough High Street watching it enveloped in a warm misty haze as if the sun were shining through a muslin curtain. Jasper, a small terrier in whom I have a half share, lay splayed out on my bed like a bit-part actor showing his all.

The late August heatwave was expected to last three days. I'd seen the sea briefly the previous year but only in poor weather and now I had the urge to make the most of the last few days of summer and be beside the seaside.

My career to date, as a private investigator, has resulted in one major success – the return of a kidnapped baby who is now toddling, throwing food and chortling at my funny faces. The baby, named Katy after me, once reunited with her mother Megan, now lives in my house in Farley Wood. Megan pays a fair rent, which means I can pick and choose my cases.

My own mother Marilyn has had a striking personality change and is also living there as surrogate gran. She isn't exactly the home-baked scone type, but Megan is, and between them they seem to cope very well. So well, that when I visit I feel like the maiden aunt who is indulged but is always just outside the cosy little circle.

Hubert Humberstone, undertaker or Funeral Director as he prefers to be called is both my landlord and friend. He has no physical attractions, being glum-faced, balding and twenty or so years older than me, but to me he is metaphorically

1

both my rock and my crampons. Mountaineering though is not a hobby of his. Hubert works hard but he manages to maintain an avid interest in footwear, the higher the arch and heel the better. He's well known in local shoe shops as the equivalent of a 'bon viveur' of stiletto and towering platform shoes. His interest is totally harmless but his prune-coloured eyes have quite a twinkle if he sees a woman totter past in a pair of magnificent height. I could feel the same way about cowboy boots and a Stetson but that's not a likely sight in Longborough.

Longborough itself is a medium-size market town, a little old-fashioned, but as house prices have risen faster than dough it's become a sought-after place to live. The new residents though have to travel long distances to their workplaces and judging by the grey faces I see in the home-coming cars some of them regret the day they moved.

Social life in Longborough is not for the faint-hearted – there's a Fuchsia Club, the Women's Institute, the Mothers' Union, the Co-op choir and one of the local schools offers courses in subjects as diverse as calligraphy and yoga. Which means for a thirty-something like me an evening in front of the TV with a glass of wine and a bowl of popcorn seems like more fun.

My love life, along with my social life, is virtually non-existent. I did go out for a meal occasionally with a police inspector called David Todman who should have husband material stamped across his forehead. He's so straight I'm convinced he thinks the missionary position's exciting. If that sounds a little like sour grapes it probably is. He's been calling in to see Megan on a fairly regular basis and Megan is so naïve she probably thinks the missionary position is kneeling in church.

I'd decided by six thirty a.m. that the weather forecast of a hot and humid day was going to be accurate. I felt I needed a holiday, even deserved one. I've just completed three 'maritals', cases where, at the end, you're never quite sure if there is a winner. The first two involved women convinced their husbands were having affairs. So I stalked and photographed and sat in my car for hours on end. And eventually I had the evidence. One man was, and one wasn't, having an affair. The first, betrayed, woman reacted as though broken-hearted and somehow I felt guilty for giving her the bad news, even though she was paying me to do just that. The second woman when told her husband wasn't having an affair replied with considerable passion – 'I knew the little shit didn't have it in him. Now I'll have to find another reason to divorce him. Bastard!'

My third 'marital' was a strange woman with luminous eyes that stared from black-framed glasses. On her first visit to me she spoke in a whisper and said she came to me because of DV. I thought she meant a divine vision but she meant domestic violence. I recommended the police and her GP but she said she was convinced her Brian was seeing another woman. If she found he was, it would give her the strength to leave him. She was fairly persuasive so I took the case on.

Armed with a photograph of Brian I'd followed him one evening to a pub on the outskirts of town. Sure enough he was meeting a woman. He stood propped at the bar for nearly three hours talking to her. I sat supposedly reading a book and drinking orange juice and lemonade for that length of time. The only problem being that he was chatting between the sparse customers to a plump, pension-aged barmaid. And when he turned round I noticed he had a black eye.

I visited the loo and when I came back he'd gone. I judged the barmaid to be a kindly, chatty soul so I came clean about my reasons for sitting in a pub for three hours reading a book. Known as Babs she was quite forthcoming. 'Poor little bugger,' she'd said. 'He comes in here once a week when his nasty bitch of a wife is out. I reckon it's the only time he gets a chat with anyone. He tells me all his problems.'

'Which are?' I'd asked.

'Well, love, you saw his black eye. He spends so much time in casualty he's on first-name terms with the staff.'

'So he's not having an affair?'

Babs had thrown back her head and laughed. 'God give me strength – is that what the bitch is saying? He's more scared of women than I am of poisonous snakes. And he's bloody terrified of her. You do him a favour love – go back to his so-called wife and tell her he *is* having an affair – perhaps then she'll divorce him.'

Later, having run through all sorts of scenarios in my mind, I came to the conclusion that the truth was always the best option, especially as I didn't want his murder on my conscience. So I told his wife the truth. She smiled smugly and handed me a generous cheque. Somehow, though, I just couldn't let it rest there and the following week I was back at the pub. I guessed Babs would have told him who I was and I appeared about half an hour before closing time. This time the pub was busier and Babs bustled between pumps and optics and hardly noticed that I had drawn Brian away to an empty table.

His black eye had reduced to a mere greenish grey now. He had receding hair that left V shapes on his head and in general he was fairly nondescript except for a rather stooped frame of well over six foot. It was only when I began talking to him that the expression 'there's nowt as queer as folk' made me realize whoever coined it was a true philosopher.

Brian began by telling me of his latest injury. 'I just don't know what to do when she starts on me – she's as good with her fists as she is with her feet.' There was a note of pride in his voice. My suggestion that he could always leave her was met at first with silence and then with a plaintive excuse –

4

'But I still love her.' As I let him talk more I realized that not only was he as dim as a forty-watt bulb, he had one main role in life – *victim*. He revelled in the attention of Babs, the hospital staff and his GP. A cracked rib to him was a badge of honour. 'Look at me,' he seemed to be saying. 'I don't lose my cool – I'm a man.' His wife, Corinne, was always contrite afterwards and he enjoyed the extra attention and pampering. It was a mutually destructive relationship but obviously fulfilled a need in both of them. Maybe one day he would tire of his frequent injuries or Corinne would go too far but somehow I doubted it. I think she was controlled enough to manipulate his injuries. Or maybe I'm being too cynical.

Anyway, 'maritals' are off my agenda for a while and as I saw the sun break through the muslin curtain I decided to find Hubert and break the news. Jasper, sensing I was leaving the room, awoke from his torpor, jumped off the bed and was hard on my heels barking excitedly for a walk. Hubert, I decided, would have to wait. Jasper's needs came first.

Outside, the air was already warm and humid. Jasper seemed to sense today was going to be different as his tail began wagging eccentrically as if in semaphore. It was then that I realized if I was going on a short holiday he would make the ideal companion. He would sleep beside me without snoring, disturb me only in the morning by gently licking my face, provide me with motivation to walk, eat my leftovers, would never argue about where we went and would be happy as long as I was with him. All he required in return was a bowl of food and water and the odd titbit. For that I had a companion who would neither tut about my calorie consumption nor notice how much I was drinking. Having sorted all that out in my mind it was only left to explain to Hubert that it was Jasper who needed to run free on some deserted beach and I was merely being altruistic.

Later that morning when I found Hubert cooking breakfast in the kitchen I told him of the sacrifice I was prepared to make on Jasper's behalf.

'I'd come with you,' he said. 'But I'm too busy. I suppose you want breakfast before you go.' He added more bacon to the grill and began cracking eggs. Hubert doesn't follow food fashions or any other fashion really. His attitude is – if your number is called, then it's called and barring accidents you'll get as long a life as you're programmed for. Eating a few extra eggs or resisting the call to sausages won't make any difference. I'm inclined to agree but I often argue with him just for the sake of seeing him animated. As he put breakfast in front of me I tried to disregard the cholesterol level while he mused aloud on a time when peasants lived on bread, cheese and ale and no one had heard of lemon grass, curry leaves, sun-dried tomatoes or polenta and when the only chef you knew was your mother.

'You're not thinking of wearing a bikini are you?' asked Hubert, abruptly changing tack.

'Why do you ask?'

He shrugged. 'I don't want Jasper running off at the shock.' His face was perfectly straight and he knew full well that I'd rise to the bait. 'I'll have you know,' I said, 'I don't look too bad in a bikini. In fact I think I look – sonsy.'

'Don't you mean saucy?'

'I do not. Sonsy means – plump, buxom, of cheerful disposition. I found it in the dictionary – I haven't just made it up.'

'I'm glad to hear it. The plump and buxom is you but I don't know about the cheerful disposition.'

'It also means *to bring good fortune.*'

'There you are then,' he said. 'Wrong on two counts.'

I didn't pursue that line any more; the trouble with trying one-upmanship on Hubert is that his brand of reality soon has me slipping on the banana skin.

After breakfast Hubert left for the first of his day's funerals telling me I could raid the fridge if I wanted to. I peered inside. It was full to overflowing. Then I rang Megan to tell her I was going away for a few days. My mother, of course, was still in bed.

'Where are you planning to go then?' asked Megan in her slow Welsh accent.

'I thought I'd look up somewhere on the Internet – Yorkshire maybe.'

'Wales is very nice,' she said. 'There's a farm near Nefyn that has a caravan.' I mumbled something to the effect that I'd think about it. I had no plans to do any such thing. A caravan in a field was not my idea of a holiday and I'd been to Wales the year before. I wanted a change. We chatted for a while about Katy but as she began yelling for attention I made an excuse and rang off.

I spent the next hour on the Internet and the telephone trying to find a hotel or a guest house that would take a small terrier. Those that did take pets had no vacancies. It was beginning to look like mission impossible and the caravan in Nefyn was becoming a strong contender, although I suspected even that must be occupied during August. I rang Megan back to find she didn't know the address or the name of the farm but as Nefyn was a very small place I shouldn't have any difficulty finding it. 'So you're telling me,' I said, 'There's nuffin' at Nefyn.'

Megan's sense of humour is purely slapstick so she answered me in her usual serious way, 'There's a lovely beach there and it's very quiet and Lloyd George's grave is not too far – that's well worth a visit. Would you bring me back some bara brith if you do go to Wales?'

I promised I would and turned to Jasper, who snuggled against me. 'Come on then Jasper – we're off to do nuffin' in Nefyn.' Jasper, intelligent enough to know by my tone of voice something to his advantage was in the offing, barked excitedly. It took me twenty minutes to pack, a minute to leave a note for Hubert, and we were ready to go. I was halfway down the stairs when the phone rang, I hesitated but only for a moment. If it were that important they'd ring again on my mobile.

Jasper is a great traveller. After a few watchful excited miles he lapses into a contented coma. On the way we stopped at a pub and he roused himself and we had lunch in a pub garden. It was a full stomach and the knowledge we were halfway there that finally made me feel in holiday mood and of course the warm sunshine and clear blue skies that seemed to hold the promise of more to come.

Nefyn simmered in the sunshine and did so with quietness reminiscent of a long Spanish siesta. The sandy beach boasted three families slothful under the shade of giant umbrellas and the sea was as waveless as a glass mirror. Jasper struggled with me to be free of his lead but I led him away from the three families, who, strangely in an empty beach, stayed close to each other. Further along the beach we were quite alone and I walked Jasper to the sea's edge, took off my sandals, released Jasper from his lead and let the sea creep over our feet. The water struck cold but Jasper was in doggie heaven dashing backwards and forwards excitedly. The heat and the excitement were soon too much for both of us and I sat by a grassy bank to recover and squint at the shiny sea. After fifteen minutes or so I carried Jasper to the car so that we could find either the farm with caravan or a guest house.

If there was a shop I didn't find it and there was no one on foot to ask. There were one or two B&Bs but they had no vacancies. Eventually though I found an elderly lady wearing a man's cap sitting reading in a deckchair outside an all-white bungalow.

'You want the Davis farm,' she said squinting at me in the bright sun. 'She's got a caravan in one of the fields. It's

about half a mile up the main road. Turn left up the narrow
road, keep on going and you can't miss it.'

The half-mile must have been a Welsh half-mile. By my
reckoning it was at least half that again and the narrow road
with high bushes each side seemed never-ending but from
the smell I did at least know a farm was nearby. When I
finally got there the farm was a grim stone building with a
collie dog lying by the doorway of the farmhouse. I parked
as near to the front door as possible and the dog raised its
head and then lowered it again. Jasper barked for all he was
worth but the collie wasn't impressed and stayed doggo. A
middle-aged woman, red-faced and scowling, appeared then
in the doorway. She looked the type who in the Wild West
would have had a shotgun behind her back. 'Yes?'

'I believe you have a caravan for rent.'

Her face relaxed slightly and she toed the dog from the
door and he moved a yard away and collapsed again in a
warm heap. 'Come on in,' she said.

The kitchen seemed dark after the bright sun but it was
hot. A smell of baking came from the gas cooker and in the
grate a small fire glowed. She noticed my glance towards the
fire but offered no explanation. 'It's two hundred a week,'
she said, 'and twenty pounds deposit for bedlinen. I'd prefer
it all in cash but I'll take a cheque.'

'That's fine,' I said. 'Shall I pay now?'

'If you want sheets on your bed, unless you've brought
your own.'

I handed her a twenty-pound note and wrote out a cheque
for the rest. From her apron pocket she produced a scrap of
paper and a scrap of a pencil and then proceeded to write
me out a receipt.

I was about to comment on the glorious day when she
seemed to read my thoughts. 'It won't last, this weather.
Take my word – make the most of what's left of today.'
From the same pocket she handed me a key. 'Don't lose

it and lock up when you go out. I'll get your sheets.' She disappeared and I heard her walking heavily upstairs, each stair creaking louder than the last. After a few moments she returned to hand me two candy-striped sheets and two pillowcases. 'The caravan is in the second field. Follow the path and try not to step in the cowpats.'

I thanked her and went out to collect Jasper. I'd failed to mention his existence and she stood at the door watching me with a slightly amused expression whilst the collie dog ignored us both.

I carried Jasper under one arm and the bedlinen in the other. The first field was full of cows and the second was empty apart from a caravan that might have once been cream but age and mud had withered it. It stood like a rusty old car, forlorn and forgotten and surrounded by cowpats. I toyed with the idea of asking for my money back but I guessed she'd refuse and I was feeling the effects of the heat and the long drive. Anyway by now it was late afternoon. It would have to do.

The caravan door creaked as it opened and a wave of hot musty air hit me. It smelt like a potting shed and even Jasper recoiled. Once the curtains were pulled and the windows opened at least I could see that the interior matched the exterior. A paraffin lamp and a box of matches had been placed on the Formica top of the drop-leaf table that I guessed hid the bed. There was no TV but there was a two-ring gas burner and a small oven. It was clean but very old and shabby. There were three cupboards – one contained a shower, which was so narrow I had to enter sideways; another was a clothes cupboard and the third contained an Elsan loo. A further 'room' contained a bunk bed.

'Well, Jasper,' I said, 'let's find civilization and go shopping.' He didn't argue. On the way I stopped off to see Mrs Davis. She must have seen me coming because as

I approached she came out holding a basket. 'Everything all right?' she asked slyly.

'Fine, Mrs Davis,' I said, unwilling to give away the idea that a week in that caravan might just cause me to lose the will to live. 'I'm going for a drive around – where is the nearest town?'

'Pwllheli,' she said, 'and I'm not Mrs Davis. This is the Euan Evans farm.'

As I drove away the thought occurred to me that this could be the wrong farm and the wrong caravan but it was too late now – Pwllheli was calling me. It took half an hour or so of driving through twisty country roads and on arrival I soon realized that I shouldn't have listened to Pwllheli calling. Sullen, bored teenagers hung around the bus bay. Many of the shops were boarded up. It had the look of a town that had somehow accepted that once having a holiday camp on its doorstep meant not only that it couldn't compete, but also that it should give up trying.

I found a small electrical shop and bought a battery-operated radio and from a gift shop a pack of cards, three paperback novels and a painting-by-numbers set. Then at the nearest off-licence I bought a box of red wine because there was no fridge to cool white wine. From a baker's that was about to close I purchased the last cream doughnut and then managed to find a small supermarket and bought dog food, a small cooked chicken, potatoes and runner beans, ready-prepared salad, long-life milk and assorted chocolate bars. I wasn't going to starve. For good measure I bought a selection of fruit and a packet of biscuits – Jasper loves biscuits. With these supplies the week at the caravan from hell wouldn't seem so bad.

Having wandered round Pwllheli and sat outside a pub having an orange juice I decided to drive back. Already I felt quite lonely; there were elderly couples and families but few people of my age. I supposed that if you had any ambition, a sleepy, half-forgotten seaside town was the last place anyone youngish and single would want to be.

By the time I found Nefyn and the farm dusk was beginning to fall and the temperature had dropped to a mellow warmth. Jasper could smell the cooked chicken and was slavering in an alarming fashion so I gave him a generous portion in his own dish and then set about unpacking my shopping. From Hubert's fridge I'd acquired cheese, some bacon and half a dozen eggs. I put together a chicken salad and washed it down with the red wine, which was barely palatable but the more I drank of it the more I liked it. I then made coffee, ate the cream doughnut and gave Jasper a plain biscuit, explaining to him that cream doughnuts were most unhealthy, especially for dogs. I don't think he was convinced.

After our meal I made up the bed, had a shower in the space that was no bigger than one of Hubert's coffins and got so claustrophobic that I made my escape after a very perfunctory dousing. Then I lay curled up with Jasper on the thin mattress of my bed and stared up at the caravan ceiling, which appeared black in the light of the paraffin lamp. It took a few moments for me to realize that the ceiling wasn't black with dirt, it was black with thousands of tiny insects. I quickly pulled the sheet over my head and although I thought I ought to be concerned about my 'plague' I fell asleep easily. Only to be woken soon after by my mobile phone. I answered it, thick-voiced, under the bedclothes.

Two

It was of course Hubert. The gist of his call was that if I were feeling lonely he would come for the day.

'I'm fine, thanks,' I said in reply.

'The weather's on the change,' he said dolefully.

'I'll cope.'

'How's Jasper?'

I had a feeling that was the real reason for his call. 'Jasper,' I said, 'is in doggie paradise.' I told him I was exploring the delights of Llandudno in the morning and with a 'Cheerio then – take care,' the conversation was at an end.

The following morning the weather was 'on the turn'. It was mild but it was no longer high summer. It was more mellow autumn but at least it was dry and after a prolonged breakfast and a short walk it was about eleven when I began the drive into Llandudno. Parking was a problem but eventually I managed to find a place in a side street some way from the sea. Jasper, fired with enthusiasm by the smell of the sea air, was highly excited. I was less so. I was easily the youngest person there. Perhaps it was the week of a pensioners' convention I thought. Arm in arm they strolled slowly or they sat looking out to sea. Many walked with sticks and I spent some time sitting on a wall playing 'I spy someone under forty'.

For Jasper the call of the sea was too much and he began pulling at the lead, so we made our way to the beach, where

I released him and he darted off to the water's edge. I was about to sit down on the sand when I heard someone yelling 'Kate – Kate!' I didn't take any notice. After all, Kate is not an uncommon name. But when the yell changed to 'Kate Kinsella – I know it's you,' I had to respond. I turned round and coming towards me was a thin woman in her thirties with a camera slung round her neck wearing white shorts and striped socks to match her multi-coloured top. She had long fairish hair and wore sunglasses. She slipped off her glasses as she came closer and she was smiling broadly. Her eyes were a clear blue, her eyelashes well loaded with mascara. There was only one problem. I didn't know her from Adam, Eve or anyone else – she was a total stranger.

'Kate – I can't believe it. Fancy seeing you here.'

My embarrassment was total. Who the hell was she? 'Hi,' I said brightly, trying to stave off the moment when I had to admit I didn't know her.

'It's been years,' she said. I crossed my fingers hoping desperately she wouldn't ask how many.

'If you're not busy,' she said, 'how about a coffee?'

I struggled for an excuse. 'I can't really. I've got my dog with me.' I pointed out from the beach to where Jasper was chasing a blue ball that bobbed about in the water. 'Jasper!' I called and he came running to examine my new companion. As promiscuous as ever he fawned and then rolled on his back hoping no doubt she would tickle his tum. She didn't. She merely said, 'Outside cafés don't mind dogs. Come on, Kate. There's one across the road with seats outside.'

It was a self-service place – all the customers, bar us, being middle-aged or elderly and mostly female – but I warmed to her and the venue when she returned to the table with coffee and two scones thickly wedged with jam and cream. Not that a coffee and a scone would help me remember who she was. She hadn't been a client. Of that I was sure. Had I met her on holiday or in New Zealand?

14

'You haven't changed a bit, Kate,' she said, as she raised her coffee cup to her lips. I began eating my scone very slowly, reasoning that if I kept my mouth full I wouldn't have to say much. 'Did you go into nursing?' she asked. I nodded. If we were going that far back there was only one place we could have met – school. So why couldn't I remember her? She obviously hadn't been a particular friend of mine otherwise surely I would have remembered her. Strong doubts about my mental health surfaced and I began to feel even more hot and bothered. I decided to risk it. 'You've changed,' I said. She smiled, revealing neat, even white teeth. And then it clicked – Helen Woods – always at the orthodontist. The same Helen whose socks were whiter than anyone else and who never ate sweets. A real swot too. She wasn't the most popular girl in school but I could remember now she'd wanted to go into politics so we'd presumed she liked being unpopular. From a gangly, toothy schoolgirl she'd turned into an attractive slim woman – what did that say about me who hadn't 'changed a bit'?

I relaxed now that I'd remembered her and we chatted a bit about our school days but strangely we didn't seem to remember things in quite the same way. The present seemed a safer option. 'Are you still nursing?' she asked.

'I'm a private investigator.'

'Wow. That sounds interesting.'

'It can be. And you?'

'I'm a freelance photographer. That's why I'm in Wales – doing some shots for the Welsh Tourist Board.'

'That sounds interesting,' I said politely. Jasper, who'd been angelic up to now, for some reason started licking at my ankle. I tried to ignore him and think of something intelligent to ask about photography. Nothing sprang to mind so I sipped at my coffee.

'Are you living with anyone?' she asked.

'No. I sort of live alone. I haven't had much luck with men.'

'I didn't until a few months ago. Then I met Paul.' She smiled with such happiness that I knew that I was in for a longish session about how wonderful he was. I suppose it's something every single dreads because it throws up all the sort of questions you want to avoid – 'What's she got that I haven't got?' being the most usual, although in this case it was fairly obvious.

I listened while she told me about her last photo assignment in India and how she'd literally bumped into him in a local camera shop. He was tall dark and handsome and, it seemed, rich. He would be, wouldn't he! Anyone I bump into is either drunk, smelly or totally obnoxious. Anyway Paul was the personification of perfect manhood. He worked as a financial advisor, was an artist in his spare time, specializing in watercolours, lived in a house by the sea in Cornwall and was a widower. They were planning their wedding for late September.

'You will come won't you, Kate?' asked Helen earnestly.

'I'll try.'

'Perhaps you could come and stay with us before then.'

This threw me somewhat. I hardly knew her. 'My mother is getting on a bit – she . . . gets a bit forgetful,' I muttered by way of an excuse.

Helen raised her eyebrows slightly, no doubt guessing I'd improvised.

'How's *your* mum?' I asked.

'She died. Two years ago – cancer.'

'I'm sorry.'

Helen gave a little shrug of her shoulders. 'I miss her so much, especially with my wedding coming up. And I haven't made many friends of my own in Cornwall – I don't know why.'

16

'It's being self-employed. It's a lonely existence.'

She smiled briefly. 'Is that it? I was beginning to think it was me.'

We chatted about India for a while, finished eating and drinking and I was raring to go. Helen was nice enough but a little serious and earnest. She wasn't the sort to go clubbing with or even have a girlie night in with. And worse, there was something – needy – about her. I couldn't quite put my finger on why I felt that. After all, she was in love and presumably he was her 'rock'.

I was about to use Jasper's toilet needs as an excuse when she said, 'Do you deal with any unusual cases, Kate?'

'In their own way I suppose they are all a bit unusual. If it starts out as a relatively normal investigation, that state doesn't last long. I'm not the world's best private 'tec.'

'Have you ever dealt with . . . ghosts?'

I laughed. 'That's for exorcists and I don't believe in ghosts.'

'I do.'

I shrugged. 'Any reason?'

'I think Paul's house is haunted.'

'There is an answer to that,' I said, not wanting to get embroiled in any supernatural mumbo-jumbo.

'What's that?'

'Sell up and move to somewhere that isn't haunted.'

She wasn't peeved at my bluntness. 'We would,' she said, 'but no one wants to buy it.'

'Why not?'

'It's isolated and fairly near the edge of the cliff . . .' She paused and I knew that another ghost reference wasn't far off. 'I think prospective buyers also think it's haunted.'

'Why would they think that?'

'They sense it.'

'Sense what? How does this . . . haunting manifest itself?'

'It's nothing tangible, at least not to viewers or even to Paul.'

'So why is the house affecting you?'

'It's got a history.'

'Is it that old?'

'No, I mean a recent history.'

'Which is?'

Helen looked out towards the sea. 'It's a very sad story . . . Paul's wife committed suicide and killed their two children.'

'Oh,' I said, shocked. 'That's tragic. Did it happen in the house?'

She shook her head. 'Not exactly but near the house. She drugged the children and herself and then walked them over the cliff edge. Paul was devastated. He was asleep in the house. He woke up and went out looking for them and saw them all smashed up on the rocks.'

'That's not something you get over easily.'

'He says at first he was in shock, then he was angry and wanted to sell up and live abroad but no one wanted to buy the house and he was too depressed to put in any effort so he stayed on.'

'But the house affects you?'

'I don't sleep very well. I hear things. It's got to the point where I'm frightened to go to bed at night.'

'Sometimes it's footsteps. Sometimes I think I hear the children crying.'

'That's horrible,' I said. 'But do you think you're just dwelling on what happened? Stress and imagination can play tricks with your hearing.'

'Do you think that's what it is?' I could see Helen was clutching at my straw of comfort. I nodded. 'Perhaps you need to move out for a while, at least until the stress of the wedding is over.'

'I've thought about that and talked to Paul about it but

he doesn't want me to do that and says that I'm being –
hypersensitive . . .' She paused and looked at me earnestly.
'You don't think I've got psychic powers do you?'

'I doubt that. I'm a psychic sceptic and I don't think you
should go down that road.'

Jasper woke from his nap and wagged his tail at me in
anticipation of either a walk or a titbit. My scone was long
forgotten and I hadn't left a crumb. I noticed now that Helen
had left half of hers. That's how slim people do it I thought.
They have that clever knack of not clearing their plate. So
simple, but so hard to do when every day as a child you were
encouraged to eat more and a clear plate was rewarded with
a round of applause. If not, you had the additional worry of
the starving children in Africa, who most certainly wouldn't
leave anything on their plates. Helen's family had been well
off, so I supposed her mother didn't worry about food left
on the plate.

'I've got to go, Kate. I'm going to Rhyl now before it gets
dark.' She leant forward and her blue eyes were bright and
eager. 'I want your business card,' she said. She handed me
hers and I rummaged in my purse for one of mine. It had a
slightly chewed appearance and as I certainly didn't want
her as a client I hoped it would show I wasn't the dynamic
type. She looked at it and murmured, 'Fancy you becoming
a private investigator.'

'There you go,' I said. 'I earn a living.'

'I expect you meet some interesting people,' she said. I
smiled but thought to myself they were only 'interesting'
in the deranged, damaged and desperate categories. I'd
faced the fact some time ago that 'normal' people do
not require my services. And I had a nervous inkling that
Helen Woods, having found me by chance, wasn't going to
let me go.

'You will come and stay,' she said, 'won't you? A long
weekend . . . soon. Then you can meet Paul.'

I could hardly wait, I thought cynically, but I nodded weakly and smiled.

The drive back to Nefyn was uneventful except for the ominous black clouds that loomed overhead. About an hour after we arrived back at the caravan the storm broke. Jasper and I huddled under the bedclothes as the wind rocked us, the thunder deafened us and the hailstones fell on the metal roof like machine-gun fire. Once when I peeked out between thunderclaps I actually saw the forked lightning through the curtains and I'm not sure who was more scared, Jasper or me. He was shaking more but I was most definitely unnerved. Eventually the storm passed over leaving only the clatter of torrential rain and puddles outside the caravan as big as ponds. 'Don't you worry, Jasper,' I whispered in his ear as I cuddled him to me. 'Tomorrow we're going home.'

Three

Arriving back at Humberstone's I knew something was wrong when I saw a little group of staff standing around a hearse. They looked far more sombre than usual. I parked my car and watched as one of the pallbearers reverently carried a tiny coffin into the chapel of rest followed by the rest of the staff. I was slightly worried because Hubert wasn't at the forefront carrying the coffin.

I rushed straight up to Hubert's flat. He wasn't in the sitting room or the kitchen. I guessed he was in his office so I thought it best to wait for him. I try to avoid too much involvement with 'downstairs'. I've never wanted to be involved in the funeral business and yet sometimes I feel that Hubert would love me to be the heir to his kingdom.

I was about to feed Jasper when he began to get agitated. I opened the kitchen door and he ran along the hallway to my office and began barking excitedly at the door. I followed, opened the door and there was Hubert sat at my desk head in hands. He quickly tried to compose himself but it was obvious he'd been crying. 'What's happened?' I asked, moving towards him and then putting my arms around him. I'd never seen Hubert cry before and like the storm it unnerved me. I was obviously squeezing him a bit hard in my anxiety.

'You'll have to let go, Kate. I can't breathe.'

'I'll get you a brandy,' I said.

'OK. But stop fussing. I'm fine now.' He didn't look

21

fine to me. His eyes were reddened blobs, his cheeks ashen.

The brandy, a treble, though he didn't seem to notice or care, brought some colour to his face. 'Sorry, Kate. This one just got to me.'

The small coffin I had seen contained the body of a three-year-old boy, starved and beaten to death by his step-father. 'I've never seen anything so tragic,' said Hubert, his eyes filling with tears. 'Little lad had legs like matchsticks. He was all covered in bruises and burns. And he had the face of an angel.' I couldn't think of anything to say so I murmured that he would never suffer again. Hubert's shoulders stiffened. 'I'd like to kill the bastard who could do that to a little child.'

'Is he in prison?'

'Yes. And his so-called mother.'

We sat in silence for a few moments. There seemed to be nothing we could say.

'Will you do me a favour, Kate?'

I hesitated but only for a moment. 'Of course. What is it?'

'Attend his funeral. It seems only his grandparents are coming. I've seen it before when children are murdered by their parents – no one wants to attend the funeral. Condemned by association I suppose. The shame of it all – it's all a bloody shame.'

'Of course I'll come if that's what you want. When is it?'

'Tomorrow.'

I'd never attended a child's funeral before although a friend of mine had quit her job as a children's ward sister because she had 'attended one funeral too many'. I dreaded it and that night in restless sleep I dreamt my mother was in sole charge of Megan's Katy and whilst she was happily swigging vodka Katy was happily playing with matches. I woke at dawn, felt exhausted and dreaded the day ahead.

The funeral was at eleven and by eight a.m. I was dressed and ready and unable to concentrate on anything else. The grandparents had left the choice of clergy to Hubert, stipulating only that the funeral should not be too religious.

When my phone rang at nine thirty I felt inclined to ignore it but it provided a diversion from waiting so I answered it. 'Hello, Kate,' said the voice. I recognized her *now*. It was Helen. 'It was so lovely to meet up with you again,' she said. 'I just had to ring you and invite you properly to Tamberlake – that's the name of the house.' I was lost for words. 'That's very nice of you,' I managed. Silence – an awkward silence.

'What about the week after next? Paul's away for a few days but you could stay on and meet him.'

A few days! 'I really am very busy, Helen.' Silence again.

'Please, Kate. I'm scared to be alone. Please. I'll pay for your time.'

That made me feel even worse. 'There's no need for that. I'll do it for old times' sake. I'll stay until Paul comes back.'

'Thank you, Kate – thank you. You really are an angel. He's leaving on Saturday. Could you come in time for lunch?'

By now I was past worrying about the day or the time. 'Fine,' I said. 'I'll be there about two.' She gave me the address and thanked me profusely again so that I felt quite churlish. Most people, I thought, would love a few days in Cornwall in the summer. I was behaving as if it was a chore.

When I told Hubert about my trip he didn't look too pleased. When I mentioned my nervous host and ghosts

23

he looked even less pleased. 'Don't you believe in ghosts then, Hubert?' I said partly to wind him up because I felt sure he didn't.

'I wish I did,' he said glumly. 'Then murderous bastards who abuse children would be haunted until the day they died. Life isn't fair though is it? They have no conscience or they wouldn't do it. Seeing ghosts needs sensitivity and imagination – that's all it is – a vivid imagination or wishful thinking.'

I didn't quite understand what he was getting at. 'You mean you have to *want* to see a ghost before one will pop up?'

He shrugged. Maybe he wasn't sure what he meant either.

The next hour dragged by. I walked Jasper while Hubert drank coffee and read the paper. Then I sat in my office and scanned my e-mail 'spam'. I'm surprised junk e-mail isn't called 'scam' because that's what they are. They feed on universal anxiety – debt, obesity and sex. *In debt? Settle your debts now! Weight loss? Lose 30lbs in a month! Penis too small? You can be extended!* Sometimes they play on sheer curiosity to get you to open the stupid things – *Hi! I've been looking for you!* I deleted my eight 'messages' without opening them and wondered if it would be worth my while to advertise myself on the Internet. How would I word mine? *Hi! Is your husband having an affair?* Or *Police too busy to help? You need an expert.* That was pushing it a bit but I could try. Maybe *Missing loved one? Make the search ours.* I quite liked that and decided to discuss it with Hubert after the funeral.

Just before ten forty-five I was ushered by Hubert to the waiting Daimler – one of two that would follow the hearse. The sun was shining, inappropriately I thought. Funerals belonged in the rain and the cold. It was ten stately minutes to the cemetery and the car's quiet dark interior gave me the chance to think about Darren – murdered brutally in his fourth year. He wasn't the only one of course. A child who'd been given the short straw in life. There were no excuses. Had he ever known any happiness I wondered. I was grateful when my short but lonely journey was over.

The officiating vicar stood at the door of the chapel to meet the maternal grandparents. On the tiny coffin had been placed a floral teddy bear. The grandmother was already sobbing and the vicar put her arms around her and hugged her tight. The Rev. Anne White was in her forties with short fair hair and the look of a kindly headmistress. She shook my hand and thanked me for coming and then as I walked into the chapel and saw the coffin, so small and surrounded by flowers, a lump caught in my throat and stayed there.

'Think of Darren,' said the vicar, 'as a tiny seedling of God, cruelly cut down before he had time to grow. He knew the love of grandparents and he had some happy times. He will always live in their hearts and now he also lives safe in the arms of Jesus.' She followed this with a special prayer for children but by then I was only aware of the tears coursing down my face.

As the coffin was carried out a medley of children's songs were relayed throughout the empty chapel. 'The Wheels on the Bus go Round and Round', and 'Incey Wincey Spider'. We walked out of the chapel and into the sunshine to the sound of 'Jingle Bells'.

After the interment Hubert told me we would be going to the catering suite at Humberstone's. Hubert travelled with me this time. I'd rather hoped we could go straight to a local hostelry. He didn't say much on the journey. Just that he was glad it was over. But it wasn't over of course. The 'refreshments' had to be endured.

Hubert sat me at one of the tables, bistro-style in pink and grey, with the grandparents Alan and Jackie. They were in their late forties, their faces ravaged with tears. Hubert brought a trolley of drinks so that we could help ourselves. We all chose brandy – neat. 'I blame myself,' said Jackie, her voice thick with emotion. 'We should have stopped her seeing that . . . monster. He's ruined all our lives. Darren was a lovely kid, so happy until *he* came into their lives. Six months with *him* and he'd killed our Darren.'

'It wasn't our fault, love,' said Alan, putting his arm round his wife. 'We warned her that he was the jealous type. We told her some men couldn't stand the reminder of another man. She wouldn't listen.'

'And now she's barely twenty and in prison.'

'Maybe she'll learn some sense and stop taking drugs. It was *him* that started her on them.'

Jackie nodded miserably and sipped at her brandy. Then she seemed to notice me for the first time. 'You're Kate aren't you?' I nodded. 'Do thank your husband for us won't you? It was ever so kind of him to pay for everything and it was such a lovely service. I keep thinking of what that vicar said. "Safe in the arms of Jesus." That comforts me.'

I blinked back a tear. This was not the time to deny Hubert being my husband.

He must have known I was gunning for him, because he disappeared as soon as Alan and Jackie left. No one had eaten any of the sandwiches but I'd sunk a few brandies and all I could do now was lie down in a darkened room and think of anything but Darren. What did spring to mind though was the tragedy of Helen's fiancé Paul. He'd lost a wife and two children and by the wife's own hand. Of course the question remained – why? I supposed that suicides where no explanatory note is left meant the grieving relatives foundered in guilt, secrecy and ignorance. Was it their fault? Why hadn't they noticed their loved one had lost the will to live? Death by suicide seemed to me a punishment for those left behind. I'd experienced the death of someone I loved but it was a freak accident and it was a consolation to know he'd died so suddenly and swiftly.

Later in the afternoon I met up with Hubert in the kitchen. He had Jasper under one arm and was back to his usual self so I said nothing about being accused of being his wife. He would be embarrassed and so would I. Plus it might upset Jasper. Instead I mentioned my forthcoming trip to Cornwall.

'I could do with a break,' he said.

'This is more baby-sitting an ex-school friend.' He was busy making tea so he didn't answer and I was still thinking about Paul's wife. 'You've had experience of suicides,' I said. 'What's your opinion?' He gave me a piercing look. 'Well it's an option. And bloody selfish.'

'Yes but sometimes it seems to happen for no apparent reason.'

Hubert set down cups and saucers. 'Misery is the reason, hopelessness. A view of the world where it's black as night and the sun don't rise.'

'You sound as if you've been there?'

'I have, Kate,' he said edgily, 'but I don't want to talk about it.' There was quite a bit I didn't know about Hubert's past but what did it matter? From Hubert's anecdotes and observing his staff they seemed a cheerful bunch, not as prone to suicide as farmers. Strange that those surrounded by death seemed happier than those who provided our food. But perhaps such close contact with death removed all the fear.

'Surely,' I said, warming to the subject, 'if people acknowledged they were miserable and depressed and sought help, at least there would be less unexplained suicides.'

'Well,' said Hubert as he poured the tea. 'I reckon depression is the new leprosy.'

'What do you mean?'

'I mean people will be kind for a while and then when you don't "cheer up" they avoid you. Misery is catching. The world is difficult enough and some people cope better than others do. But the old adage is still true, "Laugh and the world laughs with you – cry and you cry alone."'

I knew that to be true. If I ever found a boyfriend who could cope with tears I reckon I'd be in love. Most men I know don't realize that a cuddle is worth a thousand words. They don't have to solve your problems, just be gently physical. But then, as Hubert contends, if depression is contagious its not surprising men get a slightly sick expression when their woman feels low.

'By the way,' said Hubert. 'You did really well with that couple.'

'I didn't say a word.'

'You listened. That's all that mattered.' He looked at me quizzically.

'Don't look at me like that, Hubert. The funeral business is *not* my forte.'

'Well,' he muttered. 'Tell me something that is.'

'Ghost-busting?'

'Very funny. If you bust a ghost make sure you get well paid for it.'

'I'm not doing it for the money.'

'Well what are you doing it for?'

'Old times' sake.'

He raised an eyebrow. I kept quiet then. Because I still had only the vaguest memories of Helen Woods. And I had the feeling that it would be better to leave it that way.

Four

Finding Cornwall took hours but at least I couldn't miss it. Finding Tamberlake was a different matter – three random stops to ask people I was so sure were locals resulted in apologies for their only being on holiday. I began to suspect that the native Cornish hibernated in the peak holiday season and who could blame them? Eventually I stopped at an estate agent in the small town of Trevelly. A fresh-faced young man looked me up and down as if assessing whether I could afford a wooden shed in Cornwall. By his expression he guessed I couldn't. But at least he'd heard of Tamberlake and he gave me good directions although his three miles were 'country' miles and I would have guessed at six miles at the very least. The last mile always seems the longest and this mile down a narrow unmade road was no exception. High hedges occluded any view but through my open car window I could smell the sea.

The house, when I saw it between the long grass and the trees that surrounded it, was an ivy-clad Victorian monstrosity with portholes, peeling paint and an air of sad defeat. I hoped the need for a 'makeover' was only on the outside. Helen must have seen my arrival, for before I could use the brass knocker she had opened the door. She wore jeans and a white blouse tied at the front to expose her neat midriff. 'I'm so glad to see you, Kate,' she said earnestly. 'Paul had to leave yesterday and one night on my own was enough. I haven't slept.' She grabbed my travel bag and took my arm gently but I felt as if I was being dragged in.

As I glimpsed the hall I wasn't surprised she thought the place was haunted. It was gloomy and smelt of damp. Perhaps, I thought, the floral décor was trying to make a statement but I couldn't quite work out what it was. 'Wonderful isn't it?' said Helen. I supposed she was looking for reassurance so I mumbled about character and atmosphere.

'How many rooms does it have?' I asked.

'Six bedrooms, two bathrooms, three reception rooms, kitchen of course, attic and cellar. We use the cellar for Paul's huge wine collection. Come on, I'll show you round.'

'Would you mind if I had a coffee first?'

'Of course, sorry, Kate. You must be tired. Of course, we'll have lunch and do the grand tour afterwards.' That sounded good to me and we made our way below-stairs to the kitchen, which boasted a pine table that would seat eight. The Aga sat like a culinary Buddha on one wall and the sink appeared to be the original butler sink but at least with the addition of a hot tap. There was a small barred window that looked out towards an overgrown lawn and it was the sort of kitchen that needed lights on night and day. Two light bulbs covered in lampshades made of beige Bakelite lit the room but only in patches. There were several shadowy corners. 'We do have a pantry,' said Helen excitedly and showed me to a door of the walk-in pantry. It contained mostly empty pickling bottles. 'I haven't quite got round to home-made jam and pickles yet.'

'Not to worry,' I said with a nervous laugh. 'I've been pickled myself but I prefer a supermarket to do the hard graft.' She smiled as if she thought she ought to and then said, 'Paul loves all the old traditional ways.'

'Well let him do the pickling then.'

She looked at me as if I'd blasphemed, quickly composed

herself and managed a tight smile. 'Come on, let's sit down. Lunch is all ready.'

Lunch was a prawn and fresh crab salad with white crusty bread. 'This bread is delicious,' I said between hungry mouthfuls, although I did slow down when I saw Helen was pushing her food around the plate.

'I made it myself. I thought it was pretty good.'

'Clever you,' I said. 'It really is the best home-made bread I've ever tasted.' Helen smiled cheerfully, her equilibrium restored. We had strawberries and cream to follow and I offered to wash up but she opened a cupboard door and there sat a dishwasher. I was impressed with the disguise – the twenty-first century had come to Tamberlake.

There followed the grand tour of the house. The sitting room had William Morris wallpaper and original water-colours on the walls, mostly of Cornwall, and the flat-screen, multi-channel TV was encased in a double-door reproduction 'antique'.

Eventually I was shown my room and it was a relief when she said, 'You get unpacked and have a rest. I've got things to do so just relax and come down when you're ready. Supper is at seven thirty – it'll be a bit basic.'

When she'd gone I sat on the double bed and gazed at the ornate cornices, the heavy floor-to-ceiling drapes – floral of course, and with tassels – and thought that the streamlined Helen belonged not here but in some white minimalist apartment in London. I unpacked, noted I had my own TV and desk, a bowl of fruit on my bedside table alongside a cerise lamp and a selection of new paperback books. A box of chocs and a bathroom en suite and I would have been quite content. To check out if it felt haunted I walked round the room to find any cold spots and couldn't find one. I wasn't surprised of course.

A bit gloomy the house might be but I got no impression of any ghosties being likely. Although I had to admit it was far too large for one person and I would have felt uneasy being there on my own. The 'tour' hadn't included all the rooms and the attic and cellar remained unseen. One thing had struck me. There seemed to be no evidence of children ever having been in the house. There were no photographs of either his wife or children on display but, with a wife in waiting, perhaps he thought it politic to keep them out of view.

I lay back against the patchwork quilt which ill matched the rest of the room and, promising myself a quick nap, I closed my eyes. When I woke, Helen was knocking at my door telling me it was after seven. She now wore a long black skirt and a white lacy top. I felt grubby but she said the meal was ready so we may as well eat.

If only all my meals were so 'basic'. We sat in the kitchen eating crispy duck breast with red wine, new potatoes and green beans with anchovies. Helen had as much on her plate as mine but she ate only a quarter and I, of course, polished off every last morsel. Although the food was delicious the conversation was stilted and awkward, but the accompanying fine red wine soon had Helen talking about photography. Not a subject I knew much about because if I was going anywhere it was the camera I usually forgot. Over apple crumble and clotted cream I asked about Paul's job.

'It's been a bit hectic for him lately,' she said. 'A few years back he was a corporate financial advisor but he didn't feel they paid him enough so he's been freelance for the last eighteen months. I think he made a hasty decision after his wife . . .'

'Does it upset you to talk about it?'

She stroked the side of her face thoughtfully. 'Yes I suppose it does. I love Paul to bits but we never mention the past. He says the past is best forgotten and he has enough painful anniversaries to cope with anyway.'

'And you met him by chance?'

'Yes, in a camera shop. Life is really weird isn't it? We got chatting as we waited in the queue and he asked me to go for a coffee with him.'

The wine – we were now on a dessert wine – had gone to my head and I related to her one or two 'pick-ups' of mine that had no such happy endings. I'd bumped into a really good-looking guy in a supermarket. He'd taken me for a coffee. Three coffees later he was still chuntering about the futures market. He could have been talking in Mandarin Chinese, because I didn't have a clue what he was talking about. Every time I opened my mouth he talked even faster. In the end I gave up.

Helen had had similar experiences but hers were more the sudden lunge that came out of the blue. Paul, in contrast, made no unexpected lunges, had courted her with flowers and chocolates and letting her see his wine cellar.

As Helen made coffee I wondered why she had chosen me to keep her company. I didn't think it was because she liked me. The more I dredged my schoolgirl memories the more I realized, apart from the fact her socks were whiter than white and that she wore braces on her teeth, we'd had very little contact. She'd had, I remembered, a best friend called Gill who had a high-pitched laugh and a tendency to practical jokes.

'What happened to Gill?' I asked as she handed me a cup of proper coffee.

'We've seen each other a bit over the years. She's met Paul . . .' She broke off. 'To be honest they didn't get on. He thought she was nosy and flighty.'

'Is she coming to the wedding?'

'I think so.' She sounded unsure and a bit nervous.

'I'm surprised you haven't several friends who would give their eye teeth for a freebie in Cornwall.'

'I wanted you.'

'Because I'm a private detective?'

'Not exactly.'

'Why then?'

She shrugged. 'I suppose it's because you're so down to earth. You don't believe in ghosts. You see, I think Gill *does* believe in ghosts. She would turn me into a nervous wreck.'

I sipped at my coffee. 'When Paul is here have you ever been . . . nervous?'

'Once or twice but he soon calms me down.'

'Does he want to sell up and move?'

'Oh yes. This was his childhood home and it costs a fortune to keep it going. He's keen to find somewhere more modern and with less land to worry about. Three acres of land takes a lot of looking after. And it's got its own patch of private beach. I'll take you down there tomorrow. It's beautiful.'

Helen seemed reluctant to leave the kitchen and insisted that she needed no help clearing up. She guided me to the sitting room and exposed the TV screen. It was growing dark by now so she pulled the drapes and switched on lamps and left me sitting in a high-backed armchair with my feet on a footstool. I felt like grandma. All I needed was a rug over my knees.

Now that darkness had fallen the room seemed full of shadows. Behind me a standard lamp with gold tassels cast a fairly dim light and I half expected a maid to arrive saying she'd turned down my bed. I flicked the TV on and turned down the volume. I couldn't hear anything specific, no creaking boards, no running water, certainly no footsteps or voices. I could hear a slight rustle of the trees outside and wondered if a Cornish storm was brewing. There was certainly nothing that disturbed me unduly . . . except one thing. How had the children found this rambling gloomy house? Was the house itself the cause of Paul's wife becoming so deranged?

I switched up the volume on the remote and tried to relax in my granny chair. It was none of my business after all. I was simply spending a few days keeping an old friend company. Except that she wasn't an old friend and maybe I'm acquiring a more detective-like suspicious nature. Hubert would say, 'About bloody time.' He accuses me of being too trusting but this time I did feel there was a hidden agenda, but as yet I didn't know what it was.

Helen came back after half an hour or so and sat beside me in a matching chair. 'Paul rang. I told him my ex-nurse friend had arrived so that pleased him.'

'You didn't tell him I was a private detective?'

'No.'

'Why not?'

She avoided my eyes. 'It didn't seem important.'

I stared at her pointedly and eventually she looked at me. 'Do you think he's seeing someone else?' I asked.

Her response was shocked and immediate. 'No I do not! That's a horrible thing to say. We're getting married in a few weeks.'

'Precisely,' I said. 'So you want to be sure?'

'I am sure. Since his wife died I'm the first woman he's been involved with. He is not a womanizer . . .' She broke off. 'Honestly, Kate. I don't have any suspicions like that.'

'What suspicions do you have?'

'None at all. It's just my nerves. This house. Its history. It's getting to me. Paul is the one stable focus of my life.'

Her voice was wavering now as if on the edge of tears and I felt guilty for upsetting her. After all, she was a great hostess, I was well fed and watered and I was casting aspersions on her beloved. I mentally slapped my wrist and said, 'Of course he is. I'm sorry.'

'I didn't mean to get snappy,' she said. 'Would you like to see a photo of him?'

'Of course. Then I'll know who we're talking about.'

From a walnut dresser she produced two photos. Handing me the first she said, 'I didn't take this one.'

I studied it closely. Only one word came to mind. 'Wow!' I breathed. No wonder she was in love with him. He was sitting on a black stallion, wearing a tight white tee shirt, black jodhpurs and boots. He had a polo stick in his hand. Tanned, handsome and muscular – he was the stuff dreams are made of.

'And this is the one I took,' she said, handing me the second one. This showed the symmetry of his face; his dark sexy eyes all enhanced by a dark suit and a white shirt. No wonder he didn't make pickles. He wasn't the type. A man like that doesn't wear a pinny. 'Polo's an expensive sport,' I said casually.

'He plays with a friend but only when he's abroad.'

'Where is he now?'

'Argentina.'

We fell silent then. He may not be a womanizer, I thought, but any woman I knew would be more than happy to polish his polo stick.

That night I woke up twice, not because of any ghostly happenings, but because of erotic dreams of handsome polo players. They were the best dreams I'd had in ages.

At breakfast Helen looked tired. 'I had a lousy night,' she said. 'Did you hear anything?'

'Not a thing.'

'I didn't either,' she answered, but I knew by the anxious expression in her eyes she was lying. I didn't pursue it, because there was nothing I could do to alter her state of mind except be around until the gorgeous hunk returned.

'I've made us a picnic,' she said, opening the pantry door and producing a large picnic basket.

'You must have been up at the crack of dawn.'

'I never sleep beyond six,' she said. 'In fact I hardly sleep much at all.'

By ten we left to go down to the beach. I carried the basket and Helen held back the brambles and tall fronds of greenery along the narrow path. Still I hadn't seen the sea but I could smell it. Occasionally a slight breeze rustled the dry grasses and bushes and as we rounded a slight bend there was a break in the vegetation and in front of us was a vast expanse of sea. No ripples, just a glassy turquoise plate. 'It's so beautiful,' I said.

'Yes,' she said. 'This is the path his wife took. And the children of course. Going to their deaths.'

Five

Another night had passed during which I'd slept like a drunken slug. I actually felt guilty that I was sleeping so well, because Helen looked pale and exhausted. I offered to cook all the meals and help with the housework but she said she liked to keep busy. Presuming, I suppose, that I didn't. Actually I was beginning to get a little bored. During the morning I decided to take a walk down the path to the beach.

The sun shone warmly making a snug bower of the path. Two butterflies led my walk, a bee buzzed and a kestrel flew high above. As I walked I soon lost interest in the flora and fauna for two little niggles crept into my mind. The first was that not once had Helen mentioned Paul's wife's name, nor those of the children. Did that make them seem less real to her or did saying their names upset her? I didn't *need* to know their names of course. It was merely curiosity but it struck me as odd. My second niggle was, on that fateful night whilst Paul slept, was his wife carrying a torch, because unless there was a full moon she would have been walking blind.

The path dipped down quite steeply to the beach but it wasn't dangerous. Further along through yellowing grass was the cliff edge itself. I abandoned the beach path and walked towards the edge of the cliff. It was hard to miss in daylight even though there were no warning signs. At night, though, it would have been impossible to see. Going over the edge would have been easy. Easy enough to fall accidentally. I stood well back and looked down. From that angle I could see only jagged rocks.

I rejoined the path to the beach and once there I sat for a while in solitary splendour, staring out to sea and listening to the gentle swish of the sea against the sand. I would have liked a paddle but that involved sand between the toes and I hadn't brought a towel with me.

Arriving back at the house I found Helen in the kitchen slaving over a meat pie. Personally I thought she was taking the domestic goddess thing a bit far but I could eat whatever she could cook so I wasn't going to complain. She looked a better colour now but the kitchen was incredibly warm and full of the smell of fresh-baked bread. 'Guess what?' she said excitedly. I thought that maybe Paul was on his way home just as I was getting used to real home cooking. 'Gill's coming. Isn't that wonderful?'

'Why the change of heart?'

'She heard you were here and she more or less invited herself.'

'What about Paul?'

'You won't tell him will you?' Again there was that note of anxiety in her voice. Was she afraid of losing him, I wondered, or just afraid of him.

'I won't be seeing him will I?'

'Maybe not until the wedding. You will come won't you?'

'Yes. If you want me to.'

She rested her floury hands on the wooden board in front of her as though she needed support and a few seconds later her face drained of colour. 'I feel a bit dizzy,' she muttered.

I insisted she had a proper rest on her bed and I took her up to the master bedroom and helped her on to the bed. I closed the curtains and crept out of the room. I wasn't sure what was wrong with her but I wasn't going to panic yet. She'd mumbled something about Gill arriving late afternoon and that the pie was for supper.

I went back to the kitchen, tidied up and emptied the dishwasher and then with nothing else in mind I decided to explore the rest of the house. I hadn't yet seen the attic room or the cellar. The attic was up a narrow winding staircase and at the top I was surprised to find it was locked. I was both disappointed and intrigued but I went back to the floor below and quietly opened the remaining three bedroom doors. One room was obviously a guest room. The other two were empty. The two empty rooms had been redecorated with fresh white paintwork and a rose-trellis wallpaper. The wallpaper looked expensive and surely only a man could decide to have two rooms identically decorated. Had he over-ordered on the rolls of wallpaper or had he done it in a hurry for some reason? I was obviously beginning to get paranoid because I kept fretting over such trivialities. What was there to worry about after all? I wasn't marrying him, although remembering what a hunk he was perhaps I was a tad jealous.

Back in my room my mobile phone bleeped at me from the depths of my handbag. I had two unanswered calls, both I presumed from Hubert. As I tapped in his number 'Network Failure' flashed at me.

I rang Hubert from the wall phone in the kitchen. 'I've been worried,' he said. 'What's going on?'

'There's nothing to worry about. I'm just keeping an old school friend company.'

'No ghosties and ghoulies then?'

'I've slept really well, haven't even heard as much as a creaking floorboard.'

'When are you coming back?'

'I'm not sure. Unexpectedly she has a real friend coming down today so I may be surplus to requirements.'

'You've had a few queries,' he said.

'Anything . . . interesting?'

'There's a Mafia killing the police are stuck on and they thought you might be able to help with a double shooting at the Fuchsia Society.'

'Very funny, Hubert. I take it that means I've only had the usual crank calls.'

'Not that cranky.'

'David didn't phone?'

'No. Were you expecting him to?'

'It would have been nice.'

'You're not interested in him so why bother?'

'I'm a woman. I'm entitled to be illogical.'

'How's the food?'

'Terrific.'

'See you then . . . whenever.'

At one p.m. I peeped in on Helen. She was sound asleep so lunch was a DIY job. I made myself a cheese sandwich and sat in the kitchen reading a novel with a 'feel-good' factor. It was set in Tuscany amongst the olive groves. I skipped the bits about olive-growing and hoped that the love interest would hold me but it didn't and I soon got restless. I missed having Jasper to walk, because a walk with no purpose seems to me to be a waste of time. I wandered the house for a while and was about to view Paul's wine collection in the cellar when I heard a car draw up outside.

Gill, small and bouncy, stepped out of a snappy red convertible. I opened the front door and we stood looking at each other for several seconds, then she hugged me. 'I'm not going to say you haven't changed,' she said. 'You're looking good.'

'So are you,' I said. Her round face and curly dark hair made her look young, twenty-five-ish, and she looked the picture of health. 'I suppose Helen's in the kitchen,' she said, as she lugged a huge holdall through the front door. 'No, she's asleep. She hasn't been sleeping at night.'

'Huh! Who says love made you happy. Load of old tosh. Every time I've been in love I've been as miserable as sin.'

'So you're not married then?'

'Certainly not. I've never found anyone worthy enough. I just have shag buddies – much less trouble.'

Gill as I remembered had always been the outspoken type. She'd been the one to give us our sex education, although to call it 'education' wasn't appropriate. She'd always been a sexual predator and had regaled us virgins with hilarious tales of incompetent boys and ageing would-be sex athletes. Sex was something she didn't take seriously. In fact I didn't think she took life seriously at all and I felt immediately more cheery. I hoped she'd have the same effect on Helen.

I showed Gill to her room. She dropped her holdall in the doorway and cast a dismissive hand over the room. 'This Victoriana crap is awful isn't it? Why try to live in the past? What's wrong with modern stuff? It's no wonder Helen is going off her head.'

'You think she is?'

'Oh yes. I haven't seen her much over the years but she always seemed quite normal until she met him.'

'Why do you think that is?'

Gill dragged her holdall on to the bed. 'She's a typical lovesick woman, seeing booties in the tumble-dryer and an adoring father changing nappies. But Paul isn't the man for that.'

'But he did have children . . .'

'Those poor little tots,' she said soberly. 'Did anyone ask them what sort of father he was? Or did anyone ask Fran what sort of husband he made?'

'You didn't know her did you?' I asked.

'No . . . no I didn't know her. But Helen is a good friend and I may be *persona non grata* with him but I intend to stay in touch with her even if we have to meet secretly.'

I really warmed to Gill then. She was a loyal good friend to Helen and my presence didn't seem necessary at all. Except that I remembered that Helen had said she thought Gill believed in ghosts. I was about to ask her about that when she said, 'Come on, let's go raid the cellar. I could do with a drink.'

I switched on the light at the top of the stairs and the naked bulb lit the stone steps downwards. I must have hesitated, because Gill became impatient. 'I'll go first,' she said. 'I'm used to this dark hole.' I followed her down and once on the stone floor I was amazed at the size of it and the fact that there were two huge barrels on stone plinths side by side in one corner. The rest of the cellar contained rack after rack of wine. It reminded me of a Spanish bodega, cool, musty and church-like.

'What's in the barrels?' I asked.

'Sherry and brandy I think. Helen says they've been there for ages.'

'Maturing nicely,' I commented.

Gill laughed. 'Mature and needing the occasional top-up sounds just like us.'

It was Gill who chose the wine. She picked a bottle from a section marked *12*.

'These are the cheapos. Helen's only allowed these. On special occasions he chooses. Never pick one of those dusty bottles over there,' she said, pointing to a section near the barrels. 'That's the old expensive stuff. Worth a fortune so I believe.'

The wine may have been a 'cheapo' but I knew from the label it was over ten pounds a bottle because I'd seen some in our local off-licence. It was good too. Gill declined to eat and we were on our second glass when Helen appeared. Her smile when she saw Gill lit the room. They hugged and then Gill stepped backwards to look properly at Helen. 'You look like shit, Helen. What's wrong with you? You've lost weight and for God's sake you do enough cooking. What do you do with it all? Give it away to the poor of the parish?'

'Stop fussing, Gill. I eat well enough. I'm just not sleeping.'

'Pre-marital nerves?' suggested Gill.

'Of course not. I'm not in the least bit worried about the wedding.'

'It's not the wedding I was thinking of,' said Gill quietly. 'It's the marriage.'

I left them for a while, forced myself to walk the grounds twice and, soon bored, I decided to go to my room to read.

Even lying on the bed I couldn't concentrate on my book. I kept telling myself this whole scenario was nothing to do with me. But I was uneasy and Gill, who seemed so down to earth, had made me think that Helen *was* making a mistake. But then people made poor choices all the time. It wasn't the end of the world. But, of course, it had been for Fran and her children. Had she been in the depths of despair because she too thought the house was haunted or had Paul created her unhappiness? I reasoned that now Gill had arrived I could easily occupy myself finding out more about Fran and the children. If in fact there was anything to find out.

First stop, I thought, would be the local newspaper. Trevelly probably wasn't big enough to have its own newspaper office but Bude or Barnstaple might be. In the morning I'd have a day in town and try to find out a few more details about Fran's death.

I quite dreaded the evening but the meal was good. Helen produced more wine and the time passed, punctuated with giggles and guffaws and a lot of chat about not much in particular. But as the evening wore on Gill became even more talkative, more aggressive. 'Helen,' she said, 'why won't you listen?'

'Because sometimes, Gill, you talk a lot of old cobblers.'

'Would you agree that I've had more experience of men than you?'

Helen nodded reluctantly. It seemed I was to be excluded from this conversation, so I lounged back in the granny chair with my bare feet on a footstool. Outside, it was dark, the wind was whipping up and it had begun to rain heavily. The curtains were still open and I listened to the two of them argue and watched the rain beating against the dormer windows.

'Anyway,' Helen was saying, 'you haven't had a relationship for ages and yet you want me to stay single.'

'That's ridiculous. Of course I want you to have a relationship, but not with Paul. He isn't right for you.'

Gill was on the edge of her chair facing Helen, who sat bolt upright on a low-slung sofa. Helen, I noticed, seemed more spirited since Gill had arrived. She was more sure of herself, more willing to fight her corner. 'Since when have you made a good decision about a man?' asked Helen.

'Since I met Bernard.'

'Who's Bernard?'

'He's someone I've been seeing for the past year. You see, Helen, you don't know everything about *me*, your best friend, let alone a man you've only known for a few months.'

Helen seemed a little crushed but she rallied. She'd lost a round but she was still in there.

'And there's your sister,' persisted Gill. 'She doesn't like him does she?'

'My sister doesn't think anyone is good enough for me. I think she's jealous.'

'So everyone is jealous? Even your own sister? Does that make sense?'

'To me it does. You can't deny he's absolutely gorgeous.' She turned to me. 'You agree don't you, Kate?' I nodded. Gill sighed loudly.

'I know looks aren't everything but he does make me happy.'

'Does he? I haven't seen that. You've lost weight, you look pale and you're twitchy.'

'I am not twitchy and I'm not going to allow you to upset me.'

Gill looked at me and shrugged her shoulders as if to say – I've tried. But even then she hadn't quite given up. 'What about your career, Helen? You can't make a career out of cooking and cleaning. This house is huge and you do all the cleaning – surely he could afford to employ a cleaner?'

'Of course he can – we've tried but no one wants to work here anymore.'

'What a surprise,' muttered Gill sarcastically.

'As far as my career goes – I don't want to take on long assignments in faraway places. I'm doing shots for the Cornwall Tourist Board and the Wales Tourist Board. I keep busy.'

'That is true,' said Gill with a tight smile.

'Anyway,' said Helen. 'Can we change the subject? There's a favour I want to ask you both.'

'Your wish is our command,' said Gill, still sounding a little sour.

'Will you both come with me to choose my wedding dress?'

Gill didn't answer straight away. 'Yes of course,' she said eventually. 'Just promise me one thing.'

'What's that?'

'No puffed sleeves.'

Helen laughed. 'That deserves a bottle of sparkling wine at the very least. I'll go and get one.'

When she'd gone Gill went to the door to check she was out of earshot before saying, 'She's not that sure. She'd have chosen her dress by now if she was.'

'What is it *exactly* that you have against him?'

She thought for a moment. 'It's a gut feeling, but there is one word I'd use to describe him and that is *sinister*.'

'Why can't Helen see that?' I asked.

'I think she sees that trait in him as being sexy.'

'I haven't met him but maybe *I* would think him sexy.'

'You would, Kate, you would, but if you found him sinister too would you want to warn her?'

'Well yes, but she wouldn't take any notice of my suspicions would she?'

'She might . . . you being a private dick.'

'I couldn't tell her it was just a gut feeling though. I'd have to have some sort of evidence. What is it you think he's done anyway?'

Gill leant forward. 'I think he had a hand in killing Fran and the kids.'

Six

I stared at Gill. She seemed perfectly serious. 'The police,' I said, 'would have investigated things rigorously, especially with two children involved.'

'The police make mistakes.'

'Of course they do. But she walked there . . .' I broke off, aware I didn't know enough to put forward a really strong case.

'I don't know how he did it but I'm convinced he knows more than he told the police.'

'Give me one good reason, other than the fact you think he's "sinister".'

She was about to answer when we heard Helen's footsteps. 'Tell you later,' she whispered.

'Look what I've got,' said Helen cheerfully, holding up a bottle of champagne. I felt totally sober but I could see the wine had already affected Helen.

We drank the champagne and Gill, undeterred, started asking questions about Paul's plans. I guessed she was probing rather than actually being interested but Helen remained quite relaxed. 'We will sell this place, I'm sure,' said Helen.

'Does Paul want to stay in Cornwall?' Gill asked casually.

Helen sipped at her champagne. 'He has suggested we honeymoon in Argentina and if I like it we might buy a property out there.'

'Why Argentina?'

'He's got friends out there and he likes the lifestyle and prospects for his work are good.'

'What about your work?'

'Have camera, will travel,' said Helen smiling. Gill slammed her empty glass noisily on the table beside her. She was getting upset, I could see that, so I said, 'Have you got a portfolio, Helen? I'd love to see some of your photos.'

'They're in the study. I'll get them.'

When she'd gone Gill snapped, 'You did that on purpose.'

'Yes. Don't worry, they haven't got definite plans for Argentina.'

'He'll want to do a runner . . .' She broke off. 'I'll pay you, Kate.'

'Pay me for what?'

'For investigating Paul – like you're a PI – that's what you do for a living isn't it?'

'Yes but – I couldn't . . . charge you. I am quite expensive.'

'Money isn't a problem. Just say you'll do it. I'll give you as much help as I can.'

'What do you do for a living, Gill?'

'I've got my own beauty salon.'

'I'm impressed.'

'I had help along the way.'

Neither of us heard Helen come into the room. 'What help was that, Gill?' she asked, moving a low table in front of us and placing two large portfolios there for us to peruse. Gill gave a little shrug. 'A friend of mine put up the finance.'

'Was that Bernard?'

'No, it was Alan, my previous candy man.'

'Honestly Gill, I don't know why you can't find a nice ordinary man and settle down.'

'You mean like Paul?'

Here we go again, I thought. I feigned real enthusiasm for those photos just to stop them sniping at each other and I was relieved when Gill announced she was shattered and was off to bed. Helen and I followed her a few minutes later. On the way upstairs Helen said, 'Don't think too badly of Gill. She does genuinely care about me and I seem to have so few real friends.'

'I understand. I know she means well.'

That night I fell asleep easily enough only to be wakened not long after. I peered, bleary-eyed at my bedside clock. It was one a.m. and someone was sobbing. Alert and wide awake now I sat on the edge of the bed and listened. Helen was in the room furthest away but Gill was next door. I reasoned it must be Gill. I went to the door, opened it and stood in the hallway. Nothing. An owl hooted and trees rustled but apart from that all was quiet. I returned to bed and tried to dismiss it. Maybe Gill had been crying in her sleep. Perhaps she had problems of her own but if she wanted to share them she would. So, I reasoned, it was none of my business. Strangely I went back to sleep, immediately to be wakened by the unpleasant sound of magpies having some kind of dispute outside my window.

Conversation over breakfast was muted. Helen was pale with slight bags under her eyes but Gill looked fine, no red eyes or puffy cheeks. Maybe the sound had travelled down the hall like some aural illusion. Tamberlake was not haunted by ghosts, I told myself – memories maybe.

It was Gill who drove us to Bude. I was squashed in the back seat but the sun shone and Helen and Gill seemed cheerful enough, except that Gill turned to wink at me a couple of times, which seemed to suggest we were conspirators.

Helen was giving directions and we stopped on the

50

outskirts of Bude, where she pointed to a neat white semi-detached in a tree-lined avenue. 'This is it,' she said. We piled out. I'd expected a bog-standard wedding shop so this was a surprise. 'I found her in the local paper,' explained Helen. 'She makes wedding dresses to order. She's brilliant, or so I've heard from someone in the village.'

On the front door was a discreet plaque announcing – *'Your Special Day': Hand-made dresses of distinction. Mrs Lana Blake.*

Mrs Blake answered the door and showed us through to her workroom. She was a small neat woman, about fifty, wearing a plain black dress. Her grey hair was worn in a bun on top of her head and her make-up was subtle. I thought she looked rather chic like a middle-class Parisian. Her accent though was pure East London with no struggle towards being 'proper'. I could see her clients were expected to stay awhile, for a tray of tea and biscuits were awaiting us in the bay-windowed conservatory.

'Right, girls. 'Appy days. Who's the lucky bride?'

Helen raised her hand.

'I should 'ave guessed,' she said cheerfully. 'You're the one who looks worried. Never mind, my sweetheart. I'll make you the dress of your dreams. Now, 'ow long 'ave we got?'

'Six weeks.'

'Plenty of time, love. You'll need at least two fittings after this one. Just don't lose any more weight.'

'How did you know I'd lost some?' asked Helen in surprise.

'Brides always do. I reckon they think there's a law about being slim on their wedding day. You can call me Lana – me mother was a fan of Lana Turner.'

We looked a bit blank, never having heard of Lana Turner, so she waved her hand towards the tea tray.

'You two pour the tea and the bride 'ere can 'ave a look at some of my designs.'

Gill and I sat drinking tea and nibbling on biscuits while Helen stripped to her underwear to try on the samples that Lana produced from a walk-in wardrobe. 'I only 'ave two sizes of each. Brides 'ave an option of returning the dress to me for a three 'undred quid refund after the wedding. Really this is just to see what style you like.'

The first one Helen tried on had huge puffed sleeves and a full skirt. Gill made a puking motion and Lana took one look at Helen in the frothy frock and said firmly, 'Not your style at all, sweetheart.' Hastily Lana helped her out of it and produced a slinky number with neat drapes at its low neckline. A little big across the bust, it still looked sensational. Lana, using pins from a pincushion on her wrist, pinned the top and the waist to fit more snugly. Helen did a twirl, her face shining with happiness. 'Now, that fits you fine and dandy,' said Lana, obviously pleased with her alterations. 'What material do you want? Would you like a motif, a few pearls on the front, and what about the headdress?'

Helen was unsure on all counts. 'Couldn't you just alter this one? I really like it as it is.'

'Wouldn't the groom like you to have a brand-new dress? What's his name? He is a Cornishman, love?'

'Oh yes. He was born at Tamberlake near Trevelly. Paul . . . Paul Warrinder.'

Gill and I couldn't fail to notice Lana's reaction. She visibly paled. Helen was oblivious, caught in her own reflection in the full-length mirror.

'Excuse me,' said Lana. 'I'll only be a few minutes.'

Gill glanced at me and flicked her head towards the door. I made my getaway as Gill was suggesting Helen took the dress off and had a cup of tea.

I found Lana in the kitchen smoking a black Turkish

cigarette. 'What's the matter?' I asked, getting straight to the point. 'Do you know Paul?'

'No, love. Never met him.' She blew out a stream of smoke and I noticed her colour had now returned to normal.

'What is it then? You may as well tell me. I won't tell the bride.'

'That dress. She can't wear that. It 'as to look different. That was his dead wife's wedding dress. Lovely girl she was. Quite like 'elen. She had bigger boobs but she was the same type – quiet and placid. I couldn't believe it when I read it in the paper. Her and her kiddies too. Bloody tragic. It was all the talk round 'ere – small place, you see.'

'When did she bring the dress back?'

'That was about a year later. She was pregnant then. Not that she showed. I was glad to 'ave it back – nice small size.'

'How did she seem?'

'You mean was she 'appy? Yeah she seemed 'appy enough. She stayed for a cup of tea and said that her 'ubby was often away on business but that she kept busy in the 'ouse and she was looking forward to the birth.'

'And that was the last time you saw her?'

'Yeah. I just read in the papers that she walked over the cliff with the kids in a buggy . . .' She broke off. 'Whatever made her do that?' she murmured. She stubbed out her cigarette in an ashtray the shape of a shoe. 'You're her friend. What am I going to tell her?'

'Don't worry. We'll persuade her into changing the style a bit. Perhaps if we say she'll look better in cream. And we'll concentrate on the headdress. Leave it with us. A day or so.'

'Right you are, love. It did give me a bit of a turn – just imagine if 'e turns up at the wedding and there she is wearing 'is dead wife's dress.'

Helen, in the conservatory, still in blissful ignorance, had produced a notepad and was designing her own headdress. Gill looked uncomfortable and was obviously dying to know what was going on.

I admired Helen's designs and after about twenty minutes we were ready to leave. Helen and Gill walked ahead and I lagged behind. 'Give me a ring tomorrow, love,' Lana whispered. 'There's something I need to tell you. Only gossip really but you never know.'

Seven

That evening Helen gave Gill and me no chance to
talk alone. Gill was twitchy the whole evening and
we both made our excuses to go to bed relatively early.
About midnight I crept next door to Gill's room. She was
sitting up in bed wide awake.

'Sit down,' she said impatiently, 'and tell me what all
that bother was with Lana.' I told her about the dress and
about Lana asking me to phone her.

'Now do you believe me?' she asked.

'The dress is only a ghastly coincidence. It doesn't say
anything about Paul does it?'

'If you met him you'd understand.'

'Would I? I think you're more of an expert on men than
I am. The men I attract look as if they've just stepped out
of a Hovis advert.'

'Safe though,' said Gill with a slight smile.

'What exactly do you suspect Paul of? OK, he was away
on business a great deal. He may have been blind to Fran's
unhappiness but most men live in blinkers where women
are concerned. It means he was an average husband.'

'What about the fact he keeps the attic locked? Helen told
me that was a habit he'd got into when the children were
alive, as he didn't want them rampaging around.'

'So? That's seems reasonable enough.'

Gill frowned at me. 'Strange he takes the key with him.
There *are* no children now.'

'Yes,' I agreed, 'but, if you've noticed, there aren't any photographs of Fran or the children anywhere. Maybe the attic room is a shrine to them and he doesn't want Helen being reminded all the time.'

'Well I think he must have been born from a pea pod,' she said, 'because there are no photos of him either or his parents. That seems strange to me.'

'Come off it, Gill. You're being paranoid now. I'm sure he's got his faults. He may be the jealous and possessive type, he may be focused on his job, but that still doesn't make him the devil incarnate.'

Gill wouldn't be deterred. 'Let's talk about his job. That's all a bit woolly isn't it? Financial advisor – going off to Argentina to play polo and yet this dump has had hardly any money spent on it in years.'

'Perhaps the house isn't a priority anymore. He does want to sell it, after all.'

'Well he hasn't tried very hard is all I can say.'

Gill seemed to be getting more wound up rather than less. Perhaps because her arguments didn't stand up under any sort of rational scrutiny. But then how often had I gone with gut instinct rather than logic and rationality? I tried being conciliatory. 'We obviously can't stop Helen marrying him but we can be there for her if things go wrong. After all, Fran was seemingly happily married to him for five years.'

'She wasn't that happy was she? She committed suicide and took the children with her. Obviously she didn't think Paul would look after them properly.'

'I don't think that stands up. The children were very young; her bond with them would have been far stronger. And, being depressed and probably deluded, she thought they should stay with her.'

'Well,' said Gill dully. 'We don't know anything about Fran or her state of mind do we?'

I had to agree that we didn't. But Gill wasn't going to

let things drop and I was tired and getting worn down. 'OK, Gill, you win. I'll take on the case. I have to warn you, though, I'm not brilliant. I'll do my best. After all, I've nothing to lose. I'm not on a job at the moment. I'll try and find out as much as I can.'

Gill threw her arms around me and kissed me on both cheeks. 'I'll pay you well,' she said, insisting on giving me a cheque there and then.

'Just expenses only,' I said as she began writing out the cheque. 'This is one for old times' sake.'

Her idea of 'expenses' was very generous. If the investigation lasted for months I'd have to cash it but otherwise I wouldn't be taking it to the bank just yet.

Back in my room I immediately regretted agreeing. I was even beginning to feel a little sorry for Paul. After all, he had lost his wife and children in tragic circumstances. He'd found a new love and enjoyed playing polo. Did he really deserve someone trying to rake over his past? It'll be all right, I thought, as long as he doesn't find out that I've been snooping. So far he hardly knew I existed and as long as neither Helen nor Gill told him I was a private investigator he need never know.

Hubert had sent me a text message. *'When back?'* Good question I thought. Tomorrow was Wednesday. I decided to give it one more day.

The next morning Helen was on good form. The sun was shining and she planned a picnic and she wanted to take a few shots for the Tourist Board. While she and Gill beavered away in the kitchen packing the picnic basket I returned to my room to phone Lana.

'It's only a bit of gossip, love,' she began, 'but being in the wedding trade I do keep in touch with the competition. It's a few years back now but a friend of mine kitted this girl out with an expensive ready-made dress. Anyway the day she was due to collect it she rang to say the wedding was off and she wouldn't be requiring the dress. So my friend felt sorry for 'er and offered 'er all the money back and she sent 'er a cheque.'

I was about to ask what that had to do with Helen and Paul when she added, 'It was Paul Warrinder, see, and she was living at Tamberlake.'

'How long was this before he married Fran?'

'Barely six months – fast worker eh?'

'And what happened to the prospective bride?'

'That's just the point. Ali was her name, short for Alison – Alison Peters. She was never seen again.'

'Well I suppose if her relationship was over she wouldn't hang around, would she?'

'No, probably not, but it seems bloody odd to me she didn't cash that cheque.'

It seemed bloody odd to me too and I quickly decided not to tell Gill the whole story. She'd be foaming at the mouth if I did. So I decided to say that Paul had a live-in girlfriend before meeting Fran. It was years ago anyway and surely she couldn't get uptight about *that*.

We were sitting on Ilfracombe beach when I told her. Helen had got off with her camera and we sat well fed and sleepy, letting the sand slip through our toes and watching children paddling. Gill seemed relaxed and wasn't surprised about there being another woman. 'She could be a good source of information couldn't she?'

'Well yes,' I acknowledged. 'I suppose she could.'

'Where is she now?'

'I've no idea.'

Gill fell silent for a while and then said, 'If we could get into that attic room I'm sure we could find out a bit more about his past.'

'How can we do that without a key?' She looked at me pityingly as if I had no right to call myself a private detective.

'We hire a criminal, perhaps a bent locksmith.'

'Do you know someone?'

'Helen says she knows a man who does.'

A sudden breeze from the sea made me shiver. Above me the once blue skies had started changing to a motley of grey. It was the end of the conversation. We hurriedly brushed sand from our feet and packed away the picnic debris. A downpour seemed imminent and we looked for shelter; so, as it seemed, did everyone else on the beach. It was then that I spotted Helen, camera slung over her shoulder, walking briskly towards us and within minutes we were in the car just as the deluge started.

The storm that followed was intense. Gill had to come off the road because conditions were so atrocious. 'Where's the ark?' said Gill cheerfully as we watched the torrential rain and forked lightning. I believe that because cars have rubber wheels a car is one of the safest places to be in a storm but I wasn't totally convinced. Surely it couldn't be safer than under the duvet?

When the rain eased so that Gill could actually see the road she drove off at a stately pace and eventually we approached Tamberlake. Although a totally different style to Norman Bates's house in Hitchcock's *Psycho*, in pouring rain, thunder and lightning it looked grim and foreboding. But then it was a big, old house not a Barratts starter home, although, if I was getting married, I know which I would have preferred.

Over supper I told Helen I would be leaving the next day. I lied through my teeth about my landlord wanting me to return because veritable queues of clients were awaiting my services. I expected her to object but she merely said, 'Oh that's a shame. But you'll be coming back won't you?' When I explained I lived above my landlord's premises I failed to be prepared for the inevitable question. The words 'funeral director' caused wine-fuelled giggles, and I found myself hotly defending Hubert and his noble profession.

'You two really don't know what's involved – do you?' I said shirtily. I then told them an undertaker was a cross between a diplomat and a father confessor and that Hubert organized everything, flowers, presentation of the body, catering and even giving advice on finance and benefits. They still giggled and asked if Hubert was attractive. I said not to me but that my mother had enjoyed a mild fling with him.

They were still giggling when I decided to go to bed. Storms have an effect on some people or so I've heard, rather like a full moon, so I tried to excuse both of them on those grounds but I was still irritated.

I rang Hubert from my bedroom to say I'd be back early evening. He said Jasper had missed me and was I on a case?

'Yes,' I said.

'Good. I need a laugh,' he answered.

I almost wished I hadn't defended him quite so vigorously but I did look forward to going home.

The next morning I was in the middle of a dream when I woke with a start to find Gill standing by my bed. 'Caught you!' she said smiling. I wasn't amused. I was still bemused by my dream.

'What's going on?'

'Nothing,' said Gill cheerfully. 'I just thought I'd wake you up. It's gone nine o'clock and I wanted to speak to you alone.' I struggled to sit up and gather my wits but they seemed more scattered than usual this morning. 'I've found our man,' she said with a note of triumph. Still witless I said, 'What are you talking about?'

She tutted like an irritable schoolteacher. 'The man to open the attic door. Included in the price he says he'll do us two spare keys.'

'Oh good,' I said as I slid my legs out of bed to sit on the edge. All I really wanted was a cup of hot tea. Gill meanwhile was on full throttle.

'I'll take Helen out in the car somewhere and leave the back door open for him. He says it'll only take him an hour or so to bring back the duplicate keys, which he'll leave for us under a stone by the bird pond.'

'Very cloak and dagger,' I said. 'So he's local?'

'Yeah. I spun him a yarn and paid him well so he's happy.'

I wasn't happy, because it had occurred to me that he couldn't make a duplicate key without some sort of impression. I'd seen films where they made an impression from soap. So how was he going to do it? The man was obviously a criminal and what if he robbed the place or was 'casing the joint' for someone else? But it was too late now.

'What time is he coming?' I asked.

'Eleven-ish,' said Gill. 'Why?'

'I'll pretend to leave just before you take Helen out. Then I'll double back and keep an eye on him.'

'I'm sure we can trust him,' said Gill looking peeved. 'I've told him to leave the door open for you.'

'Never trust a criminal,' I said, sounding just like Hubert giving me one of his warnings. 'I'll be there to make sure he doesn't plan to make a complete set of house keys.'

By ten forty-five Gill was sitting in her car ready to drive Helen off on a bridal-shoe hunt followed by another hunt for a 'going away' outfit. I'd already put my holdall in the car when Helen gave me a hug. 'I'll be in touch. You must meet Paul before the wedding and I'm planning a hen night. Now promise me you'll come.'

'I'll certainly try.'

'I'll make sure she does,' said Gill glancing at her watch and starting up the engine. She drove off as I sat in my car.

I decided I should leave the car tucked away at the far side of the house where chummy wouldn't see it. Then I lurked in the bushes hoping it wouldn't be too long before he arrived.

He was on time. My first view was a short man of about sixty with a slight paunch, balding but with strong tanned legs. His shorts were khaki, a sort of half-combat style. As far as appearance went he was a fourth-division criminal.

But he was first division on speed. Within ten minutes he'd reappeared from the house and driven off. I waited for a few moments and then made my way to the house.

At the attic door I paused. I turned the old-fashioned round handle. It was open and I was in.

Eight

Two skylights flooded the large room with light. The sloping ceilings gave the room character, otherwise it was fairly bleak. I stood for a moment looking round trying to find the measure of the man who kept this room locked. On the left-hand side against the wall was a desk. On the desk was a single photograph, which from the doorway looked like Helen. In the corner on the right-hand side were two vast cardboard boxes of the type used for moving house. And facing me was a sofa bed above which were heavily laden bookshelves.

I went straight to the bookshelves. The bulk of the books were either about wine-making or polo or South America. I searched in vain for any books that might have belonged to Fran or the children. There were none.

Next I opened the desk drawers; there were three on each side. One contained thin files, each one neatly labelled – gas, electricity, water, car, mortgage. The mortgage file I read quickly. He'd taken out a new loan in the first year of his marriage for £100,000 on a 6 per cent fixed loan over five years. It was in his name only. The next file I came across was one labelled *Bank*. There were only his two latest bank statements in it. His current account contained £5,000 and regular varying amounts kept it topped up. I wished I had a camera, that way I could have examined everything at my leisure. Figures are not a strong point of mine but even so the irregular sums and varying times of the month and sources *did* indicate someone working freelance. His outgoings seemed to be utilities and the mortgage. There was a credit-card bill on which he owed £8,000 and which was paid regularly. Mostly the amounts were for expensive restaurant meals, some of the names of which I recognized from TV. He'd also paid a yearly subscription to a London gym.

In one drawer there were pens and notepads, stamps and elastic bands. I used a sheet of paper and a pen to write down the name of the gym and one or two of the restaurants.

In the remaining drawers was a folder with his birth and his marriage certificate and various other certificates such as his GCE 'O' levels and his four 'A' levels, all at grade A. Bright lad, I thought, and tidy too. Far too tidy. I looked in vain for photographs of Fran and the children. But in the last drawer I struck lucky. Under a pile of maps – there it was – a passport. His passport. Five years old. He'd been to Argentina several times and Bolivia. I was a bit uptight now. Who the hell was this man and what the hell was he up to?

After that I concentrated on the two cardboard boxes. The first box contained watercolours about a foot square wrapped carefully in bubble wrap. I took two or three out. I'm not much of an art buff but to me they looked very good. There in the right-hand corner was the signature P. Warrinder. He'd obviously given up painting now for there was no evidence of easels or brushes or paints. In the other box were unwrapped paintings, equally good but with one major difference – the signature. This time they were signed F. Warrinder. They were unmistakably by the same artist. He wasn't the artist – Fran had been the artist and, to my eyes, she'd been talented. And he was altering her signature.

It was then I made a decision. I was going to 'borrow' one painting from each box. I planned to get an expert opinion on them. I was making my choice from the bubble-wrapped ones when a sliver of folded paper fell out. Someone had been playing with it and rolling it into a long cigarette shape. I rolled it out flat. It was the instructions and warnings of an antidepressant called *Tourine*. I'd never heard of it. I folded the paper properly and slipped it into the pocket of my jeans. I glanced at my watch. I'd been in the attic nearly an hour – if our 'crim' was as prompt as previously, he'd be back with the duplicate key any minute.

There was one more thing I had to do before leaving the house. I wanted to check out the master bedroom. I was rushing now to have a quick reconnoitre into Paul's wardrobe. It was an oak double-door monstrosity with a deep drawer underneath. Inside, I was surprised to find at least a score of expensive suits and shirts. He wasn't into ready-mades from M&S. I had a quick peep into Helen's wardrobe and was surprised to find some expensive labels there too.

I wanted to spend more time in the bedroom but the sound of a vehicle driving up the gravel path stopped me in my tracks. I watched surreptitiously from the window and saw the little man come into the house. I stood stock still as he came up the stairs. I heard him climb to the attic, and then seconds later he was closing the back door. I saw him lift a large stone near the birdbath and then he paused to look up at the house before he walked briskly to his white van and drove off. His name was emblazoned on the side – *Robert Roberts – Handyman and General Repairs.*

I left the house then, leaving just one more job to do before leaving Cornwall, collect the local newspapers of two years ago.

I left the office with a bundle of newspapers, which had been left ready for me. I paid for them and the elderly porter at the door waved to me saying in a broad impenetrable accent, 'Don't you read all them at once my beauty, you'll go blind.'

*　　*　　*

The journey back to Longborough took two hours more than going, mainly due to roadworks, and I was exhausted when I eventually arrived back at five p.m. In the car park a Daimler was being polished by one of the pallbearers, who doubles as the car man. I only knew him as Bill. He was shouting something to me. I got out of the car. 'He's not well. The boss. Not well at all. I reckon he needs a doctor.'

'Right, thanks, Bill,' I said. 'I'll see to it.'

I hurried upstairs without my luggage. Hubert was never ill. I rushed to his flat and found him in bed with the curtains pulled. I could hardly see him the room was so dark. At first I thought he was unconscious. But the light seemed to rouse him and Jasper, who was on the far side of the bed. Jasper's whole body shook and quivered in greeting. Hubert meanwhile lay puce-coloured and sweating badly. He saw me and had trouble focusing his eyes but he managed to raise his hand, only to start coughing uncontrollably. He tried to raise himself but sank back against the pillows. 'I'm going to ring the doctor now,' I said. He didn't seem to hear me but when the coughing fit was over he closed his eyes and appeared to fall asleep.

A lanky young locum turned up at six p.m. – listened to Hubert's chest – announced it was 'something going around' but prescribed antibiotics just in case it was pneumonia. Plenty of clear fluids and analgesics every four hours, that was the usual mantra but as he left he said, 'If his breathing worsens get your husband to hospital.'

'He's not my husband.'

'OK – partner.'

I shot him an angry look.

'Well, whoever he is it's the same advice,' he said as he rushed through the door. I swore under my breath as he left.

Later when I'd had the prescription filled I plied Hubert

with an assortment of medication and insisted he drank squash by the pint. I sponged his face and hands and then left him alone to sleep. Over the next couple of hours he coughed every few minutes but I could see his temperature had reduced and he was well enough for me to leave him while I walked Jasper.

During the walk my mobile rang twice. Perhaps not being able to carry on a conversation in the street with any ease is a sign of growing older but I found it difficult. The first call was from my mother. I think she was trying to tell me she was getting itchy feet. Megan it seems was being visited quite a bit by David and I think she was tiring of playing gooseberry. I told her I'd ring her the next day and that I wouldn't be driving over, because Hubert was poorly. Telling her was a mistake. 'I'll get a taxi tomorrow morning,' she said, 'and come over and cheer him up.'

A few minutes later Gill rang. 'What did you find?' she asked excitedly.

'I can't talk now,' I said, 'I'm walking the dog. When you get a chance to see the room tonight ring me and tell me what you make of it all.'

'Anytime?'

I knew I wouldn't be getting much sleep so I agreed, 'Yes, anytime.'

On my return from Jasper's walk I collected my holdall and the Cornish newspapers from the car and went upstairs to find Hubert struggling to get out of bed. 'I don't know what you gave me,' he said. 'But I'm feeling much better. I fancy a sandwich.'

'I'll fetch you a sandwich,' I said. 'But you must stay in bed.' He lay back. 'I'm so glad you're back. I could have died.'

'Don't exaggerate. Anyway I'll be needing some help on this case.'

'Is this the big one?'

Hubert always thought one of my cases – 'the big one' – would rescue me from minor cases to the 'big time', whatever that was, in private investigation circles. Sometimes I think he becomes confused between fact and fiction. After all, who could name a real-life private investigator?

A ham sandwich seemed to settle Hubert and I left him with his medication and instructions to shout loudly if he needed me. 'What if I can't summon the strength?' he asked.

'Tough!'

'You're a hard woman.'

'No. I just don't want you milking this illness for all it's worth.'

'Have I been ill before?'

'No.'

'Well then have some sympathy.'

'Just keep drinking the squash and you'll pull through.'

As I walked back to my flat I realized we were getting more like a bickering married couple every day. It was time, I told myself, I found a man. But I hadn't had much luck so far. A little voice in the back of my head said, *Put some effort in and you might.* Another little voice answered, *You're far too busy at the moment.*

Gill rang at one a.m. I was half-asleep but roused myself. Strangely she seemed disappointed. 'There wasn't much, was there?' she said.

'Less is more in this case,' I said. 'No photos or diaries. Nothing to suggest Fran and the children ever existed. Which in itself is odd. And what about the paintings?'

'They're good. He's quite talented.'

'You didn't notice then that he altered the signatures?'

There was a momentary silence. 'You must think I'm stupid, Kate. I only looked at the top few in the box.'

'And,' I said. 'You haven't mentioned the passport.'

'What passport?'

'The one in the third drawer under the maps.'

There was a short silence. 'I looked,' said Gill. 'I couldn't find a passport.'

'You'll have to go back and have another look.'

'Is it Helen's?'

'No it's Paul's.'

I heard Gill's little gasp of surprise. 'So he hasn't gone to Argentina?'

'I suppose he could have,' I said. 'On a false passport. Or he's somewhere in the UK.'

'The bastard has got another woman.'

'Don't let's jump to any conclusions. If you can't find that passport it must mean Helen's taken it.'

'It's got to be there. It's got to be.' Gill was beginning to sound frantic now. 'Helen's so straight,' she added, 'she'd hand in a dropped pound coin.'

I wasn't sure I believed that but I murmured in agreement just to appease her.

'The only other possibility,' I suggested, 'and it's very remote, is that Robert Roberts nipped back after I'd left and stole it. But that's verging on the ridiculous – what motive could he possibly have?'

'Well . . .'

'Well what?'

'You see he's not a criminal,' she said. 'He's an ex-cop. I actually told him the truth.'

I sighed, not really being sure about the implications. 'OK – let's not panic. You go and recheck the attic and don't forget to lock the door. Ring me back from there and let me know.'

'You mean now?' asked Gill, sounding surprised.

'Yes. What's Paul going to do if he returns and finds his passport missing?'

'Who bloody cares?'

'I expect Helen will. We both think he's a dodgy character, so we don't want to put her in any danger do we?'

Silence. 'I hadn't looked at it that way,' she said thoughtfully. 'I'll go up there now.'

'Ring me in half an hour, I need to check on Hubert.'

'Will do. Thanks, Kate.'

I crept along to Hubert's room, my mind in turmoil. Thankfully he was asleep.

One hour later with the newspaper reports of the tragedy laid out on my bed Gill still hadn't phoned. Had Helen caught her in the act? Should I ring her? I tried to concentrate on reading but couldn't. After a further fifteen minutes I dialled Gill's mobile. There was no answer.

Nine

I folded up the newspapers, tried one more time to contact Gill and then gave up on the day. I was exhausted and worried but there was nothing I could do.

In the morning I took Hubert a mug of tea and he looked more chipper. 'Hardly coughed last night,' he said proudly. He peered at me. 'Did you have a good night?'

I shook my head. 'I'll tell you all about it later.'

I took Jasper for a walk and felt far more wide awake when I got back. I was just boiling an egg for Hubert's breakfast when my mobile rang. It was Gill sounding agitated. 'Kate, I'm really, really sorry. I was creeping past Helen's room and I heard her sobbing. I couldn't just ignore it could I?'

'What was wrong with her?'

'Something about a man she'd met in India. A journalist. A brief affair and it turns out he was married.'

'So are you saying she's got pre-wedding nerves?'

'Well sort of – this ex-love has got in touch to say his wife is divorcing him and he wants to carry on where they left off.'

'I wonder why she didn't mention him before in our girly chats.'

'Well, you know Helen, she likes everyone to think she's a bit of a lady. A married journo doesn't fit her image.'

'I think that's the point I want to make, Gill. I *don't* know her. She once wore the whitest of white socks, her mother died of cancer, she's a great cook and she enjoys travelling.

71

For a living she takes photos and in her wardrobe she has some very expensive clothes. That is really all I know – well – except she's in love with Paul Warrinder or says she is.'

'You sound suspicious of her,' she said after a long pause.

'I wouldn't put it as strongly as that. Just curious about her motivation.'

'What do you mean?'

'Well, is it real love or is she searching for security?'

'Better security with a fantastic-looking rich guy than an old fat ugly one. And believe me I know what I'm talking about.'

'Does she see any faults in him at all?'

'Not really. Although she did say tonight she thought he was secretive.'

'It seems Helen may have some secrets too.'

'I'm very fond of Helen,' said Gill sharply.

'I know. But how well do you know her? How often have you seen her since school?'

Gill's sharp tone changed now. 'I suppose twice a year. We've kept in touch by e-mail and phone.'

'I don't want to upset you, Gill, but she may not be the person you think she is.'

'You're just cynical.'

'No, it's being in the investigation business. It's like a woman in labour. It's not a normal birth till it's over. I'm struggling not to make two and two equal a villain without having proof.'

'You'll find the proof. He is the villain. Don't try to make Helen out as some sort of accomplice.'

'I wasn't.'

Strange that now she'd used the word accomplice it actually put the idea in my head.

'What about the passport, Gill?' I asked.

'Oh . . . I found it. Didn't I say? It was tucked in one of those magazines.'

She didn't lie well. But I couldn't carry on the conversation knowing that she thought it necessary to lie to protect her friend.

'When you want to tell me the truth, Gill – ring me again. Bye.'

I could almost sense her shock that I hadn't been taken in by her feeble lie. The passport was missing. Helen was the chief suspect. If she was protecting Paul the question was – why? What had he done? Or, more to the point, what was he up to now?

Two days later Gill still hadn't rung. My mother, though, had visited Hubert bearing grapes and lemon barley water. I noticed she was reverting back to type, her skirts were getting shorter and her make-up heavier. She would undoubtedly be on the move again soon. Hubert, though, seemed to rally in her presence and she spent a few hours with him playing cards. Maybe, if my mother was off on her travels, I'd see more of Megan and Katy, but from my mother's observations David Todman had more than a foot in the door now and I didn't fancy playing gooseberry either.

As far as investigating Paul Warrinder was concerned I had found out something. I'd phoned Helen to thank her for her hospitality. I'd caught her in the garden. 'I'm a bit worried about Gill,' she said. 'She seems really preoccupied and she's obsessed with finding fault with Paul. Do you think she's jealous?'

'She might be,' I said. 'He's young and gorgeous. Who wouldn't be? When's he coming back from Argentina?'

'There's a problem. It could be next week now. But Gill, bless her, has promised she'll stay until he gets back.'

'So, you don't feel any better about staying in the house alone?'

'I wish I did, Kate. I haven't heard anything . . . creepy . . . since I've had company but there's something making me very uneasy.'

'Is Paul likely to go abroad often?'

'Yes he is.'

'Why don't you stay in a hotel when he's away?'

'I'd be happy doing that but he says the house needs someone in it and he likes to picture me at Tamberlake.'

I swallowed hard. I wanted to say, *Come on Helen. Stop being such a wimp.* Helen wasn't stupid. She simply wanted to please and I couldn't help feeling he was taking advantage of her. Perhaps I was slow but it suddenly occurred to me that I'd taken it for granted that all three of us were scraping a living. Gill, as it turned out, had her 'candy man' and, thanks to him, her own business. And I didn't suppose photos of Cornwall and Wales brought in that much. The house had been remortgaged and Paul wasn't in Argentina, so the rich playboy scenario wasn't a sure thing. Helen had a wardrobe of designer labels. The question remained. Did Helen have money?

Asking outright about her bank account seemed intrusive, so we finished the conversation on a chat about wedding shoes and the headdress. Gill promised to ring me soon and badger me about coming down for the weekend to meet Paul. I murmured that I'd look forward to that.

Now that the wedding outfit was complete, it was all systems go. I felt like a Judas because it looked likely that Helen was going to find out some unpalatable information about her beloved. The main question being would it be best for her to know before the wedding or after? Logically it would be better for her to have any information before the wedding but emotionally she could be heartbroken.

I did need to speak to Gill again. She had knowledge of Helen's friends and family that I didn't have. I'd just have to apologize and say that being suspicious wasn't a choice for me; it was a lifestyle.

Hubert, thank goodness, was by now up and about. He was already fretting about his backlog of funerals but he wasn't quite fit enough to put in a full day. He was, however, in need of some mental stimulation, or so he said, and I needed some input from him.

We sat in the kitchen drinking coffee and I told him that I was on a genuine investigation. He smiled. 'In contrast to your fake investigations.'

I bristled at that. 'I need you to be serious,' I said. 'Helen could be in some sort of danger.'

'Right,' he said. 'Tell me the story from the beginning and my poor addled brain might just about cope.'

I told him about the house first.

'Do you think it's haunted?' he asked.

'No, definitely not.'

'Well, we know Helen's scared on her own there,' he said thoughtfully. 'I suppose that's because she knows another woman was unhappy enough to kill herself and take her children with her . . .' He paused and I was about to chip in when he said, 'What about him – the widower?'

'What do you mean?'

'Is he scared of the place? Does he think it's haunted?'

There were times, I thought, when a male perspective opened up a whole range of different concepts. I didn't of course know the answer to Hubert's question. And he looked somewhat smug. 'That business with the passport and not being in Argentina might just be his way of escaping from the house and its memories. He might not want to admit he's scared shitless too.'

'I suppose that's a possibility,' I grudgingly admitted. I did know he'd tried to sell the house but was that for his sake or Helen's? 'But he's obviously dishonest or why would he want to pass off Fran's paintings as his own? He could have sold those anyway.'

'I don't know the answer to that,' said Hubert. 'Let me read the newspaper reports and see if I can make any sense of it. Perhaps the reporter on the local rag could give you some more information.'

I flashed Hubert a huge smile.

'What did I say?' he asked, mystified.

'You just gave me an idea. Thanks.'

I rushed off then to get him the Cornish newspapers. On my return he sat with a pen and a notepad poised. He seemed pleased enough to have something to do and the thought struck me that I'd read the reports when I was half-asleep. Had I missed anything? I'd be mortified if Hubert proved he was more observant than me and judging by the determined look on his face he was out to do just that.

I took Jasper for a walk and rang Gill's mobile from a bench by the river. 'I can't talk now, sweetie,' she said. 'I'll ring you later.' Obviously Helen was around and she couldn't talk normally. Gill reserved her generic 'sweeties' for all males, just in case she slipped up.

Viewing Hubert from the kitchen doorway on my return I noticed he was making copious notes. Jasper, undecided about whom to stay with, followed me to my office, where I labelled a file and decided to call it 'Tamberlake'. I then began a list of people I needed to talk to. I put Paul Warrinder at the top of the list but I needed far more background before I met him. That way I might be able to tell truth from lies.

Gill's suspicions that somehow Paul had a hand in his family's death didn't gel with me but I conceded that he might well have caused her mental breakdown by something he did or something she found out. All the conjecture in the world wasn't going to make any difference and the moment Hubert was fully better I was going to find Paul Warrinder.

'Stop lurking in the doorway and come in.' Hubert it seems could see through the back of his head. I was impressed until I realized he could see my reflection in the murky kitchen window. The window cleaner had also been laid low with the 'bug' with no name and consequently they hadn't been cleaned for three weeks.

'Did you read these reports properly?' Hubert asked.

'I was tired,' I said, 'and there didn't seem much information.'

'That's a point I wanted to make. Take this line – *"Friends of the couple were too upset to talk about the deaths but the local delicatessen owner said they were a very sociable couple who often entertained."*'

'OK, so their friends didn't want to talk to the press.'

'Ask yourself why not?'

'I don't know.'

'And the funeral?'

'What about it?'

'It says here –' he jabbed at the paper – *"The small church of St Peter's was packed to capacity."*'

'So?'

'So, you need to get back to Cornwall and talk to their friends.'

'I did realize that,' I snapped.

'Well, I think you'll need help,' said Hubert, staring at me over his reading glasses. 'I could get in touch with the undertaker and get some inside info.'

'That would be great,' I said, with no real enthusiasm. Hubert it seemed was trying to hijack my case.

'I was thinking,' said Hubert, 'it would probably be best if I actually came with you.' I stared at him. Hubert didn't 'do' absence from his business, unless it was the annual Funeral Directors' Convention. 'I'll have to get a locum in,' he added, 'but I'm prepared to take a week or so off, because I think this is an important case.'

'Do you? I think you think I'll cock it up.'

'No I don't. And I need some fresh sea air. I'm not feeling a hundred per cent.'

'That's it, Hubert – tug at my heart strings.'

I did of course need some help. I patted Hubert on the cheek and said we'd be off first thing in the morning. 'I'll do the driving,' I said and Hubert muttered something about sharing it but at least it was settled.

Gill rang at eleven thirty. She sounded subdued and I thought that was because she harboured some resentment for my calling her a liar. 'I'm sorry I didn't believe you,' I said. 'If you say the passport wasn't there and then mysteriously it was there, then I accept that you were telling the truth.'

'I'm sorry, Kate. I did lie about finding it again. Only Helen could have removed it. I regret that now . . . I've found out something else. I haven't let Helen know but quite honestly she's not the person I thought she was and I don't know if I can stay here any longer.' Her tone was so different now from the cheerful bouncy Gill who'd arrived at Tamberlake only a few days before. She sounded near to tears. 'Come on,' I said softly. 'Tell me what you've found out.'

Ten

Gill sniffed and took a sighing breath. 'I was looking through Helen's personal photos. Just out of interest. Everything was there, all in order, neat writing underneath. Family photos, school days, first job, old boyfriends, days out, days by the sea in . . . Cornwall. And there amongst all those important moments was a photo of her sitting on a wall behind Fran and her children on the beach. I guess it was Paul taking the photo. She was smiling as if he were taking a photo of her.'

'Don't jump to conclusions, Gill. It may have been a coincidence. Were there any other photos of them together?'

'Not that I found,' she said, then added in a rush, 'I won't sleep tonight. I didn't sleep last night. I think this house is evil. There's something I can't explain. I haven't heard anything but I can feel it. There's a presence and I think that there is something we need to do but I don't know what it is.' I was quite worried. She was getting distraught and I wasn't sure what to say to make her feel better.

'Calm down,' I said. 'Take a deep breath. You have got an option. Leave there and take Helen with you. Book into a B&B.'

'She won't leave. She says she's got to get used to it . . .' She broke off. 'I just don't trust her anymore.'

'I'm coming down tomorrow with Hubert, my landlord. We'll probably stay somewhere near Tamberlake. You and I can meet up if you can shake Helen off.'

'Yeah, OK.' She sounded reluctant. Then she added, 'I wish I'd never got involved in all this. My fault . . . I want to cling on to the past.'

'I'll ring you tomorrow,' I said. 'If you call me "sweetie" I'll know Helen's around.'

I found Hubert in my office using my computer. 'I'm finding us a hotel,' he said. 'Nice-looking place near Trevelly. Food a specialty. That'll suit you.'

'Food doesn't rule my life.'

'Keeps you happy though doesn't it?'

I smiled sweetly, refusing to rise to his bait. 'I'm off to get packed. Are we taking Jasper, by the way?'

'Of course. They allow small dogs in the ground-floor rooms.'

'Good. I'm off to get packed.'

'I thought we'd make an early start,' said Hubert. 'Six a.m.'

'Fine. What car?'

'Mine's the best.'

'Well it would be wouldn't it?'

Even I was impressed when I saw a white Porsche parked outside. 'You haven't bought this have you?' I asked.

'Well I didn't steal it. It arrived while you were away. I haven't had a chance to give it a spin.'

'Are you sure you're well enough to drive?' I was, of course, only angling to drive it myself.

Hubert grinned. 'It'll be less tiring to drive it myself.'

The drive itself was slow and tedious. Hubert didn't plan to wear out his new car by thrashing it at speeds above 60mph, but I have to admit it was such a comfortable drive that I slept between our regular comfort breaks.

The hotel when we finally arrived at one o'clock was, I thought, 'twee' – all bone china cups and saucers, lace doilies and elderly couples enjoying 'civilization' at the 'Regis'.

The receptionist, a brightly painted woman in her forties, spoke in a loud high voice. 'Lunch is being served now,' she trilled. 'And this evening dinner is served at seven p.m. precisely, there's bingo at eight in the small ballroom, followed by live music.'

'I can hardly wait,' I said. Hubert and the receptionist looked daggers at me. Jasper tried to wriggle free from under Hubert's arms and we made a hasty exit to our ground-floor rooms.

The room itself overlooked the garden and there were sliding doors leading outside. It was a bit chintzy for my taste but the bed looked and felt fine and it was roomy. It was certainly more cheerful than the guest room at Tamberlake. Hubert announced he was pleased with his room and with the enclosed garden, because he could leave the door open and let Jasper run free.

Luckily we were assigned a table for two. There was a moderate choice of menu but it was three courses and the other diners seemed to be enjoying large portions. 'Have you ever noticed,' I asked Hubert, 'how well pensioners eat?'

'It's senior citizens now. You're already in training aren't you?'

I ignored his jibe. 'It does make you wonder about healthy eating, though, because I've noticed old people love biscuits and cakes and red meat and pies. How come it's done them no harm?'

'I dunno, Kate. They were the generation who only had fresh fruit if someone was ill in the house. Seems surprising they got past forty. I'm surprised I'm still here, I was brought up on suet dumplings and bread and dripping with salt.'

After the gut-busting lunch I felt like sleeping but Hubert had his agenda. 'First stop,' he said, 'the deli in Trevelly.' I wondered why that was his first stop but since he was the man with the car I didn't have much choice. I had a nervous twitch in my stomach, or was it a foreboding that Hubert really was taking over my case? Or maybe I'd simply eaten too much. Either way I felt a bit sick.

The delicatessen, tucked away in a side street, reminded me of shops in Spain or France – small but stocked to the gunnels – decorated with hams and salamis and sausage of every nationality. Those that couldn't be hung up were displayed on the marble counters covered with domed glass. Cheeses of the world were arranged with tiny bunches of black and white grapes between them. Virgin olive oils labelled as well as any wine were packed in ranks on the shelves, along with every known variety of vinegar.

There were no other customers and the owner – a big bearded man in his fifties wearing a white apron – seemed delighted we'd appeared. 'I'm Rufus,' he said. His accent, although hard to place, was not West Country. 'Are you on holiday?' he asked Hubert. For some reason he ignored me completely.

'I'm looking for olive oil,' answered Hubert. 'A good one,' he added. I was surprised, I knew that recently Hubert had occasionally used olive oil, influenced by tales of everlasting youth, but I had no idea he was going to use it as a tactic. In Hubert's youth olive oil was for purely medicinal purposes. It was warmed, poured on cotton wool and then inserted into the ear to relieve earache.

They went into a cosy huddle and then Rufus took a bottle of olive oil from the top shelf and gave Hubert a short lecture on second and third 'pressings' and would he like a taster on a piece of bread? Hubert did and I was about to intervene in this leisurely form of shopping when Hubert asked Rufus, 'How long have you had the shop?'

He smiled good-naturedly. 'I'd like to say this was the family business and I'd been here all my life. But I worked in the city, sold the London house and bought this four years ago. A dream come true.'

Hubert nodded sagely. I moved slightly nearer to both of them and Rufus smiled at me as if suddenly realizing that I was there. 'Try this new cheese, my dear – lovely dessert cheese – white Stilton with ginger.'

He cut me off a rather large sample and I nibbled away while Hubert came up with the reason for our visit. 'I paid a visit to Tamberlake, near Trevelly, a few years back.'

'Did you really? Lovely house. Run-down now I suppose. So tragic – poor Fran, and the children of course.'

'I only knew her vaguely – slight family connection.'

Hubert had missed his vocation in life. He should have been an actor. Today he was wearing his navy blazer and cream slacks, his 'away-day outfit', which he thought made him look a tad nautical. I thought he looked more like a 'lovey'. 'Was she a customer of yours?' he asked casually.

'She certainly was. Every Saturday morning. She came in here the morning she died. They loved entertaining. Every Saturday they had friends round for a meal. Quite informal I believe. It seems that Saturday night they cancelled. Her husband Paul said she was feeling low all day and couldn't face cooking. Strange . . . she seemed the same as usual that Saturday morning.'

Rufus wrapped up the olive oil as carefully as if it were a vintage wine and when I heard the price I thought of how many bottles of cheap plonk I could buy for the same money. He also asked me if I had enjoyed the cheese. 'It was delicious,' I said. 'We'll be in again before we leave Cornwall.'

Rufus smiled, well satisfied. Hubert paid him and asked, 'Do the new owners of Tamberlake shop here?'

Rufus shook his head. 'Paul's only been in once or twice since. He was living alone for a while, although I've heard there's a new woman in his life now. He doesn't seem to have much luck with women – rather like me.' Rufus threw back his head and laughed. 'My wife lasted six months down here. Too quiet I suppose and I talk food all the time so that probably drove her away. That, and the fact she fell for a local potter. There's not that much to say about clay is there?' He laughed again. I had the feeling that Rufus was either a little mad or his laughter indicated relief that his wife had left him and he'd been a happy little soul ever since.

My energy levels were beginning to flag but Hubert, in contrast, was as bright as a hopping bunny. We sat in the car and he took out his notebook. 'One thing about small places is everybody knows everybody else. The local funeral director has been very helpful. It seems Paul was accompanied to the funeral parlour by a chap called Jamie Ingrams.'

'Have you got an address?'

Hubert nodded. 'What we really need is some police input. You could ring David, see if he'll give us a hand.'

'No way!'

'Why not?'

'He's seeing Megan and I don't want to muddy the waters.'

Hubert sighed as if I was being particularly difficult and I began to get irritated. My case was being taken over. 'I think our first priority,' I said firmly, trying to re-establish my position, 'is to see the doctor who gave evidence at the hearing.'

'I had thought of that,' he said swiftly. 'But he's not at the same practice. He's now working in Devon. So that's a journey for another day.'

Wanting to be at least one up I said, 'I want to be the one to interview him.'

Hubert looked at me closely. 'I hope you're not losing your sense of humour.'

I ignored him. The funny side of life was evading me at the moment. 'I thought I'd need a cover story, so I'll be a new, enthusiastic health visitor doing some current research into isolation and depression in women with pre-school children.'

'Sounds impressive,' said Hubert. 'You haven't lost your sense of humour then?'

I didn't respond. I was too busy thinking about how best to handle the doctor. I'd brought with me several blank identity cards and, with a passport-size photo, a decent felt-tip pen, a plastic casing, a bit of ingenuity, flat shoes, a skirt, the merest flick of lipstick and a clipboard – I would become Kate Brown, HV. I'd show Hubert who was the investigator.

Hubert drove back towards Trevelly at funeral pace to the home of Jamie Ingrams. I worried about being seen by Helen so I kept my head down just in case. After all, she'd managed to spot me in Wales and if she saw me now it could ruin everything. Hubert glanced at me as I hunched down in the front seat. He had a plan it seemed. 'We're police officers from the Met, investigating the disappearance of Paul Warrinder's former girlfriend,' he said. 'What did you say her name was?'

'I didn't. Hang on, I'll try to think.'

I found it worrying that I'd forgotten her name. Eventually I came up with 'Alison' and the 'Peters' soon followed. 'What do we know about her?' asked Hubert.

'Nothing. Just that she got as far as the wedding dress and then they broke up and she . . .'

I broke off, annoyed with myself for not knowing more. Hubert became conciliatory.

'You can't find out everything in a few days. That's what we're here for.'

'We don't know for sure she's actually "*disappeared*". If he jilted her she's not going to be sending him postcards is she?' Hubert nodded and even managed to speed up a little.

I sat watching the countryside pass by. Summer was ending and the trees and fields had a parched and jaded look. Tamberlake had that jaded look too but it would have no regeneration in the spring. Two young women had had their moments of happiness there but how abruptly that had changed. Was Paul evil? Or was it the house itself? Surely in five years Fran would have known most of Paul's secrets, or at least what she'd found out that Saturday wouldn't have come as too great a shock. Sometimes the simple answers are the only answers. He was a very attractive man. Maybe he wouldn't cheat in his own back yard, but if for both women a revelation about another woman had come as a terrible shock, who knows what sort of emotional reaction there could have been. Did Helen have some inkling that he was cheating on her? Was that the cause of her anxiety? Mere suspicion but enough to blight anyone's wedding day. When he was at Tamberlake she could relax because she knew exactly where he was. And surely no woman could tolerate a locked room? And was she lying about not having a key to the attic room?

'You all right?' asked Hubert.

'Fine. Just thinking.'

'Well don't start fretting and jumping to conclusions. We've got to keep an open mind.'

'Thank you – oh wise one – I'm the investigator not you.'

'That's it, Kate – you get the bit between your teeth. This could be your finest hour.'

Somehow I doubted that but I muttered, 'Yeah, yeah.'

Jamie Ingrams lived on the first floor of a three-storey block of flats overlooking a park. He answered the entry-phone so quickly that it was as if he was expecting us.

'Police?' he enquired. We nodded with supreme confidence. Hubert introduced himself as DCI Rodney Stone and me as DI Cheryl West. Why Hubert had decided to call himself Rodney was beyond me but I supposed it was an improvement on Hubert.

Jamie was jockey-height and boyishly slim. He looked at first glance to be in his twenties but on closer inspection he had lines around his eyes and slightly receding floppy fair hair. He was probably in his late thirties. In old age he would be gnome-like.

The apartment suited his size and Hubert and I, standing, constituted a crowd. Jamie had made attempts to make the flat look bigger by mirrors and pure white walls and small black furniture. There was no clutter and no sign of hobbies. There was an arrangement of bright geometric prints on one wall adding to the modern feel. I tried to guess his occupation but couldn't. Judging from his flat he didn't bring work home.

'You've come about Alison haven't you?' he asked as he directed us to sit down. We nodded. 'Good. I'm glad the police have taken notice at last.'

'Would you like to explain that, sir?' When Hubert acted 'cop' he seemed to model his behaviour on old black and white movies. He talked slowly and enunciated every word as if he were dealing with the dull-witted. Not that Jamie seemed to notice. He was keen to talk. 'I'd given up on anyone taking any sort of action. She's been missing now for more than six years. I've tried to find her but the local police said they couldn't help me because she was an adult and, although they were sympathetic, they said they simply hadn't got the manpower.'

'Would you like to start from the beginning, sir?' said Hubert, flicking open his notebook. 'What exactly was your connection with Alison Peters?'

Jamie looked slightly surprised, as if Hubert should have known. Then he glanced at me, as if with momentary suspicion. 'She's my sister,' he said. 'Well, half-sister.'

Eleven

H ubert and I tried to keep impassive expressions.
'I introduced her to Paul,' said Jamie. 'He was a long-term friend of mine and I thought they'd get on. Alison worked in London as a fashion buyer for one of the chain stores. She loved her job but she fell for Paul, gave it up and moved into Tamberlake – all in the space of two months.'

'You didn't feel happy about the relationship?' I asked.

He shrugged. 'I was fairly neutral, I just thought it was rushed. When they started to make wedding plans, I'll admit I wasn't too pleased at first.'

'Did you have doubts about Paul Warrinder?'

Jamie shook his head. 'I could see the attraction, he's a good-looking guy and he owned Tamberlake. Alison liked the finer things of life, designer clothes, holidays abroad, good food and wine. I think she thought Paul was a good marital bet, which I suppose he was. I thought so too at the time . . .'

'But you don't anymore?'

'I had reservations. I was a great deal more upset when he married Fran less than six months after Alison left Tamberlake.'

'Did you know Fran?' asked Hubert.

'Oh yes. She was a lovely girl.'

'So you remained on good terms with Paul?'

Jamie looked sharply at Hubert. 'Are you saying I shouldn't have? He didn't jilt my sister. She decided he

88

just couldn't offer her enough. His income was a bit erratic and I think she just got cold feet about the wedding.'

'Did she tell you that?'

'Not in so many words. She was cold . . . you know. Chilled.'

'Were you close?' I asked.

He shook his head. 'No, we were never really close. We kept in touch and my mother's death brought us closer. She died of alcohol poisoning when Alison was twenty. Our respective fathers had long since abandoned us. So in effect there are only Alison and I. And since I haven't heard from Alison in six years something may well have happened to her.'

'I'm sorry to ask this question,' I said, 'but it is my job.'

He smiled at me briefly.

'Did your sister have any money?'

'Oh yes. Our mother left us a substantial house, not quite Tamberlake but in the South of England, and some capital. Mother had family money which, had she lived to old age, she'd have pissed it all away. I bought this flat and invested the rest of the money. It means I only take temporary jobs as the fancy takes me. I'm basically an idle bastard.'

Strange, I thought, how often some people never answer the question you actually asked.

Hubert gave a little smug nod in my direction.

'And Alison's share?' I persisted.

'That's the strange part,' he said, frowning. 'She's spent quite a bit enjoying herself, travelling, not working, that sort of thing. But two weeks before she left I met her quite by accident coming out of the bank. She'd closed her high-interest accounts and said she'd left just a couple of thousand in her current account. When I asked her why, she told me to mind my own business but I wasn't to tell Paul. All would be revealed later. Well I'm still waiting.'

'She sounds the impulsive type,' I suggested.

'She was *that* all right. She followed her whims. Maybe Paul fell into that category, I don't know. I think that she planned to go abroad and spend her money recklessly. I wasn't that worried in the first year. She wasn't much of a communicator. But she did send Christmas cards – always. And when someone doesn't send a Christmas card for six years you begin to doubt they are still alive.'

'What about . . .' I began but he held up a hand to silence me.

'What about tea or coffee? I'm parched.'

'Lovely. Thank you.'

He walked the few yards to the kitchen and closed the door and I didn't hear any tap running or cups rattling. 'Go and check on him, Hubert, I think he's phoning someone.'

Hubert didn't look too pleased – 'Yes, ma'am,' he said, saluting me. He came back seconds later to tell me that Jamie was indeed making a call.

A tray of coffee and biscuits eventually arrived. Jamie played mother and handed me a cup and saucer. 'Now then, Jamie,' I said, feeling clumsy holding delicate china in one hand and a biscuit in the other. 'What about Paul's reaction to Alison leaving. How much did he know about her plans?'

He paused for a moment and I felt he was carefully considering his answer.

'It came as a great shock to him of course. He looked ill that day, he was really upset. He said he'd been given no warning. She was leaving because she didn't feel ready to settle down.'

He sipped at his coffee for a few moments and then Hubert said bluntly, 'So, you're pretty sure Alison is dead?'

There was a short pause before he said sadly, 'Yes. It's just a gut feeling.'

'And who do you think killed her, sir?'

Jamie looked flummoxed. 'I hadn't thought about that. I mean, who . . . She probably died in some third-world country . . . an accident.'

'There would still have been a body, sir, third world or not.'

'Yes. You're right.'

'What about sightings, sir?'

'What do you mean?'

'Did anyone see her leave Tamberlake or get on a train or board a plane?'

'Not that I know of. She left fairly late. That might have been on impulse.'

'I see, sir,' said Hubert slowly. 'So it seems the last person to see Alison was in fact Paul Warrinder. Do you think he tried to persuade her not to leave?'

'What are you suggesting? That Paul had something to do with her disappearance? That's ridiculous. He was upset but he wasn't angry. Anyway he's not the violent type. I've known him for years.'

'I'm merely making enquiries, sir. Could we talk about Fran now?'

Jamie refilled his coffee cup and sat down. 'Can you make this quick?' he said. 'It's very painful. What I can tell you is he met Fran in a wine bar. I was there and I have to say she looked like Alison – same physical type. Six months later they were married.'

'Did she move into Tamberlake before she got married?'

'No. Afterwards.'

'Did she like the house?'

'She thought the house had bad vibes but she got used to it. She was pregnant soon after getting married and Paul didn't think a major upheaval would be good for her.'

'So you saw them quite often?'

'Yeah. Usually once a week. Saturday nights Paul would invite people. Fran did the shopping and Paul did the

91

cooking. Simple stuff, spag bol, chilli, curries. Big-bowl stuff. But we had good wine with the meal – it was great.'

'And when the children came along – you still saw them on Saturday nights?'

'Yes. The kids were in bed. They were good sleepers.'

'And Fran coped when Paul was away?'

'She had a cleaning lady three times a week.'

'We'll need her name and address. And any friends or relatives or anyone who could shed light on Alison's whereabouts.'

He shook his head. 'No, I've asked around. The cleaner's name is Carole Jackson. Number four Robin Crescent. It's just around the corner.' Hubert wrote down the address in his careful hand as Jamie scrawled down some names and addresses on the back of an envelope. 'I have contacted these people,' said Jamie defensively. 'But obviously with no result.'

Hubert was on another tack by now. 'So, Warrinder didn't have any money problems,' he muttered, as if to himself. 'They entertained, had a cleaning lady. Gardener?'

'Bill Andrews did the garden. He still does a bit occasionally. He's well over seventy.'

'So who paid for all this?'

Jamie looked a bit taken aback by Hubert's bluntness. 'Fran took care of the gardener and the cleaner. Paul paid all the utilities.'

'Fran had money too then?'

Jamie looked daggers at Hubert. 'You're at it again. Innuendo. Money attracts money. She had a pile of elderly relatives who seemed to die one after the other, so, yes, she did have her own money. But she didn't brag about it. She had modest tastes – she was the artistic type. She'd been to art school. I believe she'd sold a few watercolours. Fran didn't need to do nine to five to survive . . .' He broke off at the word 'survive', as if realizing maybe she hadn't in fact survived.

I took over again, deciding to change the subject. 'What if I were to tell you that at this moment Paul is pretending to be in Argentina?'

Jamie looked at me sharply. 'What are you talking about?'

'I'm telling you Paul Warrinder has told Helen that he is in Argentina when he isn't.'

'Well where is he then?'

'I thought perhaps you could tell me. Shall I tell you what we suspect?'

'Go ahead,' he said, obviously rattled. 'It's bound to be ridiculous.'

'I think he has another woman.'

Jamie threw back his head and laughed. 'Not Paul. You really are barking up the wrong tree. He's a one-woman man. Always has been.'

'How can you be so sure?'

'I just know, that's all.'

I decided to drop that point for the moment. 'Nearly finished with the questions,' I said soothingly. 'I'd just like to clarify what happened on the Saturday that Fran and the children died.'

He looked at me with slight suspicion. 'I thought you were here about my half-sister, after all, she's the one who seems to have disappeared. Fran's death was tragic but there was no mystery about it. I blame the doctor.'

'Why's that?'

'He prescribed those pills for her.'

'What were they for?'

'He said at the inquest that she was depressed and had trouble sleeping. It was those pills she gave the children and took herself.'

'He obviously treated her in good faith.'

'She never seemed depressed to me.'

93

'Perhaps she put on a cheerful front.'

He frowned, unconvinced. 'Maybe,' I said, 'she didn't appear depressed, because the medication *did work*.'

'Why then did she kill herself and those poor kids?' His voice cracked slightly. It struck me that he was more upset about Fran and the children than he was about the presumed death of his half-sister.

'You were fond of the children?'

'I love kids. And those two were great. I used to babysit from when they were born. Fran knew she could always rely on me to take care of them. Why did the silly cow . . .' He broke off. 'It upsets me.'

He still hadn't answered my question about that Saturday night. 'Have you any idea why Fran cancelled the dinner party? She did the shopping for it and then suddenly it was all off. Did Paul ring you to tell you?'

There was a slight pause before he answered. 'Yeah, he rang to say she was off-colour – nothing specific.'

'What time was that?'

'Afternoon, about four. I can't really remember the exact time.'

'Were you surprised?'

'Not really.'

Although I hadn't asked any difficult questions he continued to look vaguely uncomfortable, like a man losing a fight and expecting the next blow. 'What does surprise me,' I said – he looked at me expectantly – 'is that Fran didn't leave a note. By not leaving one it must have been especially hurtful for Paul. After all, no one seems to have any idea why she did it.'

He nodded as if in agreement.

'Your half-sister, just as abruptly, takes back her wedding dress and runs off. To me that smacks of Paul being responsible.'

'You're talking bloody nonsense. What on earth would

Paul have done to make them unhappy? He loved them both, and his kids.'

'Are you so sure of that?'

'I can only speak as I find. Paul is . . .' He paused and in that moment I knew exactly his dilemma. 'I'm . . .'

'You're in love with him.'

Twelve

After a few minutes Hubert drove away from Jamie Ingrams's flat and parked round the corner. I sensed he was a little peeved that I'd found out something he hadn't thought of but being curious he had to ask. 'The only reason I guessed Jamie was in love with Paul,' I said, 'and I know it sounds corny, but his eyes lit up at the sound of his name.'

Hubert muttered that he'd thought Jamie was in love with Fran.

'I'm sure he was fond of her but it was Paul he wanted.'

'But Paul isn't gay?' asked Hubert, sounding somewhat confused.

'Jamie only claimed unrequited love. Paul *could* be bisexual but he obviously didn't fancy Jamie.'

'Where does that get us then?' asked Hubert dejectedly.

'Back to the hotel, dinner and then bed, I hope.'

'That's your trouble, Kate, creature comforts, that's all you want.'

'Not quite,' I said, hoping to sound less of a hedonist. 'There are more important things in life than food and bed.'

'Name two,' said Hubert, smirking. 'And don't say sex, because you don't get any.'

'The pursuit of truth is one,' I said haughtily. Hubert laughed until he grew pink in the face. 'You'll see,' I snapped. 'Forget comfort, let's go and see the cleaning lady now.'

Carole Jackson lived around the next corner in a small semi. Hubert, living in yesteryear, expected an apron and a mop and bucket. Instead, the woman who answered the door wore embroidered jeans, a skimpy top and high-heeled mules. She was perhaps forty but she was living proof that the forties *are* the new thirties. Her make-up was immaculate and her nails, improbably long for the real thing, were multi-coloured. I did the introductions, Stone and West, because Hubert seemed a little preoccupied with her feet. Carole had one of those voices that would calm a knife-wielding maniac, and angelic features that, if recovering from anaesthesia, would immediately be a comfort. Hubert became incapable of speech and as she guided us through to her living room I jabbed him in the back with my finger. That seemed to bring him to, because he flashed me an angry look as if I'd wrecked one of his best erotic moments. Which I probably had.

Our visit didn't seem to come as a surprise. 'Have you come about Alison?' she asked.

'Alison *and* Fran.'

'You sit down. I've got plenty of time. Last time I saw the police they rushed me. Short of manpower they said they were.'

We sat down on a two-seater sofa while Carole sat on a window seat. Hubert was still mesmerized, so much so that I had to explain, 'DCI Stone is the strong silent type. But we've got plenty of time too and we thought you might be able to help us.'

'I'll do my best. I think about what happened over and over. Sometimes I think if I think about it long enough I'll make sense of it.'

'How do you mean?'

'Little things I keep remembering, but sometimes my memory plays tricks, after all, it was a long time ago now.'

'Give me an example.'

She thought for a moment. 'All right. I used to clean for Alison on Mondays, Wednesdays and Fridays from ten till four. She was ever so excited about her wedding. On that Saturday in June she went to pick up her dress. She even rang me to tell me how thrilled she was with the dress. Then when I came on Monday she was so quiet that I asked her what was wrong. I thought her and Paul had had a row but she said no and she didn't want to talk about it. At the time I thought it was because Paul had gone abroad that day and she was missing him. But now . . .'

'Now?'

'It's only a feeling if you know what I mean and I don't like to speak ill of anyone, especially when he seemed so heartbroken when she left, but . . .'

'You can tell me.'

'Yeah. You're right. It's best if I tell you,' she said. 'It was after she took the dress back that she made one or two comments about Paul. She said more to me on the Wednesday. He'd gone abroad by then and he'd be away for a week. She seemed a bit more cheerful; perhaps it was relief he wasn't in the house. She said that she didn't know him well enough to marry him and at first I thought she was planning to carry on living at Tamberlake, just staying single. But I was wrong about that. Alison was a private sort of person, a bit reserved, but I can see now that it could have been something else.'

'What exactly?'

'Fear. She was afraid of him. Too afraid to tell him she'd taken the dress back and the wedding was off.'

'Most women would baulk at telling a man news like that.'

'No,' said Carole firmly. 'It was more than that. She *had* to get away from him.'

'When did she give him the news the wedding was off?'

'I don't know. At first she'd seemed sort of relieved but the Friday of that week she closed down on me. Before that time she used to work alongside me in the house and we used to chat about everything. We were very different: she'd had a nice middle-class upbringing, I brought three sisters and myself up with no mother and a work-shy father. But we both liked to laugh . . .' She broke off suddenly and said very quietly, 'She's dead, isn't she?'

Hubert, managing to take his eyes from her feet, suddenly said, 'Do you think Paul killed her?'

'He couldn't have. He wasn't in the country. He was abroad somewhere – Argentina, I think.'

'But if he wasn't in Argentina?'

Carole uncrossed her legs. 'Alison never told me he was violent. She *was* in love with him. But I think he had secrets.'

'Most men have a few secrets,' said Hubert.

'I know that,' said Carole. 'I've been married – to a real bastard. He was a bit like Paul, good-looking; he could charm me with a handful of words. I thought he was wonderful too until the day he kicked me down the stairs and carried on kicking me as I lay at the bottom. He left me there. I lay for three hours before a neighbour looked through the letterbox and saw me. I was two weeks in hospital. He'd ruptured my spleen. I never saw him again. I don't expect the police are trying too hard to find him. Much the same as with Alison.'

Silence fell on us.

She'd told us in such a matter of fact way that it had a subduing effect on both Hubert and me.

'I'll make some tea,' she said, as if she sensed we all needed something other than pure realism. She walked out of the room, leaving us silent and Hubert looking pensive.

'What are you thinking?' he asked.

'I dunno. I was just thinking if he had killed her out of

pique there's no body and how could anyone prove he *had* killed her. Too much time has gone by.'

'Don't be defeatist, Kate. Remember that today you're a DI. I don't think he killed her because she wouldn't marry him. I think he would have taken that on the chin. His friends would have rallied round . . .'

'What did you say?' I interrupted.

Hubert looked mystified. 'His friends would have rallied round,' he repeated.

'Don't you see?' I said, trying to contain my excitement. '*His* friends – not hers . . .' I broke off as Carole came in with a tray of tea and cake.

The arrival of nourishment halted my train of thought. The fruitcake was home-made. Carole didn't eat any and neither did Hubert but I managed some. Carole sipped her tea thoughtfully and then without being prompted carried on talking. It was as if, at long last, she had her chance to tell the story. 'I came in on Monday morning,' she said. 'It was a lovely bright morning. I let myself in with the key and called out to her. It was so quiet. I knew immediately the house was empty. I checked her wardrobes. They were empty. Then I went down to the kitchen to look for a note, maybe a forwarding address. There was nothing . . . except it was obvious she'd had the usual Saturday night meal. I checked the fridge. Normally there'd be enough fresh food for at least six people but judging from leftovers they hadn't eaten as much as usual. There was something odd though . . . an envelope with my name on had fallen under the kitchen table. There was nothing inside. It was as if she was going to leave me something and had been interrupted.'

'What did you do with the envelope?'

'Nothing, I left it on the table. Paul was due home that afternoon. So I did my usual cleaning. Got rid of the rubbish, mopped the floors and polished, and vacuumed the carpets. Paul arrived back at about two o'clock. I had to tell him Alison had taken all her clothes, belongings . . . and gone.'

'How did he take it?'

Carole shrugged. 'Silently. Then after a few minutes he asked if she'd left a note. I just pointed to the empty envelope. He screwed that up and then said he was going up to the attic. I asked him if he wanted me to do my usual hours and he just nodded.'

'When you say belongings – what did you mean? Lamps, radio, CD collection?'

'Oh no, just a couple of suitcases, I think.'

'Did she take her car?'

'Must have done. It wasn't in the garage.'

'Carole, you say Alison was frightened of Paul for some reason. Could that explain why she's never been in touch?'

Carole thought for a moment. 'She would have rung me on my mobile . . . if she could . . . just to say cheerio.'

'What about her friends?'

'I know some of them. I thought her half-brother Jamie might know but he denied knowing anything about her plans. He said he was there on that Saturday night and she'd seemed perfectly normal. Her girlfriends didn't even know she'd sent the wedding dress back.'

'Did anyone report her missing?'

'No. Not that I know of. Jamie got concerned after about a year with no word but he said she'd probably gone abroad.'

'Did you tell the local police about your suspicions?'

'I didn't really get a chance. It must have been two years later when a constable asked me a few questions but, as I said, he didn't have the time.'

'And was it different when Fran died?'

'Yes. They asked more questions but they said it was obvious that due to the "balance of her mind" she'd committed suicide and taken the children with her.'

'You were still working three days a week at Tamberlake?'

'Yes.'

'And what did you think of Fran's state of mind? At the inquest Paul said she was depressed, her doctor mentioned depression. What did you think?'

Carole finished her tea and placed the cup and saucer carefully back on the tray. Hubert by my side was busily taking notes and keeping a low profile. 'She was a great mum, always cheerful around the kids. They were so bonnie . . . poor little mites. Charlotte was three, a real little chatterbox and very active. Always running and climbing and Josh was eighteen months, chubby and placid and bright as a button. As I said, when I was there she always seemed perfectly normal. I know she found being alone in the house difficult, especially when Paul was away. She asked me once to come in every day but I had other job commitments and so I turned her down. I wish I hadn't now.'

'Did you think *she* was frightened of Paul?'

'Oh no. She was frightened of the house. She was convinced it was haunted. She had trouble sleeping at night. Charlotte and Josh usually slept well but she did say on the day before she died that Josh was teething and she'd crept in beside Charlotte so that she could soothe him. The children shared a bedroom and when Paul was away she told me they all piled into the one bed.'

'Did she see ghosts or hear them?'

'No, it was odd. She said she could hear the sea as though there was a storm blowing but when she went outside she couldn't hear it. Sometimes she'd walk a little way down the path until she could see the sea, just to confirm there was no storm.'

'This was late at night?'

'Yes. I told the police but Paul denied she ever left the house at night while he was there.'

'How did he explain the fact that she'd left the house that Saturday night?'

'His excuse was he was so drunk he didn't know that she'd left the house. The police took blood samples and he still had high levels of alcohol. So that was that. The verdict was that she'd given the children some of her crushed-up tablets, taken some herself and walked out into the night and had gone over the cliff edge.'

Hubert cleared his throat as if to tell me he wanted his share of the questions.

'What type of people are these friends of Paul?' he asked.

Carole shrugged. 'Not my type, that's for sure. A bit trendy. Young, rich and with no kids. Dead shallow. Not the sort you'd go to if you were in trouble. If it would help, I've got one or two photos of them round the table. The light in the kitchen isn't that good but they always ate in the kitchen.'

She produced a photo album and eventually found two photos of a group of six people looking slightly jaded around a candlelit table with the remains of a meal in front of them. Carole pointed them out one by one. I was surprised when she told me she had their addresses. 'I know I shouldn't have done it but after about four months Paul decided to get rid of everything that belonged to Fran and the kids. Everything. He didn't even want to keep photos. He said I could have anything I wanted. I took her address book, I don't know why. At first I thought it was her diary but that had gone missing. I knew she kept a diary but Paul said the police must have lost it . . . I didn't believe that.'

'Could we borrow the address book?'

'Yeah, I'll get it for you.'

She left the room and returned seconds later with a fabric-covered address book. 'I don't think he contacted everyone in here,' she said as she handed it to me. 'There were very few at the funeral.'

'Cremation?' queried Hubert.

She nodded.

Hubert glanced at his watch and stood up. It was time to go. Even Hubert doesn't like to miss a meal he's paid for.

'There is something else . . . it's about the night she died.'

Strange, I thought, how often people leave the crux of a matter until last. 'The police asked me at the time if I knew why Fran had cancelled that Saturday night dinner with their friends. I was upset and told them that I had no idea, which was true. On the Monday I came in as usual but the police were milling around. They told me I could carry on as usual. I took the vacuum bag outside to empty in the wheelie bin. There was a black bag open on the top, I could easily see three of those polystyrene trays, several empty wine bottles and a plastic bag from the deli.'

'What did that tell you?'

She glanced at me as if I was dim. 'Those bits of packaging and leftovers told me that Paul hadn't cancelled the Saturday night dinner party. It *had* gone ahead. So he'd lied to the police. And why would he do that?'

'Why indeed?' I said.

Thirteen

Hubert sighed as we left Carole's house. 'I'm not feeling that good,' he said. His face did look pale and I thought he'd overstretched himself with the journey and the visits. I knew he wasn't exaggerating when he allowed me to drive the car back to the Regis Hotel. We arrived as the first diners were being served. Hubert rushed to his room to let Jasper out for a run in the garden. He reported back that Jasper was sulking and that we should take him with us tomorrow. I promised to take him for a long walk later and I ordered two double brandies simply because I thought we both needed and deserved them. Hubert perked up during the meal and luckily we were sat at a corner table where we could talk privately.

'We need police help on this one,' he said.

I sat for a while staring at a piece of spinach that was decorating his front teeth.

'You're not listening to me, are you?' he said. 'What did I just say?'

'We need police help? They haven't been exactly competent so far, have they?'

'You don't listen, do you? I also said that we should get in touch with the "key" man, Robert Roberts. He's ex-police, isn't he?'

I nodded. 'You've got spinach stuck to your front teeth.'

Hubert scowled and left the dining room. I sat watching the other diners but wasn't really observing them. What consumed me at the moment was why Paul should lie so blatantly. Why not tell the police they did have friends round that night? Maybe, I thought, because the police would have interviewed them and he wanted to protect them, for, after all, they knew nothing of Fran's early-morning walk to her death? Or did they? I remembered Hubert's words – 'his friends would have rallied round him'. Rallied, lied or just kept quiet? Either way there was some sort of cover-up. And I would need to talk to Carole again. Why did she no longer work at Tamberlake? Did she know too much?

Hubert returned to the table and bared spinach-free gnashers. 'Does that suit madam?' he asked.

'Don't be childish.'

The dessert trolley appeared then and after much deliberation Hubert chose fresh fruit salad and I chose strawberry torte. My motto for eating out is to rarely choose anything you can either cook or prepare for yourself. Strawberry torte was not in my culinary repertoire. I was halfway through and 'oohing' and 'aahing' at how delicious it was when my mobile rang. It was Gill. I hadn't given Gill or Helen a thought all day and wasn't quite sure how much I should tell her.

'I haven't got long,' she said, sounding breathless. 'Helen's in the bath. Where are you?'

'The Regis Hotel.'

'Paul's back in a couple of days. Supposedly ringing from Argentina. If you want access to the house, tomorrow would be good, we're still searching for the "going-away" outfit.'

'What time?'

'Eleven. I want to see you before I go, Kate. I'll ring you and let you know when.'

'OK. Do you know where the hotel is?'

'I'll find it. I've got to go now. Be careful.'

On that cryptic note she was gone. My strawberry torte lay splayed in front of me, less inviting now, the decorative strawberry on top squashed and as red as blood. I pushed the plate away.

'What's up?' asked Hubert. 'You don't leave desserts.'

'I'm full up,' I said, not wanting to elaborate.

'It's not like you,' he said. 'I'm worried. I'm off to bed before you expire from calorie deficit.'

I had one more drink in the bar, sitting alone on a chesterfield sofa and sipping at a brandy and soda. But not for long. A chubby man with glasses and a shiny pate sat beside me. 'You on holiday, love?'

'No,' I snapped. 'Murder enquiry.' He moved away so fast he nearly fell over. To help me look occupied and keep strange older men away I pulled out from my handbag the two photos that Carole had given me. I was trying to memorize their faces in case I saw any of them out and about. I guessed that Paul had taken one of the photographs and Fran the other. Paul was smiling and looking relaxed and as handsome as ever, although in the candlelight he seemed to have some designer stubble. That could have been due to the poor light. Fran was smiling but it looked false, or was I imagining that, knowing how short her life would be?

I finished my drink unaccosted by any other man, felt vaguely disappointed about that and strangely wide awake. I crept into Hubert's room to collect Jasper and we walked out into the night together. It was dark but the air was still and warm. Even so it smelt of autumn and I felt a little sad that summer would soon end.

Walking a dog at night when few people are around is a joy. You can talk and not be overheard and also not feel as if you're verging on dementia by talking totally to yourself. I put the facts to Jasper and he gave one of his quick yaps, so I take it he approved.

We walked out of the hotel car park and along a track that led eventually to a small row of cottages faced only by a bank of bushes. Most residents had their lights on and no net curtains, so I took surreptitious glances at their décor. Jasper, though, wanted to pee against their gates, so I had no time to linger and at the end of the row we turned back towards the hotel.

There were several cars in the car park. Jasper had paused for yet another sniffing session and I noticed two men in a black car talking animatedly. It was the smaller man in the driving seat I recognized – small head, floppy fair hair – Jamie. Next to him sat Paul! I yanked poor Jasper away so fast his feet hardly touched the ground. Once in the foyer of the hotel I picked Jasper up, tucked him under my arm and ran to Hubert's room and plonked him on the floor. Hubert didn't stir but his car keys had been placed neatly by his loose change on his bedside table. I grabbed the car keys and rushed out. As I got to the car park, they were just leaving. Luckily they wanted to do a right turn and the late-night traffic was building up, so I had a chance to be ready as soon as they managed to exit.

Unfortunately my night driving can be readily compared to an elderly male Sunday driver wearing a cap. My sense of direction is so poor as to be comparable with someone who has undergone a prolonged period of sensory deprivation. I wasn't sure if we were making for Jamie's place or Tamberlake but I kept behind at a safe distance and followed the tail lights.

Mile after mile swiftly passed by. The village names barely registered as I concentrated on keeping up with Jamie.

Eventually he turned left off the main road into a narrow lane. Since I was the only car behind him he'd soon realize he was being followed, so at the first widening of the lane I stopped and waited for a few minutes. When he was out of sight I drove on.

And on and on, to a village called Great Marrington where the car seemed to disappear. I drove on through the village, which did boast a well-lit pub and two street lamps. I was about to give up and go back to the hotel when I glimpsed two men at a chalet-style house, the last in the village, set a hundred yards or so back from any other house. It was built high up with two sets of stone steps to get to the front door. All the curtains were drawn and Jamie and Paul were already going inside the house. Irritatingly I caught only a glimpse of the person at the door, who appeared to be male with dark hair.

I waited in a lay-by watching the house. It was now eleven thirty and maybe they wouldn't stay long. That was the theory. I dozed for a while and then at one a.m. the house lights went out. There was no reason for me to stay now; they were obviously staying the night.

Although I seemed to be following the same route back I found it nerve-wracking in the dark and I made one or two wrong turns, so the journey back took more than an hour. The sight of the Regis Hotel was the best thing I'd seen all day.

Even though it was after two a.m. I still had one more job to do. I rang Gill, who was half-dopey with sleep, so I kept my message to a minimum – Paul was back in Cornwall but seemed in no rush to be with his fiancée.

In the morning a perky Hubert came to wake me. It was only seven thirty and already he'd taken Jasper for a long walk. My eyes refused to open properly and I felt as if I'd aged five years in as many hours. A shower and two cups of tea later I felt ready to face breakfast and the day ahead.

I told Hubert about my tailing Jamie and Paul and the fact that it hadn't achieved much. 'I wonder why he's taking such a chance?' muttered Hubert. 'You saw him, others may see him. More to the point, has Jamie checked us out and found Stone and West do not exist?'

'If it's not sex it must be money,' I suggested. Hubert merely chewed on his toast thoughtfully.

'What do you think our priority is today?' I asked. 'Because Gill is taking Helen out shopping, leaving the house empty, and we could have a really good look round.'

'What time?'

'Eleven.'

'We'd better make sure Paul isn't hanging around and before we go there I want to speak to Robert Roberts – he may have contacts.'

Hubert insisted that we take Jasper and by nine we were on our way to see the ex-cop turned locksmith.

Robert Roberts lived in a detached bungalow about four miles north of Trevelly. As we drove up he was painting his garage door. He turned and peered at us and when I told him I was a private investigator his expression registered a mixture of surprise and pity. 'Got your work cut out on this one then,' he said. 'Talk about a cocked-up investigation. Modern police work these days is all bloody paperwork and worrying about procedure and human rights. In my day Warrinder would have been worked over until he confessed.'

'So you think he's guilty then?' I asked.

'Guilty as bloody sin.'

'What of?'

He stared at my head, needing no words, he had already decided I was brainless.

'Come on in the house,' he said. 'I'm ready for a cuppa. Let the dog out, he can have the run of the garden.' Jasper, released from the car, tore twice around the garden and then began sniffing individual plants and bushes. I knew he'd pee on most of them but I doubted it would do them much harm.

Once inside the bungalow Hubert paid Roberts a compliment about his conservatory extension and Roberts responded by offering Hubert a guided tour. I was left in the lounge to stare at the Spanish-style furnishings, marble-tiled floors and terracotta walls. There were even two sombreros and a pair of castanets on the walls, which I thought was a little OTT.

When eventually they returned, still deep in conversation about grouting and varieties of wood panelling, I felt a little superfluous, although Hubert did wink at me. I knew damn well he wasn't in the least bit interested in DIY, so I guessed that he had some sort of plan.

Roberts went off to make the tea, giving me a chance to ask Hubert what he was up to.

'He's originally from just outside Longborough.'

'So?'

'So, he's got several very elderly relatives.'

My mouth dropped. 'I'm gobsmacked! You're drumming up custom and I've been sitting here like a . . . constipated prune!'

Hubert merely laughed. 'Well you're not a dried up old prune . . . yet.'

I didn't feel in the slightest bit mollified but when Roberts came into the living room with a tray of mugs, he wasn't alone. Beside him was a tall good-looking thirty-something man with a wide smile, wearing only shorts and a six pack. 'This is my son – Liam. He's a DS but soon to make DI.'

Hubert moved forward and shook hands with him. Liam then walked across to me and bent down to shake my hand. 'Hi, Kate. It is Kate, isn't it?' I nodded. I couldn't quite find my voice, because I'd looked into his eyes and they were the deepest of blues and for those few moments I was lost. It was of course lust at first sight and it was sure to be unrequited lust, so I took a deep breath and told myself to get a grip. He'd come as a real surprise. I was convinced he was adopted because he bore no resemblance to Roberts senior. He was several inches taller; his features were rugged whereas his father's were somewhat flat.

I think Hubert may have noticed I was preoccupied,

because he turned to Roberts senior and said, 'We'd be grateful for any help on this case. One of Kate's old school friends is planning to marry Warrinder in a few weeks and her bridesmaid to be – Gill – is very concerned.'

'I'm not surprised. I've met Gill. I made the key for her, partly so I could have another look round the place. He's a cocky bastard. He's got away with murder. I know he has.'

Liam picked up a mug of coffee and handed one to Hubert and the other to me and, much to my surprise, sat next to me. It was only a two-seater sofa and, as we were forced to sit so close together, his thigh was touching mine and I could smell his fresh male sweat. If I'd been wearing a corset I would have had a panic attack. My brain just seemed to close down and I had to struggle to listen to what Roberts senior was saying.

'I was a DS when Alison went missing. Not that she was reported missing until she'd been gone for more than a year. One or two basic enquiries were made but it seems she'd been planning to go, taking money out of her bank accounts some days before. She took her belongings and her car and the thinking was that if she'd wanted anyone to know where she was she would have contacted them.'

'And is that what you thought?'

'No. And I never will. Warrinder killed her or got someone else to do it, but with no body and no back-up there was nothing else I could do. The superintendent, one of those graduate fast-trackers, was good at moving paper and charming the chief constable, but he didn't know his arse from his elbow and he gave us no bloody support.'

'What about motive?' I asked.

'Money,' he said. 'She had cash. Quite a lot. We made a few basic enquiries when we were eventually alerted but there was no trace of her or her money. She had new credit cards that were never used. Now, you tell me of a woman with new credit cards who doesn't use them.' He didn't give me a chance to refute that. 'She's dead, I tell you. Only death stops a woman spending.'

Hubert sat nodding in agreement and Liam whispered in my ear. 'My mother liked spending, he's biased.'

'Is she . . . ?'

'No she's not in the shopping mall in the sky. She's in Devon spending her new husband's money.'

'I'm sorry,' I murmured, not being able to think of anything appropriate.

'Don't be sorry. I still see her. Dad's grateful his pension isn't being frittered away and the new husband has so much money he's delighted to have a new wife to spend it for him.'

It's true, I thought, there is 'nowt as queer as folk'. But even thinking that, to me Liam seemed normal enough, and at that moment I was prepared to believe he was a virtual saint. Lust is addling your brain, my inner nag murmured to me but I knew given the slightest opportunity I'd be struck deaf.

'Kate, are you listening? Robert's got something to say about Fran's death.' Robert looked across at us. 'Liam, save your comments for later. Kate's around here for a few days.'

'OK, OK. I'll tell her the family secrets in private.'

Robert didn't look pleased at that comment but I think it was more that he wanted to expound his views rather than watch his son flirting with me. 'The investigation was slipshod . . .' he began. 'It was a total farce. In his statement Warrinder said he woke at eight thirty a.m. Fran wasn't in the bed beside him, so he presumed she was with the children. He went downstairs and there was no evidence of them having had breakfast, and the double buggy was gone, so he assumed they'd gone for an early morning walk. It seems she liked to be out of the house at every opportunity. It was a lovely morning so he wasn't surprised or worried that she'd gone out. He had a leisurely breakfast and it was nine thirty before he decided to go and look for them. He said he walked down to the beach, there was no sign of them there, then he came back up from the beach and took the cliff-top path. After that he came straight home and phoned the police.'

'It sounds plausible so far,' I said.

Roberts turned to Hubert. 'What do you think?'

Hubert frowned. 'So far I can't see what else he could have done. What did the police do?'

'That's where I think it went pear-shaped. Warrinder rang the local police in Trevelly. It's a police house, blue light outside, police constable inside with a wife and two kids. He's not overworked. The odd scrap to sort out on a Saturday night, a bit of low-grade nicking, the odd car being taken for a joyride. Anyway, Warrinder rang him and told him he couldn't find his wife and kids. To which the answer was – ring her friends and phone back at eight p.m. if he had no joy . . .' He paused. 'Well, you can see the progression, can't you . . . ? In the event they didn't find their bodies until the next morning. By which time they'd been battered to buggery on the rocks.'

I felt myself shivering. Roberts spoke with a passion and, although it was good to have him on the team, his doubts had held no sway in the past. All this mulling over what had happened still wasn't evidence. Nothing seemed concrete and real. It was all supposition.

Hubert glanced at his watch. If we were going to have another look round Tamberlake it was time to go.

Roberts noticed. 'If you're going to the Warrinder place I'll come with you.'

'Dad – don't get involved,' said Liam, sounding worried. 'Your blood pressure went up last time. Leave it to Kate.'

'She's an amateur. We're professionals. You come as well.'

Liam glanced enquiringly at me. I nodded. I was pleased.

Robert was setting the burglar alarm as we left the bungalow. He turned to me. 'There was insurance money,' he said.

'They wouldn't pay out on suicide though . . . would they?'

'Not for suicide, but for murder. They were all insured. His life, two hundred thousand, her life, a hundred thousand, and the kids, fifty thousand pounds each. Makes you think, doesn't it?'

It certainly did.

Fourteen

I knew little about life insurance but again suspicion was not enough. We were following Roberts senior and son. I regretted not telling them I'd seen Paul the night before, just in case Paul was at the house.

In the event all seemed quiet. The sun shone and there was a gentle breeze and Tamberlake looked fairly tranquil. Gill had managed to leave the back door open, although I did see Robert with a huge bunch of keys and I wondered if he could pick locks as well as make keys.

Once inside, Hubert and Roberts went off together. Liam looked enquiringly at me and asked, 'Well where do you want to start?'

'I'm not even sure what we're meant to be looking for.'

'My dad is looking for a body. He's nosed around here before. He had to leave the force on health grounds because of this case. He was forced out. They found out his blood pressure was a bit high and after that he didn't have much choice but to go. He was a thorn in the superintendent's scrotum.'

I could tell Liam shared some of his father's choice turns of phrase but it didn't help me to know exactly what I was meant to be looking for. 'How would you dispose of a body in and around this house?' I asked.

He looked thoughtful and stared at the kitchen table. 'Chopping it up is as good a way as any – if you can face it. That way you can leave the pieces in different locations. But

Deadly Choice

believe me, Kate, there are many people murdered whose bodies are never found. Their graves exist somewhere, but hiding places are so many and varied, including the sea. Well-weighted bodies can stay on the seabed for ever.'

'There is one way he could have got rid of some of the body parts,' I said. 'It's a bit far-fetched but still feasible.'

'Fire away.'

'What about well wrapped up and carried in luggage to Argentina?'

All credit to Liam the gorgeous hunk, he didn't laugh. 'An arm or a chopped-up leg would be easy enough to carry but would the X-ray machines pick it up? Even if the airport staff thought it was a joint of meat, I don't think it's legal to carry fresh meat in passenger luggage.'

'No, I suppose not,' I agreed. Even so, I hadn't given up on the idea entirely. 'What about in the boot of a car? Across the channel by ferry and for a start there's the whole of France to dump the body parts.'

He nodded. 'It's been done before.'

Strange, I thought, here was a man I fancied like mad and, far from flirting with him, we were discussing the disposal of body parts.

'Dad's convinced Alison's body is here somewhere,' he said. 'He even asked for bits of the premises to be dug up.'

'Which bits?'

'Parts of the garden where new plants and bushes had been put in. The gardener was interviewed but Warrinder had been abroad at the time of planting, so a dig was vetoed.'

I was about to tell him that I'd seen Paul locally when he was supposedly still in Argentina. He was a man who always purported to be away at crucial times and yet Fran had died with him in the house. Any further discussion was cut short when Hubert and Roberts appeared.

Roberts looked flushed and angry. 'I'm going to nail the bastard if it's the last thing I do. His passport's gone. He's in some racket up to his neck. I don't know if it's drugs or money-laundering. I think he's leading a double life and travelling on a false passport . . . I'm telling you, Liam, I won't rest . . .'

'Yes, Dad, you will rest and it'll be the long one. Is he worth dying for?'

Roberts took a deep breath. 'I know I get agitated but I was in the force all my life and when you see these well-educated prats more concerned about figures and budgets than catching criminals it just makes my blood boil.'

To defuse the situation I said, 'Let's get out of here. It's not giving us any answers.' Then I added, 'Has Hubert told you Warrinder is already in the area? He wasn't due until tomorrow.'

'Where is he? And why didn't you tell me?' snapped Roberts.

'Hang on, Dad,' said Liam, looking daggers at me. 'I didn't know anything about this.'

'I want to know where he is . . . now! Don't worry, I'm not planning to take him apart limb from limb. But I'd like to see what he gets up to.'

Liam looked at me and I could see he wasn't best pleased. I shrugged and looked apologetic but it was too late now to stop Roberts. 'He's at Great Marrington,' I said. 'Last house of the village.'

'East or west side?'

'East, I think.'

He raised his eyebrows as if my being unsure of direction was a further indication that I was brainless. The three men went into a brief huddle to exclude me, I suppose, and I stood like a lemon for a few minutes.

By now I was feeling uncomfortable anyway at the four of us trespassing and wanted to get away. Also time was pressing, Hubert was only able to stay for a week and we only had the one car. I could of course hire a car and stay on alone. I had to admit, but only to myself, that I felt overwhelmed. The police had closed the case. Fran and her children had been cremated and although Alison was technically a missing person, she was just one of thousands of the missing not sending Christmas cards. Roberts hadn't managed to make headway whilst he was in the force and now the passage of time had blunted any leads. It was also more than likely that those who had lied at the time would continue to lie.

We went our separate ways but not before I'd given Liam my mobile phone number. 'If you think of anything,' I said casually.

'I'll be in touch,' he said as he briefly clasped my hand.

In the car I asked Hubert why I'd been excluded from their conversation.

'No sinister intent. We've been invited to lunch at their place tomorrow.'

'We haven't got time for that,' I said irritably.

'A working lunch. We need them both on our side. Liam can get us information. Anyway, since when has lunch been such a hardship for you?'

I didn't of course have an answer to that and it would mean seeing Liam again. So I smiled. 'Where to now then?' I asked.

'I fancy a pint.'

'That means I have to do the driving.'

'My turn today. You can drink tomorrow.'

Hubert drove to Trevelly and into the spacious car park of the Crown and Anchor.

'We need to keep local so that we can catch any gossip,' he said as he locked the car. I looked around the car park; ours was the only car. He noticed my scathing glance. 'It's early yet. It could be crowded inside.'

It wasn't. Inside, there were far more horse brasses than customers. Three old men sat playing dominoes in a dim corner and the young barman was busy doing the *Sun* crossword. It didn't augur well on the gossip front. The barman looked up as we walked to the bar.

'What can I get you, my beauties?' he asked. He had a pale, round face, hazel eyes and fair-cropped hair, and he'd taken lessons in 'camp'.

'I'll have a pint of the local bitter,' said Hubert, his voice seeming lower than usual.

'Good choice, sir, if I may say so. And for the young lady?'

'I'll have an orange juice.'

As he poured the beer he seemed eager to talk. 'Down here on holiday are we, sir? Taking in the lovely Cornish sights?'

Hubert shook his head. 'Not exactly. I've come seeking information about my niece, Alison Peters. She went missing from around these parts.'

I was impressed with Hubert's quick thinking, because I was pretty sure he'd only thought of that on the spur of the moment. The barman was by now opening my bottle of orange juice. 'She was living up at Tamberlake, wasn't she?' he asked, although he obviously knew that she had been. Hubert nodded.

'I've only worked here a year but people still talk about her and the woman who jumped off the cliff with her kids. I reckon the house is jinxed. Some old places are like that.'

He handed me my juice and then Hubert surprised me. 'You go and find a table, Kate. I'll be with you in a minute.'

Find a table! I thought. There was nothing *but* empty tables. But I did as I was told and found a table near a book-lined wall. It was one of those themed pubs which is a cross between a library and an auction room. Hubert seemed to be talking very quietly to the barman and I was intrigued. What the hell was he asking him that he should exclude me? They were talking together for several minutes and I began to get just a little irritated. I'd finished my orange juice by the time Hubert returned. 'Contain yourself,' he said before I could open my mouth. 'I'll explain all.'

Even then Hubert sipped at his beer thoughtfully and I grew more impatient.

'Come on then, spill the beans. What on earth did you find to talk about with the barman?'

'Drugs.'

'Drugs,' I repeated like a parrot.

'Yes. Robert is convinced Warrinder is involved in drug dealing. It's a belief that marred his career, because he managed to persuade the superintendent of the day that Tamberlake was Cornwall's main storehouse for hard drugs. Paul and Fran were married by then, Fran was pregnant and at six a.m. one morning a "crack" team . . . my little joke . . . battered down the door dressed all in black and heavily armed. They found nothing. Not even any wacky baccy. The chief constable apologized and Roberts is convinced there was some sort of compensation payout for Warrinder. It seems the Warrinders have lived in Cornwall for generations and had used their money for many good causes. It was embarrassment and recriminations all round.' He paused to take breath.

'You didn't find *any* of that out from the barman, did you?'

'Be patient, Kate. The superintendent of the time was transferred, he took all the blame but of course it had been Roberts who had instigated the whole thing. Any promotion he may have hoped for was scuppered and when he still carried on making waves – they encouraged him to go.' He paused to sip his drink. 'I'll put

121

you out of your misery. I asked the barman who his supplier was.'

My ears caught the words but I was having trouble actually believing it. 'Whatever made you think he'd have one – just because he's gay and camp?'

'Nothing to do with that. His skin had a pasty look and I thought the pupils of his eyes seemed abnormal.'

'I'm very impressed,' I said. Actually I felt peeved that I hadn't noticed but I supposed that was because I'd been distracted by his voice. 'I'd be even more impressed,' I added, 'if he'd told you.'

Hubert grinned. 'He did. I told him I'd got chronic pain and he said he could tell I wasn't a cop. I don't know how he knew that, but he told me there was a wine bar in Newquay – the Marigold. There I was to ask for a man called Big Charlie and if I said Gay Gordon sent me he'd give me what I wanted.'

Suddenly I was worried. Neither of us knew anything about the drugs scene. I read the papers and heard of schoolchildren using and selling drugs, but no one had ever offered me any and in Longborough I wasn't aware of any scene. 'You're getting out of your depth,' I said. 'Silly nicknames are always a bad omen.'

'I haven't done anything yet. Anyway, I'll only be meeting a supplier. It's the dealers we want and, according to Roberts, Warrinder could be big time.'

I sighed. 'I'm getting dodgy vibes about all this.'

'I'll get you another orange juice,' said Hubert, patting my arm, 'and something with chips that'll chase them away.'

I watched Hubert's retreating back and thought, *A portion of chips won't do it this time.* We were merely amateurs and to me illegal drugs spelt only violence and death. There only had to be a whisper that we were not genuine tourists and we could be in trouble. After all, this patch of Cornwall was only small and the Cornish were known for their smuggling abilities. All that differed was the merchandise.

When Hubert came back I asked him when he was meeting Big Charlie.

'Tonight,' he said. 'What's wrong with tonight?'

'Nothing, but I'm coming with you.'

'Oh no you're not.'

'Oh yes I am.' Then I added feebly, 'It is my case after all. You have bodies to attend to in Longborough.'

'You're being silly. People buy drugs every day. It's not dangerous as long as we don't take them.'

I stared at him long and hard. 'Honestly, sometimes I despair, for a man of your age you can be very naïve.'

Hubert merely grinned. 'Look on it as an adventure, Kate.'

'I think,' I said miserably, 'it's one adventure we could do without.'

Fifteen

During lunch I realized Hubert was determined to follow the drugs line of enquiry, although how he expected buying a few quid's worth of crack cocaine would aid our investigation I didn't know. All he did was murmur about 'little acorns' and refuse to say any more.

We did agree our next priority was to try to talk to as many friends and associates of Paul as possible. I had a feeling that Paul had kept *his* friends close and Alison and Fran's at bay. Hubert produced a map of Trevelly and the surrounding area and found out that two people on our list of six 'regulars' lived near enough to walk to Tamberlake approximately two miles away. We'd already seen Jamie, so it left a mere five to go. Which didn't sound like many on paper but the reality always works out to be more difficult.

We walked Jasper for a short distance but he seemed glad enough to snuggle down on the back seat. We left the back window open just in case we forgot about him. The weather remained warm and mellow but sun through glass can heat a car to suffocating levels, so we were both conscious of Jasper's welfare.

Our first call was to Michelle Ford. The terraced house, modest but attractive, with hanging baskets on the porch and rose bushes in the front garden, was situated on the outskirts of Trevelly. Hubert parked the car directly outside. 'What's our cover story?' he asked.

'Journalists?' I suggested. 'We're done with the police angle.'

He shook his head. 'No, it's too easy to say no to journalists.'

I thought for a moment. Jamie would undoubtedly have told them the police were snooping around and our descriptions would have been circulated. 'What about saying we're really insurance investigators trying to establish if Alison is dead or alive? After seven years of being missing with no contact, someone can be pronounced dead – can't they?'

Hubert nodded but still looked uncertain. 'I think it's time to come clean. Just say you're a PI and leave it at that. If they won't talk to us we'll have to think of something else.'

In the event it didn't matter, there was no reply to our loud knocking. So loud that an elderly toothless neighbour came out and said in a crackly voice, 'It's no use knocking. She doesn't get home till late.'

'How late is late?' I asked.

'Between seven and half past. Shall I tell her who called?'

'No thanks, we'll come back.'

'Right you are.'

A bit dejected we drove on to the next address. The home of Harvey Trenchard. A modern detached house this time, low-level, with vast picture windows and what looked like solar panelling on the roof. It reminded me of a goldfish bowl and although the house was well back from the road, almost hidden by an array of trees, as we drove through the open gates it wasn't long before we glimpsed a man at the window watching our arrival.

He came to the door, a short round man, in his early forties, wearing gold-rimmed glasses that reminded me of an agitated owl. I decided Hubert was right. 'Kate Kinsella,' I said, 'private investigator, and my associate Hubert Humberstone.'

'I don't want to talk to you,' he snapped. 'I've lost two

good friends in recent years and I don't want to rake up the past.'

It was obvious if I didn't say the right thing now he was going to slam the door in our faces, so I took a deep breath. 'Helen Woods is a long-standing friend of mine. She wants to marry Paul, of course she does, but she thinks the house is haunted and I wondered if you'd ever noticed anything unusual at Tamberlake.'

Harvey moved his glasses further down his nose and stared at me above the rims. His eyes were cold brown pebbles. 'When a house has seen tragedy, it's bound to leave its mark,' he said. 'But I've never experienced anything untoward there. The best person to talk to is the estate agent who has tried to sell the house on at least two occasions.'

'Fine. Thank you,' I replied. 'The name of the agents?'

'Brant and Brant. Trevelly High Street.' With that terse reply he did indeed slam the door.

'Pompous prat!' I proclaimed as we turned to go.

'Calm down,' said Hubert. 'One of the group will talk to us.'

'I don't think so,' I said despondently. 'They lied en masse about being at Tamberlake on the night Fran died. I can't see them recanting now.'

We walked back to the car in silence. I turned once to see the 'owl' watching us from his glass bowl. I found him quite sinister and wondered how he afforded a house of that size. 'What do you think he does for a living?' I asked.

Hubert smiled at me and patted me on the head. 'No use guessing. Roberts will know and if he doesn't, Liam will find out for us.'

I brightened at the sound of Liam's name and the fact that I'd be seeing him for lunch the next day.

It took only a few minutes to find Brant and Brant but it was a surprisingly busy office with a team of three sitting in front of computers and each having a potential customer in front of them. The young receptionist wore a short skirt, a flimsy white blouse, high heels and a switch-on smile. I told her we were interested in buying Tamberlake and with a big apologetic smile she told me it wasn't on the market but there were other large houses which she was sure I'd love. We took a seat and she handed us details of four houses which she was sure would fit our 'requirements'. I flicked through the brochures, for they were brochures and not flimsy two-pagers.

'I reckon,' I whispered to Hubert, 'she's seen your car and thinks you're my sugar daddy.'

'Hmm. If I were,' he said thoughtfully, 'I'd want you to look like a rich bitch. Dripping gold and diamonds, with blood-red three-inch fingernails and six-inch heels.'

'Pigs might fly,' I said as my eyes glazed over at the most expensive of the houses – a cool £3,000,000. 'And they'd be flying if, between us, we could afford the porch and the conservatory in these houses.'

'You have no ambition, Kate, that's your trouble.'

Since he hadn't bothered to look at the prices I didn't respond and a few minutes later one of the prospective buyers was being guided to the door and having his hand firmly shaken. The redundant negotiator now turned his attention to us. In his early thirties, short and dapper, he wore a navy suit and white shirt. His hair was thick and dark and had a crimpiness that was probably natural but looked artificial. He struck me as the type who would wear sunglasses on the dullest day. 'Hi, I'm Simon Viner,' he announced with a wide smile, thrusting his hand at us and shaking our hands vigorously. He guided us to his desk, lifting out the chair for me, but his attitude changed immediately we mentioned Tamberlake. 'You do know it's not up for sale?'

'Oh yes,' I said innocently. 'But we've heard a whisper that the owner, Paul Warrinder, is planning to marry and he's thinking about selling again.'

Simon's small mouth curved a little. 'Well, I hope he gives us another crack at selling it.'

'You've had problems with it?' queried Hubert.

'No, not at all. In fact an American wanted to buy it, convinced it was really "Mandalay".' Noticing Hubert's puzzled expression he added, 'From the novel by Daphne du Maurier.'

'Oh yes. I remember,' said Hubert. 'I saw the film.'

'When was it you tried to sell it?' I asked Simon.

'The first time Mr Warrinder put it on the market was about five years back. I'd just started work here. I was too junior to deal with it then. But when his wife was alive, we did have one or two interested besides the American.'

'Why didn't it sell then?'

Simon shook his head. 'I got the impression that Mr Warrinder didn't really *want* to sell. It was an inflated price and he refused to drop.'

'Do you think that was because he was emotionally involved with the house?' I asked. Simon's answering glance made it obvious he'd never given that a thought.

'Could be. The Warrinders have lived there since Victorian times. Old man Warrinder – didn't marry until he was fifty – and young Warrinder's mother died in a car crash. The story is the family money had all been given away to good Cornish causes and there was only the house left to the only son and heir. These big houses do take considerable maintenance . . .' He paused as if remembering he was a salesman. 'Now, I can show you more modern houses, easy to maintain, some with solar panels.'

'I saw one of those yesterday. I thought it was like a goldfish bowl.'

'I'm surprised. Our new boss, Mr Trenchard, designed his own.'

Time for a hasty exit, I thought, but I kept my cool. 'I would have thought Brant would have been the owner.'

'Mr Brant and his daughter have just sold up and moved abroad. We'll be called Trenchard soon.'

I smiled at him. 'I'm sure it'll be Trenchard and Viner before very long. Thank you so much for your help. We'll be in touch.'

His face grew slightly pink and his final handshake at the door was even more energetic.

'Phew!' I breathed as we walked away. 'Why the hell did Trenchard send us there?'

'A wild goose chase?' suggested Hubert.

'Or just trying to wear us out. At this rate Helen will be celebrating her first anniversary before we come up with anything concrete on Paul.'

Again we checked our list, deciding to make it our last house call of the day. Our other visit was to be the druggie wine bar in the evening. The name of the second female on the Saturday night list was Diane Brandon. Her apartment in a large Edwardian house was in a quiet avenue of trees on the approach road to Trevelly. There were no nets at the window and an intercom system. There seemed to be no sign of life. I pressed the first of the other two buttons and there was still no response. The top-flat occupant did respond. 'I'm looking for Diane,' I said into the microphone panel.

'She's on holiday. Won't be back till the weekend,' came the voice from above.

'Cheers.'

I felt despondent as I got back in the car. All we'd managed was to receive the order of the elbow from one friend and by now they would all be forewarned and forearmed. Why would they change their stories now? To admit they met up as usual on the Saturday night that Fran killed herself would be pointless unless they had a reason to tell the truth.

Hubert, sensing I was losing heart, said, 'Come on, we'll have a few pre-dinner drinkies at the hotel and take a taxi tonight.'

'It's only five,' I said.

'By the time we've given Jasper a walk and fed him it'll easily be six and then we need to freshen up – it won't leave that much drinking time.'

Nothing ever goes quite according to plan and as we walked through the lounge a voice called out, 'Kate!'

I turned to see Gill coming towards us. 'Why didn't you phone me?' I asked.

'I did,' she said indignantly. 'You were switched off.'

Hubert, not waiting to be introduced, slunk away to walk Jasper. Gill looked a little flushed and worried. I ordered a pot of tea and we sat alone in a corner of the lounge by the potted plants. 'I'm going tonight,' she said. 'I've had a huge row with Helen. She's found out you're back and making enquiries. In the end I told her I was paying you to investigate Paul. She went ballistic. She was a different person. Shouting that we were both jealous bitches who couldn't find a decent man of our own. And Paul was practically the Son of God and how dare we suggest he'd done anything criminal?'

'So what do we do now?' I asked.

Gill shook her head. 'I wish I'd never got involved. The way I feel at the moment I won't be coming to the wedding.'

'Has anything else happened? Does she know he's in Cornwall at the moment?'

Gill grimaced. 'No . . . she doesn't. I don't think she'd have believed me anyway.'

Our tray of tea arrived delivered by a heavy-footed waitress with a sour expression. I poured the tea and handed a cup to Gill. 'She's not as innocent in all this as she appears, you know. That photo of her sitting on the wall behind Fran and the children wasn't a coincidence. She'd been seeing him for a few weeks before Fran died.'

'She admitted that?'

'Not exactly. She said it was merely an innocent friend-ship and that they'd only met for coffee or afternoon tea.'

'Maybe that's the truth,' I said.

'Well one thing was true,' she agreed. 'They had met in a camera shop. But everyone in Cornwall knows of Paul Warrinder. It's a small place and old man Warrinder funded amongst other things two libraries and a park. They were always in the local newspaper. There was a full-page spread for his wedding to Fran.'

'So, she knew of him long before he met Fran?'

Gill nodded. 'It's no wonder the poor cow topped herself and the children. She must have found out for sure that day. Maybe someone let the cat out of the bag that night at the dinner party. She goes to bed, the bastard lying fast asleep beside her, and she decides that she and the kids would be better off in the next world.'

I had to agree Gill had probably got it right. Their so-called friends must have felt guilty and so declined to admit they were even there that night. There may of course have been a massive row and perhaps they had left earlier than usual.

'And there's another thing,' she said, as she added another spoonful of sugar to her tea. 'I searched his pockets and found a card from a gambling casino – Knightsbridge – pretty exclusive by the looks of it.'

From her pocket she produced the card. Gold-embossed and gold by name – 'The Golden Globe'.

It seemed to me that, far from going abroad, Paul was spending regular amounts of time in London. But were the gym and a casino the only reasons?

'How did you leave it with Helen?'

'Frosty to say the least. I don't think she'll be wanting either of us at the wedding.'

We sat silently for a while. 'I think we should call the whole thing off,' said Gill eventually. 'She isn't the friend

131

I thought she was and if she makes a mistake that's her lookout.'

I felt inclined to agree with her and was about to say, *Yes, let's forget it,* when I remembered Roberts and his suspicions. Suspicions that bordered on obsession, but he was an experienced detective and I couldn't ignore that.

'You go back to London, Gill. Hubert and I have got contacts now. I can't let it go. It's not really about Helen, is it? It's about the two other women involved with Paul who both came to sticky ends.'

'You think Alison is dead?'

'Yes. I do. And I think Paul murdered her. But how the hell we can prove it I don't know.'

'Wow, what a mess,' she sighed. 'But . . . there is something I could do. I could check out the gym and the casino for you. Even if I only found out the membership fees and where he stayed in London.'

'That's a good idea.'

Gill glanced at her watch. 'I must go. It'll be really late when I get back.'

I walked with her to the car and I watched her drive away until she was just a little flash of red in the distance. An image that reminded me of the red of the collapsed strawberry gateau. A cold shiver snaked down my back and I didn't know why.

Sixteen

We arrived in the dining room a little late, to find our usual table for two in the corner was gone, usurped by a man with two walking sticks, so it would have been churlish to object. We were shown instead to a table for four and I prayed no one would be sat with us. Eating with strangers can be hell. How people manage it on cruises I'll never know. Of course, everyone is a stranger at first but there are some people who should definitely remain in that category.

During the first course, which was called 'seafood surprise' as opposed to prawn cocktail, I told Hubert about Gill's visit and that I felt uneasy. He told me I was worrying too much. 'Next step is you starting to believe Tamberlake really is haunted. It's best if we concentrate on the drugs angle at the moment.'

'We don't even know if there is a drugs angle.'

'True,' he agreed, 'but we still need to eliminate it.'

'I've done nothing about those watercolours either. I'd like to know if they are as good as I think they are. After all, why would Paul alter Fran's signature on them if it wasn't worth his while?'

'Who knows? Does he have any talents of his own? He may have been jealous.'

If that was Hubert's psychological angle I wasn't convinced, but I supposed it was a possibility.

'There was that photo of him on a horse playing polo,' I

133

said. 'Supposedly in Argentina. Probably a mock-up taken in some local park.'

'Don't get impatient,' said Hubert. 'This is complicated. It could take weeks, even months. Look at poor Robert Roberts – he's been pursuing Warrinder for years and he hasn't made much progress.'

'That's really cheered me up.'

'Think of it this way. Roberts has got us on his side now.' I wasn't convinced that was really to his advantage but I didn't say so.

Our main course had just been served when we were interrupted by the late arrival at our table of two large middle-aged Americans both wearing shorts. My heart sank. After introductions and handshakes Hubert announced he was a funeral director. I thought that might have caused a real hiatus in the 'getting-to-know-you stakes', instead Franklin and Beatrice didn't bat an eyelid, because they were aficionados of English graveyards.

Luckily Beatrice wasn't as talkative as Franklin and I could have learnt more about epitaphs and who was buried where, than most people get to know in a lifetime. But I was only half listening. I couldn't concentrate on official graves when I was concerned with the unofficial, unknown grave of a young woman.

After our dessert Hubert and I made an apologetic escape with Franklin's raucous 'We'll be seeing you folks!' ringing in our ears.

In the taxi, which thankfully had turned up on time, Hubert made it plain I was to sit still and keep my mouth shut. 'Are you actually going to part with good money?' I asked. He nodded. 'Don't worry, I'll buy the gear, then hand it over to young Roberts tomorrow and he can deal with it.' I still wasn't happy about Hubert taking such a chance, but he still sounded cautious so I tried to relax and enjoy the drive.

It had crossed my mind that Hubert might have been planning to sample the goods. After all, he didn't smoke and he rarely took as much as an aspirin, so I thought he might be tempted by curiosity and a misplaced sense of adventure. But now I realized he was far too sensible – he just wanted to meet a supplier – all in the cause of our investigation.

It was just after nine when the taxi driver dropped us off just outside the Star Light Wine Bar. He promised to pick us up just before midnight. It was dark outside and nearly as dark inside. The bar was obviously named after its interior, because the ceiling held myriad star-shaped lights and the chairs and tables were the brightest chrome. But the light remained so subdued that the few customers milling around seemed to be moving in the shadows. I found a table near a wall and watched as Hubert approached the bar. He came back in high dudgeon claiming, 'Daylight bloody robbery! Two glasses of cheap plonk and it cost more than a whole bottle of a good supermarket wine.'

'That's life,' I said. 'Just wait until you find out how much your little packet of crack will cost.'

'I've heard it's not that expensive.'

'Not at first maybe. But an addict is in no position to haggle once hooked. They have to pay the going price.'

'Just sip that wine slowly, Kate. You can buy the next round.'

'It's no wonder you're a rich man.'

Hubert scowled and his face appeared to be strangely mottled in the 'star' light.

We sat in silence watching a few more customers arrive. Mostly young men, smartly casual. A sign on the door had announced 'No jeans or trainers'. There was some hugging and shaking hands, except that soon it became obvious that the hands were still being held and that the hugs became a lover's possessive clasp. It took Hubert a little time to realize what was going on. 'This is a gay men's club,' he said in astonishment.

'Well at least *I* won't be bothered,' I said smugly.

'What's that supposed to mean?' asked Hubert, his eyes roving over the increasing huddles.

'You could well be a source of . . . interest.' He couldn't see that I was merely winding him up and he turned to gaze at me with an anxious expression. 'They'll see I'm straight.'

'It's not stamped on your forehead.'

He didn't say another word for a while, then, as if he'd been mulling the issue over, he muttered, 'If someone did . . . proposition me . . . what do I say?'

'I'd suggest "get lost" but if you want to be more subtle just say you're not alone.'

'Will that work?'

'Probably not, if they like a challenge.'

'You're being a real pain.'

My comeuppance came about fifteen minutes later when a group of women arrived together, some of whom looked very butch. One with short-cropped hair and vast shoulders kept looking my way. I wasn't nervous, just a little disconcerted, but an hour and one more drink later we began to relax. Nothing riotous was going on, in fact the atmosphere felt safe and friendly. Apart from a few casual glances, no one bothered us.

'There you are,' I said to Hubert. 'In the gay world we are not fanciable.'

'I'm not fancied in any world,' replied Hubert, gloomily staring into his wine glass.

It was nearly eleven when Hubert spotted his quarry. 'That's him,' he whispered in my ear. My eyes scanned the little groups around the bar. 'Don't make it obvious,' he urged. 'He might get suspicious.' I didn't see why he should but I could tell Hubert was quite excited by the whole thing. 'Which one?' I whispered back.

'The big bloke over by the corner of the bar – that's Big Charlie.'

I looked across to the bar as casually as I could. Big Charlie had his back to me and was talking to the barman. He was well over six feet tall with broad shoulders, a square head, and was all dressed in black. 'He looks like a cop to me,' I said. 'Do be careful.'

Hubert finished his drink. 'Just stay here,' he said. 'It won't take long.' He walked over to the bar and, as the barman began serving another customer, Hubert stood alongside Big Charlie and engaged him in conversation. It wasn't long before Hubert and Big Charlie strolled off towards the gents', Big Charlie first, followed a few seconds later by Hubert.

I debated for a while about buying myself another glass of wine. Neither of us was driving, so I approached the bar, having to negotiate a small group of women. They smiled at me as I eased past them and the big butch one said, in a surprisingly soft voice, 'If you're on your own you can always stand with us. I'm Denise, known as Den.' So I bought my drink and stood listening to their chat, which centred mostly on their jobs, clothes, food and diets and holidays. I was enjoying myself just listening when a crop-haired blonde with a face like a cherub asked me what I did for a living. I'd blurted out the truth before thinking. 'Hey, that's cool. How did you get into that? Come on, tell us all about it.'

Much to my shame I forgot about time and Hubert. I was enjoying myself, they were a lively crowd and they seemed interested in my job. In a lull in the conversation I glanced at my watch. I'd been chatting for half an hour! Where the hell was Hubert? The look on my face alerted Den. 'What's up?'

'I'll have to go. My . . . colleague . . . he should have been back by now.'

'Where did he go?'

'The gents'.'

I'd already moved away when she grabbed my arm. 'I'll come with you.'

She strode ahead with me following. At the door of the gents' she held up her hand. 'I'll go in first. No one will argue with me – tallish balding guy, isn't he?' I nodded.

I heard her open the cubicle doors and a flustered-looking man came rushing out. When she reappeared it was simply to shake her head and ask, 'Was he alone?'

'No, he was with Big Charlie.'

'Shit!'

'You know him?'

'Everyone knows him. He's a thug. What in God's name did he want with him?'

'He was trying to buy crack cocaine. It was a lead in our investigation.'

'A bloody dangerous lead.'

I could feel the panic rising in me now. My chest felt tight, my mouth dry.

'There's a back entrance,' said Den. 'Come on.'

We rushed past the ladies' and a staff room to the door at the end of the corridor. As Den opened it a security light came on, showing a small walled area with overflowing bins. There was no sign of Hubert. 'I'll check outside the gate,' said Den. She heaved the tall wooden gate open and looked around outside. I meanwhile had spotted something on the ground near the bins. Even with the security lights on it looked like oil. I bent down and rubbed my finger in it and stroked it on to my hand. It was blood. I couldn't move and I began to heave. Den helped me to my feet. 'Now, don't panic. You'd better call the police.'

'And say what? A friend of mine went off with Big Charlie to the gents' loo to buy crack cocaine. I don't think they'd have much sympathy.'

138

I'd begun to shiver now. I had a feeling I wasn't going to see Hubert ever again. I couldn't think and I allowed Den to guide me back to the bar. As we ended, a bell for time was being rung. 'Your best bet,' said Den, 'is to go back to where you're staying and ring the local hospital.'

'I've got a taxi booked for midnight,' I murmured.

'Right, I'll come with you.' She propped me up by the bar, where her friends had gathered round wanting to know what was going on. Someone thrust my handbag towards me and then Den, with her hand under my elbow, guided me outside to the car park. The taxi was driving in at the same time and we bundled in and he drove off. Even though I tried to keep calm, tears pricked at my eyelids and I couldn't think. I had no idea what to do next.

'Have you got any friends in the area?' asked Den.

'Friends,' I echoed. Then like a ray of sunlight through fog came my answer. 'I know an ex-cop.'

'Ring him, ring him now.'

I scrabbled about in my bag and finally found Roberts's business card. I punched out the wrong number twice until Den grabbed my mobile and the card and did it for me. Roberts sounded wide awake. I gave him a garbled account. 'Don't worry, Kate. Go back to the hotel and stay there. Lock your door and don't answer it to anyone. I'll get Liam and his mates out looking for Big Charlie's car. We know the number. Don't you worry, we won't pussyfoot when we do find him.' Never mind Big Charlie, I thought, what about Hubert?

The bar was closed at the Regis but Den had a word with the night porter and he appeared minutes later with a bottle of brandy. 'Sorry about your trouble,' he said. 'Make sure you give me a replacement tomorrow.'

Luckily Hubert had left his room key in reception, because I'd forgotten all about Jasper. As I approached Hubert's room Jasper began to bark. When I opened the door with

Den still in attendance he seemed more interested in Den than me. She was obviously a dog lover and next door in my room, whilst she made a fuss of Jasper, I poured two large brandies into teacups. I was still shivery and on the verge of tears but the brandy's fiery warmth braced me a little. It was odd, I thought, that I should be relying on a woman I'd only just met, but it was her calm masculine style that was so reassuring. I supposed we could scour the country for Hubert but where would we start? If the police did find Big Charlie he would probably admit to supplying drugs but not to . . . what? Abduction? GBH? Murder? I downed another brandy. 'Hubert's dead,' I said aloud.

'You can't know that,' said Den. 'You're going to have to get a grip.'

I knew she was right but I couldn't. I had visions of Hubert crawling away to die. In pain, lonely.

'I've got to go and look for him,' I said. 'I can't stay here.'

'Didn't that ex-cop say to stay here with the door locked?'

'Yeah. But I've got to *do* something.'

'Let's wait for an hour or so and see what happens.'

Her quiet voice calmed me for a few seconds. Then the thought galloped into my mind that in an hour or so Hubert could have bled to death. Judging by the amount of blood in the yard he could have bled to death in minutes. Please, Hubert, I pleaded silently. Please still be alive.

Seventeen

D en did her best to make me talk about something
other than Hubert and although I tried to respond I
could only do so pacing the room. She was, it seems, a
fire officer and at any other time I would have been really
interested – but not now. Images of Hubert lying dead by
some roadside kept coming to mind. Jasper's interest in Den
had now waned and for a while he followed me as I walked
back and forth. Then after a few minutes he sat at the door
to the garden wagging his tail and barking. I opened the
door and he rushed off into the dark.

I was so consumed with worrying about Hubert I didn't
notice how long Jasper had been gone. 'There's no sign of
Jasper,' said Den, peering out into the garden. 'I can't see
him.' I stood at the door and called him but he didn't come
running. The garden was walled, with the gate as the only
exit. After that a short path led to the car park. There was no
way he could escape – unless the gate had been left open. It
was then that Jasper gave a short sharp yap.

I rushed out into the garden and found Jasper frantically
trying to burrow beneath the gate. I opened it and he
immediately tore off towards the car park. As we ran
after him the security lights came on. There were at least
twenty parked cars and we lost sight of Jasper amongst them.
Den and I stood calling him and finally he responded with
excited yapping. The sound was coming from beyond the
furthest car, somewhere in the bushes and the flowerbeds.

141

And there lying face down was Hubert. I knew it was him because I recognized his new casual shoes. His hands were outstretched and he was clutching a syringe, the needle shining in the semi-black. It was Den who took charge, rolling him on his side, checking his airway. 'He's still alive,' she said. From her trouser pocket she produced a mobile phone. She rang 999 while I stayed on my knees looking in horror at Hubert's face. His lower lip was bloody and swollen, his eyes puffed and closed. There was blood covering his face and the rivulets had dried into his neck. He was breathing but only just. I rolled up his sleeves to see if he'd been pumped full of heroin but in the poor light I couldn't see the needle puncture.

I held his hand and began talking to him. 'Come on, Hubert. Hang on. You're going to be all right.' All the usual stuff. I wasn't convinced he could hear me but it was worth a try. Den rushed off to get a blanket and I changed tack. 'Don't you dare leave me,' I said directly into his ear. 'I can't carry on without you.' He made a slight gurgling sound and I thought at first he was trying to respond but he was only attempting to spit out a loose tooth. I pushed the tooth back into the socket and then Den came rushing back with the blanket. I'd just covered him when I heard the ambulance siren. No sound ever could have been more welcome.

The paramedics were quick and efficient. An oxygen mask was strapped to Hubert's face, an intravenous line was put in place but when they asked what exactly had happened to him I couldn't say. 'Is he a druggie?' the younger paramedic asked me as he carefully removed the syringe from Hubert's hand. 'No way,' I said. 'He's a funeral director.' It was a daft answer but I wasn't thinking that well. My knees were beginning to buckle and I had a desperate need for confirmation that he would survive. But my nursing experience told me that though the paramedics would do their best there were no guarantees.

Once he was stabilized I walked behind them, planning to be with him in the ambulance, but I was told I would have to follow on behind. Den came to my rescue again. 'I'll drive you. I only had a sip of the brandy.' Words couldn't express at that moment how grateful I felt towards her. I muttered, 'Thanks a million,' and we quickly made our way to Hubert's car.

We followed close behind the speeding ambulance, with its silent flashing blue light. It all seemed surreal, like watching an accident documentary. But this *was* for real and Hubert's life was on the line and I felt sick.

Mile after mile passed by. 'Where the hell are we going?' I asked Den. She sped round a tight bend like a rally driver and said, 'We're on the Exeter road.'

'Exeter?' I asked in amazement.

'Yep. Not all the local hospitals have A&E departments. Don't worry, the hospital will know the ambulance is on its way. They'll be all geared up for him.'

The journey seemed to last for an eternity but eventually we arrived and as we parked the car I could see Hubert already being trundled hurriedly into the A&E department.

There was no need for me to run anymore, so we walked slowly and I took deep steadying breaths. Hubert, I knew, would immediately be whisked away into the resuscitation area and there I would be in the way.

The middle-aged male receptionist wore a white tee shirt from which bulged muscular hairy arms. He wanted the usual information: name, address, date of birth, next of kin. I was standing by the desk, feeling distinctly odd and fixated on his hairy arms. I didn't know Hubert's year of birth. His actual birthday was in December but even though I knew the date I couldn't remember it. How could I then say I was his next of kin?

Mr Muscles stared at me and I tried to focus on his name badge. It took me a few seconds – *Norman Jacks*. 'Are you all right?' he asked. My head throbbed, my eyesight seemed dulled and his voice sounded so quiet, as if he were speaking down a long rubber tube. I felt a hand on my shoulder and Den guiding me to a chair and sitting me down with my head between my knees. Thought processes were still in action, though, because I realized that at least it would give me time to do a little mental arithmetic.

When my head resurfaced I was able to tell him 10th December 1948 and my name was Kate Humberstone – daughter. The year was a mere guess but I thought the 10th December was his correct birthday. Norman Jacks filled out the appropriate forms and we joined a sad little band in the waiting area. Every time a door opened our eyes looked towards the person entering for some sign it was us they were looking for.

Waiting in A&E is a lesson in patience but who wants it? Some people just can't cope and a scruffy drunk who had wandered in with a bleeding head wound was one. A security man with a mere half of Norman's muscles attempted to quieten him down. A stream of foul language, mostly unintelligible, followed and when the drunk lashed out at the security guard Den was on her feet and in an instant she had him in an armlock and began wrestling him to the floor. The security man was meanwhile using his walkie-talkie to summon back-up. The drunk by now was lying very still and gingerly Den got to her feet and looked down at him. She looked worried. After all, in the present climate, if she'd injured him, or worse still he was dead, she'd be either sued or imprisoned for five years.

Two more security men burst in then, hauled the drunk to his feet and unceremoniously plonked him into a wheelchair and pushed him away. I wondered where they were taking him but I didn't care and the relief all round that he'd been dispatched was palpable in the air.

Den also looked relieved as she sat down beside me, pink-faced and breathing only a little faster than normal. 'I didn't expect all this on a girls' night out.'

'You were great,' I said admiringly.

'Yeah. Being in the fire service keeps you fit.'

Now that the waiting area was quiet again we sat silently and in the silence anxiety clawed in the pit of my stomach. Why was it taking so long? When would someone speak to me? I'd already decided that the next medical-looking person to come through the door would be waylaid. For all I knew, Hubert could be in a corridor somewhere. I'd read the newspapers about the elderly lying in corridors for hours, even days. Patience is only a virtue, I decided, when nothing is to be gained by being impatient. If I was playing the 'daughter', then I was going to be a stroppy one and fight for my 'father's' rights.

I stood up and announced to Den, 'I'm going to find out what's going on – now!'

And then, as if conjured from nowhere, a young woman wearing a white coat and a stethoscope strung around her neck like a badge of office walked up to me. 'Are you Kate?' I nodded. She was smiling. 'I'm the registrar, Dr Sophie Morgan. I've just come to tell you you can see your father now. He's going to be fine . . .' She carried on explaining something about X-rays and cracked ribs but somehow the information wasn't penetrating. '*He's going to be fine*,' was all that mattered. She led me to a curtained cubicle and, before pulling back the curtain, said, 'I'll need to talk to you again later. Please come and find me before you go. He's still very sleepy due to the heroin.'

I caught the slight note of reproach in her voice but I managed to remain silent. Hubert was going to live and that was all I cared about at the moment.

145

He lay slightly propped against white pillows. His intravenous infusion continued in his left arm. Both eyes were puffed and blackening and until the swelling went down he would be unable to see. I thought at first he was asleep but then he spoke, 'Will the girls still fancy me now?'

'Did they ever?'

'That's my Kate,' he said. 'I can't see a thing at the moment but I knew it was you.'

'How?'

'Footsteps. You're a bit of a clomper.'

'Shall I go and exchange myself for a ballet dancer?'

'I'm too spaced out for all this, Kate. I keep drifting off. I was set up.'

'Even I guessed that. Was it Big Charlie?'

'Yeah. And two others. One was the barman from the Crown and Anchor. The other was skinny and weasel-faced. I did try to fight back . . .'

'Don't worry about that. The odds were against you.'

'I've been a bloody fool.'

'We both have. You just need to rest up and get better now. What did they say is wrong with you?'

'Didn't the doctor speak to you?'

'Yes . . . but I didn't take it in.'

'Call yourself a nurse?'

'No, at the moment I call myself an anxious relative.'

He grinned through swollen lips, showing one loose front tooth hanging lower than its twin did.

'I wouldn't smile for a while,' I said.

'That tooth,' he said, 'has got to be saved. The doc doesn't hold out much hope. She said I was long in the tooth anyway.'

'A dentist will sort you out.'

'I'm lucky. I've got three broken ribs, bruised kidneys, a half-knocked-out tooth, black eyes and a bloodstream full of heroin, so at the moment I can't feel a thing.'

'When does the doc say you can get out of here?'

'Forty-eight hours if my waterworks function again.'

'Great. I think you ought to go home then, don't you?'

He fumbled for my hand, patted it and said cheerfully, 'Stop talking, Kate. Go home. Go to bed. If I'm lucky some nubile young nurse will give me a blanket bath, so I'm in no rush to go back to Longborough.'

'You'll be lucky. You have to be at death's door to get a blanket bath these days.'

'You're a real killjoy.'

'You wait and see.'

I kissed him on the forehead and was about to leave when he asked, 'Is Liam with you?'

'No. A woman from the wine bar called Den has been my guardian angel.'

'You mean, she's a . . .'

'Yes, a lesbian. So what?'

'Well just because you can't find a man doesn't mean you should go the other way.'

'I *could* find a man if I wanted to. And I am *not* going the other way. It's not a matter of choice.'

As Hubert grunted and pretended to snore I made my exit.

Den was still waiting for me in reception. She looked tired now and as I approached she was wearily running her fingers through her hair. I told her about Hubert's condition and that the heroin was keeping him cheerful. We still had the drive back to Trevelly, so I offered her Hubert's room for a few hours' sleep and she agreed. 'I'm not on shift tomorrow,' she said, adding, 'and I'm glad. I feel shattered.' I too felt drained but the awful anxiety had gone.

Den insisted on driving, she was obviously impressed by the car and she was a good, if fast, driver. Her night vision was considerably better than mine.

We'd been driving along for about three miles when

147

my mobile rang. It was Liam. He and his dad had been scouring the countryside for Hubert and Big Charlie and I had forgotten to ring him. I apologized profusely and told him all about Hubert.

'Just as long as you're OK. We haven't found Big Charlie yet but we will, and the others. Make lunch a bit later tomorrow, say two p.m.'

I was surprised lunch was still on. I hadn't given either Helen or Gill or Warrinder a thought. I was at that stage in an investigation when it seems to be going nowhere and where my spirits sink. I'd experienced it before and knew it would pass but there was one thing I simply had to do. I had to confront Paul Warrinder as soon as possible.

Eighteen

The next morning at nine a.m. I rang the hospital. Hubert was both 'satisfactory and comfortable'. I knocked on Hubert's door but Den didn't respond, so I left her to sleep on for a while and rang the hotel manager. He'd heard about Hubert being found unconscious in the car park and was sympathetic and said he'd send up two breakfast trays.

Den was awake by the time breakfast arrived and we ate together in Hubert's room. By the time we'd eaten enough calories to last twenty-four hours I'd told her the whole story. She was a good listener and she told me the drug scene in Newquay was particularly active. 'There's two Cornwalls,' she said as she finished off the last morsel of toast, 'one for the middle-aged and elderly – all cream teas and Cornish pasties – and the other Cornwall for the young – surfing, sex and drugs.'

'So what are the police doing about it?'

She shrugged, pushed her tray to the end of the bed and sat back against the pillows.

'They try, but who's going to give away their supplier?'

'Where does it come from?'

Den's expression revealed she thought I'd led a sheltered life. 'Have you been abroad lately?'

I shook my head. 'I went to New Zealand nearly two years ago.'

'I go to Holland quite often. I've got a good friend there. Back in the UK, customs officials just aren't there to monitor

149

all the flights. I could have walked through any time with a suitcase full of drugs.'

I finished my coffee and took both trays and placed them outside the bedroom door. Drug smuggling, it seemed to me, was too big a leap from possible murder and it complicated everything. If Warrinder was a drug dealer and smuggler and Fran had found out, surely divorce was the answer and not suicide and murder. She could, of course, have shopped him – so why didn't she? Did Alison disappear so completely because, once she found out, she was afraid for her life? Then she must have made a conscious decision to start a new life, not even daring to send her half-brother a Christmas card. In the event that she had evidence of Warrinder being a major drug dealer, surely she would have been offered police protection. That was a question I could save for my lunch with Liam.

Later, when Den was ready to go, I offered her a lift but she declined, saying she'd already booked a minicab. I waited with her in reception and we exchanged telephone numbers, vowing to keep in touch. As we hugged each other goodbye, she murmured in my ear, 'Take care, Kate. There is always someone bent on the inside. It only takes one.' I asked her to explain but the minicab driver was already sounding his horn impatiently and she hurried away.

'Thanks a million,' I shouted after her.

I took time that morning deciding what to wear. In the end I decided on a denim skirt, a tightish black tee shirt and a pair of mules with heels. Checking myself in the mirror I decided Liam would be impressed that I'd scrubbed up so well. Jasper was lying in his basket fast asleep after chasing around the garden. He'd been slightly subdued since finding Hubert and I debated with myself if I should disturb him or not. In the end I chose to leave him behind but asked one of the porters, Jimmy, to let him out for a run mid-afternoon.

I arrived for lunch on the dot of two, which was just as

well, because I was quickly ushered into the kitchen and there to greet me was a huge bowl of pasta with a prawn, bacon and cheese sauce. I wasn't a bit hungry but Liam was and he couldn't wait to eat. I was impressed with his cooking but I was more impressed with the fact that he didn't *talk* about the food or his cooking prowess. He asked first about Hubert but I got the impression he wanted to satisfy his stomach and curiosity could wait. So I simply said, 'He's OK – thanks.'

'Come on then, Kate. Eat up. You look the sort who enjoys her food.' If he was saying I was fat, he said it with a smile and a twinkle in his eye, so, hungry or not, I polished off the lot.

Once he'd eaten he was anxious to talk. Mostly about his father. 'I know you're only trying to help a friend but it's fired up my dad's obsession. He's out now seeing a chap in Devon who he used to work with years back. I tell him he's wasting his time but he doesn't listen.'

As I listened to him I began to wonder about Liam. Without any real justification at all I had the feeling that he wanted his father to stop trying to nail Warrinder, for reasons other than health. 'What are you worried about most?' I asked. 'Your dad getting sick, or are you trying to hide something from him?'

'What the hell are you talking about?' The twinkle had gone from his eyes, to be replaced by an angry glint. Here goes another potential romance, I thought. When would I learn to keep my mouth shut? 'I only meant that perhaps you're trying to protect your dad by not letting him know all the facts.'

'What facts?'

'Well, it seems the drugs scene is flourishing in Cornwall, Newquay especially, and I wondered if the police were . . . well . . . turning a blind eye.'

He stared at me. 'You're really asking about bent coppers, aren't you?'

'I suppose I am. Every force has got one or two, or so I've heard.'

'Really?' he said. 'Is that what you've heard?'

Was I being that irritating or was that a touch of guilt in his voice? I couldn't be sure but I couldn't just leave it there. 'I've read about huge hauls of cannabis and cocaine,' I said. 'What happens to it?'

'Everything we find is dealt with by the civilian property officer, logged in and sealed with a number and date. Not only is the item manually accounted for but it's also put on computer.'

'And who destroys it?'

'It varies.'

He was being deliberately evasive. The temptation would be as great as if pound notes were about to be destroyed. Some would succumb. And I was beginning to wonder if he was one who would. Liam stared at me for a moment then smiled. 'I reckon you're in the right line of work after all.'

'That's good,' I said. 'Cos I'm stuck with it.'

'Rest assured,' he said, 'that everything is done to ensure that any drugs do not leave the property office until the court case, when they may be produced as evidence. The court then passes a Drugs and Paraphernalia Order so that the drugs may be destroyed.'

'And the destruction?'

'That takes place at local headquarters. The drugs are incinerated in the presence of a senior officer not below the rank of superintendent. Satisfied?'

'Yes . . . but . . .'

'But what?'

'The drugs could still be siphoned off at source. A little bit here, a little bit there, even before getting to a police station.'

'Yes, and the chief constable might be a pole dancer. Let's get off this subject, Kate, before I get really irritated.'

Fair enough, I thought, and changed the subject. 'What plans has your dad in mind for nailing Warrinder?' I asked.

Liam shrugged. 'He knows I'm the voice of caution but he also knows he can take more risks than I can, because he's no longer in the force. I'm sure he thinks he won't be prosecuted – but he will if they find out.'

'For what?'

'Skulking around Tamberlake. He's had keys to that place for ages.'

'So, he still thinks Alison is buried there?'

'Oh yes. Nothing, bar a severe hammering, will shift that idea from his head.'

'Maybe he needs some help.'

'You're thinking of going there with a pickaxe and a shovel are you?'

'No, but tomorrow I'm planning to see Helen and if everything goes according to plan I'm going to meet Paul Warrinder – see what I make of him.'

Liam sat back in his chair grinning.

'What's so funny?' I asked.

'It's just that you seem to think a bit of feminine intuition will crack the case like an elephant stamping on a walnut.'

'I do not! But it's best to know the enemy. Meeting him would be a help. Then at least I'd know what we were up against.'

'He's as slippery as baby oil on smooth tiles. You won't trap him with words.'

I thought about that for a moment. 'Didn't they get Al Capone on tax evasion?'

'They did. Has Warrinder, to your knowledge, been evading tax?'

'No, but if he could be arrested on a minor charge,'

I said, 'once he was in custody he could be questioned more fully.'

'Don't you think he was questioned before? We didn't use the thumbscrews but he told us nothing that would incriminate him.'

'What about the fact that it seems he hasn't been to Argentina, and if he has, he was travelling on a false passport?'

Liam smiled. 'A false passport is an offence but lying about where you are isn't.'

I realized then I wasn't going to win any arguments with him so I simply said, 'I still need to meet him.'

'Just be very careful.'

Strange, I thought, how contrary is human nature. The more you are exhorted to 'be careful', the more exciting the risk seems.

I left on a cheerful note, with Liam promising to ring me and fix up a proper dinner date. 'On one proviso,' he said. 'No shop talk. We talk trivia.'

'I can do trivia,' I said. He opened the car door and then kissed me full on the lips. Not bad, I thought. Not bad at all.

I was driving away feeling exceptionally cheerful when my mobile rang. I parked the car and rummaged in my bag. It was Helen.

'Kate. I hear you're in Cornwall. Paul's back. He's been a bit naughty – he came back early from Argentina but he's had a stomach bug and he didn't want to burden Gill and I with his being ill, so he stayed with a friend.'

'That was thoughtful of him.'

'You really must meet him. Come for lunch tomorrow.'

'Love to.'

'About one?'

'I'm looking forward to it.'

Warrinder was indeed slippery. I didn't think he would give himself away, but someone else surely would.

I drove on to Exeter to visit Hubert. In daylight the journey didn't seem so far and I managed to find a parking space after driving around the hospital grounds a mere twice.

Hubert sat in a chair by his bed, wearing a striped hospital dressing gown. At first I thought he was asleep but then I noticed one eye was slightly open. The bruising was more pronounced now and the heroin had obviously left his system. I was impressed, though, that his tooth was back in place. He pointed to his tooth. 'Some medic fixed it,' he said. 'He told me it was superglue and I don't think he was a dentist.' I smiled and sat down. 'Don't just sit there grinning. Get me out of here, Kate. I can't stand it. I won't be getting a blanket bath and the baths here aren't clean.'

'I'm surprised you can see well enough to notice.'

'I'm serious, Kate. The hotel is cleaner, the bed's more comfortable and the food's better. I'm coming out.'

'Don't think I'll be blanket-bathing you, because I won't.'

'I wouldn't let you, you can be ham-fisted.'

'I'd butter me up if you want to get out of here.'

He stood up unsteadily.

'Sit down again,' I said. 'You'll have to sign a form first.' He sat down again like a sulky schoolboy and I went off to find the nurse in charge. I found her in the nurses' station looking frazzled. Her attitude suggested that, as long as Hubert signed the appropriate forms, he could crawl out on all fours. He was just one less for her to worry about.

When I returned Hubert was waiting by the door wearing his own bloodstained clothes. In fact he was holding on to the door. I realized guiltily that I'd been too preoccupied to remember he might have needed clothes and toiletries. He grabbed the forms, I provided a pen and he signed them using the doorframe to rest them on. On the way out I handed them in at the nurses' station to be countersigned and then the frazzled ward sister managed a tight smile. 'Any problems,' she said, 'see a GP as a temporary resident.' In other words never darken our doorstep again. I thanked her, Hubert muttered his thanks and then, with him hanging on to my arm, we made our way slowly out of the hospital.

Once in the car, Hubert murmured that he felt very weak and within a mile or so of the hospital his head had slumped forward and he was asleep and snoring.

Back at the Regis, as I helped Hubert into reception, Jimmy the porter rushed forward to help support him, as his legs didn't seem to be responding. We managed between us to get him to his room, where the porter helped him on to the bed and removed his jacket and trousers. Hubert's white vest was bloodstained, so between us we removed that and slipped on his blue silk pyjama top. 'What a poser,' I said. Hubert grunted but obviously didn't appreciate the comment. After Jimmy the porter had left I went next door and released Jasper.

When he saw Hubert he barked and circled and his whole body quivered with joy. Then he managed to scrabble on to the bed and snuggle down beside him. Hubert raised a languid hand and stroked Jasper's head. A few minutes later they were both asleep and even the hotel manager's knock at the door didn't wake them.

'How is he?' he whispered as he peered in on the sleeping duo.

'He'll be fine now he's back here.'

'What would he like for dinner? Chef can rustle up anything your dad fancies.'

'Perhaps some grilled plaice and mashed potatoes?'

'No problem. Soup? Dessert?'

'He likes jelly and ice cream and tomato soup.'

'Fine. Anything you need, just let me know.'

I thanked him profusely and he gave me an old-fashioned bow and left.

As I closed the door I thought Hubert was right. The Regis Hotel was a better bet on the healing stakes. Hospital was fine if you were unconscious and unable to worry about hygiene shortcomings, the awful food, the noise and the lack of fresh air. In his own room Hubert could have peace and quiet and Jasper to aid his recovery.

By the time Hubert's dinner tray arrived he'd slept for three hours. A young waitress brought up the tray and gazed at Hubert asleep with his mouth wide open. 'Bless him,' she murmured as she placed the tray on the coffee table.

As she closed the door Hubert woke and with his half-open eye spied the tray. 'You go down to the dining room and eat. If you think you're going to sit here and watch me eat you can think again.'

'If you're sure you can manage . . .' I began. He didn't let me finish, he just waved me away, so I sloped off to the dining room desperately hoping that Beatrice and Franklin wouldn't decide to keep me company. They did. And they wanted to know all about Hubert's attack. I half expected them to ask about the state of Hubert's bowels but they didn't go quite that far. Having established that the police had a name and description of the assailants, I was then subjected to a discourse, during my main meal, on the American judicial system and its superiority. Franklin believed that capital punishment was the only answer to every crime from mugging to murder. He was so bellicose and convinced he was right, I merely listened and vowed to have meals in my room from now on. I soon grew so tired of his pontificating that I declined dessert, saying I had to check on Hubert.

I found him sitting out in his blue silk pyjamas looking more chipper. 'I was starving,' he said. 'I feel so much better now. I can think clearly again.'

I knew Hubert well enough to know that he had an idea, but he thought his ideas were solutions and I hoped his 'clear thinking' wasn't another scheme that should be kept locked in the labyrinthine depths of his mind.

'London,' he said.

'What about London?'

'We shouldn't be here in Cornwall. The answer is in London.'

'What answer?' I asked.

'Whatever Warrinder is up to – he's not doing it in Cornwall.'

Nineteen

That night I sat propped up in bed watching television but unable to concentrate. Maybe the answers were in London and not Cornwall but at the moment there were more loose ends locally. Loose ends! Who was I kidding? We'd achieved nothing between us. Hubert's beating and a dose of heroin were hardly an achievement. In a week I'd managed to find out that Warrinder either had a false passport or he hadn't been to Argentina at all, also that their friends had lied about the night Fran supposedly committed suicide, and that was the sum total of actual knowledge. I lay awake for hours trying to plan some sort of strategy but apart from getting Hubert safely back home the rest was a blur.

The next day Hubert's eyes were virtually open but he didn't have much energy and seemed to be content to lie in bed watching television and waiting for his meals to be delivered. I rang my mother, Marilyn, and she told me, with a hint of *I told you so* that David and Megan were 'getting serious'. I told her I was pleased but I don't think she believed me. She'd had a taste of surrogate grandmotherhood and now the great wide world was beckoning her. Her latest venture, she informed me, was to buy a camper van and 'see Europe'. I doubted Europe wanted to see her, and I wondered how someone who was always broke could afford a camper van, and I guessed some fool bank manager had given her a loan. But I didn't ask. I did ask about my god-daughter Katy, who it seems is *'a little peach'*.

159

Hubert is occasionally psychic and just before I was about to leave for lunch at Tamberlake he looked up from the television and stared at me for a few moments.

'You've been talking to your mother.'

'How can you tell that?'

'A look comes over your face,' he said.

'Worried? Anxious?'

'No,' he said, shaking his head. 'Mystified. Like you've seen the ghost of things to come and you don't like it.'

'My mother is such an airhead she—'

'Just be grateful you've got a mother. She is an airhead but given half a chance you would be too. And she's not good at choosing men, so you do have that in common.'

'Are you trying to depress me?'

'No,' he said, trying to look the innocent.

I changed the subject before I did get depressed. 'I'm off to see Helen at Tamberlake. She's cooking lunch. You'll be all right on your own – won't you?'

'Jasper's here,' he said. 'We'll be fine.' Jasper awoke from sleep, nuzzled Hubert's hand and wagged his tail. I was surplus to requirements.

I arrived at Tamberlake as the looming black clouds decided to shed their cargo of rain, and in the few seconds it took me to reach the front door I was soaked. I hadn't worn a coat, just a long summer skirt and a white blouse. They clung damply to me as I waited for someone to answer the front door.

It was Paul Warrinder who answered the door. He was better-looking in the flesh than in photographs. His smile was warm, his teeth perfect. His eyes, although dark, almost black, reminded me of pools of petrol, with those shiny flecks of colour in them.

'Come on in,' he said. 'You look as if you need to dry off.' He guided me to the downstairs cloakroom, where I towel-dried my hair and dabbed at my clothes.

Helen was there to greet me when I came out. 'It's good to see you again, Kate. I thought after the trouble with Gill you might not speak to me again.' She didn't give me time to reply, before suggesting we had a glass of wine in the sitting room. 'Don't worry about Paul, he's in the kitchen preparing lunch. He's making pizzas.'

'From scratch?'

'Yes. He's a great cook and he loves it, so I just leave him to it.'

Helen poured out the Argentinian wine. 'I have to explain to you,' she said, 'about how I met Paul. I did meet him in a camera shop but it was before Fran . . . died. We just chatted. After that I seemed to see him quite often, just around and about with his children. We were *not* having a relationship. I thought he was gorgeous-looking but he wasn't free and I wouldn't chase after a married man.'

'What was he buying in the camera shop?' I asked.

She frowned. 'A camera . . . why do you ask?'

'I just wondered. He's keen on photography then?'

'Oh yes. That's one of the things we have in common.'

I sipped at my wine, one glass would have to last unless I was prepared to take a taxi back to the Regis and leave Hubert's car behind. Helen stared into her wine glass. 'I hope Gill and I will make up soon,' she murmured. 'I *really* want her to come to the wedding.'

Helen was far more edgy now that Paul had returned. I was about to ask her *why* when he appeared at the door to announce that lunch was ready. We dutifully followed him to the kitchen, where a mega-size pizza had just been removed from the oven. He'd also made coleslaw and provided a huge salad. If nothing else, Helen would at least be well fed. I couldn't resist another glass of wine and halfway through the meal I began to feel pleasantly mellow. So mellow that when Paul asked if I enjoyed being a private investigator I was able to say that it '*had its moments*'.

161

'Helen told me,' he said, looking me straight in the eye, 'that Gill was convinced not only had I killed Alison but that somehow I was responsible for Fran and the children's death. That was very hurtful, as you can imagine.'

I nodded. I didn't know what to say. Helen murmured, 'Paul, darling, don't let's get heavy. Gill means well.'

'I'm not getting heavy, sweetheart,' he said evenly. 'I just want to get the record straight for Kate. I've had enormous bad luck recently. It hasn't been easy, but meeting Helen has given me another crack at happiness and I don't want anything to spoil that. I'm sure you can understand that, Kate.'

I nodded again, feeling like one of those toy dogs dangling in the back of a car. In truth I was wary of putting my foot in it. The less I said, I reasoned, the more he would talk.

'I've heard via my friends,' he continued, 'that you've been asking questions about me. The latest rumour is that I'm a drug dealer and that our Saturday night dinner parties were drug-fuelled orgies and that's why Fran . . . did what she did.' He paused, still looking me straight in the eye. 'I'll admit I told the police that we had cancelled the dinner party that night but I did it to protect them. They knew nothing about Fran's death and they were devastated by the news. What use would it be subjecting them to police questioning when there was nothing to say?'

'That makes sense,' I said to mollify him. Then I finished the last mouthful of pizza on my plate, murmured that it was delicious and sipped at my wine. It gave me a chance to decide how to make a comment more of a question, and one that might prove illuminating. 'I can't help wondering,' I said, 'about Fran's state of mind that evening. Feminine curiosity, I suppose.'

Paul shrugged. 'Looking back, she seemed a little subdued but I wouldn't say depressed. She always looked forward to Saturday nights. It gave her a break from the cooking,

162

because I always cooked and cleared up afterwards. She got dressed up and the children went to bed early, which gave us a chance to have a quiet drink before our friends arrived.'

'You said she was subdued – was there a reason?'

Paul sat back in his chair and ran his hand through his hair. 'As I said, in retrospect I think poor Fran had been subdued since Josh was born. I think she had post-natal depression but she insisted it would pass and – her words – she didn't want her "emotions artificially tampered with by medication". I should have insisted earlier but I did insist in the end because she couldn't sleep at night, saying that she could hear things. I thought with medication and proper sleep she'd be OK but I was wrong. Very wrong.'

'Were you surprised she didn't leave a suicide note?'

A pained expression crossed his face. 'I don't think the word "surprise" is adequate. I was in total shock. Numb. It was as if I was walking through fog. Nothing made any sense. If you're talking about raw emotion, when the fog lifted – I was angry. Very angry. Fran had every right to kill herself, but to take my babies with her, with no explanation, was unforgivable.'

There was silence then. I could see Paul's hand trembling slightly and his eyes glimmered. It was Helen who broke the silence. 'Time for coffee,' she said quietly.

Over coffee I changed tack. 'What about Alison?' I said. 'Where do you think she's gone?'

'To be honest, I don't care,' he muttered under his breath. Then added, 'Don't get the wrong impression. I loved her. I wanted children by her. She wanted to be free, I suppose. This house is a job in itself. I think she saw the future and didn't like what she saw. She wasn't particularly domesticated. She saw the restrictions and got out.'

'Weren't you . . . a bit surprised she didn't give you an explanation?'

'There you go again,' he said, with the briefest of smiles.

'I was hurt that she couldn't talk to me. Not wanting to marry me was, of course, her choice, but we could have remained friends.'

'Would that have worked?'

He looked thoughtful. 'No. Probably not.'

'Were you . . . concerned when she didn't contact her half-brother?'

He smiled. 'There you have me, Kate. This time I was surprised. They were fairly close. I have to admit it was only when Fran died that I did wonder if Alison too had killed herself or gone adrift in some out of the way country.'

'Why would she have killed herself?'

'No particular reason. But she too could be a little unstable at times.'

'But you didn't do anything to find her?'

'No. Why should I?'

Why indeed? I supposed if I was engaged to a bloke who went AWOL I wouldn't necessarily think he was a missing person – just that he didn't want anything more to do with me. I'd have still wanted some sort of explanation, but then life doesn't always give you explanations. Life's a bitch. I guessed that was Paul's attitude too.

Helen had remained very quiet but now she'd obviously had enough of the serious stuff, because she began to bustle about, noisily clearing the table. With two of Paul's exes being supposedly 'unstable' and her afraid to be in the house on her own, I did wonder if her IQ only reached double figures, and tried to remember if she'd shown any promise at school. My abiding memory was still of her white socks and the braces on the teeth, so she hadn't shone academically, because I certainly couldn't remember ever asking to cadge a look at her homework. Was she 'unstable' too? Or was Tamberlake responsible? She refused my offer of help to stack the dishwasher but forced a smile. 'We're having our usual Saturday night dinner party tomorrow. You will come, won't you?'

'You mean the same friends that—'

She didn't let me finish. 'Of course. They're incredibly loyal, aren't they, darling?'

He stood up and put his arm around her. 'I don't know how I would have survived without them.'

Twenty

The next day Hubert had resumed life in the world of communal dining. We were given a table for two and Hubert was fussed over like a minor celebrity. Whilst I'd been at Tamberlake the previous day the police had arrived to take a statement. Big Charlie and the barman had disappeared but they were hopeful that they would be caught. I remained sceptical.

Hubert dropped his bombshell once we'd finished our mammoth breakfast. 'I'm going home,' he said. 'But don't think I've lost my nerve, just because I was nearly killed. The locum isn't coping that well and I don't want my reputation put in jeopardy.'

I stared at him and he looked away. He was scared. His brush with death had upset him more than I'd realized. 'Couldn't you hang on for one more day? I could drive you home tomorrow.'

He shook his head.

'Please think about it. You're not well enough to drive. We could go straight after breakfast tomorrow.'

Eventually he said, 'Oh all right, but I don't want you gadding off and leaving me on my own all day.'

'Fair enough,' I said. 'We'll gad together. Picnic? Pub lunch? A paddle in the sea?'

Hubert's eyes lit up. 'I haven't had a paddle in the sea for years.'

So we did just that. I ordered a packed lunch via reception

and by ten thirty, Hubert, Jasper and I were driving to the beach. The sun shone thinly but promised warmth to come and after hiring a windbreaker and two deckchairs we planned to spend the day reading the papers, eating and throwing sticks for Jasper. It took Hubert a while to get the courage to remove his socks and shoes – he doesn't own sandals – and roll up his trouser legs. He strode off to the water's edge at a brisk pace, hesitated for a few seconds then took the plunge until the sea lapped as far as his ankle bones. He paused for a few more seconds looking out to sea with a hand over his eyes, then he turned abruptly and walked back to our little camp in the sand. 'Too bloody cold,' he said gloomily.

'What did you expect for your feet – the Caribbean?'

As he picked up a towel he looked hopefully at me, as if he'd like me to dry his feet. My eyes stayed resolutely on my newspaper. Not that my mind was on the usual array of bad news and health scares. I hadn't told him I was invited to the Saturday night soirée. It was time to broach the subject. He didn't respond at first, other than with a grunt that I interpreted as disapproval. 'I think his looks have swayed you,' he said. 'Now that you've met him and found out he can cook pizza – he must be a saint.'

'I only said I thought he *might be* telling the truth. Innocent until proved guilty and all that. But, saying that, I think that I think he's a pompous prat and, for all his posturing – as cold as the sea you've just paddled in.'

'Robert Roberts thinks there's no doubt.'

'Yes. But he's the old school of cop – convict at all costs.'

'I think he talks a lot of sense,' said Hubert, slipping his socks back on. 'And he was willing to lay his career on the line because he was convinced that Warrinder is guilty of murder.'

'Evidence of that is not forthcoming. There's something I've missed.'

'Just the one thing?'

'Warrinder bought a camera . . .' I tailed off. Something told me it was significant but I had no idea why. Then realization dawned. It was merely the fact that it was an *item*. Like a computer.

'I've got it!'

'What?'

'In the whole of Tamberlake, and that includes the attic, there is no computer.'

'Don't get carried away,' said Hubert, giving me a worried glance. 'Lots of people don't have a computer.'

'Not people like Warrinder. The cleaner, Carole Jackson, she'll know if he's ever had one.'

'I'm flummoxed,' said Hubert. 'I reckon you've had too much sun.'

'No. I'm convinced this is a lead. Come on, Hubert, you've had your paddle. Let's get to work.'

In my enthusiasm I hadn't given a thought to *which* camera shop. Hubert remained flummoxed. 'So what?' he said. 'Warrinder buys a camera. Next we'll be checking out where he buys his loo paper.'

It was hard to explain why I thought it was significant. Warrinder had encroached on Fran's artwork and just by chance he meets a professional photographer. I'd thought Helen had been the one doing the chasing – now I wasn't so sure.

I'd never seen a camera shop in Trevelly, so we started on the inland towns of Bude and Launceston. In Launceston we struck lucky. There in the main street was a camera shop, its small windows crammed with every type of camera. Unfortunately I assumed the young man at the counter was a shop assistant, so that when I asked him how long he'd worked there he replied sharply that he was the owner and had been there for fifteen years. Tall and lanky, with fair cropped hair, a pale skin with no signs of crow's feet, I thought that, whatever secret he had in the youth stakes, I wished I had it too.

'I wondered if you could help us,' I began, then hesitated. I didn't want to mislead him into thinking we actually wanted to buy a camera, but he might not cooperate if we told him the truth. 'A girlfriend's fiancé bought a camera here about six months ago and he recommended it but I don't know the make.'

'What do you want it for?' he asked.

'Taking photos, of course.'

'No, I meant for holiday snaps or more impressive, professional stuff?'

'My friend is a professional photographer – it's a wedding present. So we'd like the same one.'

'Name of buyer?'

'Paul Warrinder.'

'Hang on. I'll look through my records.'

He disappeared into a back room and Hubert began browsing amongst the glass-encased cameras.

Within a few minutes he was back with a sales docket. 'That was easy enough,' he said. 'Thought I recognized the name. He's been in a couple of times.' Then he added with a slight frown, 'It's an expensive one. But it wasn't a camera – it was a Sony camcorder – nine hundred pounds worth.'

Now I really was lost for words but Hubert came to my rescue. 'I think we'll just have a middle-of-the-range camera,' he said, pointing to one in the glass case underneath the counter. 'Good choice,' said the owner. 'Takes a fair photo does that one.'

Hubert paid on his credit card and, as we walked out into the street, muttered, 'I've never owned a good camera before.'

'Well aren't you the lucky boy,' I said, feeling peeved

that I wasn't any wiser now that I knew Warrinder had bought a camcorder. So what? I was more interested in his lack of a computer. Perhaps he had a computer somewhere else or he'd got rid of it because it contained something incriminating – like a suicide note.

When I suggested this to Hubert he snorted, 'I've never known anyone write a suicide note on a computer.'

'It could be a new trend for the twenty-first century. People end relationships via e-mail now.'

'Very few,' he replied, unconvinced.

Back in Trevelly I drove towards Carole's place. We saw her emerging from a local shop with several plastic bags of food. She was grateful for a lift and invited us in for a cup of tea. Whilst she put her food away and Hubert admired her legs I asked her about the computer. 'When Fran was alive,' she said, 'he had one in the study upstairs.'

'You mean the attic?'

'Yeah. I only went in there once a month to give it a bit of a dust. He was tidy.'

'And after she died?'

'That was when he took to keeping it locked. I thought he'd put all their belongings up there – toys, photos, clothes, that sort of thing. He cleared the house of their personal stuff about a week after they died. Didn't want to be reminded, I suppose.'

'So, you don't know what happened to the computer?'

'No idea, love. Is it important?'

'Could be. I'm not sure. What about a camera? Did he have a camera?'

'He did. He was always taking photos. He took a real pride in it.'

'You don't know where he had the films developed?'

She sat down wearily on a kitchen stool and crossed her legs. She was wearing a short denim skirt and mules with a slight heel. The view kept Hubert dumbstruck. 'I don't know where he went,' she said slowly, 'but she used a shop in Newquay – one of those gift shops, I think, that do other things on the side.'

As Carole looked so tired, I didn't want to outstay our welcome. 'Just one more question,' I said. It was one of those little niggles that had been troubling me. 'How often exactly would you say Paul went away?'

'I can tell you that. Every month while Fran was alive. That was the week I did the attic.'

'Did he always go abroad?'

'Mostly, I think. I did once joke to Fran that maybe he was a spy . . .' She hesitated. 'Look, I may as well tell you . . . when I was up in the attic I did have a nose round. Not that there was much to find, but one day I did find a card with an address scrawled on the back. I remember thinking that perhaps he wasn't always working . . . if you know what I mean?'

I nodded. 'You couldn't by any chance remember that address?'

She put her head on one side and rested her hand on her face. 'It was London, Kensington. A flat.' Well that narrowed it down, I thought. She closed her eyes. 'Something Mews . . . a herb.' I waited. 'I've got it – Rosemary Mews.'

'And the number?'

She shook her head, still with her eyes closed. 'I think . . . I can't be sure, it was either eight or three.'

'You are a genius,' I said delightedly. 'Thanks so much.'

'Lovely woman,' said Hubert as we got back in the car.

'Lovely clever woman,' I said as we drove away.

My mobile phone trilled as we approached the Regis car park. 'Is that Kate Kinsella?' a male voice enquired. 'You don't know me, my name's Bernard.'

'Gill's boyfriend?'

Silence.

'I have some bad news. I got your number from Gill's diary . . .'

I felt my mouth dry. 'What's happened?'

'Gill was involved in an accident two days ago. Early this morning they switched off the life-support machine and I'm sorry to say that she died half an hour later.'

Twenty-One

I tried to speak but my brain and mouth seemed one big void. Not Gill, I thought. It couldn't be true. It didn't seem possible. 'An accident?' I managed to croak.

'Yes. In central London. A motorbike courier knocked her down.'

'Have they got him?'

'No. He didn't stop.' Bernard's voice had a shocked robotic sound.

'I'm so sorry. I don't know what to say. She was . . .' I paused, about to trot out the old clichés used when someone young dies.

'I don't even know why she was there,' Bernard continued. 'There's a perfectly good gym locally but she wanted to try a more expensive one. She said she might meet some celebrities.'

'Are the police convinced it was an accident?' I asked quietly.

'You mean . . . it could have been deliberate?'

'Yes. It's a possibility.'

'Oh my God!'

'I'm sorry if I've made things worse.'

'Nothing could be worse than losing her.'

'I know,' I murmured. 'I'll meet you in London. We can talk . . .'

'When?' he asked dully.

'Two days – Tuesday . . .' I paused. 'Have you told Helen yet?'

173

'I tried but she wasn't answering her phone.'

'Leave it to me,' I said. 'I'm seeing her tonight.'

He gave me his address and phone numbers and then, barely audibly, he said goodbye.

Hubert frowned in puzzlement. 'Gill's dead?'

I nodded. I didn't want to talk about it; I had to mull it over quietly. He patted my knee and we drove on in silence.

At nearly eight p.m. I arrived at Tamberlake, parked the car and sat for a few minutes watching the sky darken. The news of Gill's death had really shaken me and I wondered how much she had told Bernard about the situation. I dreaded the evening ahead. When would I tell Helen? Before the meal? Afterwards? She'd get no sleep whenever I told her. This was my chance to meet Paul's clique of friends, possibly my only chance. I made my decision. I would tell Helen tomorrow. And I was determined that this night would be a turning point.

Paul greeted me at the door, kissed me on both cheeks and, with an arm around me, led me to the kitchen. I was the last to arrive. He introduced me as, '*The* Midlands Sleuth, an old school friend of Helen.'

Jamie Ingrams and Harvey Trenchard sat between two women, the elusive Michelle Ford and Diane Brandon. Michelle was a redhead in her forties wearing jeans and a black low-cut top. She was striking rather than attractive – her long nose and thin face was saved from severity by soft blue eyes. Diane in contrast had neat features but small grey eyes. She wore a long brown skirt and a cream top. She was Miss Average in looks and below average in friendliness. She stared at me and didn't respond to my cheerful hello. I guessed she was in her late thirties and I couldn't help finding it strange that not one of the four seemed to have a partner.

Trenchard stared at me too and murmured something to

Diane, whose little grey eyes darted briefly over my body like a shop assistant deciding dress size at a glance. Paul began pouring wine. Helen checked the oven and then placed a basket of French bread and a bowl of salad on the table. Michelle smiled at me. 'What exactly are you investigating in Cornwall? Rumours are abounding, I can tell you – everything from drug dealing to Satanism.'

'I'm just ghost-busting and catching up with old friends.' I glanced at Helen, who'd sat down to await Paul's triumphant offering from the oven. Surprisingly she winked at me. 'I'm sure Helen's told you the full story,' I said, hoping she was going to help me out.

'I have,' she answered. 'I've told them I think this place is haunted and Jamie's extremely worried about the whereabouts of his half-sister.'

Michelle, far from being sympathetic, laughed. 'Jamie, you know your half-sister was slightly eccentric. She'll turn up.'

'Why do you say she was eccentric?' I asked.

Before she could answer, Jamie angrily snapped a piece of French bread in half. 'Kate, take no notice,' he said. 'Michelle is a frustrated old bag who hasn't had a man since 1990.'

'And you are an old queen who hasn't had a man . . . not a proper man . . . ever!'

'You two,' said Paul as he put on oven gloves, 'are like bickering four-year-olds. Take no notice, Kate, they just do it for effect.'

Paul served his Italian chicken dish, strong on garlic, tomatoes and basil, and the conversation turned to cars, holidays and the forthcoming wedding. It was Diane who first mentioned Fran. She'd been drinking wine steadily and far from being merely unfriendly I realized that she'd been getting maudlin drunk. 'It was this time last year that Fran—'

'Drop it!' snapped Trenchard.

'No I won't! Fran and the kids were my friends. I'm not going to pretend they didn't exist. Paul might be able to do that but I can't.'

Paul winced slightly. 'Life goes on. I couldn't grieve for ever.'

'Since when has a mere six months been for ever?'

Helen now looked uncomfortable and she stopped eating and began pushing the food around her plate. Paul placed a hand over hers and Helen tried to smile. 'Don't deny me happiness, Diane. I never thought I'd feel like this again.'

Diane's answering smile was more of a sneer. 'You said exactly that after Alison had left and you met Fran.'

He shrugged. 'I can't help it if love came knocking once more.'

I looked over to Helen, who I expected to be a little upset by all this, but she merely smiled at me and began clearing the used plates. 'I think,' said Paul, 'we should have a special bottle of wine tonight.' There was a murmur of agreement, or maybe relief that the conversation had ended. As he went to the cellar, Diane looked at her wristwatch. 'Last year at this time Fran went down to the cellar seeming fine. She came back, pale and shaking, saying she felt a bit faint. Strange how much Paul drank from then on. He was drinking whisky when usually he sticks to wine.'

'Maybe he was worried about her,' said Trenchard. 'You really do have a nasty suspicious mind.'

'You wouldn't notice if your own socks were on fire,' said Michelle.

Trenchard laughed. 'I'm never quite that pissed.'

'You were that night,' retorted Michelle.

'Was I? I don't remember.'

'I remember. We all drank too much . . .'

'We usually do,' he interrupted, 'and don't forget we were on the spliff as well.'

Michelle didn't answer but Diane, looking furious, snapped, 'Which is why we were told to keep our mouths shut and deny we were ever here.'

'Paul was only trying to protect us all,' said Trenchard. 'Don't forget I drove home that night.'

'Yes, and God knows how we got away with that,' said Diane. 'We could easily have been seen.'

Trenchard shrugged. 'It was late. Most of Trevelly is asleep by ten thirty.'

'Anyway, I was talking about Fran . . .'

At that moment Paul walked back in, carrying two bottles of wine, and, after a short silence punctuated only by the sound of popping corks, he poured the wine into fresh glasses. He was handing the glasses round when Diane looked at me and cocked her head towards the door. 'Excuse me, Paul,' she said. 'I need to throw up.' She left the room and a few seconds later I followed, saying, 'I'll just check on Diane.'

I saw her at the open cellar door, obviously waiting for me. As I approached she said quietly, 'I'm not stupid and I'm not even that imaginative but I'm sure Fran found something in the cellar that night.'

'But she was hearing things more than seeing them, wasn't she?'

'If she'd heard something she would have told us. I'm sure she saw something. She came back into the kitchen and she was scared. When I heard she'd committed suicide I wasn't that surprised, but I was surprised about the children.'

'What on earth could have frightened her in the cellar?'

Diane shook her head. 'I wish I knew. I've been down there and I couldn't see anything . . . scary.'

'Has it got a history?'

'Nothing I've heard of. It wasn't built over a burial site, so she didn't see the walking dead.' Then she touched my

177

arm. 'Come on,' she said. 'I'm full of Dutch courage. Come down with me.'

She flicked on the light at the top of the stairs and we walked carefully down the steep steps to the main body of the cellar. 'That night,' I asked, 'why *did* Fran come down here? Was it just for another bottle of Vin Ordinaire or was it something a bit more special?'

'Just stocking up on the cheap stuff. We were all knocking it back a bit.'

I started having a look round but since I didn't know what I was looking for it seemed a bit pointless. The one overhead light bulb didn't provide much light and I was about to suggest we were wasting our time when there was a click as the light was switched off and the door above closed. From dim light to complete dark was a shock.

'Where are you, Diane?' I asked, arms outstretched like antennae.

'Over here.'

I followed the sound of her voice and we grabbed hands and stepped towards what we hoped was the direction of the stairs. Disorientated, we took a little time to find the bottom step. Like two old grannies we began walking up the stairs. Halfway up we heard the key turn in the lock.

Twenty-Two

Sometimes only one word will do. We both began screaming 'Help!' in unison. It was mere seconds later that the light was flicked on and the door opened. Helen stood at the top of the stairs. 'I've been looking for you two upstairs.' She sounded like a mother looking for two unruly teenagers.

'Did *you* switch the light off?' I asked.

'No. It was probably Paul.'

I swore under my breath and we went back to the kitchen. 'You locked the girls in the cellar, Paul,' said Helen mildly.

'Did I? I thought you were in the bathroom,' he said. 'I passed by the cellar and I guessed I must have left the light on, so I turned it off and locked the door. Sorry.' He flashed a quick boyish grin towards Diane and me. Diane sat down, dragging her chair noisily on the tiled floor.

I sat down too, hoping at some point we'd move to somewhere more comfortable, but it seemed less likely now. Michelle looked a little glassy-eyed, Trenchard was talking about the housing market to no one in particular, Jamie followed Paul's every move and Diane had slunk into a depressive state and was staring into her glass of wine. Only Helen seemed calm and sober. Paul had a smug self-satisfied look on his face, as though he was watching the plebs from some seat of majesty. I obviously didn't know him, but on our short acquaintance I had summed

179

him up – he was shallow, devious and cold. Everything he said was so plausible and yet . . . my thoughts were interrupted by a sudden urge to get away. I needed to see Helen alone and, if I made my getaway now, Paul would wave me off at the door.

When there was a lull in the conversation I asked Paul to recommend a minicab firm. 'I'll ring them for you, Kate,' he said. 'What time?'

'As soon as possible. I've got an early start in the morning.'

He left the kitchen then, presumably to use the landline, and I moved and sat by Helen and whispered to her, 'Ring me tomorrow. I have to speak to you privately.'

'What about?'

'Gill.'

Then she really surprised me. She whispered back, 'Come here at ten o'clock. Paul should be out by then. He's going into Exeter.' I glanced around the table; no one seemed interested in the two of us together in a huddle. I nodded to her, just as Paul came back.

'Twenty minutes,' he said cheerfully. 'Time enough for a brandy.'

In the minicab on the way back to the Regis I realized that I hadn't found out who was the last to leave Tamberlake on that Saturday night a year ago. Trenchard had said he'd driven home but was he alone and was he the last to leave? Was Paul indeed the last person to see Fran that night?

Hubert seemed preoccupied in the morning with phoning Humberstone's and getting back to 'normal life', if undertaking could be called normal. I left him at the hotel and drove out to Tamberlake. There was no sign of Paul and only Helen's car was in the drive.

She met me at the front door looking cheerful and I felt almost traitorous to be bringing her bad news. As she produced a cup of coffee I debated with myself how best to tell her. She sat down and stared at me. 'What is it, Kate? What's happened?'

'It's Gill,' I said. 'There's been an accident. A road accident . . . I'm very sorry . . . she died in hospital.'

The colour drained from Helen's face, I grabbed her hand and, although she was dry-eyed, she'd begun to tremble. 'What happened?' she asked.

'She was hit by a motorbike courier . . .'

'And he didn't stop?'

'That's right.'

'Where?'

'In London.'

'Where in London?'

I stared at Helen. This wasn't the Helen I thought I'd got to know. Her voice had a steely quality. I'd expected tears but not this cool interrogation style. 'Where?' she repeated.

'In Soho. She'd been to a gym.'

'The Health and Fitness Palace.'

'Yes. How did you . . .'

She looked at me, disengaged her hand and said, 'I can't tell you anything, Kate. You'll just have to trust me.'

I couldn't help it. I stared at her. The new Helen wasn't the timid, slightly dull bride-to-be I'd thought she was. From the far reaches of my memory I had a flash of a school 'do'; friends, parents, all packed into the hall for the school play. I wasn't involved, being unable to act, but Helen had played Lady Macbeth. I'd managed to slip out during the performance and slip back in for the final curtain. There was more to Helen's past than her white socks, but what the hell was she up to now?

'I want you to help me search the cellar,' she said.

'It's been searched already.'

'Who by?' she asked.

'The police had a quick look round and Robert Roberts has had a good snoop.'

There was no surprise in her expression at his name. 'His eyesight isn't too good,' she said. 'I want us to go down there with a torch and if necessary move every wine bottle.'

'That'll take some time – what if Paul comes back? And I've promised Hubert that I'll be back by eleven thirty.'

'Well we'll have to get a move on, won't we? I've got a strong torch for both of us – the light down there is useless.'

Armed with a torch each, we made our way down the cellar steps. 'You have a good look round the barrels and that corner,' she ordered. 'I'll start on the vintage stuff.'

'Fair enough,' I said. 'But what exactly are we looking for?'

'Evidence.'

'Aren't you taking pre-marital nerves a bit far?'

Even in the gloom, her answering expression said it all. She had real reservations about marrying Warrinder. 'Don't stand there with your mouth open, Kate. Let's get on with it.'

I crawled on the dusty floor; I shone my torch on individual bricks, looking for any signs of disturbance. Helen meanwhile was taking out bottles and checking the empty racks. I found some mouse droppings but otherwise not so much as a toffee paper. I was struggling up from the floor and resting my hand on one of the barrels when something glinted at me. A piece of glass, I thought, stuck in the rings. I positioned my torch at a better angle and saw it more clearly. Circular, tiny – not glass at all – but a contact lens.

Twenty-Three

'Don't touch it!' shouted Helen. 'I'll get an envelope.' She rushed upstairs and returned in a few minutes with a pair of rubber gloves and an envelope. Delicately she removed the lens and placed it in the envelope. 'Well done, Kate. I don't know how you managed to see it.'

'What are you going to do with it?' I asked, because it was obvious she had a hidden agenda and I'd been relegated to sidekick status. Not that I minded. It was a great surprise to see Helen being proactive, but what had caused the change of heart? One moment Paul was a perfect specimen of manhood, now he was under the gravest suspicion.

'I'll take it to the Robert's now,' she said, smiling. 'They'll know what to do.'

As we parted, she said, 'You're leaving Cornwall today?'

'I'm going to London to see Bernard, Gill's boyfriend.'

'I'll be in touch. I'll let you know about the contact lens.'

'Was it Alison's?'

'Could be. She wore them.'

I thought it strange that Helen should know that, when no one else had mentioned it, but I supposed that maybe it was like wearing a wig, the less people who knew, the better. It was still odd that Helen should know.

I was driving away when Paul's car came into view. I smiled and waved with mock cheerfulness and after a brief surprised glance he waved back. I continued driving but I felt the urge to turn around and tell Helen to take the greatest care, because I had a gut feeling that she was in danger.

Back at the Regis Hotel, Hubert had paid the bill and was obviously keen to make his getaway. He was standing in the doorway waiting for me, with Jasper straining at the leash beside him. 'I've checked your room,' he said. 'Let's go.'

We were ten miles or so into the journey before I told him about the contact lens. 'Well done,' he said. 'I reckon a contact lens could be as good a way of identifying a body as teeth.'

'We haven't got a body.'

'Just a question of time,' he said. 'Just a question of time.'

It was early evening when we arrived back at Humberstone's. As we'd driven through Longborough I'd noticed a new picture-framing shop. It certainly wasn't an art gallery but it did have a few paintings on easels in the front window. It seemed worth a trip and I resolved to take my two stolen watercolours there in the morning. I doubted I would get a valuation but any opinion might help. After all, what was the point of Paul trying to pass them off as his own if they were valueless?

Later that evening I rang Helen on her mobile, she didn't reply and I didn't leave a message. I rang the Roberts home; there was no reply there either. Finally I rang Megan. My mother had left the day before – destination unknown.

In the morning I felt exhausted. I decided to take the train to London and I rang Bernard to tell him I'd meet him on Euston Station. He sounded very low and I hoped I wasn't going to make things worse for him. Death by hit and run was bad enough, but to know or suspect that it wasn't an accident, but murder, was going to be hard for him to bear.

Hubert was busy in his office downstairs, catching up on his paperwork, so I rang down on the internal phone to tell him I was going to London by train. 'In that case, take plenty of food and drink,' he said. 'You won't survive if there's a delay.'

I packed a picnic. Survival was possible but irritability and low blood sugar were a certainty, so I took his advice . . . just in case.

Before going to the station I decided to visit the art shop. It wasn't open by nine a.m. and I was about to walk away when a middle-aged woman, with plaited hair, wearing a long floral skirt and a green puff-sleeved blouse, emerged from an elderly Beetle car, produced a set of keys and opened the shop door. 'Come in,' she said cheerfully. 'You are a customer, I suppose, and not a bailiff?'

'I'm not exactly a customer but I would like some advice . . . if you can spare the time.'

'Time is on my side,' she said. 'Customers are thin on the ground. Yesterday not a single soul passed my threshold. I tell a lie – the postman came delivering yet more bills.' She placed the plastic bag she was carrying behind the counter and said, 'Now, how can I help?' I took the two watercolours from my holdall, giving her the one signed by Fran first. 'I wondered if you thought this was any good.'

She gazed at the painting for a few moments. 'Not bad, fine use of light, quite delicate. I like it. Pity it's a copy.'

'A copy?' I queried in surprise.

'Yes. It's not an original.'

'Are you sure?'

'I'll check but I'm sure.'

She began taking the back apart, removing the thick card that held the painting in place. 'What on earth . . . ?' She paused, for underneath the card were several tiny flat packets wrapped in opaque cellophane. She stared at me. 'You look surprised,' she said, handing me the collection that had been pressed between one piece of card and another. She removed the second piece of card to reveal the painting. 'Yes, it is

185

a copy,' she said. 'But I could probably sell them for a tenner.'

I wasn't listening. I'd opened one of the tiny packets. They were negatives. I turned my back to her and held them up to the light. Tiny images of children. Children who'd been torn from innocence into a perverted adult world. Each negative had some sort of number code in the corner and each child had a name. I felt sick. I'd expected Warrinder to be involved with drugs, but not this.

'Are you all right?' she asked.

I dithered for a moment. 'Yes. I'm fine. Could you put them back for me?' She fixed the packets back in place and reassembled the painting. I couldn't have managed, because my hands were trembling. 'Would you check this one out too?' I asked her, handing her the second painting. Carefully she unclipped the back. This time there was no false backing and when she examined the painting she judged it to be an original. I returned the paintings to my holdall, thanked her and left the shop.

Outside, I took several deep breaths. As I walked away I caught a glimpse of the shop owner watching me go. I wanted to rush to the police with the negatives there and then but I needed to think carefully before I did anything.

At the train station I tried to think rationally. Would I achieve anything in London when Warrinder was in Cornwall? Prejudice had blinded me to the possibility that he might be involved in paedophilia. I'd thought him too good-looking, too self-assured. I'd assumed that somehow I'd recognize a paedophile by his shifty eyes or lack of self-confidence with women. I supposed he could be a mere purveyor of child pornography rather than a paedophile himself, but either way he had no moral objections to distributing vile images of children. I presumed he was touting his negatives in photographic form because the FBI and the British police were now monitoring the Internet much more closely. Had Fran found out about his activities? It seemed likely that she had, but what had she found, something in the cellar that night? Surely if she'd found a contact lens she'd have removed it? What the cellar at Tamberlake needed was a complete forensics team. But would finding negatives of child pornography in the back of watercolours be enough evidence to force a search of the cellar? I decided that perhaps London could provide a few answers if that was where Warrinder conducted his activities.

On the train I mulled over events, trying to separate the facts from conjecture, but I felt defeat was staring me in the face. If Warrinder was into some sort of organized child pornography ring, he'd covered his tracks well. 'Mummy, Mummy!' a child screamed out from further along the train. The sound echoed in my head. Warrinder's victims would also be crying, 'Mummy, Mummy!' only there would be no answer. The child's cries strengthened my resolve. If I had to take risks then I would. The police had been following the rules and Warrinder was still able to continue his activities. But not for much longer.

The train was approaching Euston when I realized that I had only the vaguest idea of what Bernard looked like. I'd arranged to meet him at the bar on the concourse, because it gives such a good view from above.

As the train stopped and I stepped out, a middle-aged man, balding and with glasses, smiled at me. He'd decided to meet me off the train, I thought, so I stepped forward towards him, smiling back, and he walked straight past me to the elderly woman behind me.

In the packed bar, I searched and listened for a possible Bernard whilst berating myself for being so stupid. Did I think I was going to recognize him by his voice? I ordered a glass of red wine and took it to the front of the bar, where there was a seat vacant beside a young girl who looked Japanese and who appeared to be a student catching up on her note-taking. I sipped at the wine and every so often checked the main bar by craning my neck. No one seemed to be looking for me, so I presumed Bernard was expecting the train to be delayed and would arrive soon.

One wine was enough during the day, so I drank coffee after that. Two coffees drunk very slowly and an hour had slipped by. Another coffee, another half an hour.

It was becoming obvious that Bernard wasn't going to show up. There was only one thing to do, I'd have to go looking for him. I checked his address in my diary and stood up. As I reached the door, I had one last look at the customers milling around. A man standing by the bar, pint in hand, glanced at me and then looked away. He wasn't Bernard, being far too young, in his late twenties or early thirties. He wore a suit with the tie loosened. A briefcase on the floor was clamped between his feet. Remembering Hubert's theory that shoes can tell a story, I glanced at his. Black and shiny, lace-ups, they looked brand new. My one final glance at the back of his head revealed his hair was short and very neat – I had him sussed – he was a soldier on leave.

Outside on the concourse, I began walking towards the underground taxi rank. Still on alert for Bernard I paused at 'The Sox Shop' to have a final look around. Briefcase-and-black-shiny-shoes-man caught my eye but he ducked away and I told myself that I was being paranoid if I thought he was following me.

I walked briskly down the stairs and waited behind three men in the first taxi bay. After a short wait a taxi drew up, the driver wearing a white turban and an expression of stubborn resignation. I gave him the address in Gospel Oak and he grunted in response as we swept into the usual volume of heavy London traffic. At the second set of traffic lights a black cab drew alongside us and I glimpsed 'shiny shoes' obviously on the lookout for me. Obvious, because he was deliberately peering into the cab. He *was* following me.

Twenty-Four

As the taxi neared Gospel Oak I kept peering behind but, if we were still being followed, the other taxi had either stopped or rerouted.

My driver remained mute and sullen but I gave him a generous tip and expected at the very least a slight twitch of the lips in return. He merely managed a slight nod of the head.

Bernard's house was a four-storey, Edwardian house, white with potted artificial trees outside. I was ringing the bell and banging on the door when it began to rain. I stood under the porch wondering what to do. I braved the rain to check there wasn't a spare key under the pots, then ran next door hoping he was on good terms with his neighbours. It seemed he was. A white-haired elderly woman answered the door and at the mention of his name her eyes lit up. The porch sheltered me from the rain but she didn't invite me in. 'Lovely bloke,' she said warmly in a strong London accent. 'He's a real friend to me. I live here on my own, can't make the stairs anymore. Him and a friend brought my bed downstairs – I don't know what I'd do without him. That poor Gill. He's heartbroken . . .'

'Have you seen him today? Mrs . . . ?' I interrupted her.

'It's Mrs Ball. Call me Alice. No, love. Saw him last night. I made him a nice pie and took it round to him about six o'clock. He brought back the dish just after seven. He said he was going down the pub.'

190

'Did you see him again?'

'I was pulling my curtains across about nine and he passed by with a wave.'

'I'm a friend of Gill's,' I explained. 'He was due to meet me at Euston but he didn't show up. I wondered if you had a key.'

A flicker of anxiety crossed her pale, lined face. ''Course I have, love. Hang on, I'll get my coat.'

She spent some time checking that she had her own key, produced an umbrella and a walking stick and we made our way slowly next door. As she opened the door she said, 'Ever so modern this place. He keeps it lovely.' Once the door was open I could see what she meant – pure white walls in the hall, with black and white prints arranged in groups. The floor was a shiny parquet and both hall lamps were white-shaded. 'Kitchen's that way,' said Alice, pointing to a closed door at the end of the hall. 'His living room is on the left.'

The living room was a further ensemble in white and black, two white leather sofas, more white lamps and an atmosphere that made a statement. To me, it revealed that this room's function was to impress others but that not a lot of living took place there.

'Is this how it always looks?' I asked Alice.

She nodded. 'Oh yes. Bernard is very particular.'

'What about Gill? Did she help choose the furnishings?'

'I don't think so, Bernard wouldn't let anyone choose for him. Anyway, she only came round about three times a week. She didn't stay the night.'

'But I thought she lived here,' I said, puzzled.

Alice gave me an old-fashioned look. 'You don't know Bernard at all, do you?'

'No. I've never met him.'

'Well, I'm not saying he didn't love Gill, because he did. He thought the world of her but he couldn't help himself.'

191

'In what way?'

'Well, he was gay, dear. Always bringing different men here. He couldn't find the right man. If he'd seen one a few times, he'd bring him round and introduce him to me, and some of them were lovely. I mean, you'd never know . . . they weren't like nancy boys. And they were all very nice to me.'

Alice followed me into the kitchen and I noticed that even a short walk made her breathless, so that in the kitchen she had to sit down. The kitchen too was in monochrome, alleviated by some stainless steel. I left Alice catching her breath while I went upstairs.

I found him in bed. Lying tidily under a black duvet, head on a white silk pillow. An empty bottle of vodka and an empty packet of tablets for lowering blood pressure sat on his bedside table. A trickle of vomit had escaped from his blue mouth and it was obvious he'd been dead for some hours – the hours I'd been on the train. I guessed he'd been drinking and taking the tablets at the time I'd phoned him.

I didn't rush to ring for the police. First I had to get Alice out of the house. In the kitchen she sat looking slightly bemused, as if she'd forgotten why she was there, but if she noticed any change in my expression she didn't comment on it. 'I've never been upstairs. Same as down here, is it?'

'Yes,' I said. 'Just as tidy. Come on, let's get back to your place.'

I had to help her to her feet from the scoop-shaped chair. 'I bet he's at the undertaker's arranging Gill's funeral,' she said. I stayed silent as she added, 'That's where you'll find him.'

In Alice's living room I helped her take off her coat. 'I'm only eighty-eight,' she said, trying to catch her breath, 'but I feel at least a hundred today.'

'Do you fancy a cup of tea?' I asked.

'That would be lovely, dear,' she said.

I was relieved to be in the kitchen and have a chance to think. If I waited for the police there would be all sorts of questions. Before I knew it I'd have blurted out words like murder and paedophilia and I'd probably be locked in a padded cell. On the other hand Alice needed to know something might be amiss. Elderly and frail, she relied on Bernard for a feeling of security. I had to find out if there was anyone else she could rely on.

'Alice,' I said as I came back in with a tray of tea and the biscuit barrel. 'Have you got any friends or relatives nearby?'

'There's Maggie round the corner,' she said. 'She's younger than me but not that steady on her feet. She pops in once a week.'

I poured the tea and she was giving me a funny look. 'What have I done?' I asked. 'Don't you take milk in your tea?'

'It's not that,' she said. 'There's no biscuits in that barrel. Don't you know people keep money in biscuit barrels? Anyway, it's not airtight, biscuits go soggy in there.'

'Wouldn't burglars know you kept money in there?'

She glanced at me as if I should have more sense. 'I'd tell 'em where my money was. Nowadays you can't win. If I clobbered him I'd go to prison and if he clobbered me he'd probably never be caught and if he was and he said he was sorry he'd be let off because the prisons are too full.' She paused, took a deep breath and fell silent.

I stared at the biscuit barrel. *Don't you know people keep money in biscuit barrels?* No, I didn't know. What do people keep in wooden barrels? The answer had been there all the time.

'I expect Bernard will be back soon,' said Alice.

'I think something may have happened to him,' I said.

I took her hand and she must have seen the anxiety in my eyes. 'He was in the house, wasn't he?' she asked. She didn't wait for my reply. 'I knew he hadn't gone out. My hearing is still good and I would have heard him.'

'I want you to ring Maggie now and ask her to come round. I'll wait here till she arrives.'

I tapped out the number she gave me on my mobile and handed it to her. She stared at the mobile phone nervously and then shouted loudly into it. 'Hello, Maggie. It's me. Could you come round? There's been a bit of bother.' Alice listened intently to the reply. 'She'll be about ten minutes,' she said. 'Her false teeth are in soak. That's a joke, they're always in soak. She only puts them in for special occasions.'

We drank tea in silence and then Alice said, 'Killed himself, did he?' I nodded. 'Did he leave a note?' she asked.

'I didn't see one but I didn't have a proper look round.'

'I bet he did. He was very organized.'

'I've got a confession to make,' I said. 'I haven't rung the police yet.'

'Nothing they can do, is there? Not now.'

'I haven't called them yet because I . . . don't want to get involved.'

'You too busy?' she asked sharply.

'It's not that, I'm a private investigator and I'm on a case.'

Alice gave a sharp intake of breath. 'Well, well, fancy that. You're not investigating Bernard are you?'

'No. I was at school with Gill.'

Alice stared into space for a while and I could see it was dawning on her that Bernard really was dead. Her eyes became teary and she rubbed her hands together as though she felt cold. 'Alice,' I said. 'I want you to be brave and ring the police. Explain Bernard hasn't left the house but you let yourself in and you couldn't get up the stairs but he's not answering. You think he may be dead.'

'I bet they don't come.'

'I'm sure they will but I'd rather you didn't mention me at all. I'll give you my mobile phone number. Any problems – ring me.'

On a page from my notepad I wrote out my number in bold and handed it to her. She looked at it sadly. 'But I haven't got a mobile phone.'

'Just ring on your own telephone.'

'Oh,' she said. 'I didn't know you could do that.'

I heard the front door open and Maggie, a thin bird-like woman, walked in hurriedly, taking off her wet coat and plastic hood as she did so. I wasn't surprised she didn't wear her false teeth very often, they seemed too large for her small mouth and they moved as she spoke. She glanced suspiciously at me. 'What's up?' she asked Alice.

I saw this as my opportunity to leave. Maggie looked the determined type and I could imagine her trying to stop me leaving. 'I'll be off then, Alice,' I said. 'Remember what I said. Any problems with the police – ring me.'

'You'll come again, won't you?'

I nodded, smiled at Maggie – who scowled in response – and left.

Outside, the rain hit the pavements and the street was deserted. I'd wanted to get away but now I wasn't sure what to do or where to go next. After a minute in heavy rain I realized finding shelter in the nearest tube station was my best option. But finding that tube station proved difficult and a small hotel, the Haven, on the corner of Alice's road tempted me. Partly because I needed a haven and partly because the flashing neon vacancy sign caught my eye. It was more a B&B than a hotel but at least it would be dry and from there I might be able to see if and when the police arrived.

Inside, it smelt of damp overlaid with air freshener but the proprietor, a rotund man called Derek Benson cheered me up with a ready smile. 'Come on sweetheart,' he said, picking up my holdall. 'I'll show you one of our best rooms.'

Upstairs the room he offered me was large, clean, with an en suite shower and loo. 'We don't do evening meals, love,' he said. 'Breakfast is between six thirty and eight thirty. How many nights?'

'Two – maybe more. Would that be all right?'

'That's fine. No problem. There's a couple of pubs that serve food nearby, but if you don't fancy going out in the rain then I can do you sandwiches and soup. Nothing fancy – ham, cheese, cheese and onion, cheese and pickle, corned beef with or without pickle, egg, egg and cress, egg and tomato . . .'

I laughed. 'I get the picture. Egg and cress sandwiches please. And soup – tomato?'

He grinned. 'Yeah. We do tomato.'

Once he'd gone, promising me sandwiches in fifteen minutes, I had a quick shower and then rang Hubert. I didn't tell him about Bernard, just that I was staying at the Haven Hotel in Gospel Oak and that everything was fine. I got the impression he didn't want to talk, although he did tell me the death rate was up and he was extremely busy. I also rang Helen but there was no reply. I didn't leave a message, after all, telling her Bernard was dead was hardly likely to raise her spirits. It did occur to me that, now she suspected Paul was involved in some sort of crime, she might do a runner. If she'd known he was involved in paedophilia, she would have been out of Tamberlake faster than a pro's tennis ball.

Only a few minutes late, Derek produced my supper on a tray. The plate of sandwiches rose volcano-like on the plate but I'd eaten nothing for hours and, although the egg and cress palled after a while, I ate them all. Then I stood at the front window watching and listening for the police. Just after nine I rang Alice. She sounded tearful, the police had been.

'Everybody's been tramping in and out. They've taken my poor Bernard away.'

'I'm sorry,' I murmured, at a loss for something to say. 'But it was what he wanted.'

'Bless him,' she said sadly. 'He was only forty-five. He'd got years in front of him. I didn't think he was the type.'

I couldn't answer that. After all, I hadn't even known he was homosexual.

Next morning after breakfast I rang for a minicab to take me to the address in South Kensington. I assumed Warrinder might have stayed there or, if not, someone there might have known him.

The rain had stopped, the sun shone thinly and the driver didn't stop either talking or shouting abuse at other drivers. We had one or two near misses and by the time we arrived in the less than fashionable part of South Kensington my nerves were on edge.

Rosemary Mews was set in a Georgian terrace, some of which had long since lost its grandeur. The paintwork was grey with age and the window frames had begun to rot. Dead leaves and litter accumulated near the front door and the panel of apartment numbers had been vandalized, so that one edge had been lifted. The basement flat saw the worst of the rubbish, a wheelie bin had overflowed and a plastic bag had exuded its contents over the tiny patch an estate agent would call a patio. The basement was in darkness and there was no sign of life. I looked up. A light showed on the second floor.

I selected an identification card from my selection and slipped it round my neck. I looked up and down the road. A small band of camera-carrying tourists, wearing shorts and trainers regardless of age or size, were leaving a hotel opposite. I took out my mobile phone, so that I felt less conspicuous, and pretended to be making a call. I was doubtful about this venture but I told myself this is what private investigators did – lie and snoop and go up blind alleys in the hope that there would be some light at the end of the alley.

I pressed all four of the entrance buttons. And I waited. Then I tried again. Silence. Either no one was in or they weren't prepared to answer the door. I tried once more and then decided the only thing I could do was come back later.

This time I took the tube to Oxford Street and decided to spend the rest of the day window shopping and going to the cinema. I'd just walked into Marks and Spencer's when my mobile rang. It was Helen. 'Where are you?' she asked. She spoke so quietly I had trouble hearing her.

'M&S,' I replied.

'Have you been to the flat in South Ken?'

'Yes. No one was in.'

'Paul's on the move. He's coming to London to buy wine.'

'I'm going back there this evening.'

'No, don't!'

'Why not?'

There was a pause before she said, 'Thanks for calling. See you at the wedding.'

'Is he there?'

'Must go. See you. Bye.'

I hadn't really had a chance to tell her about Bernard but I didn't think it would help her to know. She'd sounded scared enough anyway.

Twenty-Five

I expected Helen to ring back but she didn't and when I tried an hour later the phone was switched off.

The day passed exceedingly slowly. I drank numerous cups of coffee, lunched in a pub, read two newspapers, completed a crossword and still had hours to spare. Eventually I decided to visit a cinema for the first time in years. I settled for the latest *Terminator*, because I thought that at least the action would keep me awake.

By seven p.m. I was back in South Kensington and the lights in three flats were on. This time it seemed even less of a good idea but I took a deep breath and rang the basement flat bell. A man's voice answered the entryphone. 'I'm Jacky Bates,' I explained, 'from Environmental Health.'

A timid-sounding voice said, 'Not again . . . I suppose you'd better come down.'

He stood in the doorway wearing a red baseball cap and grey sweatsuit. His skin also had a greyish tinge and his eyes were narrow and a watery blue. I guessed he was in his forties. I looked down at his feet, he was wearing trainers. 'Just back from a jog?' I asked cheerfully. He didn't reply. He just flicked his head towards the open door. I paused for a moment. I didn't like the look of him but, living in the basement flat, he probably saw more comings and goings than most and I judged it was worth the risk.

There was no hall, the front door leading straight into the living room. It smelt of stale cigarette smoke and damp. By the side of an unlit gas fire was a sleeping poodle in a plastic dog bed. In a cage on a stand near the window a budgerigar stood on his perch. An assortment of sagging chairs and a threadbare carpet completed the décor and, although there was a computer switched on with the screensaver swirling, there was no TV.

I produced a notebook and pen and began asking questions – name, date of birth, had he noticed any problems? His name was George Eccles, born in 1958, and there had been complaints before – cockroaches. He picked up a pair of plastic glasses from beside takeaway food containers and perched them on the end of his nose. 'Do you want a cup of tea, Miss Bates?' he asked.

'Mrs.' I said quickly. 'No tea thanks.'

'Well, I want one,' he said. 'You can have a look at the kitchen if you want. It's very clean.'

I followed him through to the kitchen, which was cluttered but wasn't a health risk. As he busied himself filling the kettle, I said, 'We had a complaint from one of the residents here about . . . rats by the rubbish bins.'

'Who complained? I haven't seen any rats.'

'I can't give you a name. Tall, thirties, good-looking. I don't think he lives here permanently but when he does it appears he complains to us – not me personally – I'm new.'

George shook his head. 'From the basement I only see their shoes or their back view. There is a bloke I see occasionally that wears flash shoes.'

I tried to keep my voice neutral. 'Which flat?'

'The one above me. It's quiet usually but when he is there he has a lot of visitors. Noisy buggers.'

Once the tea was poured George wandered back into the living room. From under a pile of newspapers he produced an ashtray and rolling tobacco and began rolling a cigarette. 'Want one?' he asked. I shook my head. Once he'd skilfully rolled the cigarette I noticed how thin it was. I'd seen cigarettes rolled that thinly before, by men eking out their small tobacco allowance. Ex-prisoners.

'Do you have a job, Mr Eccles?'

George shook his head. 'Nah. I used to work . . . once. I don't miss it. I'm quite happy here with my pets.'

It was then that I turned to look at the budgie and the dog. They hadn't moved. They couldn't. They were not alive and, looking more carefully at them, they had never lived. Even more unnerving was the sound of footsteps above. I thanked him and left within seconds. I did pause at the door to say, 'I can't see any problems here, Mr Eccles, and my report will make that clear.'

He slammed the door, irritated, I think, that I had left so abruptly. I rushed up the steps and then made my way to the front door, but not before noticing that the lights were on in the ground-floor flat and the curtains closed. I stood on the doorstep and knew that there was no point in my being there any longer. Taking calculated risks was one thing, but being foolhardy was quite another. If Warrinder perceived the net was closing in, I didn't think he would hesitate to silence me. I was well worth taking out if I was all that stood in his way. I imagined a few lines at the bottom of the *Evening Standard*. *'A Private Investigator, Kate Kinsella, age 34, has now been missing in London for a week. Her landlord has offered a £10,000 reward for news of her whereabouts.'*

Dream on! I thought. I'd just taken out my mobile to ring Helen and had my back to the road when all hell broke loose. Sirens wailed, brakes screeched, shouts of 'Go–go–go!' echoed and seconds later I was felled to the ground. Completely disorientated and crushed by the weight on top of me, I felt my wrists being roughly handcuffed. 'I haven't done anything,' I screamed above the noise of shouting and footsteps thundering up and down the stairs. I was hauled to my feet and, although I noticed my 'assailant' was a cop with a huge girth, it was the ashen face of the man two cops were leading out – Jamie – that silenced me.

Then I was hurriedly frogmarched to a waiting police car, where I was bundled into the back seat to sit beside a young sour-faced female police officer whose most noticeable feature was a thin line of black hair on her top lip. 'What the hell is going on?'

'You'll find out. Think yourself lucky you're not in the van with the other smack heads.'

I looked to the 'van' – several men were being pushed in like cattle. 'I was only visiting,' I said.

'That's what they all say.'

'Do they all say they're private investigators too?'

She looked at me warily. 'Are you on a care in the community order?'

'I am not!'

'Well just shut up! You can say your piece at the station.'

I soon found that was not as easy as it seemed. For some reason we were driven to West End Central police station, which heaved with police, drunks, and assorted criminal types. Our arrival added to the chaos and even the desk sergeant looked bemused. 'Quiet!' he screamed. A brief lull descended. 'Take this new lot to the cells. I'll get them processed as soon as I can.'

As I stood there in the crush my mobile sounded. I struggled to remove it from my pocket, because of the handcuffs. 'I am entitled to one phone call,' I said. She scowled and removed it from my jacket pocket. Then she held it to my ear. It was Helen. 'I've been arrested. I'm at West End Central police station.'

'Pass the phone to an officer. I'll explain.'

I handed my mobile to my personal cop, who glowered at me as I said, 'My friend wants to confirm who I am.'

She snatched the phone and listened. Helen seemed to be

giving her chapter and verse and the call was only marked by the odd 'Right', 'OK', 'I'll pass that on',' 'Yes', 'Thanks', 'Will do'. Whatever Helen had told her, it had worked. My handcuffs were immediately removed and she shouted above the noise, 'Sarge, I need a DCI in an interview room. Urgent! Like, now!'

'Interview room three,' he shouted back. I was quickly ushered through a coded door and into the calm of a long corridor. At interview room three, the door was opened for me and my PC said, 'I'm Debbie. Do you fancy a tea or a coffee?'

'I'd love a coffee.'

'Take a seat and I'll be back in a minute.'

Once I sat down I was aware of how fast my heart was beating. I took a few deep breaths and told myself I'd be out of here soon. I'd had a few surprises. The first was being floored from behind by a heavyweight cop, the second was seeing Jamie amongst those arrested, and now there was this huge change in attitude from the police. Perhaps, I surmised, PIs were held in slightly higher regard than I'd previously thought.

Debbie returned with a china mug of coffee and a tall man in his early thirties in a pale grey suit with a red tie. The suit looked expensive. He had friendly brown eyes, an easy smile and a full head of dark hair. 'I'm DCI Anthony Carson,' he said as he offered me his hand. 'I'm pleased to meet you, Kate.' His voice gave him away – expensive schooling, university, fast-tracker. Very attractive and probably married. All the 'pleased to meet you' bit had me worried. I smiled and remained mute.

'You'll be glad to know we have resumed surveillance on the house. I'm afraid there was some lack of communication between the Drug Squad and SO5.'

I relaxed back into my chair, suddenly aware of how tired I felt. What exactly was I supposed to say now?

'You look all in,' he said with a smile. 'I think the least I can do is to drive you home.'

'Hotel. The Haven in Gospel Oak.'

'Right,' he said briskly. 'When you're ready.'

'Hang on,' I said. 'There is something else. One of the men arrested at the house is a friend of Paul Warrinder. He's young-looking, slim – Jamie . . .'

'Thanks.' He looked towards Debbie. 'Get him separated from the rest. Make sure he's cautioned and I'll be back to interview him as and when. He can sweat it out for a few hours.'

Once outside and sitting in the car, a black BMW, I felt so comfortable that I worried I would fall asleep and then wake up feeling even worse. I tried to stay awake by asking him about the drug bust. 'Were any drugs found?' I asked.

'No idea,' he said. 'But then I'm not with the Drugs Squad.'

'Who are you with?'

'SO5.'

'And what does that mean?'

'I thought Helen would have told you.'

'What's Helen got to do with it?'

As we stopped at traffic lights, he glanced at me sharply. 'You really don't know, do you?'

'Know what?'

'That Helen is working undercover for SO5.'

My mouth opened and closed. I was surprised but angry with myself for being so stupid. I *had* noticed her change of attitude but I'd put that down to her realizing Warrinder was a criminal and wanting him to be caught.

'So what is SO5?' I asked.

Twenty-Six

'I'll tell you all about it over a meal,' he said. 'What do you fancy – Chinese, Thai, Mexican, Indian?'

'All food sounds good to me.'

'Good. I can't stand fussy women.'

I found myself liking DCI Carson more and more and resolved to find out if he was encumbered in any way.

In Belsize Park he stopped outside the Curry Garden on a yellow line, which made him seem somewhat adventurous. Or was that a warped view after being with the very proper David Todman on a few occasions?

The waiter greeted him by name and found us a table for two by the window. 'I used to live round here,' he explained. 'A grotty bedsit but it was home for a while.'

'After your divorce?'

'Yes,' he said. 'How did you know?'

'Just a guess.'

The restaurant's low hubbub of voices I found quite reassuring. They were having fun, enjoying the food and being . . . normal. I felt far from normal, so much so that I asked Anthony to order for me. I felt far too drained to make a decision even about food.

He'd ordered a spicy prawn pancake to start but I could only nibble at it. I wanted to talk at that moment, not eat.

'Tell me about SO5,' I said, 'and about Helen. I still can't believe it.' He smiled and topped up my wine glass. I could still drink and the wine was already having an effect.

'Helen's one of our newest operatives,' he said. 'SO5 is an operation that's been under way covertly for eighteen months. Paedophilia isn't just about men sexually abusing children. It's big business and, where there is money to be made, someone will come out on top. And Paul Warrinder is one such Mr Big. We've been on to him for some time but have had no real evidence. We decided to put Helen in mainly because she looked like his dead wife and because she's a damn good actress and a good cop.'

I was still mystified. 'I hadn't seen Helen since school but Gill spoke as if they met regularly.'

'Yeah, well. They did meet over the years, but Helen didn't tell Gill she was in CID.'

'Why not?'

'Helen's married to one of our best undercover men. The fewer people who knew about her the safer he was. Anyone who works undercover lives a strange half-life of lies and deceit and has very few friends outside the force. Undercover agents can't afford to trust anyone.'

'So, the forthcoming wedding was a set-up?' I said unnecessarily.

He nodded. 'We would have come up with an excuse to delay it if he hadn't been charged by the due date.'

'What about the Cornish police?'

'They don't know about our operation. The Roberts duo were a bit of a pain but they have proved useful.'

'And was poor Gill murdered?'

'Yes. We're ninety-nine per cent sure that she was.'

'Why?'

'She'd been making enquiries about Warrinder at the gym. We do have a suspect in our sights but we want Warrinder as well.'

When the main course arrived I took a deep breath and tried to look enthusiastic about it but I wasn't.

'So what happens now?'

He glanced at his watch. 'He's arriving by train any minute now. He's being followed.'

'And then what?'

'We'll arrest him at the house.'

'Have you got the evidence this time?'

'We think so. Since the FBI began checking suspect computers, the paedophile rings have had to become more ingenious – smuggling images via other means. For Warrinder that included specially made wine bottles that could take negatives in the base.' He paused. 'But, of course, that isn't what makes the most money.'

'What does?'

'The actual trafficking of children from around the world.'

'You mean for supplying paedophiles?'

'Yes. It doesn't get much publicity. The public would be sickened. When the children start to grow up and get more difficult we know they are murdered. "Snuff" movies still exist. The children are often orphans or they have been sold by their parents for what is for them a large sum of money.'

I was stunned into silence. The whole idea of selling children to be abused is so horrific that it's hard to comprehend. I didn't want to think about it but now it was head-on and I felt real hatred welling up for Warrinder and all those involved.

'Is he making vast sums of money?' I asked. 'I glanced at his bank accounts and they seemed normal.'

'Yes. He has other personas, false passports and bank accounts in foreign banks. Rich paedophiles will pay huge sums to fulfil their desire for a young child to use as a sexual plaything.'

My appetite had disappeared totally by then and when his mobile rang and it was obvious he would have to leave I breathed a sigh of relief. 'I'm sorry about this,' he said. 'I'll have to go.'

'What's happened?'

'They've lost Warrinder. They didn't even see him get off the train.'

He paid the bill and the manager offered me a 'doggie box' but I refused. Anthony drove me the short distance to the Haven Hotel, stopped the car and then kissed me briefly on the lips. 'I'll be in touch,' he said. I wasn't going to hold my breath. I liked him and that was worrying. He was obviously a driven man and his work would always be his number-one woman. He probably drank a lot and I'd been there before. Still, on this investigation I'd been kissed twice and I didn't know why. Were my pheromones in overdrive? It was hard to understand.

I put him out of my mind, sat in the hotel lounge and rang Helen's mobile. Not only did she not answer, there was no ringing tone. I tried again – still nothing.

I asked Derek in reception if he knew of any overnight coaches to Cornwall. He looked a bit concerned that I wanted to leave. 'I'll obviously pay now for the two nights, but I've had some bad news and I need to get back to Cornwall as quickly as possible.'

'I'll ring round for you,' he said, still looking concerned.

I sat in the lounge and rang Hubert to tell him I was returning to Cornwall.

'What for?' he asked bluntly. 'You'll wear yourself out.'

'I know, but when this is over I'll be going back to my "maritals" and I promise I won't moan.'

'That'll be the day,' he said. 'You just take care. I need you back here.'

'What for?'

'Light relief.'

Derek came back to me with news that there was a coach leaving at eleven p.m. from Victoria coach station.

It took me about five minutes to pack my bag and return

208

to the bar, where I drank a steadying brandy and ordered a minicab. Derek bustled in ten minutes later with a brown paper bag. 'A few sandwiches,' he said. 'You look a bit peaky.' Strange, I thought, how an act of kindness from a virtual stranger could make me tearful. There are more heroes than villains in the world, I told myself, and when it seems that criminals, drug dealers and paedophiles are everywhere, there are more kindly Dereks and Alices than the rest. Remembering Alice, I rang her to find out how she was coping.

'I'm not too bad, dear, thank you. Maggie's here with me at the moment and we're on the port and lemonade. She's going to stay the night . . .' She broke off and I heard them laughing. 'She's not legless yet but she says she's getting that way.'

The call cheered me even more and, when my minicab arrived, Derek carried my bag out for me and we gave each other a quick hug.

I arrived in Cornwall feeling exhausted. I'd dozed on the coach in short bursts only, because the student who sat next to me had been determined to tell me his life story. Thankfully he was only twenty, so it took a mere two hours, and his life had been incredibly uneventful, but politeness dictated I responded at appropriate moments.

It was grey-skied and threatening rain when I finally reached Tamberlake at mid morning. Helen's car was outside and although I knocked loudly at the front door there was no response. The back door was open and I called out, 'Helen! Helen!' several times as I went from room to room. Finally there was only the attic and the cellar left. I checked the cellar first – that was empty – then I went back up to the attic. The key was in the lock. I called out, 'Helen!' once more as I turned the key. I felt some resistance but pushed the door open.

Helen lay on the floor, her hand raised as if trying to bang on the door. She was still breathing and her mouth was moving. She whispered the same word twice before I finally understood. 'Hypo . . . hypo.'

'You're diabetic?' I yelled, as if she were deaf. She managed to nod slightly but her eyes were closed. She was semi-conscious and I prayed she still had her swallowing and cough reflex intact. 'You have to swallow – can you?' I didn't wait for an answer, I was scrabbling in my bag for some leftover chocolate and a can of fizzy drink Derek had packed into the brown paper bag. The fizzy orange drink was full of sugar. I removed the ringpull and, lifting her by the shoulders, encouraged her to drink. It trickled down her chin and she coughed once or twice. 'Don't choke,' I said. 'Just drink it!' I was aware I was panicking inside and it was beginning to show on the outside. 'Now suck the chocolate,' I said, placing a square into her mouth. I checked to see that it had dissolved before slipping in another square. Then I gave her more of the sugary fizz. It was a miracle I'd seen before. After a few minutes her eyes opened and, although she seemed to have trouble focusing, she muttered, 'Kate. That was a close call.'

'You're telling me.'

She struggled to sit up properly and I encouraged her to eat more chocolate and finish the drink. 'Well, I reckon you owe a man called Derek who owns a B&B a drink.'

She looked at me blankly and I didn't bother to explain. After a few minutes she felt well enough to stand up and I helped her downstairs, where I put the kettle on for some hot sweet tea.

Helen's colour gradually improved as she drank the tea. 'Why didn't you tell me you were a diabetic?' I asked, trying not to sound peeved. I could have added other questions about her being married and being in the police force but I didn't think it was the right time.

'I've only been a diabetic for two years,' she explained. 'I was stabbed and the doctors seem to think the shock may have affected my pancreas. I usually manage to keep my diabetes well controlled but I had less breakfast this morning . . . you won't tell anyone I was hypo, will you?'

'No, of course I won't . . .' I paused. 'Who locked you in?'

'I don't know. I was searching the attic room again just in case I'd missed something. I'd left the key in the lock. I didn't hear a thing. When I came to leave, I was locked in. If you hadn't found me I'd be dead by now.'

I finished my tea and realized that she had to know that Warrinder was still on the loose. 'They lost him at the station,' I told her. She bit her lip. 'He's an evil bastard. And I've been sleeping with that monster for months.'

'Isn't that taking the line of duty too far?'

'I did volunteer, no one forced me. I wanted to do it. If you knew the children, if you'd heard them cry for their mothers – it's a small price to pay to rid the world of scum like him.'

We fell silent and she began to look slightly anxious. 'What's up?' I asked.

'He's on the run and this is the place he'll come to. He'll realize the game is up, so he's got nothing to lose.'

'Are you going to ring the local police?'

She shook her head. 'No, they'll come here mob-handed and someone will warn him off.'

'So, what do we do?'

'The only thing we can do. Wait for him.'

Twenty-Seven

W e sat half concealed behind a curtain, staring out on to heavy rain for two hours waiting for him.

Now that I knew Helen's true mission she wanted to talk. Far from being a professional photographer, she was a mere amateur. It had provided the ideal cover for her activities. After she'd left school she'd gone to university to read criminology.

'Why keep it a secret?' I asked.

'It wasn't exactly a secret but I'd only kept in touch with Gill from school and I knew if I told her I wanted to join the police graduate entry scheme she'd take the piss because she always thought I was a bit on the wimpy side. Plus, if I failed, I didn't want her to know. Once I'd got my degree I was fast-tracked and now I'm an inspector but I plan to make superintendent.'

I was impressed. Helen had always been very feminine but she obviously had real guts and determination. And she could lie as well as any psychopath.

'All that and you're married too?'

'Yes.'

'Do you want to talk about it?'

'Not really. It's hard. We don't see much of each other and we're nearly always in some sort of danger.'

'At least it's not boring.'

'Sometimes boring would be heaven. This isn't the sort of job anyone can do for long. In fact I've been told to take a year off undercover work and I may not be allowed to be connected with paedophile crimes again.'

'Why's that?'

'After a long time you get hardened to it. It's blatant and in your face and your initial repulsion turns more towards acceptance. You find you begin to sympathize with the perpetrators . . .' She broke off. 'Don't get me wrong, Warrinder isn't sexually interested in children. He's into money and power – that's what turns him on. The really scary thing is that he seems so normal. He's been kind and gentle towards me. He's treated me like a princess. He's played with my mind.'

I guessed at this point in her assignment she was beginning to get screwed up. It's one thing to live with a cruel, unfeeling monster and know exactly how he'll react to circumstances, quite another to live with a dual personality, knowing that the dark side is there just below the surface.

It was about two thirty when we heard the rumble of a lorry. I peeped out to see a brewery lorry, on the back of which were a few wooden barrels and several smaller metal barrels. The driver stopped and sat in his cab smoking a cigarette. Helen was on her feet.

'Hold on,' I said. 'He might be waiting for Warrinder. Let's get up to the attic. He might come in to check on you – if he comes alone we might be able to overpower him.'

'It might just be a delivery,' she said.

'No,' I said, pulling her towards the door. 'I think that Alison is in one of those barrels. And they want to remove the evidence.'

Helen clapped a hand over her mouth. 'But there couldn't be anything in the barrels – there was brandy in one and sherry in the other.'

'There's a trick involved somewhere,' I said, trying to sound convincing. 'I'm sure she's in one of the barrels.'

From the attic we could just about see the lorry but we

couldn't see the driver. We'd been watching for a few minutes when a car drew up and out stepped Warrinder and Trenchard. They began talking to the driver, still in his cab. We couldn't handle three men – it was ridiculous. 'Let's call the police,' I said. Helen shook her head. 'By the time they get here they'll be gone. He can't be allowed to escape this time.'

'Well, we can't just stay here and watch them go.'

'I don't intend to. Warrinder wanted me dead, so maybe my cover is already blown. He'll come looking to make sure I'm still locked in here and to finish me off if I'm not already dead.'

'I still think we should call the local police.'

'Yeah. OK,' she said reluctantly.

I'd just started rooting in my shoulder bag for my mobile phone when we heard footsteps. 'Too bloody late,' I muttered. Helen signalled for me to stand behind the door. I looked in vain for a weapon. What was I supposed to do – trip him up? Helen got on the floor and lay on her side looking towards the door. 'When he's inside,' she whispered, 'take the key from the outside and lock us all in.'

The footsteps became louder and it sounded as if there was only one of them. I began to tremble. Warrinder was young, fit and strong. Helen may have been a policewoman but she was slight and if it came to a fight I imagined she'd be fast and nimble but no great shakes at fending off a sharp left hook. As for me, I'd rather try to talk my way out. I could be brave as long as I didn't even try to think about the consequences. Once I thought blood and loosened teeth, my insides turned to jelly.

The key turned in the lock. As he slowly opened the door, I could see him in the space between the door and the frame. He stared at Helen lying on the floor and then half turned as if satisfied. It could have only been seconds but it seemed longer, because he changed his mind, turned and put one foot into the room. I sharply slammed the door in his face. He staggered backwards and then righted himself and charged into the room like an enraged bull. I was backing away terrified when a punch caught me in the jaw. I was aware of falling and then Helen's voice saying, 'Hands up you bastard.' The world was spinning but I saw the gun in her hand. He kicked the gun away and the shot reverberated round the room, loud as a cannon. It landed near me and I made a grab for it but he too lunged for it at the same time. Helen had dived on to his back and was yanking back his head by the hair. But he had the gun and it was aimed at me. He was momentarily distracted by the sound of the lorry's engine starting up. I kicked him between the legs. Helen was still hanging on to him like a monkey and now had an arm around his neck. It made no difference. He shot me.

A red-hot poker entered my left arm and stayed there. I don't know if I screamed but things became very black as I fell to the floor. I was vaguely aware of the sound of footsteps, scuffling and shouting, but the only thing that seemed real was the searing pain in my arm.

Helen's face came into view as she bent down to tell me the ambulance was on its way, and when I next squinted around I was alone and blood was steadily trickling down to my fingertips. I heard another two shots being fired. How long I was left alone I don't know, but I knew I was both frightened and outraged. I held up my left arm with my right to lessen the blood flow and managed to get to my feet. It was slow progress but I managed to get down the stairs. I was aware I was leaving a trail of blood but I didn't care. For all I knew, he'd shot Helen too.

Outside, I was staggering around when the ambulance and the police arrived. I slumped to the ground and saw a pool of blood gathering around me. Just before an oxygen mask was placed over my nose and mouth, I looked into the blue eyes of a uniformed PC. He supported my shoulders as the paramedics struggled to find a vein to put up an intravenous infusion. 'I'm Mark,' he said. 'Don't go to sleep. You're going to be just fine.' I tried to focus on his face. When I did finally get him into focus, I saw that apart from largish ears he was very attractive and I reasoned that if I could still work that out I wasn't quite at death's door. I clung on to his hand and begged him not to leave me.

So he stayed with me in the ambulance and during my time in the A&E department. He was still there whilst I was having my third unit of blood. By then I knew his life story and that he was free and single. I'd been given an injection for the pain and the euphoria was such that I even saw being shot through a rosy glow. It wasn't so bad. My silver lining was the lovely Mark sitting beside me, holding my hand and hanging on to my every word.

I remembered little about the operation on my arm but, when I came round from the anaesthetic, Mark was still there and I wondered why. I began to feel anxious. Where was Helen? Had they caught Warrinder? 'Are you here to protect me?' I slurred at Mark.

'It's my day off. I've chosen to spend it looking after you.'

'Thanks a million,' I said as I drifted back to a warm and cosy sleep.

Helen visited me the next day and I was well enough to ask questions. Warrinder had escaped . . . in a way. He'd run towards the beach pursued by Helen and Robert Roberts, who'd been in the area – 'snooping', Helen called it. But he hadn't taken the path to the beach, he'd taken the cliff-top path and just kept on running.

'I feel cheated,' said Helen. 'He's dead but in a way that doesn't help. He should have stood trial.'

She looked pale and upset. 'You need a good long holiday,' I said.

'I'm taking one. I'm resigning from the force. I want my marriage to work and I don't think it will if I have to associate with any more low life. Nigel didn't think he'd play the jealous husband but knowing I slept with Warrinder has affected him. It's affected us both.'

'You're worn out. Take a holiday together, somewhere exotic. You may feel differently when you get back.'

'I don't think so. There is something else . . . have you been interviewed by the police yet?'

'Today sometime, so Mark told me.'

'That gun wasn't legal,' she murmured. 'Nigel insisted I had one. If SO5 finds out I'll be dismissed.'

'I only saw Warrinder with a gun and that's what I'll say.'

'Thanks, Kate. I'd rather resign than get the push.'

'What about Jamie?' I asked.

'Jamie and Trenchard have sung like canaries. They were the chief henchmen. And Trenchard himself is a paedophile. I hope he rots in prison.'

'And the barrels?'

'You were right, Kate. It was horrific – Alison had been chopped in half, wrapped in formaldehyde-soaked sheets then encased in strong plastic. Warrinder needed help, of course – he paid a vast sum to a local cooper. He'd rigged up a foil bag, just like the ones in wine boxes, so that, when the tap was opened, out came the sherry and the brandy. Of course, no one carried on until the bag was empty.'

'Was she killed in the cellar?' I asked.

'I'm not sure. Cause of death seems to be strangulation. The three of them, Warrinder, the estate agent from hell and the cooper, sawed her in half and then stuffed her body into the barrels. They cleaned up the cellar floor – leaving just the one clue – the contact lens. I think Fran found it or maybe she'd already found the other one in another room, and she either confronted him or decided she couldn't carry

217

on living, knowing that her husband and the father of her children was a monster.'

I was beginning to feel tired now, and my arm throbbed, but I still wanted to talk and, even though the ward manager passed by my bed showing me five fingers, I didn't want to be hurried. 'I suppose the only consolation,' I said, waving cheerfully at the ward manager, 'is that a major paedophile ring has been broken and that's down to you, Helen. You risked your life, because if he'd found out you were working undercover you'd be dead.'

She shrugged. 'That's the nature of the job. Anyway, you've had your share of altercations.'

'How do you know that?'

'I didn't meet you by accident. It was a set-up. Gill didn't know what was going on but the cheque she gave you wasn't her money. SO5 paid indirectly. I told her I wanted you to investigate the so-called "ghosts" but it was to be a secret between Gill and me that I paid.'

'Why Gill and me?'

'We checked out a few school friends. Gill was an obvious choice, because we'd stayed in touch. Paul would have been suspicious if I didn't invite a few friends. Gill just got too involved and I had to try to put her off, hence the row, but she was dogged and she died because she couldn't let go.' She managed a half smile and patted my hand. 'And you, because you knew nothing about me and in a crisis you could have proved useful. You should be flattered. The police thought your investigation clear-up rates were pretty good.'

I didn't know what to say to that. But one other thing did trouble me. 'Tell me your secret,' I said. 'How did you get Warrinder not only to trust you but to fall in love with you and want to marry you?'

She was about to reveal all when Mark walked in. 'I'll tell you another time,' she said. 'And thanks for taking the bullet for me.'

I was disappointed all round. Warrinder had avoided a trial and prison and I'd been denied her feminine secrets.

'Hey, come on, cheer up,' said Mark as he kissed my hand. 'I'm taking some annual leave so that I can drive you back to Longborough.'

My disappointment left me as abruptly as a rainbow fades. Whatever 'secrets' Helen had, I wasn't doing so badly.

It was that night, listening on the hospital headphones to the news, that I heard the antidepressant drug 'Tourine' had been taken off the market. People already taking it were advised to see their GPs. One of the side effects, it seemed, was to increase depression in some people. Six people had committed suicide whilst on the drug.

The death of Fran and her children would always remain a mystery now, for the one man who was most likely to know the cause had taken the easy way out. My consolation was to also hear on the news that a major paedophile ring had been broken and that several young Argentinian children had been rescued from a semi-derelict house in South London.

Two days later I was back in Longborough. I hadn't told Hubert I'd been shot. He'd have come dashing down to Cornwall and he couldn't afford the time or the worry. He saw me from his office, being helped out of a car, and came out to meet me.

'What have you done?' he said, seeing my arm in a sling.

'I've only been shot,' I said. 'It's not major.'

'Well, I call it major. Another cock-up, was it?'

'No! We got a result.'

'That makes a change. Welcome home.' He looked questioningly at Mark. I made the introductions and we went upstairs to Hubert's kitchen, where he began busily making us a meal. Jasper was delirious with excitement, although most of it was reserved for Mark.

Mark had gone to the bathroom when Hubert put an arm

219

around me and said, 'You do realize he is a toy boy. He's years younger than you are.'

'Yes, I know. I'm in the first throes of love. Great, isn't it?'

'I'm going to lose you one of these days,' he said sadly.

'We'll see,' I said, giving him a peck on the cheek. 'I'm on a roll at the moment though, Hubert. Men seem to be clamouring for me.'

'It won't last.'

I didn't let his pessimism affect me. Instead I felt a real surge of optimism. I'd stopped a bullet, found an attractive man or two, and once my arm was better there would be no stopping me, in life or in the bedroom.